The New York Times
Book Review

125 YEARS OF
LITERARY HISTORY

Edited by Tina Jordan with Noor Qasim

CLARKSON POTTER / PUBLISHERS

NEW YORK

Cover photo credits: Red and blue circles: The New York Times.
Yellow circle: Helen Bevington, by permission of Stephen
Bevington and family. Orange circle: Hal Fiedler (illustration);
Joan Didion (text), by permission of her agent, Lynn Nesbit.
Green circle: Edward Fella.

For a full list of text and photo credits, see page 366.

Library of Congress Cataloging-in-Publication Data
Title: The New York Times Book Review / editors of
The New York Times Book Review.
Description: New York : Clarkson Potter, 2021.
Classification: LCC Z1003.2 .N49 2021 (print) |
LCC Z1003.2 (ebook) | DDC 028.10973—dc23.
LC record available at https://lccn.loc.gov/2021004171.
LC ebook record available at https://lccn.loc.
gov/2021004172.

ISBN 978-0-593-23461-7
Ebook ISBN 978-0-593-23462-4

Printed in China

The New York Times:
Editors: Tina Jordan with Noor Qasim
Editorial director: Caroline Que
Visual editor: Anika Burgess
Project manager: John Cruickshank

Clarkson Potter/Publishers:
Editor: Angelin Borsics
Cover design: Ian Dingman
Contributing designers: Jan Derevjanik and Benjamin Tousley
Production editor: Mark McCauslin
Copy editor: Ihsan Taylor
Production manager: Kim Tyner
Compositors: Merri Ann Morrell and Nick Patton

10 9 8 7 6 5 4 3 2 1

First Edition

Reading at Columbia University on September 28, 1994.

For my mother, Marlis Anderson Jordan, who instilled in me a love of reading (and ferried me to the Emily Fowler Public Library once a week for an armload of books when I was a kid), and in memory of my father, Terry Gilbert Jordan, a professor whose vibrant intellect and curiosity helped shape the way I read and think to this day.

Contents

SIXTEEN PAGES

WITH BOOK REVIEW SUPPLEMENT.

NEW-YORK, SATURDAY, OCT. 10, 1896.

A BOOK REVIEW SUPPLEMENT.

We begin to-day the publication of a Supplement which contains reviews of the new books, the announcements of the publishers, an epitome of the leading articles in the domestic and foreign magazines, information and comment relating to art, and other interesting matter which may appropriately be associated with the literary and art news of the day. This Book Review Supplement will appear hereafter every Saturday morning. We commend it to the attention of our readers, who will observe that its form will enable them easily to preserve the successive numbers.

The Birth of the Book Review

As we celebrate the 125th anniversary of The New York Times Book Review, take a trip with us back to the earliest years of the newspaper to look at how its literary coverage began—and how it grew before being spun off into the Book Review we know today.

It all started in the very first issue of The New York Daily Times on September 18, 1851. Peer carefully at the old, yellowing pages, densely speckled with six columns of tiny, often smudged type, and there—in an article on Page 2 headlined "Snap-Shots at Books, Talk and Town"—the paper laid out its ambitious plans for covering books and the publishing industry.

"The book-men are just now bidding upon the summer's surfeit of literature, and sometime, it may be worth our while to take our readers into the rooms of this traffic," the newspaper announced. "We shall sometimes too . . . take note of the books of the day—unravel their narrative into a newspaper column and give the public, whom we have taken in hand to serve, a running synopsis of their story. And if we give, now and then, a critical shot at their manner, method or morals, we shall do it with all the modesty, and perhaps the occasional misses, which belong to our swift shooting."

No time was wasted. The next day the paper introduced a column about authors and artists called "Limnings of Literary People," and on September 22 the first book reviews appeared. They included such gems as *The United States Post-Office Guide* and an apparently execrable novel called *Kenneth:*

A Romance of the Highlands, the review of which began, "Mr. Reynolds is a bad specimen of a very bad school of writers."

Book reviews, which were published at least once a week, were crisp and to the point. D. J. Browne's *American Muck Book,* for example, got a one-line rave as "doubtless a most valuable aid to the farmer, who admits science to the help of agriculture." Two 1851 novels that we now regard as important were not reviewed: Herman Melville's *Moby-Dick,* which came out a few weeks after The Times began publishing, and Nathaniel Hawthorne's *House of the Seven Gables,* which had been published in the spring.

The second half of the 19th century was filled with riches: "There were literary giants, and pygmies, too, upon the earth," wrote Francis Brown, who edited the Book Review from 1949 until 1971. "It was the period of Trollope and Dickens and Thackeray, of Whitman, Longfellow, Tennyson and Baudelaire, of Darwin and Huxley, of the Russians Turgenev, Dostoyevsky and Tolstoy." With a few notable exceptions, the paper covered every important book published during those decades.

Villette, by Charlotte Brontë, was hailed as "a first-class work." An unnamed critic struggled with *Leaves of Grass,* first calling Walt Whitman "a literary fraud" and then confessing, "Still, this man has brave stuff in him. . . . Since the greater portion of this review was written we confess to having been attracted again and again to *Leaves of Grass.*" Of Charles Darwin's *On the Origin of Species,* the paper's unnamed critic wrote, "Shall we frankly declare that, after the most deliberate consideration of Mr. Darwin's arguments, we remain unconvinced?"

The blockbuster novels of the day were often first published in serial form, usually in magazines like *Harper's* and *Scribner's,* and The Times covered new chapters with fanfare. "The first sheets of *Bleak House*—Dickens's new novel—have been received in advance of their publication in London, for *Harper's Magazine,*" the paper reported on March 16, 1852. "They have the clear ring of the true metal." Although an editor once railed that "a serial story has ever been our special detestation. We have a horror of anything published in parts," The Times nonetheless published some serials of its own, including Thomas Hardy's *The Hand of Ethelberta.*

The Times's book coverage extended well beyond reviews and serials. Holiday gift guides, publishing news, literary scandals, poems, summer reading and recommendations for children could all be found in the pages of the paper. In 1871, an editorial remonstrated against the moral depravity of "flash literature"; in 1875, a male author penned an essay about the difficulties of dressing his female characters (the opening line: "What shall I put on her head?"). Dime novels—the pulpy Westerns that were blamed for social ills, like comic books in the mid-20th century and violent video games today—figured in countless news stories.

Charles Dickens, Mark Twain and Walt Whitman were among the subjects of early author profiles, some reprinted from other newspapers and magazines, others written for The Times. When a correspondent visited Émile Zola in Paris in 1885, he found it "not a luxurious apartment. . . . Straight-backed chairs were arranged against the walls in gaunt precision. . . . A spiritless attempt at a bric-à-brac collection was nailed to the walls, and a few vases, suggestive of a New York boarding house, adorned the mantelpiece." When a writer called on Alexandre Dumas *fils,* he described the house—at

"No. 98 Avenue de Villiers"—as "glaringly white, three-storied, with a capacious *porte cochère,* which could hold half a dozen carriages and still not be uncomfortably crowded."

Authors like Dickens, William Makepeace Thackeray and Oscar Wilde were front-page news when they came to America on speaking tours; sometimes the paper began covering their visits the moment they disembarked from the ship.

Literary stories great and small were considered newsworthy. A letter of support Louisa May Alcott sent to the American Woman Suffrage Association was reprinted in full, as was Twain's remedy for a cold: "Plain gin was recommended, then gin and molasses, then gin and onions. I took all three." When Wilde fell victim to card cheats in New York, readers learned about it in a piece headlined "Oscar Fleeced at Banco."

Authors' marriages, illnesses, arrests, writing habits, children, money problems and vacations were fodder for stories. So were their deaths: When beloved authors were dying, The Times issued deathbed updates—in Whitman's case, for months—that we would now find intrusive.

Given the breadth—and depth—of literary coverage appearing throughout the paper in those early decades, it was perhaps no surprise that someone decided to corral all those stories and reviews into a dedicated book section. That someone was Adolph S. Ochs, who established the Book Review as a stand-alone supplement shortly after he became publisher of the paper in 1896. And thus was born The New York Times Book Review, a publication that over the course of its 125-year history has been known variously as "the Saturday Review of Books and Art," "the Sunday Book Review," "the NYTBR" or, mostly internally, simply "TBR" (not to be mistaken for the current acronym for "to be read," though you can understand the confusion).

"In this publication was carried out an idea of the publisher of The Times that a newspaper book

NO HOPE FOR WALT WHITMAN.

THE AGED POET MAY LIVE THREE OR FOUR DAYS LONGER.

PHILADELPHIA, Dec. 21.—All hope of Walt Whitman's recovery has been given up by his physicians, who say, however, that he may last as long as three or four days. He takes little or no nourishment, and was very weak to-night, but still maintains his cheerful disposition. He has been told his exact condition by the doctors, but he remarked to his nurse, "We may beat them all yet."

Dr. Alexander McAllister of Camden was called in by Dr. Longacre, and is now attending him regularly. The two physicians made an examination of their patient to-day, and found that his right lung is entirely collapsed and his left one two-thirds gone. His heart is the strongest organ. Only the doctors and the nurse are allowed to see the poet. Not even his brother, who called at the house to-day, was allowed to see him. His presence at the house was announced to "Walt," who sent down his love.

Dr. McAllister said to-night that he didn't think death would be sudden, but that he would sink away gradually. Dr. Buck, a friend of the poet, now in Canada, who is the possessor of all his manuscripts and knows all of his affairs, has been telegraphed for, and is expected to arrive at the bedside to-morrow or next day.

WALT WHITMAN STILL SINKING.

DOUBTFUL IF THE POET WILL BE LIVING THIS MORNING.

PHILADELPHIA, Dec. 26.—Dr. Buck, Walt Whitman's biographer, who is constantly with the poet, said this morning that he was so weak that it was doubtful if he would live until morning.

He dozed during the early part of the morning, and at 10 o'clock showed signs of sinking. His heart, which has been his healthiest organ during his illness and has been acting regularly, failed him to-day and became very unsteady. His pulse, which has been as low as 65, ran up to 95, and his respiration increased, his breathing becoming short gasps. He was lower at 5 o'clock to-day than at any time during the week. At 10 o'clock this evening his pulse fell to 88, and he appeared much easier, although he was very weak.

No nourishment was taken by the poet to-day, the only thing that passed his lips being an occasional sup of water. He appeared perfectly rational and clear-minded, but showed no disposition to talk, not even to his closest friends, and answered all questions put to him in monosyllables. The attending physician receives numerous letters and telegraph dispatches daily, asking after the sick poet's condition, but he has become so weak that they have discontinued showing them to him, as he apparently takes little interest in them.

AT HOME WITH EMILE ZOLA

HE TALKS FREELY OF HIS LIFE, HIS BOOKS, AND HIS WAYS.

HOW HE CAME TO WRITE THE MORE FAMOUS WORKS—HIS TOWN QUARTERS AND HIS LOVE OF COUNTRY LIFE.

News stories from early Times books coverage.

A woman reads at the New York Public Library, 1952.

review should be a literary newspaper, treating newly published books as news and containing besides other news of literary happenings," Elmer Davis wrote in *History of The New York Times, 1851-1921.*

"Books as news" remained the Book Review's watchword for years. "Literary criticism, an excellent thing in its way, but, properly speaking, a means rather than an end, has never been the chief object of its existence," the Book Review reiterated in 1913. "An open forum for the discussion of books from all sane and honest points of view is always accessible in The New York Times Book Review."

As time passed, the Book Review evolved, shedding its "books as news" dictum and embracing literary criticism, essays, theories and ideas. It became a lens through which to view not only literature but also the world at large, with scholars and thinkers weighing in on all the people and issues and subjects covered in books: philosophy, art, science, economics, history and more.

J. Donald Adams, who was appointed editor of the Book Review in 1925, later recalled: "When I took over, The Times thought that all you had to do was to tell people what was in the books. I wanted to make the Book Review something more than that." Under him, reviews became more opinionated and the coverage broader and deeper. "Dissent in itself can be exciting, can bring light into gray corners," Francis Brown wrote in a short history of the Book Review in 1968. "As our culture becomes more and more unified, diversity is a quality to be cherished and cultivated, and how dull it would be, how stultifying, to find ourselves in agreement on politics, aesthetics or what you will—and most of all on books, which by their very being testify to the diversity of man."

The Book Review didn't just explain to its readers; it began engaging them, stimulating them and occasionally angering them. It provoked—and encouraged—lively debate and the exchange of ideas, all while helping people figure out what book to pick up next.

In many ways, the Book Review's history is that of American letters. In this book, we'll highlight that history, drawing on our vast and varied archive to examine the ways the Book Review has shaped literary taste, informed arguments and driven the world of ideas in the United States and beyond. We've pored over more than 6,000 issues to bring you the best, worst, funniest, strangest and most influential coverage from our pages.

James Baldwin wrote for us, as did Langston Hughes. Toni Morrison was a regular contributor. Eudora Welty was briefly on staff and reviewed the likes of E. B. White, Virginia Woolf and S. J. Perelman. Here we have reviews by Margaret Atwood, Thomas Pynchon, Tennessee Williams and Nora Ephron. Presidents—Theodore Roosevelt, Bill Clinton, Herbert Hoover—wrote reviews, and so did musicians, poets, playwrights, scholars, Nobel winners, tycoons and Hollywood stars. Where appropriate, some reprinted reviews have been edited for clarity—and, quite frankly, to shorten them, since they often ran to many thousands of words.

We'll bring you the Book Review's most fascinating interviews, with everyone from Willa Cather to Gabriel García Márquez, as well as essays by Paule Marshall, Haruki Murakami and Walter Mosley, to name a few. We'll showcase a handful of our best letters. And along the way we'll show you how American reading tastes and book-buying patterns shifted, how literary criticism evolved and the ways in which history—particularly both world wars—shaped what was written and published. Yet even though the literary landscape has changed dramatically over the past 125 years—driven, in no small part, by the influence of the Book Review—some things remain the same: As an editor's note from 1897 points out, "Life is worth living because there are books."

TINA JORDAN
DEPUTY EDITOR,
THE NEW YORK TIMES BOOK REVIEW

A Review of the Review

PARUL SEHGAL

Halfway through *Lolita*, Humbert Humbert—relaxed, triumphant and a mere pinch of pages away from his downfall—stops to extol the wonders of America. He has dragged his 12-year-old quarry on a road trip across the country, a perversion of a honeymoon. He slips into French to marvel at all they have seen. "*Nous connûmes,*" he purrs, borrowing "a Flaubertian intonation"—*we came to know*—and enumerates each guesthouse and motel, each unsmiling landlady.

Nous connûmes—we came to know. It has felt like the mood of the moment, with the reappraisal of monuments, real and metaphorical, in our midst—writers included. There have been fresh considerations of William Faulkner, Flannery O'Connor, David Foster Wallace and others, as their private papers and private lives have come to light. *Nous connûmes* Nabokov himself; this past year brought forth a swarm of studies and, in March, an anthology dedicated to *Lolita* alone. The morality of the novel, and of its creator, are litigated with hot urgency, as if Nabokov, dead some 40 years, lingers in the dock somewhere.

Not a surprising moment, then, to be asked to explore the archives of The New York Times Book Review on the occasion of its 125th anniversary, a moment for celebration but also for some more challenging introspection, a moment to examine the publication's legacy in full. My brief, you could say, was to review the Book Review, to consider the coverage of "women, people of color, L.G.B.T.Q. writers"

and changing mores in criticism. But what revelatory news could I possibly bring? The word "archive" derives from the ancient Greek *arkheion*, sometimes translated as "house of the ruler." Who wanders there with any illusions?

What could those reviews contain? Some misjudgments, to be sure—masterpieces misunderstood in their time. A few preternaturally sensitive assessments. Fluorescent condescension and stereotype. Above all, the pleasant and dubious satisfactions of feeling superior to the past.

And yet. In recent years, The Times has faced scrutiny of the racial and gender imbalance in its reviews. One survey, which looked at nearly 750 books assessed by The Times in 2011, across all genres, found that nearly 90 percent of the authors assessed were white. But what about the reviews themselves: the language, the criteria? When "women, people of color, L.G.B.T.Q. writers" *were* reviewed, how was their work positioned? What patterns can we trace, what consequences? And what do we do with this knowledge—how can it be made useful? When we come to know, what do we really see?

To wander through 125 years of book reviews is to endure assault by adjective. All the *fatuous* books, the *frequently brilliant*, the *disappointing*, the *essential*. The adjectives one only ever encounters in a review (*indelible, risible*), the archaic descriptors (*sumptuous*). So many *masterpieces*, so many *duds*—now enjoying quiet anonymity.

What did I find? Those misjudged master-pieces—on Dreiser's *Sister Carrie*: "It is a book one can very well get along without reading." The sensitive assessments—consistently by the critic and former editor of the Book Review, John Leonard, an early and forceful champion of writers like Toni Morrison, John Edgar Wideman and Grace Paley. Fluorescent condescension and stereotype—on N. Scott Momaday's *House Made of Dawn*, which went on to win the 1969 Pulitzer Prize for fiction: "American Indians do not write novels and poetry as a rule or teach English in top-ranking universities either. But we cannot be patronizing." Oh, no?

The inaugural issue of the Book Review was published in 1896. It featured 10 reviews, all unsigned, along with lists of new books and literary happenings. An essay in the form of an imaginary conversation poked fun at novelists' stock phrases. On Laurence Sterne: "that 'shorn lamb' of his has been pulled hither and thither enough to be the toughest jerk mutton in the world."

Since 1924, the Book Review has run bylines. Contributors are not, for the most part, professional critics (a vanishing breed) but what Ford Madox Ford called "artist-practitioners"—the moonlighting novelist or specialist. Curiously, many seem to speak in one voice throughout the years, with that signature, seignorial remove.

That tone isn't merely a function of the rhythms of the short review; it flows from the house style. Reviewers almost never use "I," long discouraged by the paper, but the magisterial "we." What flaws did "we" discover in this slight but promising novel? Why do "we" go to fiction? (This last example from my—our?—own work.)

"We" can be a coercive little word. A forced embrace, a leash. It's Humbert's pronoun—*"nous"*—his way of speaking for Lolita. It presumes consensus; it presumes that "we" are the same. Margo Jefferson, a former book critic at The Times, has spoken about the peculiarity of the convention. "'We' meant that our readers were our students and our followers," she said. "It implied we were omni-scient narrators, leading them toward the best, the wisest, the most educated conclusions."

How unselfconsciously, how *affectionately*, that notion of consensus was once assumed—and inscribed. How specifically the reader of the Book Review was imagined and catered to. In a summer reading column in 1915, the Book Review recom-mended titles for the "intellectual enjoyment that appeals to 'the tired business man' on holiday."

As I reached midcentury in the archives, I kept bumping into one particular reviewer with a plump, paternalistic style and the Dickensian name of Marshall Sprague.

Sprague! I'd innocently turn a corner and find you back at it, comparing a woman writer to a trout—*as praise*.

His own best-known book—a study of the frontier (what else?)—was titled *A Gallery of Dudes*, a fair description of these pages at the time.

(A moment to appreciate the obituary of Francis Whiting Halsey, the Book Review's first editor, whose death in 1919 was presented as a sort of apotheosis of literary masculinity: "Overwork on a 10-volume history of the European War contributed to his last illness.") It was a clubby world put into a panic by the success of "the lit'ry lady," as a 1907 article termed her. Early issues of the Book Review were lively with alarm. Why Are Women Using Male Pseudonyms? How Dare Women Write From the Point of View of Male Characters? Why Are Women's Books Selling So Well? *"Is Woman Crowding Out Man From the Field of Fiction?"*

The suave "we" would not yet accommodate women, or others, and the reviewer acted as sentry, patrolling the pronoun's borders. For years the novelist Anthony Burgess, chief fiction reviewer of *The Observer* in London, was said to decide which women would be permitted to leave the "ghetto" of female writing. The longtime Times staff critic Orville Prescott enjoyed prerogatives of his own. (The paper's staff critics, of which I am now one, operate independently of the weekly Book Review.) In 1948, Prescott dismissed Gore Vidal's novel *The City and the Pillar* as "pornography"—an odd claim given the lack of sex in the book. I suspect that what Prescott really found so objectionable was the absence of shame in a love story between two men. Meanwhile, in the Book Review, C.V. Terry took a different view, but no less ugly: "A novel as sterile as its protagonist." Vidal and his publishers claimed that the Book Review refused to run paid advertisements and had him blacklisted for years.

Truman Capote's Southern Gothic *Other Voices, Other Rooms* was published that same month, and featured that famous author photograph: young Capote, lovely and sulky, splayed across the back jacket, making the kind of eye contact that can still make you flush, some 70 years on. Carlos Baker's review was an extended shudder. "The story," he

wrote, "did not need to be told, except to get it out of the author's system."

Note that language. It reappears in the reviews of the interlopers—the nonwhite writers, women writers and especially L.G.B.T.Q. writers. Their books are not written, they are not crafted—they are expelled, they are excreted, almost involuntarily. James Purdy's work—his "homosexual fiction" (this from a Wilfrid Sheed review)—represented "the sick outpouring of a confused, adolescent, distraught mind" (that from Prescott). Katherine Anne Porter's work received a clinical and distressing diagnosis: "The pellucid trickle has lately clouded." The charge can be twisted into a form of perverse praise, as if writing were a sort of bodily instinct. In a review of *Dust Tracks on a Road*, John Chamberlain wrote that the "saucy, defiant" Zora Neale Hurston was "born with a tongue in her head, and she has never failed to use it."

Where Black writers are concerned, another pattern can be detected. Reviewers might impute cultural importance to the work, but aesthetic significance only rarely. And if aesthetic significance was conferred, it often hinged on one particular quality: authenticity. The convention was so pronounced that a writer named Elizabeth Brown addressed it in her 1932 review of Countee Cullen's stinging satire *One Way to Heaven*. "Most of us have not yet reached the stage where we can appreciate any story about colored people at its face value without always straining to find in it some sort of presentation of 'Negro life,'" Brown wrote. "It is, therefore, from one who frankly knows little about the subject, an impertinence to say that Mr. Cullen paints a convincing picture of life in Harlem; but one can at least say that the picture is sometimes amusing, sometimes very moving, and at all times interesting."

That presumption—that the work of the Black writer was always coded autobiography, and *only* coded autobiography—was so entrenched, it feels startling to see the Black novelist praised purely for technique and inventiveness, to see an artistic lineage located, as in Wright Morris's review of Ralph Ellison's "Invisible Man," which named Ellison as a descendant of Virgil and Dante.

Authenticity was valued up to the point it contravened the (white) critic's notions of Black life. In his review of James Weldon Johnson's novel, *The Autobiography of an Ex-Colored Man*, Charles Willis Thompson, an op-ed writer for The Times and frequent reviewer, objected to Johnson's depiction of a lynching as an ordinary affair, attended by familiar figures and recognizable types. The author "knows more about such cases than I do," Willis concedes— Johnson worked as an anti-lynching advocate for the N.A.A.C.P.—but smoothly sails on. "I have never seen a lynching, but I have talked to many who have and they all tell me that the lynchers are the toughs and riff-raff of the community." Furthermore: "I have seen lynchers after the event, and they verify this description."

I can hear the muttered objections. Times were different. How crude, how predictably "woke" to apply present-day standards to the past. But I'm not referring to just the real relics, many of which provoke more amused incredulity than offense. (My particular favorite is an agitated essay from 1900 in which a "Mrs. Sherwood" inveighs against the fashion for heroines who smoke and befoul their fragrant feminine breath: "the sweet south wind over a bank of violets.")

To dismiss these reviews as mere fossils requires a series of awkward and dishonest contortions. Reviewers like Sheed and Prescott might have handled the work of gay writers with tongs, but the public didn't. *The City and the Pillar* and *Other Voices, Other Rooms* both made the Times bestseller list. And if these judgments were simply a matter of their times, would it make sense for Zora Neale Hurston to sound quite so exasperated in 1950? "It is assumed that all non-Anglo-Saxons are uncomplicated stereotypes," she wrote in an essay

titled "What White Publishers Won't Print." "They are lay figures mounted in the museum where all may take them in at a glance. They are made of bent wires without insides at all. So how could anybody write a book about the nonexistent?"

To my mind, the most persuasive evidence against treating such reviews as irrelevant artifacts is the letters to the editor. If the critic assumes (or imposes) consensus with that peremptory "we," in the letters, we see the reader recoil. *"We" who?*

In 1974, the writer Rebecca West excoriated *Conundrum*, Jan Morris's landmark memoir about her gender transition. Throughout, West refers to Morris as "Mr. Morris"—"one feels sure she is not a woman." West scorned the fact that Morris had transitioned as an older woman: "a woman who has had the equivalent of a hysterectomy, one who cannot offer the same facilities for love-making as a woman who was born a woman. And having changed sex so late in life, she is unlikely to attract the men that, earlier, would have made good husbands or lovers." To top it off, she objected to the "spirit of passionate advocacy," with which Morris wrote, as if "he [sic] had had to make the change from man to woman against a host of opposition." *Surely not.*

The responses were scathing. How could West pronounce upon the validity of Morris's sense of herself as a woman? How could she reject emotions she had not felt? "If this were an account of the first Everest ascent, should a reviewer doubt its honesty simply because no one had ever climbed the mountain before?" one reader asked. "Or, more to the point, because the reviewer had never wanted to himself?" Another reader, recuperating at home from a hysterectomy, wrote in furious solidarity with Morris: "I expect to have just as good a relationship now as formerly, and in fact, am waiting impatiently for my doctor's OK to go ahead."

But reviewers like West weren't firing off these broadsides from their desks unsolicited. These reviews were commissioned; they passed through multiple layers of editing. West's views on gender were far from a mystery. Christopher Hitchens would memorably describe her feminism as "above all concerned with the respect for, and the preservation of, true masculinity." A strange assignment, to say the least.

Perhaps not. In recent years, the paper has been grappling with its history of reporting on L.G.B.T.Q. issues, especially during the height of the AIDS epidemic. According to the paper's former executive editor Max Frankel, the longtime publisher Arthur Ochs Sulzberger instructed The Times to avoid the subject of gay life as much as possible. The stylebook did not allow the word "gay" to be used until 1987; the preference was for the clinical "homosexual."

How can one cover—let alone judge—what one refuses to see? What one is institutionally mandated to ignore?

There's a Jasper Johns sculpture called *The Critic Sees*. It features a pair of round-rimmed glasses. Where one expects two eyes are two open mouths instead, in mid-pronouncement.

It was 1981, and Toni Morrison was lonely. Not for readers or praise—she'd written four acclaimed books by then; her readership was wide and admiring. "My complaint about letters now would be the state of criticism," she said in an interview. "I have yet to read criticism that understands my work or is prepared to understand it. I don't care if the critic likes or dislikes it. I would just like to feel less isolated."

The relaxed, reflexive contempt of reviews of the past cannot be disentangled from their failures as pieces of criticism. They might stand in harsh judgment of the writer, but as examples of writing they're *soft*. They rarely quote the book, or offer more than perfunctory summary. We hear little of style, of argument or technique. I'm reminded of Richard Brinsley Sheridan's 18th-century play *The Critic*, which features two malicious critics, named

Dangle and Sneer. That's what these pieces do. They hover and mock, or patronize, the reviewer keeping his hands in his pockets all the while. He builds no case—he feels no need; the identity of the writer, the source of that obsessive fascination, appears to be all the evidence required for his scorn.

The opposite of "dangle and sneer" isn't "genuflect and revere." It's the work of vigorous reading, of research, curiosity, the capacity for surprise—*criticism*, in short. In a 2006 interview, Maxine Hong Kingston pined for "better criticism"—not kinder reviews: "I don't mean they praise my work more, I mean that they understand what the work is about and there is more willingness now to read a book by a minority person and to criticize it as literature and not just see it as anthropology."

In time, one begins to see calls for this kind of coverage in the Book Review itself. The section becomes self-reflective, critiquing a literary culture it had a powerful hand in creating. We see Bharati Mukherjee's 1988 front-page essay on immigrant fiction, in which she questioned the racial underpinnings of the fashion for literary minimalism. Meg Wolitzer's 2012 essay "The Second Shelf" asked why women's literary fiction is taken less seriously than men's, why women are derided for the narrowness of their subjects but punished if they take risks. If "a woman writes a doorstop filled with free associations about life and love and childbirth and war, and jokes and recipes and maybe even a novel-within-a-novel," Wolitzer wrote, "she risks being labeled undisciplined and self-indulgent."

A ghostly feeling settled over me as I read this essay. I'd seen the reviews Wolitzer was referring to—not just of her contemporaries but of generations past, that long, ignoble lineage. The contributor who, in 1905, sniffed that the woman writer would always paint on a small canvas, ask the small questions; his descendant in 2001 who berated a novelist for squandering ambitious experimental techniques on the deeply undeserving subject of a young girl's coming-of-age story. Another prickly feeling followed—that I've been reading writers who'd produced the very book Wolitzer imagined, as if they'd absorbed her piece. I think of Lucy Ellmann, who also contributed to the Book Review around that time. In 2019, she published *Ducks, Newburyport*, a thousand-page doorstop—all in one sentence, no less—about "life and love and childbirth and war, and jokes and recipes" (and a mountain lion). The novel won awards, raves; no one that I recall accused it of indulgence. The review or essay written in protest doesn't merely seed the work of the future; it can clear a path for its reception, creating the vocabulary and terms by which it will be received.

My copy of *Lolita* is all foxed pages and spindly spine, battered and beloved. It's my mother's old copy and still bears traces of her cigarette ash. Looking at the passage again now, I understand for the first time, shamefacedly, its irony. Humbert boasts of all he has seen, but what does it amount to but a few squalid motel rooms, variations in bathroom tile? "Nous connûmes" *nothing*. It's the very story of the novel—all that Humbert refuses to see about the girl he calls Lolita, about himself.

To look at the past is to look, for the most part, at what *can be seen*, what can be assessed. The number of women reviewed in an issue, the cruel jokes. I'm haunted by what cannot be quantified, what cannot be known—the long legacies of the language in the reviews, and how they creep into the present. How "reckonings" pass for restitution. I'm haunted by the notion of jettisoned novels and aborted careers—of novelists but also would-be reviewers. See, I know something of how language can be used to thwart and intimidate, about worlds so closed they awaken the great, self-preserving question: Why bother?

But bother I did; bother I do. In part because criticism, when I came to it, felt like freedom. The critics I first loved spoke with a note of defiant truthfulness; they were impatient with cliché, puffery and scolds, contemptuous of anxious gatekeeping. I'm not referring to academic critics but regular reviewers, whose only credentials were nerve, wariness and style. V. S. Pritchett, Anatole Broyard, Randall Jarrell, Elizabeth Hardwick, Margo Jefferson. They were so often transplants, immigrants, dropouts. Their notion of "we" was expansive and frequently full of playful provocation.

There are old, imperishable debates about whether criticism is itself an art form (depends who's doing it, I say). What cannot be in doubt is that criticism is itself a form of mythmaking, itself a story. And like any other story, it ought to withstand scrutiny, both of itself and what it purports to protect—for the desires of criticism and literature lie tangled together. "Stanley Elkin says you need great literature to have great criticism," Morrison once said. "I think it works the other way around. If there were better criticism, there would be better books."

Parul Sehgal is a book critic. She was previously a columnist and senior editor at the Book Review. She is the recipient of the Nona Balakian Award from the National Book Critics Circle for her criticism.

The steps of the New York Public Library on May 3, 1979.

1896

1921

CHAPTER ONE

The New York Times
SATURDAY REVIEW OF BOOKS AND ART.
NEW YORK, SATURDAY, JANUARY 3, 1903. SIXTEEN PAGES.

Contents

The New York Times
SATURDAY REVIEW OF BOOKS AND ART.
NEW YORK, SATURDAY, DECEMBER 7, 1901. 56 PAGES.

CONTENTS

ARCHITECTURE AND FURNITURE

A Novel Estimate of Books.

Has New York Advanced in the Fine Arts?

TOPICS OF THE WEEK.

The New York Times
SATURDAY REVIEW
NEW YORK, SATURDAY, OCTOBER 12, 1907. 16 PAGES.

TRUE FRIENDS.
By MARY E. KILLILEA.

THE REAL SHAW.
A Fellow Fabian Presents Him as a Serious Man with a Serious Purpose — Has Deliberately Undertaken to Make Sociology Joyous and Popular.

FEARS MAN IS A FAILURE.

TOPICS OF THE WEEK.

The New York Times
SATURDAY REVIEW
NEW YORK, SATURDAY, NOVEMBER 21, 1908. 16 PAGES.

BALLADE OF THE DREAMLAND ROSE.
By BLISS CARMAN.

W. J. LOCKE'S FRANK VIEWS
NOVELIST'S NOT UP TO POSSIBILITIES

TOPICS OF THE WEEK.

The New York Times
Review of Books
PART SIX. NEW YORK, JANUARY 12, 1913. 8 PAGES.

THE GREATEST CENTURY.
The Thirteenth the Most Really Constructive, the Most Spiritual, and the Most Philosophical Period in History
By THOMAS WALSH, Ph. D.

TRUTH ABOUT GISSING.
By H. G. WELLS.

The New York Times
Book Review and Magazine
SUNDAY, AUGUST 8, 1920. THIRTY-TWO PAGES.

THE LEADERS OF GERMANY
Illustrated by Césare

On October 10, 1896, "the Book Review became the newspaper of the rapidly expanding book world," *The Literary Digest* proclaimed in a 1919 piece celebrating Francis W. Halsey, the Book Review's first editor. "A paraphrase of The Times motto, 'All the news that's fit to print,' would have described the Book Review, 'All the books that are fit to be read.'"

It was the age of Rudyard Kipling, Ezra Pound, Edith Wharton, William Butler Yeats. In his history of the Book Review, Francis Brown noted, "It was a period of ferment, of individuality . . . and while the Book Review did not interpret the period as a whole in the sense of answering the why and the how, it did answer the what by reflecting and recording temper and mood."

The Book Review—which started at eight pages—exploded in size during its first 25 years. Often it was 32 pages; for special issues—such as holiday issues—it was as many as 56. Its basic format did not change until 1911, when there were two important developments. First, publication moved from Saturday to Sunday with the hopes that it "will be read with more thoughtful attention . . . when the subscriber is free from the cares and demands of weekday vocations." And second, the lead review began appearing regularly on the front page.

In 1920, the Book Review merged with The New York Times Magazine, an experiment that ended abruptly two years later.

The First Issue

The eight-page inaugural issue of The New York Times Saturday Book Review Supplement, dated October 10, 1896, featured news stories on the cover—including "Oscar Wilde's Forlorn State," about the author's suffering in jail, and one that should sound familiar: It was about how book sales at department stores were threatening independent bookstores.

There were 10 reviews. The one of *One Day's Courtship and the Heralds of Fame* began, "Mr. Robert Barr is a reasonably ingenious, versatile, fairly well informed writer, and frequently an irritating one." Of Emile Richebourg's *La Jolie Dentellière*, the critic offered what was clearly an insult: "This novel belongs to the class—a very large class—of French novels that seem to be written with a view to the stage as their ultimate destination." (The equivalent, perhaps, to a reviewer today noting derisively that a book reads like a movie treatment.)

There was also a piece that derided the use of cliché in fiction, lists of publishers' forthcoming titles, news of magazine articles, a page on art-world doings and a rather strange little piece reprinted from *The London Standard*—perhaps used to fill extra space—that had absolutely nothing to do with books or literature. "Science Has Neglected Eggs" was about keeping eggs fresh. "The egg problem seems one that might advantageously be taken up by those interested in developing poultry and eggs as a domestic industry."

In "Notoriety by Negation"—reprinted from a British journal called *The Saturday Review*—an unnamed critic took a few vicious swipes at the popular novelist Marie Corelli. The Times noted the critic's "savagely contemptuous" tone, adding that the motto of *The Saturday Review* "seems to be 'Anything to give pain.'"

All of the Book Review's early issues were, as Elmer Davis explained in *History of The New York Times, 1851–1921*, printed "in the form of loose sheets, folded into the rest of the paper. Those who didn't care to carry the Book Review about with them—they rarely failed to 'look over' it—let it blow away in the wind, so one morning the management of The Times was attracted, and rather aggrieved, by a cartoon in *Life* entitled 'The Littery Supplement,' and depicting a citizen desperately trying to struggle out of an elevated station through a heap of discarded sheets of The Times Saturday Book Review."

The New-York Times.

SATURDAY BOOK REVIEW SUPPLEMENT.

COPYRIGHTED. SATURDAY, OCTOBER 10, 1896. 8 PAGES.

BOOKSELLERS IN CONCLAVE

Steps to be Taken to Combat the Department Stores.

The National Association of Booksellers, Newsdealers, and Stationers held their fourteenth annual convention in Boston on Tuesday and Wednesday of this week. Nearly one hundred delegates were present on Tuesday. Eighty-six of them represented eight unions. Fourteen States were represented.

A committee, which had been appointed to consider the subjects, presented a long list of resolutions advocating that all dealers friendly to the order be admitted; that the publishers of all ten-cent periodicals be asked to furnish their publications to dealers at a uniform rate of 7 cents; that the organization request Harper & Brothers to print the selling price of their magazine, 35 cents, on its cover; that the cause of the abuse and unfair treatment that has until now been accorded to book publishers should cease. All booksellers, stationers, &c., were earnestly requested to join in order that an appreciable force might be felt to emanate from them. Women engaged in the book and news trade also were requested to join in separate unions in the different cities and towns.

Before the morning session closed, the Committee on Nominations brought in the following list of officers, recommending them for the ensuing year: President—J. F. Martin, New-York; First Vice President—F. A. Salisbury, Providence, R. I.; Second Vice President—J. E. Gray, Everett; Secretary—J. H. Riley, Providence; Treasurer—J. H. Nolan, Providence; Sergeant at Arms—B. Lewis, Boston; Executive Committee—M. Moy of Pawtucket, H. N. Borden of Boston, F. J. Hayden of Providence, F, R. Sampson of New-York, W. D. Madigan of Lancaster.

At the afternoon session about 150 delegates were present, and later 175. The election of the officers recommended by the Nomination Committee in the morning session was first acted upon. The list as given was carried through, with the exception of T. F. Martin, who was the candidate for President favored by the fifteen New-York delegates. Against him the Eastern delegates arrayed Mr. Michael F. Moy, who twice before had been elected, and on a vote being taken he was elected.

At the session on Wednesday the relations existing between publishers and newsdealers were fully discussed. It was decided to acquaint the publishers with the competition that dealers are meeting with and to seek their aid in lessening the evil.

An extended discussion was then entered upon as to the best means to adopt to do away with the competition dealers are meeting with from department stores. It was decided to appeal to the dealers throughout the country and organize for the purpose of endeavoring to secure legislation which will exact a tax from department stores for every department which they conduct outside of the principal line of business in which the proprietors are engaged. The dealers in Illinois are making strenuous efforts to obtain such legislation. It was decided, on motion of Mr. J. J. Daley, that the Secretary be authorized to send circulars to the trade, requesting a boycott on all publishers who do not treat the trade justly. The decision whether or not to send the circulars was left to the discretion of the Advisory Board.

JERSEY'S HISTORICAL SOCIETY.

Efforts Newark Is Making to Prevent Removal to Princeton.

The proposal to remove the library and collections of the New-Jersey State Historical Society from Newark to Princeton will be formally presented to the society for consideration a second time at a special meeting called to meet next week. Last Spring the Trustees of Princeton University made an offer of free accommodations to the society provided the removal should be made. The present quarters in Newark have long been inadequate. For about half a century the society has had its home in that city.

Last Spring, after the Princeton offer was made, a meeting of the society was held and the offer was considered, but it was finally decided to postpone action, in consequence of promised efforts to raise funds sufficient properly to provide for the needs of the society in Newark. How successful these efforts have been is not yet made public, but a report will be made at the meeting next week, and it is expected that a vote will be taken as to the acceptance of the Princeton offer.

An article in The Newark Daily Advertiser, urging further help for the movement to retain the society in that city, declares that "a large majority of the members of the society are citizens of Essex County, and local pride would peremptorily forbid the transfer of the society's collection to Princeton. The best interests of the society itself, as well as of the Newark Free Library, to the purposes of which the society's library is invaluable, preclude the thought of allowing the Historical Society to leave our city. But to retain the society and its collection some kind of terms must be offered. The society is living under intolerable conditions, its priceless collection is in hourly danger of destruction, it has no accommodations, and, therefore, a large part of its collection is boxed, and some of it lies in the vaults of the Public Library. If Newark is to retain the Historical Society, it must help to provide a decent home for the society.

"It is disagreeable to contemplate the possibility of such a reflection upon the intelligence and local pride of the Newark community as a vote by the Historical Society to remove to Princeton, and we cannot believe that the necessity will be made apparent when the society meets next week to take that extreme action. It is more agreeable to believe that the danger of losing an institution which belongs to half a century of Newark's history will bring forward citizens ready to pledge enough to erect a new building for the society."

OSCAR WILDE'S FORLORN STATE

Punishments He Undergoes—His Release Not Far Off.

What appears to be the best kind of information concerning the present condition of Oscar Wilde is given in the October number of The Bookman. Its authority is "an English official whose position has made him personally cognizant of the actual facts." The Bookman says:

"From this source we learn that Mr. Wilde's physical state is very distressing. He is unable to assimilate food, and an enteric disorder which has become chronic has reduced him to a condition of great weakness. He is governed by the silent system, and this is rigidly enforced, so much so that he has several times been punished for half involuntarily turning his head in chapel to get a glimpse of the person seated beside him.

"We were inquisitive enough to ask the nature of his punishment on these occasions, and were told that it consisted in having his 'rug' taken from him. The rug in question is a strip of rag carpet which serves as a substitute for a mattress, being spread upon the surface of a deal door which is his only bed; so that, when under punishment, he sleeps upon the bare planks.

"The gentleman who made these statements is persuaded that Wilde will lose either his life or his reason as the result of his imprisonment; but he probably underrates the extent of human endurance. The sentence, under the English system of commutation, has only some six months more to run, and it is generally understood that at its expiration Mrs. Wilde will rejoin her husband. As she has in her own right a settled income of £800 a year, they will probably make their future home in some obscure Continental town."

TO STEAL BANCROFT PLATES.

A Burglar's Attempt at the History Building in San Francisco.

Last week Wednesday an attempt was made in San Francisco to steal some of the plates of H. H. Bancroft's "History of the Pacific Coast," valued at $10,000. The burglar failed of accomplishing his purpose, but the case possesses some interesting features. He began his work shortly after 6 o'clock in the evening, and at 6:15 o'clock the next morning was caught by R. J. Weir, one of the members of the Bancroft Company, and A. McKenzie, the janitor.

The man was recognized by Weir, but, for some reason, Weir did not have him arrested, and the officers of the company refused to discuss the case. The man had been connected with the building, it is believed, or with the Bancroft family. No one would tell why the company protected the burglar or what was the cause of his attempted theft. The Chronicle says it is supposed that he was known about the building and succeeded in hiding himself in some place until the cellar was closed at 6 P. M.

There are 120 boxes of these history plates, and each weighs about eighty pounds. The man moved thirty-four of them to the elevator in the rear of the basement. He must have used a truck. They weighed nearly a ton and a half in all. After he put them on the elevator he tried to raise them to the level of the sidewalk, but the elevator would move upward only five feet. The burglar then went away, and did not return until daylight.

At 6:15 A. M. he came back, driving a large two-horse express wagon. He stopped in front of the door, opened it, and jumped down on the elevator to lift the boxes to the sidewalk. Weir and McKenzie, who had been watching, rushed at him, and he surrendered without a word. Weir made no attempt to arrest or detain the man, but became somewhat reconciled, and he was allowed to go off with his wagon.

C. O. Richards, son-in-law of Hubert H. Bancroft, and manager of the business, would not discuss the case with a Chronicle reporter. He tried to belittle it, and said that the work was probably that of "a hypo fiend," who tried to steal a few plates and sell the metal in them. Mr. Weir, in a pleasant way, told some parts of the story, but absolutely refused to tell who the burglar was, why he tried to steal the plates, or why he had been so quickly released. It was impossible for Detectives Ryan and O'Day to discover the cause of the attempted stealing. For the thirty-four boxes of plates the man could have obtained as metal about $65, though it would cost the Bancroft Company $10,000 to replace the plates if stolen or injured.

Some persons at first believed that men who had business troubles with H. H. Bancroft tried to seize the plates for the purpose of compelling him to come to a settlement with them. Another theory was that the burglar believed he could store the plates away and demand several thousand dollars for their return. The Chronicle says: "These theories fell through, as the plates really have no commercial value."

ARDITI'S REMINISCENCES.

His Career as Operatic Conductor in London and New-York.

Signor Luigi Arditi, of whom Lumley said that, "taking all qualities into account, a more able conductor never reigned in this country," has just published in London a volume of reminiscences, which have been edited by the Baroness von Zedlitz. An advance notice of the work, in The London Daily News, contains the following:

Politics he does not touch upon, although as Signor Arditi is known to have been the friend of Mazzini and other Italian patriots of his period, and later on was a more or less intimate acquaintance of Garibaldi, his recollections of political personages would, we think, be quite of equal interest. The book, however, deals with Arditi's career from the time when he and Bottesini spent two months on a sailing vessel from Genoa to Cuba, down to the present day; and, despite some padding, it is crammed with good things concerning the musical celebrities whom the veteran conductor has met. It was, for example, thanks to Alboni, that Arditi still shows a bald head. His hair came off after a boyish illness; but Alboni had a superstition against a wig, and, clutching it off Arditi's head, threw it to the other end of the singers' waiting room. This was in 1850, and in New-York; but Arditi afterward wore the wig furtively at home, and it was the first object which met his wife's eyes when she unpacked the portmanteau which he had taken on his honeymoon.

Then there is a story about Mario, who, in New-York, to Grisi's intense disgust, was haunted by a middle-aged spinster who had conceived a tender affection for him. The lady was said to be a Miss Coutts, but her real name was Giles, and she had previously been a similar annoyance to Charles Kean. She followed the Arditis on board ship, wearing a bonnet trimmed with orange blossoms, whereupon Grisi wickedly suggested a committee of gentlmen to drop her into the sea. It was on this American tour that on a bitterly cold night in Washington, Grisi, in place of the white draperies of Norma, wore a fur cloak, and Mario, as Pollio, held over her a huge coachman's umbrella, because the snow had broken down the roof. From America, in 1856, the Arditis came to London, and Mme. Arditi was immensely surprised, on being introduced to Bosio, to find that eminent prima-donna ostentatiously taking a pinch of snuff. Signor Arditi has much to say about Giuglini, Sontag, Titiens, Piccolomini, Viardot, and others. He also prints an interesting letter from Viardot concerning the first performance of Verdi's "Macbeth" in Dublin, where the irrepressible gallery boy, when the nurse and doctor appeared during Lady Macbeth's sleep-walking scene, seriously inquired, "Well, is it a boy or a girl?"

There is an anecdote about Titiens, who, in the scene with Pollio in "Norma," rushes to the gong, but who instead struck Giuglini fairly on the nose with the heavy gong stick, to the immense delight of the Dublin gallery. There is another good story about the rehearsal of "Roberto," in 1862, when the Bertram could get no response from his demons. Mapleson made no appearance, and Arditi, flinging down his baton, cried: "Where the devil is the impresario?" At that moment a huge black cat walked leisurely from the wings to the footlights, amid roars of laughter from the band. Arditi also prints a pleasant little mot of Rossini. When Mme. Arditi was first presented to him, the great composer bowed and said: "Now I know why Arditi composed 'Il Bacio.' ('The Kiss.')" Again, when Arditi had done Rossini some trifling service, the composer was profuse in thanks, and cordially offered him as a souvenir "one of my wigs," which were arranged on stands on the cheffonier.

When we come to more recent times the narrative becomes of personal rather than of general interest. Still here and there we find many interesting facts and amusing anecdotes. Christine Nilsson's nervousness when studying is exemplified by the statement that while singing to Arditi she used to tear the trimmings and laces off her dress by continually fingering them, to the despair of her lady companion, Mrs. Richardson. As an agreeable incident of Nilsson's first appearance in "Mignon" at Baden Baden, Arditi cites two letters of congratulation sent round to the artist's room by Viardot and Pauline Lucca. Rival vocalists are not usually so generous. Arditi alludes to the London production of "The Flying Dutchman," which he conducted in 1870, and records the surprise of himself and of Ludvig Straus that the overture was encored. That surprise was certainly not shared by anybody else.

Signor Arditi more than once accompanied the company of her Majesty's opera to the United States, and he records that at St. Louis a man walked twenty miles in the hope of "hearing Queen Victoria sing in her Majesty's troupe." At Cleveland, too, they did not want "Sonnambula," but "H. M. S. Pinafore," suggesting that Mlle. Marie Marimon should appear as Buttercup "because every one in Cleveland knew Sullivan's music." Again, in America it is necessary to be identified at the bank before a check can be cashed. In New-York, the cashier stated he did not know Arditi. "Have you ever been to the opera?" asked the conductor. The reply was in the affirmative. "Then," retorted Arditi, turning round, taking off his hat, and showing the back of his bald head, "look at that." He was at once recognized.

"Later on Arditi conducted the opening performance at Mme. Patti's private theatre, and he speaks with pardonable amazement of the fact that at the supper 450 bottles of champagne were drunk. At Liverpool, in the course of the Harris tour of 1888-9, he was shadowed by the police. At last he turned round upon the Sergeant, who saluted, and smilingly asked, "How did you like our men last night? We played the stage band in 'Aida' for you." Then came Arditi's tour with the Carl Rosa troupe, and finally, last year, the production of "Hansel und Gretel." Signor Arditi gives a list of his works, of vocalists who have sung under his baton, and so forth, besides portraits of eminent conductors and artists, and fac similes of letters from Viardot, Patti, Rossini, Garibaldi, Titiens, Giuglini, Gounod, and numerous other celebrities. His literary style is at times a little prolix; but the book on the whole is usually most interesting; while that it is highly amusing may be gathered from the good stories which, mostly in a greatly abbreviated from, we have quoted.

IN THE PUBLIC EYE.

In some comments on Harold Frederic's dispatch to THE TIMES explaining how William Morris declined the Poet Laureatship, The Rochester Union adds that Morris was a friend of Lord Rosebery, in whose gift the appointment was, and who was said to be inclined to make him Poet Laureate. Lord Rosebery's inclinations in this respect, it is said, were so well known that Morris intimated to him through a friend that he could not accept the post if it were offered. The result was that Rosebery went out of office without making an appointment.

If Victor Hugo had not been a great writer he would have been a notable artist, but who ever knew that Robert Louis Stevenson was a draughtsman? And yet he was. He never wrote a better book than "Travels With a Donkey in the Cevennes," and he originally made a series of illustrations for it. The London Studio will reproduce these sketches, and, besides, some humorous cuts of Stevenson's, engraved by him, which he made while spending a Winter at Davos.

Two eccentric French journalists, MM. Leroy and Papillaud, started from Paris, January, 1865, and without a sou in their pockets, depending on writing alone, reached Hongkong. They went through Italy, Greece, and Egypt. These literary tramps insist that they lived entirely by means of copy. M. Leroy, besides using his pen, made his pencil serve him. The French Journal "En Route" describes their journey so far. Our fearless scribes, when last heard of, were making for Japan.

There is a proof reader's tale about the late H. C. Bunner. When his delightful "Love in Old Clothes" was set up it quite nonplused an aged and worthy proof reader. The matter was written in a perfect Elizabethan style, whose words have additional letters, and some balance is kept up of clipping pronouns. The proof reader could not be made to understand it, and so he corrected every variation in his proof from Victorian English—if we admit that there is such a modern fixed vernacular. This proof reader, celebrated for his accuracy, was, however, born when spelling was in a state of transition, and so all modern copy was a bother to him. In one of Mr. Bunner's longer ventures he describes somewhat himself when he was a clerk in a large house in New-York, which concern imported South American products. In this romance, there is a description of crude Para rubber, and the author must have been an expert with this peculiar substance, so cleverly does he dwell on its characteristics.

The death of Dr. Julian Thomas, who was better known under his sobriquet of "The Vagabond," deserves more than a passing comment. Julian Thomas was a Virginian who after the civil war became a journalist, and was connected with a paper in New-York. In 1874 he went to Australia, and was associated with The Melbourne Argus. In Australia he advocated many reforms, and urged the founding of colonial lunatic asylums. In 1891-2 he was Secretary of the Royal Commission of Chantus, appointed by the Victorian Government. Dr. Thomas was keenly alive to colonial interests, and called public attention to the French and German aggressions in the South Sea. In his extended travels he visited all parts of Australia, New-Zealand, and China and Japan were well known to him. Dr. Thomas was sixty-five years old when he died.

Things to Avoid in Book Plates

Here the Book Review weighed in, a trifle pompously, on book plates, advising against comic or grim designs.

VERY MUCH HAS BEEN WRITTEN ABOUT BOOK plates in the sense of regarding them as bits of paper to be stuck into volumes, their adhesiveness as proprietary labels being dwelt upon to the exclusion of their artistic quality. A man having a library is supposably endowed with some literary taste. When he puts his plate into a book he not alone indicates proprietorship, but the idea is suggested that his volumes are to be preserved.

Though a person may be fastidious to his visiting card, he often shows indifference to the quality of his book plate. In selecting a subject for your ex libris, you may follow somewhat your own fancy, inclining toward heraldic emblems, if you please, but beware of comicalities. It is nothing less than lèse-majesté to put a comicality, with your name under it, on a grave, honest and dignified book. Punning book plates are worse than poster ones.

When you have decided what you want, consult an artist. He will, if he knows his business, simplify or bring out clearer your idea. Above all, eschew careless incapable engravers or etchers. Art is always poor when it is cheap. Remember that a book plate perpetuates as nothing else will coarseness and crudity.

There is a tendency of late (Germanic, possibly) to be gruesome in the composition of a book plate. So skeletons and death's heads from "Danse Macabre" have been copied. This illustrated pessimism is in bad taste. Life is worth living because there are books, and so let us open a tome with a happy thought, even if it were written by Schopenhauer.

"Can Any of Your Readers Furnish Me With a List of Books?"

The Book Review began running letters soon after its first issue in 1896, but these usually arrived in a trickle, with one or two tacked at the bottom of a page where space permitted.

By 1898, though, correspondence had exploded, and the letters section, called "Comment and Query" (the "query" portion was soon spun off into its own page), sometimes filled two pages. It was the internet message board of its day, lively and topical and bristling with opinions. Debates about books and reviews could—and often did—rage for months.

When there wasn't any simmering controversy, the editor posed questions to generate discussion.

For example, on December 31, 1898, in a note affixed to the top of the letters page, he invited readers to submit their lists of the best short stories ever written, saying he would be "glad to hear from them."

The letters page also served as a recommendation engine: From the very beginning, people wrote in seeking literary inspiration from fellow readers, who were only too happy to oblige.

To The Editor:

———

Can any of your readers furnish me with a list of books suitable for working girls, that would be good from a moral and not too poor from a literary point of view, and yet exciting enough to interest them? I confess I don't think they would appreciate Jane Austen, and yet I don't care to try Marie Corelli or Rider Haggard. If any of your readers could make any suggestions on the subject, they would greatly oblige.

A READER OF THE NEW YORK TIMES
New York, April 16, 1898

1896 ———————————— **1897** ———————————— **1897** ————————————→

The first issue of the Book Review is published on October 10, 1896.

The Book Review anoints the 50 best books of 1896. The No. 1 novel is J. M. Barrie's *Sentimental Tommy.*

Publishers Weekly reports that 5,703 new books and new editions were published in 1896.

I would like to make a few suggestions in response to the inquiry regarding books for working girls.

I presume the inquirer had in mind books of fiction in which the action is quick and interesting and free from much "philosophizing," or short stories, and given that the taste of the working girls in question has not been too much spoiled by a diet of *Family Story Paper*, I see no reason why there should not be a large and choice variety for them to select from. There are *Betty Alden*, by Jane G. Austin, and *The Green Door*, by Mary E. Wilkins; also Cooper's *Last of the Mohicans*, and Conan Doyle's *Refugees*.

Nearly all the titles given are of books read by myself before the age of 14, and I judge from the pleasure and food for reflection they afforded that they might be suitable to the intellect of the average working girl.

S.S.G.

East Orange, N.J., May 4, 1898

———

I think that "A Reader of The New York Times," whose letter appeared in the issue of April 23, will find *Ramona, In the Golden Days, All Sorts and Conditions of Men, A Singular Life* and *Rudder Grange* "exciting enough to interest working girls."

The "working girls" to whom I read aloud *Rudder Grange* confessed that it was "the first book they ever listened to without going to sleep." Their interest was unabated and they never failed to be present while the story lasted. Probably Stockton's other writings would have equally attracted them, but the readings were brought to an unexpected close. Surely it is something to bring amusement and brightness into dull lives.

There are, of course, working girls and working girls, and some of them may see nothing in *Rudder Grange*, as some of us can find nothing satisfactory in Rider Haggard or Marie Corelli.

A FRIEND OF THE WORKERS

New York, May 1, 1898

———

In making a selection for working girls, it is wise to bear in mind that a considerable percentage of them read with pleasure and appreciation novels every bit as good from a literary standpoint as do the girls in higher walks of life. I have in mind a cashier in a retail Avenue A butcher's shop who reads no novels at all but English literature and history, a packer at Macy's who reads only good poetry, a saleslady at Wanamaker's who reads "purpose novels," a cigarette girl who reads constantly such authors as Thackeray, William Morris, Walter Besant.

EDWIN WHITE GAILLARD

Librarian, Webster Free Library

New York, May 12, 1898

1898 —————————————
The Book Review runs a front-page piece on the importance of the bicycle, "which has become a force in latter-day letters."

1899 —————————————
The Book Review recommends Kate Chopin's *The Awakening* in its summer reading issue, calling it "clever" and "particularly poignant."

1900 —————————————→
In a front-page editorial, the Book Review rails against "heroines who smoke" in novels.

THE NEW YORK TIMES BOOK REVIEW

32

Early Book Review Headlines That Didn't Mince Words

FICTION, GOOD
AND OTHERWISE

~

PRURIENT AND
WORSE YET---DULL

~

Bad Prose as Well as Bad Verse.

~

FEVERISH FICTION.

~

A Painstaking but Dull Book.*

~

SUNDRY NOVELS

Some Worth Reading and Others
Not Worth the Printing

~

WELL-WRITTEN STORY:
UNPLEASANT CHARACTERS.

~

DULL CONFESSIONS BRIGHTLY REVIEWED.

~

WORTHLESS EDITION OF
A POOR ANTHOLOGY.

George Bernard Shaw, *Plays: Pleasant and Unpleasant*

In the beginning, only some reviews were signed—the ones by well-known critics and scholars. In 1905, the editor noted that the annual holiday issue was "remarkable for the large number of valuable contributions . . . from writers of eminence in their respective fields." This practice, however, was the exception, not the norm; unnamed pundits regularly took potshots at authors, poets and dramatists, some of whom began writing directly to the paper's publisher, Adolph Ochs, asking that he intercede on their behalf. Ochs's replies were courteous but firm. "I should be pleased to have notice taken of your book," he wrote to one Mr. Miller in 1901. "Of course in such matters, as you will readily understand, I do not interfere; in fact cannot do so without totally demoralizing our organization. Our high standing as to the literary character of The Times is due to the utmost freedom given for the honest expression of the opinion of the writers."

This review of George Bernard Shaw's plays, though, later caused quite a stir, probably because it crossed the line from "honest expression" to mean-spiritedness.

MR. SHAW IS ALWAYS SMART AND GLIB, AND he is not more demoniac or less human in any one of these plays, as a whole, than in another. They are all readable, if one likes to read Shaw's stuff, and for the sake of good measure he has written a long introduction to each volume, in which he sets forth again in his fluent, showy way, his barren philosophy and his unbounded self-esteem. He has not a touch of the poetical in his composition, and the critic and satirist who is not a bit of a poet cannot reasonably hope to win wide renown as a dramatist.

Of course, this criticism, and any other that may conceivably be made against these pieces, has been "discounted," as the phrase goes, by the author in his preface, wherein he proclaims his own artistic and literary kinship with the great. But this clever, voluble jack-of-all-trades . . .

1901
The French poet Sully Prudhomme wins the first Nobel Prize in Literature.

1901
Booker T. Washington publishes *Up From Slavery,* which the Book Review says is "a simple and unaffected biography."

1905
Mark Twain's 70th birthday celebration at Delmonico's is front-page news. The menus are inscribed with one of his famous lines: "Be good and you will be lonesome."

THE NEW YORK TIMES BOOK REVIEW

cannot be judged by his own comic standards when he puts his wares in the open market.

Mr. Shaw's new book is one which a multitude of readers would find intolerably dry. The moral of *Widowers' Houses* they would fail to comprehend. There are two or three passages in *The Philanderer* that seem capital burlesque. Probably a plumber's assistant would laugh at them if they were read aloud to him. *Mrs. Warren's Profession* has an unspeakable subject and the details of the story are unlikely. This play is too harsh and repellent, too bitter in its view of life, too dry and inconsequential to be acted.

A smart bit of historical perversion is called *The Man of Destiny,* and its subject is a supposed incident in the life of Napoleon. This shows, as some scenes in *The Devil's Disciple* (acted here last winter, but as yet unpublished) show, that Shaw has the instinct of stagecraft and the knack of devising situations, and that if he had a poet's gift he might become a real dramatist.

A striking portrait of the author serves as frontispiece in Vol. 1. His face is long and narrow, the brow high, the eyes shifty, the nose large, broad and blunt at the tip, the hair and beard scant Not a handsome man, surely and one who, except for the oddity of his dress and his views, and the unusual opportunities he has enjoyed to publicly exhibit both, would never have attracted much notice. And, to conclude, it should be borne in mind that there are ten thousand men and women in America and England writing smart, partly original, wholly unactable plays.

Shaw on February 3, 1889.

"Mr. Shaw's new book is one which a multitude of readers would find intolerably dry."

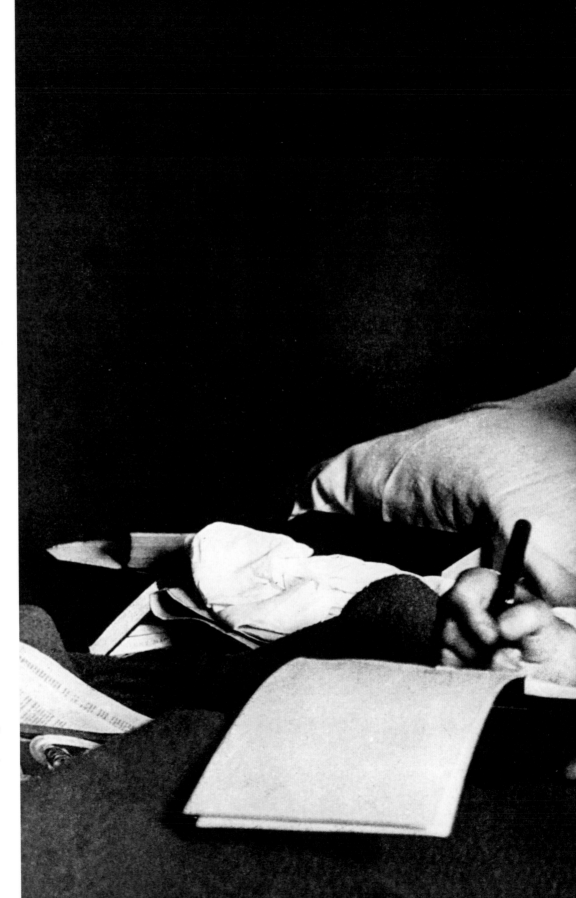

In 1902, The Times reported that Mark Twain "does a good deal of his work in bed," adding that the author once scolded a group of writers complaining about the difficulties of creative work. "Writing is the easiest thing in the world," he told them. "Just try it in bed sometime. I sit up with a pipe in my mouth and a board on my knees, and I scribble away. Thinking is easy work, and there isn't much labor in moving your fingers significantly to get the words down."

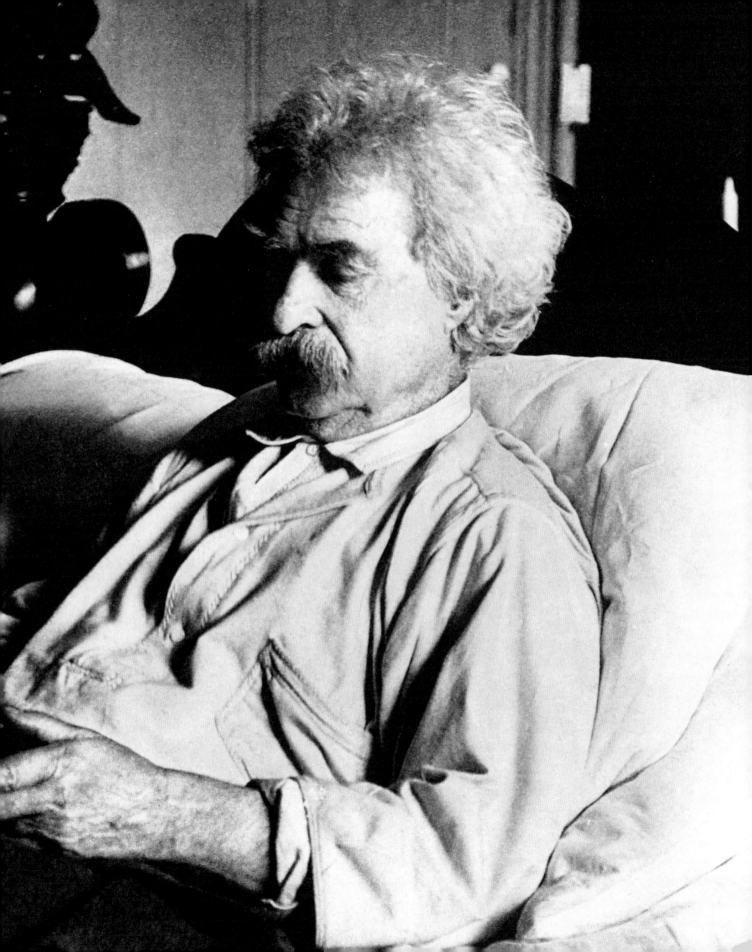

Henry James, *The Two Magics*

Sometimes the anonymous Book Review critics got it wrong; sometimes they got it very, very right. This assessment of the book that included "The Turn of the Screw" said of the horror novella, "The very breath of hell seems to pervade some of its chapters."

COMING IMMEDIATELY ON THE HEELS, AS ONE may say, of his painfully elaborate treatment of an almost worthless subject in a story called "In the Cage," this newer volume by Mr. James is doubly gratifying. We should not care, certainly, to recommend it offhand as agreeable reading for habitually light-hearted or light-minded persons, though, to be sure the second of the two stories which make up its contents, "Covering End," is a perfect example of pure comedy.

But it is to the longer tale that we desire to direct attention. "The Turn of the Screw" is such a deliberate, powerful, and horribly successful study of the magic of evil, and of the subtle influence over human hearts and minds of the sin with which this world is accursed, as our language has not produced since Stevenson wrote his "Jekyll and Hyde" tale.

Mr. James's story is perhaps as allegorical as Stevenson's, but the allegory is not so clear. We have called it "horribly successful," and the phrase seems to still stand to express the awful, almost overpowering sense of evil that human nature is subject to derived from it by the sensitive reader. We have no doubt that with such a reader Mr. James will invariably produce the effect he aims at. But the work is not horrible in any grotesque or realistic sense. The most affecting argument against sin we have lately encountered in literature, it is nevertheless free from the slightest hint of grossness. Yet while the manner of his story is always graceful, the very breath of hell seems to pervade some of its chapters.

Just what the story is would be unfair to divulge here, but a boy of 10 and a girl of 8 figure in it prominently, and they are so lovely in their outward semblance of childlike innocence. Yet these children are accursed, and are shown to have daily, almost hourly, communication with lost souls, the souls that formerly inhabited the bodies of a vicious governess and her paramour who, in the flesh, began the degradation of their victims. The awful "imagination of evil" this fair boy and girl must possess, the terrible precocity which enables them to deceive their pastors and masters as to their knowledge of their ghostly mentors, are set with perfect clearness against the narrative to produce the thrilling effect.

A Christmas house party, with ghost stories told around the fireplace, develops "The Turn of the Screw" in a tale of a ghost seen first by an innocent child, and this leads to the production of this ghost story read from the faded manuscript of a gentlewoman who had had experiences with the possessed children. The style of the manuscript, in spite of the insistence upon the woman's penmanship, is obviously the style of Mr. Henry James. But one appreciates not the less the touch in the statement that it was read "with a fine clearness that was like a rendering to the ear of the beauty of the author's hand."

A portrait of James published in The Times in 1916.

"'The Turn of the Screw' is such a deliberate, powerful, and horribly successful study of the magic of evil."

"Your Worship of Kipling"

In his reply to a somewhat cranky missive, the editor of the Book Review laid out its basic philosophy.

"YOUR WORSHIP OF KIPLING."

To The New York Times Saturday Review:

Is there never to be any let up in your worship of Kipling? I can put up with a considerable of that sort of thing; but you have brought it close to a state of nausea—and if, as I conjecture, Kipling is not hopelessly conceited, he must be nigh sickening of it himself.

TIMES READER.

New York, May 15, 1899.

To The New York Times Saturday Review:

Is there never to be any let up in your worship of Kipling? I can put up with a considerable amount of that sort of thing, but you have brought it close to a state of nausea—and if, as I conjecture, Kipling is not hopelessly conceited, he must be nigh sickening of it himself.

TIMES READER
May 15, 1899

The editor responds:

Although the above note is anonymous, this need not diminish the force of the appeal contained in it. The editor has, in fact, concluded to violate the ancient rule not to notice anonymous correspondence and accordingly gives "Times Reader" a hearing. "Times Reader" will be glad to know that the present number of The Saturday Review has been prepared with a special desire to please him (or her). So far as our most eagleish eye has determined, this present number of The Saturday Review does not contain a single article about Kipling, save of course the present, and for this "Times Reader" will not blame the editor. But it will be impossible to give "Times Reader" any guarantee of future immunity from Kipling. The Saturday Review must give the news of books. Its topics must be timely. Otherwise it would not remain long alive. The editor seriously hopes that "Times Reader" desires to see The Saturday Review continue its existence for many years. "Times Reader" is a candid friend, the kind of friend the editor likes to hear from. But these friends should always extend their candor one point further. They should send their names with their friendly admonitions.

Later

The above had been scheduled for a Kiplingless paper, and had been written in perfect good faith, when, late yesterday afternoon, there came to the editor news he had long had an inkling of but could not print until now—news of Mr. Kipling's new edition of his works. This seemed to us a most important piece of news and could not possibly be "held over." Will "Times Reader" please pardon us—or at least credit us with good intentions? And will he not understand that an editor, who aims to print the news, is far from being a free agent?

How a Christmas Classic Came to Be

The Book Review often reprinted Clement C. Moore's famous poem during the holiday season. In 1899, it published this brief history, which drew a fascinating reply from a reader.

THE MERRY CHRISTMAS SEASON ALWAYS awakens fresh reference to the name of another who quite by accident made the whole Christian world his debtor. Clement C. Moore, a man of profound learning, earned worldwide and enduring fame as the author of "A Visit From St. Nicholas," more familiarly called "The Night Before Christmas." No poem written by an American has had so wide a circulation or been translated into so many languages. The human spirit beats in it, the true Christmas spirit pervades it, and it will be dear to the hearts of children as long as children continue to hang their stockings on Christmas Eve—and may that beautiful custom never die out!

Moore, who gave this old Dutch legend its poetic form, was born (July 15, 1779), reared

CHRISTMAS CLASSIC IN AUTHOR'S HAND

"A Visit to St. Nicholas," Written by Clement C. Moore 100 Years Ago and Known to Every Child

'Twas the night before Christmas, when all through
the house
Not a creature was stirring, not even a mouse;
The stockings were hung by the chimney with care,
In hopes that St. Nicholas soon would be there;
The children were nestled all snug in their beds,
While visions of sugar-plums danced in their heads;
And mamma in her 'kerchief, and I in my cap,
Had just settled our brains for a long winter's nap;
When out on the lawn there arose such a clatter,
I sprang from the bed to see what what was the matter.
Away to the window I flew like a flash,
Tore open the shutters and threw up the sash.
The moon, on the breast of the new-fallen snow
Gave the lustre of mid-day to objects below,
When, what to my wondering eyes should appear,
But a miniature sleigh, and eight tiny rein-deer
With a little old driver, so lively and quick,
I knew in a moment it must be St. Nick.
More rapid than eagles his coursers they came,
And he whistled, and shouted, and called them by name;
"Now, Dasher! now, Dancer! now, Prancer and Vixen!
On, Comet! on, Cupid! on, Donder and Blitzen!
To the top of the porch! to the top of the wall!
Now dash away! dash away! dash away all!"

Page of "The Night Before Christmas" in the Handwriting of its Author.

A LITTLE book bound in red morocco holds the kernel of the children's celebration the world over of Christmas. To look at it no one would dream its hidden words are even now vibrating in the hearts of countless children, yet the 'neath its bright covers ing the original manuscript when it was presented to the society by T. W. Moore, a relative, some fifty years ago, is a letter in which the writer tells how the verses came to be written and how it happened that they were eventually published.

1907 —————————————
Theodore Dreiser republishes *Sister Carrie,* which the Book Review pans: "It is a book one can very well get along without reading."

1910 —————————————
Mark Twain dies. The paper reports that, on his deathbed, he called for his copy of Carlyle's *French Revolution.*

1910 —————————————→
The Book Review wonders if "the beautiful and ultra-virtuous American heroine of fiction" can possibly be "true to life."

1896–1921

and spent practically all his days in this city. His father had a stately mansion, a house that stood on a hill where the east side of Ninth Avenue, between Twenty-second and Twenty-third Streets, now is. It commanded a magnificently extensive view of the river and beyond, and the land was terraced to the water's edge.

Moore devoted his life to the education of young men for the ministry. He became Professor of Greek and Oriental Literature in the Episcopal Theological Seminary. As a relaxation from his serious work, Dr. Moore amused himself by writing stories and verses for the entertainment of his children, and "The Night Before Christmas" was written to aid their jollification while celebrating the holiday season of 1822.

A young lady from Troy, while on a visit to the home of Dr. Moore, saw the verses, and was so pleased with them that she begged the privilege of making a copy of them to show her friends at home. The following year, without consulting Dr. Moore, she sent the poem to the editor of the *Troy Sentinel*, in which it was printed on Dec. 23, 1823. The pleasure with which it was received, and the popularity which it immediately secured, mollified the good doctor's displeasure over its publication.

On July 10, 1863, Dr. Moore died at his summer home in Newport, R.I., at the ripe old age of 84 years. His place in the affections of his fellow men is secure as long as there is a pair of childish lips to murmur that happy closing line in his poetic version of the jolly old Dutch legend of "The Visit of St. Nicholas":

Merry Christmas to all, and to all a good night.

A week later, the Book Review printed a reply from a reader:

It is not so long ago that Clement C. Moore's old residence in New York's Chelsea was torn down. I remember it well. The whole block bounded by Twenty-second and Twenty-third Streets and Ninth and Tenth Avenues was, as late as 1855, a hill, with high stone walls supporting it on the street and avenue sides. I used to take my sled up in front of the old mansion and slide downhill, out at the northwest corner of Twenty-second and Ninth. That was the mansion in which "The Visit of St. Nicholas" was written. And those were the days before horse cars, when omnibuses ran in summer and big stage-sleighs in winter, for the snow stayed on the ground weeks at a time. I saw that old hill dug down and carted away, and that winter, 1856 I think it was, the rain collected and froze in the excavations and I skated there. But I will say no more, or I shall ramble too long and too far.

GEORGE W. VAN SICLEN
The night before Christmas, 1899

1911 — The Book Review switches to Sunday on January 29.

1911 — In an op-ed, the Book Review wonders if there is a connection between the divorce rate and the public's appetite for saucy novels.

1912 — Edgar Rice Burroughs publishes *Tarzan of the Apes.*

Charles W. Chesnutt, *The Marrow of Tradition*

Our reviewer found this fictional account of the rise of the white supremacy movement and the Wilmington insurrection of 1898 to be "too bitter" in places but conceded he was likely far from impartial.

MR. CHARLES W. CHESNUTT FORMED HIS STYLE and tested his strength in writing stories such as might be supposed to please his white readers and to place them in the attitude declared by Dr. Johnson to be correct when considering the performance of the dancing bear, but with *The House Behind the Cedars* he took a new stand and began to exhibit the darkness of the educated black man's lot, the hopelessness encompassing him, the dismal fate sure sooner or later to overtake him.

In his *The Marrow of Tradition,* published this week, he pursues the same policy, but the action includes an entire town and a large family connection, thus having a much wider scope than the former novel. The chief actors are white, and the main object of the story is to exhibit the deterioration in character and conduct caused by the effort to oppress the negro. The suffering of the dark race is made manifest also, but the book closes leaving the moral victory with them. "The negro question," says Mr. Chesnutt, "will trouble the American Government and the American conscience until a sustained effort is made to settle it upon principles of justice."

He shows his readers a mulatto physician, brilliant in his profession, the founder of a hospital, a good citizen, unimpeachable in any way, excluded from consultation because of his color. He shows the doctor's wife, the legitimate daughter of a mulatto and a white man, deprived of her inheritance and of her name by white women who conceived themselves to be doing their duty to their family and to society by suppressing her father's will. He shows a negro accused of a crime which he knows to be the work of a white man, but suppressing his knowledge and facing the terrors of lynching that his silence may possibly save the life of his former master, to whom the truth would be fatal. He shows white men planning to change the laws made during the Reconstruction period and allowing themselves to be led into falsehood, even into perjury, rather than tell the truth under the circumstances which would make them ludicrous in the eyes of the negroes. Last of all, the natural result of the forces set at work in the earlier chapters, he shows a town given over to bloodshed and terror, in the midst of which two who have most cruelly wronged the negroes are compelled to humiliate themselves before two of the despised race.

The book is skillfully written, and although certain occasional touches seem too bitter, or quite unfair, who shall say that to an impartial reader, to a Hindu or Chinese critic, they might not seem entirely impartial? They are certainly indications of feeling among the best class of negroes among whom the white men of the South should find allies in the task of justly and fairly settling the negro question.

Fiction has been so powerful an element in the relations of the North and the South that it cannot be neglected in contemplating the condition and prospects of the section, and Mr. Chesnutt's book should receive as much attention in the South as was given to *Red Rock* in the North. The two deal with persons of widely differing character, but neither pretends to generalize. Mr. Page's martyr doctor who gave his life to save that of a negro criminal, and Mr. Chesnutt's mulatto physician, his only son slain by a rioter's bullet, would understand one another. The two books should bring together men of their mind and spirit.

"The main object of the story is to exhibit the deterioration in character and conduct caused by the effort to oppress the negro."

Chesnutt writes in the library of his home in Cleveland, Ohio, May 1904.

Why Miss Alcott Still Lives

When *Little Women* was first published in 1868, the paper's reviewer wrote, "While occupied with something far graver and less agreeable, we pushed *Little Women* quietly within the reach of two younger critics, and soon had them silent for a time." The book met with the children's approval: "You ought to read it, though!" they said.

NOTHING CHANGES THE CHILD. BORN INTO AN age of iron, an age of steam, or an age of electricity, he is precisely the same, with the same primal reversion to ancestral tastes. He will read stories of war and hunting, and will long to use a wicked gun; he must pass through the barbaric period.

So must his sister, but for her the stories of the human giant and fairy are substituted. The human giant, the girl of 5 or 6 who performs all the household work of her father's small establishment; the domestic fairy, who bestows good gifts upon her entire family by charming an aged millionaire, or a dying miser, or an alienated grandparent, or a long exiled third cousin, are always favorite with girls.

It is because Miss Alcott ministered to the phase of childish feeling that her books have so long held sway among American girls, and it is small wonder that the appearance of two as plays and of one with 15 clever pictures sets them among the chief favorites of the holiday season.

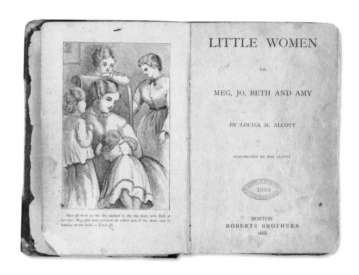

Yet, looking merely at their incidents and at the characters of their small personages, one is puzzled to see why they should be longer lived than a hundred ephemerals which have opened their wings to flutter about the Christmas candles and closed them to fall into forgotten slumbers. Their success is one of the strongest illustrations afforded by juvenile literature than, in art as in life, it is above all character that counts. Miss Alcott, as all the world knows, grew to her noble womanhood in a home which surpassed in quaintness anything which she would or could describe. She and her sisters had every opportunity to perform giant labors, and all manner of uses for fairy wands, and she, the strongest and the cleverest, found need for all her strength and cleverness, and when she wrote of the March family she merely described life as she knew it.

As Scotland to Burns and Sir Walter, as courts to Metternich, such was a New England home with plenty of nothing but love and courage to her. She had no need to rectify and enlarge, to cull anecdotes from the records of children. She had only to unveil the mirror of her heart.

A Form of Busybodyism

In its early days, the Book Review quite enjoyed issuing knuckle-rapping editorials like this one, which was written after the paper published a news story about censorship in an Illinois library.

THE NEW YORK TIMES THE OTHER DAY CON-tained an account, partly ridiculous and partly disgusting, of the tribulations which a library at Evanston has got into by undertaking to regulate the reading morals of that community. It appeared that the chief censor was the librarian, and her principle of exclusion was simple. Any book that contained any sentence to which any respectable person objected was thereupon "taboo." At least that is the only way in which we can account for the fact that pretty much all the recent novels that amount to anything or have anything to say were on the blacklist of this singular institution.

Of course there are in every community, and in an American community in larger numbers than in any other except a British, plenty of people endowed with a heaven-born itch for minding other people's business. The less they know about the business the more eager they are to mind it. But to interfere with the reading of other people and to insist that they shall read nothing but what you think good for them is a form of busybodyism in the pursuit of which much annoyance may be inflicted. It is to this that the busybodies of Evanston appear to have devoted themselves with great success, aided, or yielded to, by the authorities of the local library. If the Prurient Prudes find something in a current book which it would not be good for such a child to know, the offending volume must therefore "go." It matters not that it may be a work of genius by a writer of distinction and bear the imprint of a respectable publishing house. If somebody with a cultivated sense for indecency finds it indecent it is doomed. On such principles the volumes on the shelves of the Evanston library will soon be reduced to the goody goody class, which no sane soul can find interest in reading.

What sort of protection to the public morals is it to proscribe any book that any old woman of either sex and of any age may find "immoral" and then to publish the fact of that proscription? One would rather live under the Russian censorship than under that. The Russian censor is at least a male.

1912

Harper's finds Zane Grey's third novel, *Riders of the Purple Sage,* to be "too bludgy," and publishes it only after the author pleads with them. It is a huge hit.

1912

After the *Titanic* sinks, the paper publishes a poem about the tragedy by Thomas Hardy. Hundreds of readers then send in their own apparently bad poems, causing the paper to scold them for their "audacity."

1913

The Book Review issues a stern editorial against immoral books: "A bad book is much more dangerous than a bad play or a bad picture."

1896–1921

DRACULA
By BRAM STOKER

"To absorb you, to startle you, and to linger with you creepingly after you have read it."

PAPER 50 CENTS.
FOR SALE AT ALL BOOKSELLERS.

Arthur Conan Doyle at Home

One of the Book Review's most popular features, "Authors at Home," began in late 1897. These profiles were meant to "picture the subjects in relation to their environment and to draw them forth on conversations regarding their own work."

In 1901, the Book Review collected 22 of the stories and sold them as a book, *American Authors and Their Homes,* saying that "the volume, which as a piece of bookmaking leaves nothing to be desired, will, we are quite sure, be largely read by the admirers of the authors." The series continued for several more years, and in 1902 featured the home of Sir Arthur Conan Doyle, who was then as popular in this country as he was in Britain.

The Times had not always been a Doyle fan. It ran a blistering review in 1892: "Appreciation of Dr. Doyle's *Adventures of Sherlock Holmes* has to do with one's personal zest for the marvelous. You may care for one detective story, but when there is a round dozen, you may get a fit of indigestion. . . . Sherlock Holmes, with all his mise en scène, has too much premeditation about him. You get a little weary of his perspicacity."

SIR A. CONAN DOYLE, AUTHOR OF *SHERLOCK Holmes* and *The Hound of the Baskervilles,* when at home lives in a modest red brick residence, with many a gable and many a balcony in the neighborhood of South Norwood. Those who have made his literary acquaintance chiefly through the medium of his detective stories would probably find him a totally different appearing individual from the man they expected to see. There is nothing of the lynx-eyed, nothing "detective" about him—not even the regulation walk of our modern solver of mysteries. He is just a happy, homely, genial man, tall, broad-shouldered, with a hand that grips you heartily, and that in its sincerity of welcome is very likely to hurt. He is brown and bronzed, for he enters liberally into all outdoor sports—football, tennis, bowls and cricket. He is a capital amateur photographer, too. But in exercise he most leans toward tricycling. He is never happier than when on his tandem with his wife, starting a 30-mile spin.

It will probably surprise most people to learn that Dr. Doyle is still a comparatively young man. He was born in Edinburgh in 1859. He went to Stonyhurst, in Lancashire, at 9, and there had a school magazine, which he edited, and in which he wrote the poetry. At 17 Dr. Doyle began to study medicine. At 19 he sent his first real attempt, a story entitled "The Mystery of the Sassassa Valley," to *Chambers's Journal,* for which he received a guinea.

It was in 1882 that Dr. Doyle started practicing in Southsea, where he continued for eight years. By degrees literature took his attention from the preparation of prescriptions. In his spare time

Opposite: Doyle and his wife Louisa perch atop a tandem high-wheel bicycle in front of their London home, circa 1895.

he wrote some 50 or 60 stories for many of the best magazines. But Dr. Doyle was not entirely satisfied with his successes, and so for a time he turned his attention to another branch of literary effort. He devoted two years to the study of fourteenth century life in England—Edward III's reign. The period has hardly been treated in fiction at all, and he had to go back to early authorities for everything.

The result of this work was *The White Company,* which has gone through many editions. Then it was that Mr. Doyle made up his mind to go to London and start as an eye specialist—a branch of the profession of which he was particularly fond. He took rooms in Wimpole Street, had a brass plate put on the door, and started. But orders for stories began to come in, and at the expiration of three months he forsook medicine altogether.

Dr. Doyle's literary method is interesting. He invariably conceives the end of his story first, and writes up to it. He gets the climax, and his art lies in the ingenious way in which he conceals it from his readers. A story occupies about a week in writing, and the ideas have come at all manner of times—when out walking, cricketing, tricycling, or playing tennis.

The original of Sherlock Holmes, Dr. Joseph Bell, is an eminent practitioner of Edinburgh. Dr. Doyle frankly confesses his indebtedness to him, and tells how he was impressed by him in his student days. He says, "I was a clerk in Dr. Bell's ward. A clerk's duties are to note down all the patients to be seen and muster them together. Often I would have 70 or 80. Dr. Bell's intuitive powers were simply marvelous. Case No. 1 would step up. 'I see,' said Dr. Bell, 'you're suffering from drink. You even carry a flask in the inside breast

pocket of your coat.' Another case would come forward. 'Cobbler, I see.' Then he would turn to the students and point out to them that the inside of the knee of the man's trousers was worn. That was where the man had rested the lapstone—a peculiarity found only in cobblers.

"All this impressed me very much. He was continually before me—his sharp, piercing eyes, eagle nose, and striking features. There he would sit in his chair with fingers together—he was very dexterous with his hands—and just look at the man or woman before him.

"The remarkable individuality and tact of my old master made a deep and lasting impression on me, though I had not the faintest idea that it would one day lead me to forsake medicine for story writing."

In an interview, Dr. Bell acknowledged that Dr. Doyle was "one of the best students I ever had. He was always exceedingly interested in anything connected with diagnosis, and was never tired of trying to discover all those little details which one looks for.

"In regard to the practical application of those powers of observation, there is a system by which they may be cultivated, and I try to teach it to my pupils. The fatal mistake which the ordinary policeman makes is this, that he gets his theory first and then makes the facts fit it, instead of getting his facts first and making all his little observations and deductions until he is driven irresistibly by them into a direction he may never have originally contemplated.

"After all, there may be much more in life for a man if he keeps his eyes open. There is a problem, a whole game of chess, in many a trifling occurrence, if one learns how to make the moves."

Dips, Drops and Thrills
at Coney Island

Conan Doyle was a bona fide celebrity in this country, and the Book Review—and the rest of the paper— covered his personal life as thoroughly as it did his fiction. The author takes a summer cottage at Montauk! He sees a ghost! He has problems with his dinner jacket! He attends a cricket match! He is fined for driving his automobile in excess of 30 miles per hour! In 1914, when he visited Coney Island, it merited a news story.

CONAN DOYLE LIKE BIG BOY AT CONEY

With Lady Doyle and Detective Burns, He Does All the Stunts.

LAUGHS AT EVERYTHING

Bands Play "God Save the King" and Crowds Cheer Titled English Visitor.

Sir Arthur Conan Doyle, Lady Doyle, his wife, and a party of fifteen friends, including William J. Burns, the detective, and William F. Kenny of Brooklyn, visited Brighton Beach and Coney Island last night. Sir Arthur saw everything that was to be seen and did many of the things for which Coney is famous.

SIR ARTHUR CONAN DOYLE, LADY DOYLE, and a party of 15 friends visited Brighton Beach and Coney Island last night. Sir Arthur saw everything that was to be seen and did many of the things for which Coney is famous.

Scenic railways, dips and drops of all kinds, and absurd attractions like the Crazy Village in Luna Park appeared to please him immensely. He was either laughing outright or smiling broadly from the time he started.

The visit of Sir Arthur to Luna Park was more of a triumphal entry than anything else. As he stepped under the big front arch, the band began "God Save the King." Everyone in the park, it seemed, knew who was coming in, and those nearest Sir Arthur cheered him with vigor.

In Luna Sir Arthur entered right into the frolic of a Sunday night at Coney. First he shot the chutes, then he took the seemingly perilous Whip ride, and finally he went into the ridiculous Crazy Village. And he enjoyed it all—particularly the Whip, which he pronounced thrilling. The Infant Incubators were also visited and Lady Doyle was presented with a doll to which she had taken a fancy.

Castle House, the new summer dancing pavilion in Luna, held the visitors for some time. After she had watched several amateur and professional demonstrations of the one-step, the maxixe and other new dances, Lady Doyle was heard to remark that she saw nothing objectionable in the dancing.

After more than an hour of hilarity in Luna, Sir Arthur and the party went to the Coney Island Police Station, where Capt. Samuel McElroy and Lt. Samuel Hammond received them.

A visit to the Brighton Casino concluded the evening's entertainment. It was after midnight before Sir Arthur and Lady Doyle left Coney. When asked what he thought of the island, Sir Arthur said, "Coney Island doesn't give one time to think. I'm trying to get myself together. But I certainly had a good time."

Du Bois on May 31, 1919.

W. E. B. Du Bois,
The Souls of Black Folk

In this essay collection—now widely accepted as a foundational text of American intellectual history— Du Bois famously posited that "the problem of the 20th century is the problem of the color line." In it, Du Bois also detailed his now-storied critique of Booker T. Washington's emphasis on economic advancement. Rather than evaluating the work on its own merits, however, this review explicitly pits Du Bois against the clearly favored Washington.

IT IS GENERALLY CONCEDED THAT BOOKER T. Washington represents the best hope of the negro in America, and it is certain that of all the leaders of his people he has done the most for his fellows with the least friction with the whites who are most nearly concerned, those of the South. Here is another negro "educator," to use a current term, not brought up like Washington among the negroes of the South and to the manner of the Southern negro born, but one educated in New England—one who never saw a negro camp-meeting till he was grown to manhood and went among the people of his color as a teacher. Naturally he does not see everything as Booker Washington does: probably he does not understand his own people in their natural state as does the other; certainly he cannot understand the Southern white's point of view as the principal of Tuskegee does. Yet it is equally certain that *The Souls of Black Folk* throws much light upon the complexities of the negro problem, for it shows that the key note of at least some negro aspiration is still the abolition of the social color line. For it is the Jim Crow car, and the fact that he may not smoke a cigar and drink a cup of tea with the white man in the South, that most galls William E. Burghardt Du Bois of the Atlanta College for Negroes. That this social color line must in time vanish like the mists of the morning is the firm belief of the writer, as the opposite is the equally firm belief of the Southern white man; but in the meantime he admits the "hard fact" that the color line is, and for a long time must be.

The book is of curious warp and woof, and the poetical form of the title is the index to much of its content and phraseology. To a Southerner who knows the negro race as it exists in the South, it is plain that this negro of Northern education is, after all, as he says, "bone of the bone and flesh of the flesh" of the African race. Sentimental, poetical, picturesque, the acquired logic and the evident attempt to be critically fair-minded is strangely tangled with these racial characteristics and the racial rhetoric.

While the whole book is interesting, especially to a Southerner, and while the self-restraint and temperateness of the manner of stating even things which the Southerner regards as impossibilities, deserve much praise and disarm harsh criticism, the part of the book which is more immediately concerned with an arraignment of the present plans of Booker T. Washington is for the present the most important.

The writer admits the great value of Booker Washington's work. However, he does not believe so much in the gospel of the lamb, and does think that a bolder attitude, one of standing firmly upon rights guaranteed by the war amendments, and alluded to in complimentary fashion in the Declaration of Independence, is both more becoming to a race such as he conceives the negro race to be, and more likely to advance that race. "We feel in conscience bound," he says, "to ask three things: 1. The right to vote; 2. Civic equality; 3. The education of youth according to ability," and he is especially insistent on the higher education of the negro. The value of these arguments and the force of the statistics can best be judged after the book is read.

Many passages of the book will be very interesting to the student of the negro character who regards the race ethnologically and not politically, not as a dark cloud threatening the future of the United States, but as a peculiar people, and one, after all, but little understood by the best of its friends or the worst of its enemies outside of what the author of *The Souls of Black Folk* is fond of calling the "Awful Veil." Throughout it should be recalled that it is the thought of a negro of Northern education who has lived long among his brethren of the South yet who cannot fully feel the meaning of some things—and which the Southern-bred white knows by a similar instinct; certain things which are—by both accepted as facts—not theories—fundamental attitudes of race to race which are the product of conditions extending over centuries.

"For it is the Jim Crow car, and the fact that he may not smoke a cigar and drink a cup of tea with the white man in the South, that most galls William E. Burghardt Du Bois."

1914

The paper determines, after surveying 25 famous poets, that John Keats's "Ode on a Grecian Urn" is "the best short poem in English."

1914

The Times publishes an article headlined "Tango, Motors, Golf and 'Movies'—Enemies of Books."

1914

Scholars and critics chastise the paper for asking them to name the best short story in English. "You have asked a question to which there is really no answer," one writes tartly.

Ida Tarbell, *The History of the Standard Oil Company*

Tarbell, one of the most famous muckrakers—writers who helped expose Gilded Age corruption—originally wrote her investigation of John D. Rockefeller and the Standard Oil Company for *McClure's* magazine.

AS READABLE AS ANY "STORY," AND WITH rather no more of romance than the average "business novel," is this history of the rise, development and ultimate success of the Standard Oil Company. Incidentally, too, it is a history of the petroleum oil business from its first discovery and use as a "patent medicine" to its present position as fourth in the list of exports from this country. That the telling of this story should have been undertaken by a woman seems strange, perhaps, but Miss Tarbell was born in the Pennsylvania oil regions, and in her girlhood days was in the center of the sphere of agitation that has existed from the time of the discovery of oil up to the present. Her people were oil people.

Honest the writer has tried to be to both sides to the various controversies. Her records of these are digested from an enormous mass of statistics contained in almost numberless lawsuits, investigations by congressional and legislative committees, records of hearings brought about by investigation of charges against Standard Oil.

Her text is what she alleges to be an oft-repeated assertion by Mr. Rockefeller that "the oil business and its regulation belonged by right to them"—the Standard Oil Company, of which he was president. "John D. Rockefeller's one irreconcilable enemy in the oil business has been the oil producer. Whenever he has had the chance he sought to persuade the producers to do what he would have done had he owned the oil fields—keep the supply of crude oil short."

Beginning with the discovery of crude petroleum floating on the surface of Oil Creek by Samuel M. Keir, and his exploitation of it as a cure-all about 1850, followed with the belief of George H. Bissell that petroleum was a possible illuminant and lubricant, and the confirmation of that belief by Prof. Silliman of Yale and the subsequent development of the fields through experimental borings, the history traces the slow growth until the oil fever was at its height in western Pennsylvania.

At that time there was in business in Cleveland a commission firm known as Clark & Rockefeller. They had but little capital, but Mr. Rockefeller saw the great possibilities in refining petroleum. He took in Samuel Andrews as a partner. They improved the methods of refining, and Henry M. Flagler, Stephen V. Harkness, and William Rockefeller were brought into the business. These men in 1870 established the first Standard Oil Company. This was a couple of years after John D. Rockefeller had discovered the possibility and value of railroad rebates and had secured them from the railroads that were hauling his crude oil from the fields and carrying his refined oil to the seaboard. That matter of cheap transportation, the writer asserts, was the keynote to the success that Mr. Rockefeller achieved.

"That the telling of this story should have been undertaken by a woman seems strange."

When there was a row over this question of rates Mr. Rockefeller found an old charter for the South Improvement Company which granted practically limitless business powers. This he had resuscitated and under a secret arrangement got a lot of his competitors to go into the "trust" business under its provisions—the first thing of the kind ever established in this country. The producers found out about the company of refiners that had banded together to limit and control refining of oil and after a series of suits succeeded in having the company's charter revoked. But before this was done Mr. Rockefeller had managed to get most of the 25 Cleveland refineries under his control, and thus became the greatest of producers and shippers in the West. The railroads were after his trade and got it by rebates that no one else could get, though freely promising similar rebates to others who would ship as much oil as Rockefeller did. This none of them could do, even in combination. The oil producers raged and stormed and held meetings and had railroads investigated and tried legislative action—all in vain.

With the discovery of a means of pumping oil over the mountains from the fields to the tidewater refineries, oil producers were sure they had found a way to destroy the domination of the Standard Oil Company. Railroads tried in

Tarbell in 1905.

Other Classic Muckraking Books

HOW THE OTHER HALF LIVES: STUDIES AMONG THE TENEMENTS OF NEW YORK, BY JACOB A. RIIS
1890

The Book Review did not yet exist when Riis's famous treatise was published, but it received a long review in the paper: "The title explains itself, for it is true 'that one-half of the world does not know how the other half lives.' The question is, Does it care?"

OTHER PEOPLE'S MONEY AND HOW THE BANKERS USE IT, BY LOUIS BRANDEIS
1914

Although this detailed investigation into the misuse of investment funds is now considered a classic, the Book Review found it lacking in 1914: "The book is merely the revamping of old material, without new scandals, or original thought."

THE JUNGLE, BY UPTON SINCLAIR
1906

After finishing this novel—which famously exposed the seamy conditions inside Chicago meatpacking plants—The Times's reviewer wrote, "We lay aside *The Jungle* with a conviction that it is not, after all, a great and epoch-making work."

every way to block the building of the pipelines, and a dozen local "wars" resulted. But when Mr. Rockefeller was convinced that both crude and refined oils could be piped, he took the one way out of the difficulty. Agents bought out rival refineries in New York, Philadelphia, and Baltimore. All the terminal and refining facilities that were worth anything were acquired. And when the pipelines, built with the money of the producers, were completed and in good working order, they found that they had no purchasers for their goods except Standard Oil, which had now spread out to control the markets of the world by building huge tank steamers to transport oil in bulk. There was nothing to do but get discouraged and sell the pipelines to Mr. Rockefeller and his associates.

Goaded to desperation at the baffling of all their plans, the producers now attacked the very life of the Standard Oil Company, maintaining that all its business was illegally in the hands of nine trustees. Suits brought in Ohio proved successful, and the trust was ordered dissolved. Producers thought this an opening of the door to free competition. Mr. Rockefeller thought differently. He had secured a charter in New Jersey for another Standard Oil Company under which business could be carried on as secretly as ever, and he merely smiled when the old trust was dissolved and kept consolidating his interests and extending their scope under the Jersey charter until they are more firmly entrenched than ever.

And there this story leaves them, probably the most perfect business machine in the world, with a worldwide practical control of the refining and distribution of the cheapest illuminant and lubricating material on earth.

The Brouhaha Over Edith Wharton's *The House of Mirth*

New York society was outraged by the publication of this novel. Here's how the drama unfolded.

April 1, 1905 | The Book Review takes note of a serialized novel by Edith Wharton, noting that "Mrs. Wharton's serial in Scribner's, *The House of Mirth*, develops in a rather grim fashion."

July 8, 1905 | Book Review editors write a poem to Edith Wharton after reading the latest serial installment of *The House of Mirth*.

August 12, 1905 | Edith Wharton appears on the cover of the Book Review. The accompanying note from the editor says: "This is the first portrait printed in The New York Times Book Review in eight years or more, and the departure from custom is surely justified. The recently printed assertion that *The House of Mirth*, like most 'society' novels, promised to reach no logical or dramatic conclusion, and was likely to end, as it were, 'in the air' with a question mark, seems to be sufficiently disproven in the latest installment, in which the drawing together of the meshes of the plot is readily observed. Indeed the novel has a well-wrought plot which cannot fail to develop a striking denouement."

TO EDITH WHARTON.

After Reading the July Number of Scribner's Magazine.

SIBYL, endowed with a magical vision,
    Critic and scribe of our social melee;
    Splendid the past in your Vale of Decision,
    Keen is the wit in your tales of today.
Under your spell we have sauntered in bowers
Where Petrarch and Guido perhaps sang their lays.
Changing your mood, you have brightened the hours
With scintillant views of our own divorcees.
Now, in your guidance, we're threading the mazes
That wind and bewilder beyond comely portals—
Offended by Vanity's ugliest phases,
Shamed by the weakness of poor fellow-mortals—
Piercing recesses where scandal has birth,
In the halls of that House of so dubious Mirth.

October 15, 1905 | The New York Times Magazine publishes a feature on *House of Mirth*, calling it "a novel of remarkable power," and letters begin pouring into the Book Review.

To the Editor:

———

As usual, Mrs. Edith Wharton has written an interesting book—interesting in story and in style. She has also given it a good title. The milieu in which she has placed her dramatis personae is as fascinating as it is trite and vulgar. If this is a true picture of society, written with the art and knowledge of one who is said to be a member of it, what an appalling picture it presents! *The House of Mirth*, with its spacious halls, barren of all nobleness, empty of all high ideals, might truly be called *The House of Dearth*.
M. L. LIVINGSTON
Fort Hamilton, Oct. 30, 1905

The New York Times.

SATURDAY REVIEW OF BOOKS--PART II.

LITERARY SECTION OF THE NEW YORK TIMES.

NEW YORK, SATURDAY, AUGUST 12, 1905. 12 PAGES.

THE THUNDERER'S WHIM

New Venture of The London Times in the Field of Book Selling—Its Circulating Library.

THE London Times has, on what appears to be a considerable scale, gone into the business of selling books and running a circulating library of the sort on which the English reading public so largely rely for their supply of books. In its contracts with the publishers of the books which it proposes to sell or circulate it is stated that The Times stipulates not only for the discount accorded to the large distributing agencies, but also that a certain amount shall be expended for advertising in its columns, and that no like arrangement shall be made with any other newspaper for a fixed time; this was stated originally to be five years, but to have been reduced to one year.

⁂

THIS embarkation on lines somewhat novel, though not entirely so, for The Times has naturally caused much comment in the "trade" and in papers which are not prepared or desirous to follow in the footsteps of the great London journal. Some of the comment has been sharply adverse, and some of that has been distinctly amusing. The criticism by The Saturday Review of London showed something like a recrudescence of the "bitter and brutal" wit for which it was once celebrated. Our own Publishers' Weekly seizes the opportunity to discuss the possibility that The Times will enter the publishing field also, for which it predicts insurmountable difficulties, and it makes a running comparison of the present venture with the policy of the department stores in the matter of bookselling not flattering, as may be assumed, to the newspaper. But The Times is by no means without defenders. In The Sphere Mr. Clement Shorter points out several features of the situation which adverse critics have ignored. He says that there is no question of underselling, that the amount to be expended for advertising by the publishers selling to The Times is no greater than it has been customary for the publisher to spend, and that the paper has for some time been the largest single purchaser of books in the kingdom and has already found sale for some $10,000,000 worth. He expresses the opinion that the new enterprise will be of real and marked advantage to authors, publishers, and readers.

⁂

WHETHER this view be correct or not, we suppose that it is fair to assume it was not deeply considered by The Times except as it bore on the probable profits of the new line of business in connection with its older line of publishing a newspaper. It entered on the experiment undoubtedly with the opinion, if not the conviction, that it would in the long run and on the whole be profitable. If it shall turn out that way, it will probably be continued and expanded and the example will be followed by others. That, in this heartless world, is the way in which business questions are treated by business men, and though it is open to the suspicion of the terrible vice of "commercialism," it has prevailed since men began to barter among themselves.

⁂

THE world has wagged along under it not without a certain progress perceptible when we compare sufficiently widely separated periods, and we are inclined to think that the way will not be abandoned within a time worth while trying to predict about. There has long been a conflict between the

policies—economists like to call them the "principles"—of division and of concentration of employments and occupations. For some time past the latter policy has seemed to be making the greater advance, but in reality there has probably been going on a process of adjustment depending, after all, on the profit of one or the other or of a combination of the two. It is not a peaceful method, and it has its disagreeable consequences. But the peace that does not pass understanding is usually secured by fighting it out. The present-day enterprise of that newspaper which the Chancelleries of Europe used to call "the Thunderer" is interesting in the possibilities of development in the newspaper world it suggests. If a book shop and circulating library, why not an intelligence office and railway and steamboat ticket bureau, a lecture course, or a gymnasium?

A RECENT PORTRAIT OF EDITH WHARTON.

Photographed by Gessford, N. Y.   Copyright, 1905, by Charles Scribner's Sons.

SWINBURNE'S LYRICS.

A Consideration of Their Quality Based on a New Selection of the Poems, Arranged and Commented Upon by William Morton Payne.*

Written for THE NEW YORK TIMES SATURDAY REVIEW OF BOOKS by
MONTGOMERY SCHUYLER.

NO lover of English poetry will dispute that an anthology of Swinburne reduced to the proportions of a vade mecum is a desideratum. Such a selection has been attempted twice before, once by Richard Henry Stoddard in 1884, and once by the poet himself in 1887. Neither of these compilations is what lovers of poetry required, a "Golden Treasury," to use the title that Mr. Palgrave made both current and classical, of Swinburne's verse. For it is what that same Palgrave, with that sureness of critical appreciation which showed itself not so much in what he said about his poets as in the selections he so unfailingly made from them of their best, described as "the brilliant lyrical gift" of Mr. Swinburne that alone needed or deserved the honors of an anthology in order to give in manageable compass the measure of his poetical claims. Mr. Stoddard's selections included his poet's essays, to use the selector's words, "in the narrow province of Greek tragedy" and "in the broad world of the English drama," as well as "in the enchanted region of romantic verse." By attempting so much he would have beclouded and confused Swinburne's performance as a lyrical poet, even if his selections had been such as perfectly to represent it, which they were far from being. He was obliged to make, in the first place, much too big a book, a volume of over six hundred closely printed and double-columned pages. The poet's own selection must be dismissed as, upon the whole, an illustration of paternal fatuity. Rubinstein, when he was asked which of his own songs was his own favorite, made frank and humorous answer, "Oh, always the last." This uncritical attitude toward the Benjamins among his bantlings seemed to be that of the poet in becoming his own anthologist. Most admirers of his "brilliant lyrical gift" would agree, doubtless, that it was most brilliant exhibited in the first two series of the "Poems and Ballads." From the first he has chosen just one, and that the comparatively inconsiderable "Itylus"; from the second only two, "A Forsaken Garden," which of course nobody could spare, and "A Ballad of Dreamland," which most Swinburnians would willingly spare in behalf of any one of at least half a dozen other pieces

*SELECTED POEMS. By Algernon Charles Swinburne. Edited, with introduction and notes, by William Morton Payne, LL. D., associate editor of The Dial. Square 12mo. Pp. xii.-373. Boston, U. S. A., and London: D. C. Heath & Co. 1905.

I just finished *The House of Mirth* and hope to soon forget it. I had read the extravagant praise of it by reviewers, but it seems to me to be a detestable story, detailing with microscopic minuteness the downfall and death of a beautiful and virtuous girl. One is not introduced to one charming, pleasant, attractive person in over 400 pages. Mrs. Wharton and her men and women are always talking to the gallery. They are always straining to say bright things, and the stilted, rapierlike, Henry Jamesy style becomes wearisome.

I think the whole story produces a bad taste in the mouth, points to no moral, and as to the title, it should be changed to *The House of Lies*.

NEWPORT
New York, Nov. 15, 1905

———

This is an answer to the reader who signs herself Newport. I attribute the feminine gender without hesitation, as women are not apt to spare each other. Although Newport has read *The House of Mirth* and "hopes to forget it," it seems to have made a sufficient impression upon her to call forth such a torrent of ill-merited abuse. We who have read Newport's criticism hope soon to forget it. As a strong adherent of Mrs. Wharton and of her literary style, I take up the cudgels on behalf of the large majority who voice my sentiments. We prefer "the extravagant praises" of an army of reviewers to the harsh, badly expressed, and uncalled-for remarks of one unsympathetic critic.

LENOX
New York, Nov. 24, 1905

———

These here letters signed Lenox and Newport give me a pain; anyone would think from the fuss made over 'em that the writers was real swells. The one feels better because what Mrs. Wharton says is only too true, while the other pretends to be real mad at having his set misrepresented. Mrs. Wharton's book ain't in the same class with Thackeray's or George Eliot's, but she has the up-to-date society novelists beaten to a frazzle. The only criticism I can make is that she would have been fairer to the smart set if she had run in a few pure, high-minded, cultured representatives like me who are doing our best to discourage bridge and make the ladies stop smoking cigarettes.

OCEAN GROVE
Brooklyn, N.Y., Dec 13, 1905

———

I would like to express a few opinions in reference to criticisms of Mrs. Wharton and her book, *The House of Mirth,* by some readers of your publication, and to criticisms in general written by the "average reader." If our friends must make public their likes and dislikes of certain authors and their books, why should they not be a little more moderate in tone and thought, and not, like the country boy who, desiring to cut a sapling, took an axe in hand, when a pocket knife would have sufficed.

E.D.
Brooklyn, Dec. 28, 1905

———

I am an "average reader" and I do not like axe-swinging under my nose. Therefore, I wish to point out to "E.D." that this department of the Saturday Review of Books is sacred to the "average reader." We most of us want to know what the "average reader" thinks of a book, not merely his pocket-knife views, but his axe-swinging views as well. Upon the "axe-swinging" opinion of the "average reader" depends the fate of every book. What capable reviewers say is interesting, what the "average reader" actually thinks of a book is vital.

JAX
Northampton, Mass., Jan 4, 1906

The Book Review Turns Ten

"Since the announcement was made of the tenth anniversary of The New York Times Book Review, we have received many letters from persons of distinction in various walks of life," the Book Review announced on October 13, 1906. "Of course the world of literature is most largely represented, both by authors and by publishers. But the writers represent also the pulpit, the bar, the bench and the world of business."

The New York Times Book Review seems to be doing the best work of any paper of its kind in the country. The book reviews are very dignified and interesting; I read them every week with a great deal of pleasure.
ELLEN GLASGOW

I congratulate The New York Times Saturday Review of Books on its tenth anniversary. I read it with interest. Its criticisms are independent. Even the letters it prints from idiots (I recall, for instance the people who can see no humor in *Alice in Wonderland*) add to the gaiety.
JUDGE ROBERT GRANT

I have found The New York Times Saturday Review of Books of rare excellence. From the beginning it attracted and has held my attention. It is worthy of The New York Times.
ANDREW CARNEGIE

It is my belief that the publication of this supplement has rendered a most noteworthy service to literature. It has furthered an intelligent knowledge on the part of the book-reading public. I should hope that the interesting material presented in the literary supplement may have an influence on the readers of the political and financial sheet which otherwise they might not have been ready to interest themselves.
GEORGE HAVEN PUTNAM
G. P. Putnam's Sons

I can't do without The New York Times Saturday Review of Books. I read it every Saturday morning before dressing, and even creep down the cold stairs to the rear door to get it while the gas is still burning in the basement. The reviews are always good, thoughtful and just. But the influence of the "best-selling" lists is really in many instances harmful. I have been in stores when I was frankly told that not any but the six best-selling novels were handled, unless specifically ordered by a customer.
WILL N. HARBEN

For an all-around presentation of book news for the average intelligent man, don't think The New York Times Book Review has its superior. If you were only as enlightened on the subject of spelling reform as you are on most topics, I should consider you as near perfection as possible!
HENRY HOLT

The New York Times.

SATURDAY REVIEW OF BOOKS.

LITERARY SECTION OF THE NEW YORK TIMES.

NEW YORK, SATURDAY, OCTOBER 13, 1906. 20 PAGES.

Tenth Anniversary Number.

CONTENTS.

MR. HOWELLS'S ENGLISH TOWNS.

As a companion volume to his "London Films," issued last year, the Harpers will publish about the end of the current month further fruits of the recent visit of William Dean Howells to England. The new book bears the title "Certain Delightful English Towns." In it Mr. Howells takes the reader in that charming, easy-going, and companionable way which is his own to Exeter, Bath, Wells, Bristol, Folkstone, Canterbury, Oxford, Chester, and other places as rich in associations. Mr. Howells, in spite of all the pleasure he takes and leads you to take in these mellow old English places, looks at them always with American eyes. He is always keen for the details which link the history of the mother island with that of the younger nation on this side of the water. The view is an outside view, of course, and in so far superficial, but it is not less interesting or less full of suggestion on that account.

THE AUTHOR OF "A KENTUCKY CARDINAL" CORDIALLY PRAISES THE NEW YORK TIMES BOOK REVIEW.

The rounding-out of ten years of life for the New York Times Saturday-Book Review is an event of dignity and weight in the history of our critical literature. It was mature when it began; and it has added to its youth as it has added to its years. Both the gravity of its judgments and the freshness of its temper render it a vital force, and the multitude of those who look to it for serious guidance, or from lighter motives, testify alike to its solid character and to its range, its sunniness, its readableness. Where else may one find such a weekly gathering and sampling of the grapes that some day may be vinegar, or some day may be wine, or some day may be—neither!

James Lane Allen

A NOTE FROM JAMES LANE ALLEN.

AMERICAN POLITICS.

PHILIP LORING ALLEN, the well-known journalist, has finished his volume on American politics and politicians, and the Fleming H. Revell Company is rushing it through the press for early publication. Mr. Allen was a witness of every climax he describes, and so writes authoritatively about "America's Awakening." He tells how the "awakening came," about "Graft Among the Fathers," the work of Roosevelt, La Follette, Jerome, Folk, Cleveland, and other politicians, campaign methods and the changes in them at the present time, "The Trend Towards a Pure Democracy," "The Moral Wave and the Average Man," &c.

In the opening chapter Mr. Allen gives a résumé of the history of "bossism" and the reforms it led up to. In the course of this chapter he writes:

"Things is different" nearly everywhere. The country seems, in fact, to be emerging from a period when the rule of some boss or other was accepted as the normal and unalterable condition of American life. Some Americans lived under extremely benevolent despotisms, some under conditions most galling. The cause and cure of bossism had been for twenty years one of the most prolific topics of discussion in print. There were hierarchies of State bosses, city bosses, and ward bosses, interrelated, through natural co-operation within the party and secret and corrupt understandings between opposite parties. All of them received defeats now and then, but two successive defeats against the boss-made candidates was something almost unprecedented. Scholars began to study the boss as they would a scientific specimen, analyzing and describing his complicated activities. His average lease of power was solemnly computed at eight years. And the final proof of his acceptance as a permanent force was furnished when publicists began to point out that, instead of being an unmitigated evil, as the reformers had always insisted, the boss really performed some very useful functions for society.

ELINOR GLYN'S BOOK.

A NEW story by that gay and frivolous person, Elinor Glyn, is announced by the Harpers for publication Oct. 18. The story is called "Beyond the Rocks," and by all accounts trips audaciously along the ragged edges of a dangerous situation. Elizabeth, Ambrosine, Evangeline, previous inventions in the spiciness of girlhood created by this author, are all, it is said, outdone by Theodora, who plays the leading part here. This Theodora is married to a man of fifty-odd, excellent and rich, but—dull. Thereafter she meets another man who she thinks ought to have been her husband. And there you are. The scenes are laid in Paris and London, and you can trust Mrs. Glyn to avoid anything more than pleasantly shocking.

OUR TENTH ANNIVERSARY.

The Principles Which Have Guided The New York Times Book Review—Opinions of Its Services Expressed by Many Distinguished Persons.

THE present number of THE NEW YORK TIMES SATURDAY REVIEW OF BOOKS begins the eleventh year of its publication. The letters from various persons of the various sorts and conditions to which it makes its appeal show, in a manner most gratifying to its conductors, how complete has been the success of that appeal. The success, indeed, has been not only gratifying, but surprising to the projectors of THE NEW YORK TIMES BOOK REVIEW. Like the expenses of the Department of Agriculture, according to the naïve report of its earliest chief, it has "exceeded their most sanguine anticipations."

This is very likely to be the case with reference to any attempt to meet what, to the attempter, seems to be a "long-felt want." Either it is a failure and does not meet any popular demand at all, or else it meets a larger demand than could in a "conservative estimate" be expected. In 1896 every, or almost every, daily newspaper in New York maintained a "literary department," and for convenience this department was relegated to a certain day or days of the week, partly in its own interest, partly to meet the general exigencies of the publication of which it was an integral part. It was an entirely obvious suggestion that this department could and should be made a separate part of the publication. Entirely obvious, but, like Columbus's trick of standing the egg on end, it had not happened to occur to anybody. When you began to think about it it offered manifest advantages. The head of the family might hand over the literary supplement to his wife, women being, in America, quite notoriously the reading sex, while he solaced himself with the market reports and "quicquid agunt homines." Truly the ideal of a family newspaper is that which at once divides itself according to the ages, sexes, and conditions of the members of the family and answers their several and heterogeneous needs.

The first attempt to carry out this obvious notion which had not occurred to anybody was not very imposing. The first number of THE NEW YORK TIMES SATURDAY REVIEW OF BOOKS, written or compiled, naturally, exclusively by the staff of THE NEW YORK TIMES, consisted of eight pages of its present size, or four pages of the size of the newspaper. A page, at the utmost a page and a half, of the larger size would have held the ordinary literary department. The first number was swollen to four pages, not by advertisements, for there was not an advertisement in it excepting that the last of its eight pages was given to announcements concerning the Sunday edition of THE NEW YORK TIMES of the following day. It was swollen by the inclusion of a page about "art," which was early dropped by reason of the urgency of the literary claims upon space, by pages of publishers' announcements and so forth, so that the strictly literary department, the reviewing of current books and periodicals, did not, after all, much exceed that which all the morning papers, or nearly all, were devoting to the same subject matter.

From that small beginning it is a great stride to THE NEW YORK TIMES SATURDAY REVIEW OF BOOKS which most of its readers know. The REVIEW has acquired a large separate circulation. It is recognized as one of the most noteworthy attractions of the journal of which it is an outgrowth. It has on occasion expanded itself to fifty-six of its own pages, and frequently to forty-eight, its normal or average size being with difficulty kept down to sixteen pages.

L. M. Montgomery, *Anne of Green Gables*

When the first volume of this now-beloved series appeared in 1908, the Book Review found the character of plucky, outspoken Anne to be wanting: "All the other characters are human enough."

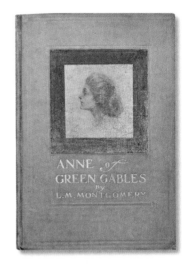

A FARMER IN PRINCE EDWARD'S ISLAND orders a boy from a Nova Scotia asylum, but the order got twisted and the result was that a girl was sent to the farmer instead of a boy. That girl is the heroine of L. M. Montgomery's story, *Anne of Green Gables,* and it is no exaggeration to say that she is one of the most extraordinary girls that ever came out of an ink pot.

This author undoubtedly meant her to be queer, but she is altogether too queer. She was only 11 years old when she reached the house in Prince Edward's Island, but, in spite of her tender years, and in spite of the fact that, excepting four months spent in the asylum, she had passed all her life with illiterate folks, and had had almost no schooling, she talked to the farmer and his sister as though she had borrowed Bernard Shaw's dictionary, Alfred Austin's sentimentality, and the reasoning powers of a justice of the Supreme Court. She knew so much that she spoiled the author's plan at the very outset and greatly marred a story that had in it quaint and charming possibilities.

The author's probable intent was to exhibit a unique development in this little asylum waif, but there is no real difference between the girl at the end of the story and the one at the beginning of it. All the other characters in the book are human enough.

1914 ——————
A reporter examines the things patrons scrawl in library books. Balzac's novels are roundly criticized: "I shall need to be fumigated after this."

1914 ——————
The paper reports that in a new trend, authors—Booth Tarkington, Ida Tarbell—have begun appearing in the movie versions of their books.

1915 ——————→
The review of Somerset Maugham's *Of Human Bondage* notes that "it is not meant to provide pleasant voyaging for the weary."

Other Famous Pans

COLLECTED POEMS,
BY WILLIAM BUTLER YEATS
1896

Though he would go on to be awarded the Nobel Prize for literature in 1923, the Book Review was not an early fan of the Irish poet, calling this volume "as discouraging as a breakfast of cold porridge."

THE GOLDEN BOWL,
BY HENRY JAMES
1904

Perhaps because of its primary theme—adultery—the paper took a dim view of this novel: "It seems to me to present Mr. James at his worst."

SISTER CARRIE,
BY THEODORE DREISER
1907

"It is a book one can very well get along without reading," an unnamed critic sniped of Dreiser's novel about early-20th-century urban American life.

HOWARDS END,
BY E. M. FORSTER
1911

Though this socially astute novel is often considered to be Forster's masterpiece, the Book Review was not a fan. "Mr. Forster . . . evinces neither power nor inclination to come to grips with any vital human problem."

ULYSSES,
BY JAMES JOYCE
1922

The paper's reviewer, Dr. Joseph Collins, called Joyce's masterwork "the most important contribution that has been made to fictional literature in the 20th century," but stressed, "The average intelligent reader will glean little or nothing from it—even from careful perusal, one might properly say study of it—save bewilderment and a sense of disgust."

BUDDENBROOKS,
BY THOMAS MANN
1924

When Mann's master work was finally translated into English, the Book Review's unnamed critic found it "immature," adding sourly, "One has a suspicion that Mann likes death scenes."

TENDER IS THE NIGHT,
BY F. SCOTT FITZGERALD
1934

"Bad news is best blurted out at once," the Book Review said of this novel, published eight years after *The Great Gatsby*. "*Tender Is the Night* is a disappointment . . . not the work of a wise and mature novelist."

Literature in the Trenches

BY LT. CONINGSBY DAWSON

War was still raging in Europe when the Book Review commissioned this essay from a lieutenant in the Canadian army—who, in his civilian life, was a novelist.

I HAVE BEEN ASKED TO SAY SOMETHING FOR The New York Times Book Review on literature in the trenches. There isn't any. There isn't any in the sense that people living in America would understand. The life that men lead in the trenches is greater literature than was ever penned. When a man gets a rest from fighting he doesn't want to spend his time in the same ecstatic atmosphere in which he has been existing close to No Man's Land; what he wants is something that will give him contrast.

As far as my own personal taste is concerned, when I was in the trenches I would far rather read a penny dreadful than a novel by Jane Austen. The book which would have given me the greatest delight is an unexpurgated edition of *The Lives of the Notorious Pirates*.

Literature in peace times consists for the most part in the expression of noble purposes which nobody practices. As far as fiction is concerned its chief interest is as to whether the hero kissed her in the drawing room or the pantry. When a man gets to the front there is no "her." He lives his noble purposes unconsciously and doesn't want to read about them. Therefore the kinds of books he likes to read are the sort of reflection of himself that a concave mirror gives of a very thin man.

Since I have been on the Western front, I have discovered only one man who loved literature, a Shakespeare enthusiast. I had lost my way and stumbled into a strange dugout. I don't think I had been there five minutes before we found ourselves in a heated discussion over a highly technical point in the sonnets. My chief object in calling in at the dugout was to discover the shortest way back to my battery. Shakespeare did not seem of vital importance at the moment. I only commenced the conversation as a means to an end. When I got up to go, the officer in question volunteered to see me on the road. It was pitch black and there was occasional shelling. Nevertheless, he poured out his soul about Shakespeare. We came to a crossroad where ammunition limbers were going up. We climbed on one and continued talking. Not so far away to our left was the Hun front line, with that wonderful phantom city made of flares and rockets and lights shooting up. As we rode upon the limber through the blackness and the ruined country we forgot the tension and horror of our environment. Presently we came to a point which I recognized, dismounted and tumbled into a trench. After fumbling our way a little further we came to my kennel. It was toward 3 A.M. before my enthusiast for Shakespeare left me. He was one of the few men whom I have met in France whose love for literature and the imaginative world outran his dog-tired love of sleeping.

One has a strange feeling about books when he is in the immediate presence of death. I remember an anecdote about a famous Swedish writer which partly illustrates my mood. The watchers by his bedside thought that he was dead. Suddenly he raised himself up.

"Now I could write," he whispered. They were his last words.

In the light of my experiences at the front I know what he meant. The petty personal problems which we cloak in words and call literature seem so ignoble a presentation of men and women who are planned for immortality and live in an infinite world. I went to France fully intending to keep a record of what I felt and saw there. I soon found that what I felt and saw was too grave to put on paper; I cheapened myself in my own eyes in the attempt.

Yet there are moments when one's old love of self-expression survives. I remember a night on the Somme when I was forward as observation officer. We had a dugout in a shallows trench in which we were supposed to take shelter during shelling. The Huns knew with absolute certainty the location of our observation station and used to place their shells so near to us that they would frequently blow the candles out with the concussion. I was fairly new to the game then and I thought it was an officer's duty never to take cover during shelling, but to stand up making a pretense that he enjoyed it. I have learned better now. On this particular night the moon was shining brightly over the recent battlefield. A great number of our unburied dead were lying where they had fallen and one could distinctly hear the scurry of the scavenger rats. Some hundreds of yards away, etched against the horizon, were the ruins and blasted trees of a battered town. Behind that was the miraculous metropolis, of which I have already spoken, consisting of Hun signals, flares and rockets. In the immense silence which prevails after a period of shelling, I began to plan

Dawson.

my next novel. I tried to think what there could be after the big experiences I was having that would be worth writing about. It seemed to me that nothing personal could ever again be worth recording. An army does not think in individuals; it thinks in crowds. The individual soon learns that he is of no importance, save as far as he marches in step with his battalion. Something like that happens to a writer when he has seen the populations of cities go over the top in an attack. It is the big motive that shoves the individuals out of the trench and into heroism that alone is worth mentioning.

And yet the front has its humor as well—a grim kind of humor. This spring I was sent forward into a town which we had recently captured to discover an officer. The stones of the houses had already been knocked down and the Hun was doing his best to blast them into powder. I had reached a certain point when suddenly the Hun barrage descended. I knew that if I didn't complete my errand I should have trouble coming back later, so I made up my mind to try to find my illusive friend. I had hunted about for some time and the shelling was becoming more intense, when from underground a music-hall gramophone voice commenced singing: "All that I want is someone to love me, and to love me well—very well."

That finished me. "You can love yourself," I thought, and promptly beat it.

Literature! There's heaps of it at the front and no one to write it down. Men say and do more exquisitely poignant and noble things every day than have ever been penned.

With the following examples I will end: In a certain attack the Hun set to work to knock out our artillery. He commenced with a heavy shelling of the batteries which lasted for some hours; this he followed up with a barrage of gas shells. The gunners' only chance of protecting

"The life that men lead in the trenches is greater literature than was ever penned."

themselves from the deadly fumes was to wear their gas helmets. All of a sudden when the gassing of our batteries was at its worst along our front, S.O.S. signals were discerned.

Word came through that our infantry were being badly strafed and were expecting a heavy Hun counterattack. You cannot lay a gun or set fuses in a gas helmet. If our infantry were to be saved, some of the men at the batteries must sacrifice themselves. Without an order from anyone, the fuse-setters and gun-layers tore off their helmets. Our guns opened up.

The unmasked men lasted about 20 minutes; when they had been done others removed their only protection and followed their example. This went on for two hours. They weren't going to let their pals in the trenches down. The spirit of the new literature after peace is declared, if I know anything about men, is going to be the spirit of those gunners. We're not going to write the kinds of books that let our pals down. We've finished with the old indecencies and doubts. The sacrifice of the trenches has taught us better.

1915 ——————————————————
The publishing house Alfred A. Knopf is established.

1916 ——————————————————
An editor's note in the 20th anniversary issue reiterates that the Book Review "distinctly does not lend itself to faddism."

1920 ——————————————————→
On June 2, 15 famous American writers cable Thomas Hardy to wish him a happy 80th birthday.

A World War I
Reading List

After the war, bookstores were flooded with military memoirs. "No one can possibly read these stories, told so frankly, so simply, so artlessly by the youths to whom the tremendous business over war became the commonplace of existence, without tears that burn the eyes," the Book Review opined in 1917.

THE FIRST HUNDRED THOUSAND,
BY IAN HAY
1916

"Here is a book which gives the experiences of an actual soldier," the Book Review said, adding that the book was so simply and vividly written that it "is likely to endure when most of the other war books are forgotten."

FROM MONTREAL TO
VIMY RIDGE AND BEYOND,
BY LIEUTENANT CLIFFORD
ALMON WELLS
1917

This collection of letters, sent by a Canadian lieutenant who was killed in action at the Battle of Vimy Ridge, "was not written for the public," the Book Review noted. "But it is profoundly moving and interesting, with a universal note in it these days, when the war is coming so close to us all."

CRUMPS,
BY LOUIS KEENE
1917

This memoir, by a Canadian soldier, "takes the whole thing a good deal as a college boy takes a big football game; it's all something of a lark, a glorious great game, and even the horrors are touched on with a latent feeling that they are, in their own way, humorous. There is the story of the right hand of a dead man sticking out of the trench in the position of a man trying to shake hands, 'and as the men filed by they would often grip it and say, "So long, old top; we'll be back again soon."'"

PRIVATE PEAT,
BY HAROLD R. PEAT
1917

"Private Peat gives us an intimate picture of the daily life of the trenches," the Book Review said, "of the weariness and boredom of many of the days, of the pastimes of the soldiers, of the exchanges of words and signs that used, but do not now, to pass between the men in the opposing trenches. . . . In the end he is terribly wounded, lies two days without succor, finally to be reached and saved."

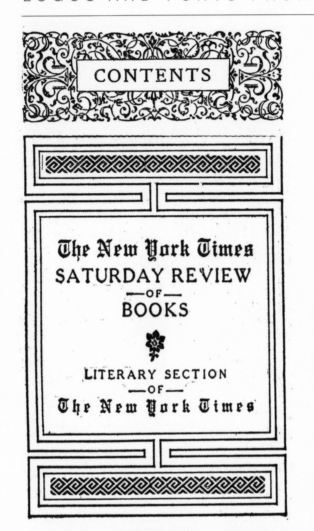

CONTENTS

The New York Times
SATURDAY REVIEW
—OF—
BOOKS

LITERARY SECTION
—OF—
The New York Times

Books Worth Reading Again.

"When a new book comes out, I read an old one."—Emerson.

XV.

Authors at Home.

XXVIII.

London Literary Letter.

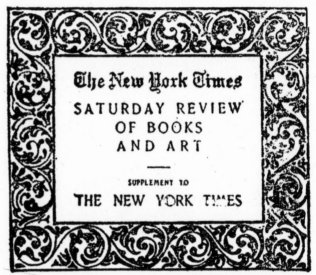

The New York Times
SATURDAY REVIEW
OF BOOKS
AND ART

—

SUPPLEMENT TO

THE NEW YORK TIMES

The New York Times
SATURDAY REVIEW

VOL. XIII.
No. 47.
$1 per Year.   NEW YORK, SATURDAY, NOVEMBER 21, 1908.   16 PAGES.

Three Hundred Leading Spring Books

The Book Review's biggest issues were its seasonal announcements, which were packed with advertisements and lists of forthcoming books from every publisher of note. What makes this one particularly interesting is the early infographic, which charted the books by category.

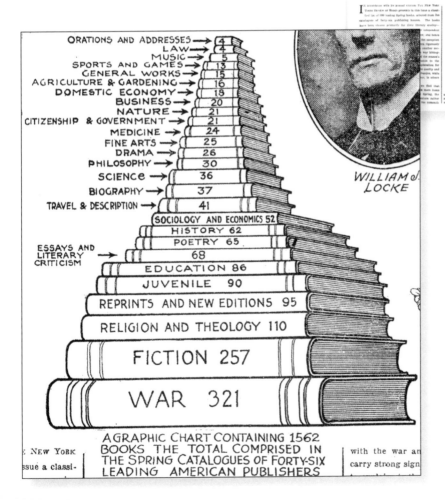

A woman reads about Picasso in Central Park on May 3, 1979.

1921

CHAPTER TWO

1946

The New York Times
Book Review and Magazine

SECTION THREE

SUNDAY, MARCH 27, 1921.   THIRTY-TWO PAGES

WHAT PEACE HAS DONE TO EUROPE
By HERBERT HOOVER

The New York Times
Book Review

Section 3

SUNDAY, JUNE 10, 1923   THIRTY-TWO PAGES

CONRAD, SCULPTOR OF WORDS
The Art of Prose "is Matter Both the Colors and the Shapes"

Drawn from Life by Conn.

The New York Times
Book Review

Section 3

JANUARY 3, 1926   THIRTY-TWO PAGES

MT. EVEREST, CHALLENGER OF MEN
Human Courage Shown at Its Highest in the Last Expedition

Mount Everest.

The New York Times
Book Review

Section 4

SUNDAY, OCTOBER 25, 1931.   THIRTY-TWO PAGES

AN ANARCHIST EXPLAINS HERSELF
Emma Goldman Tells the Story of Her Tempestuous Life

Emma Goldman.

The New York Times
Book Review

Section 5

SUNDAY, APRIL 25, 1936   TWENTY-FOUR PAGES

A MEMOIR OF UNCOMMON CHARM
Nora Waln's Remarkable Record of Her Life in China

Nora Waln.

The New York Times
Book Review

Section 6

SUNDAY, AUGUST 4, 1935   TWENTY PAGES

A NEW NOVEL BY WILLA CATHER
In "Lucy Gayheart" She Returns to the Scene of Her Early Work

Willa Cather.

The Book Review began this era as part of The New York Times Magazine. It was a brief, two-year marriage, and not a particularly happy one, thanks to the volume of book advertisements, especially at Christmastime. On October 15, 1922, the two were officially divorced.

In the 1920s, under the editor J. Donald Adams, the Book Review—though remaining chatty in tone— began challenging the "books as news" motto. Slowly, reviews became more opinionated and wide-ranging. There were still breezy, gossipy columns about authors and publishing, but longer, more thoughtful pieces and profiles—Willa Cather, Robert Frost—began to appear. It is during this time that we begin to see glimpses of the Book Review as we know it today.

Agatha Christie, *Murder on the Links*

In 1920, the Book Review gave Christie's first novel, *The Mysterious Affair at Styles,* a rave ("though this may be the first published book of Miss Agatha Christie, she betrays the cunning of an old hand"). The reviewer who tackled her second novel, *Murder on the Links,* liked it just as much—and was particularly besotted with Hercule Poirot.

HERE IS A REMARKABLY GOOD DETECTIVE story which can be warmly commended to those who like that kind of fiction. The author introduces again the suave and capable Belgian detective, Hercule Poirot, who made his first appearance in her previous detective story, *The Mysterious Affair at Styles*. Aside from being a very successful detangler of criminal mysteries, he is also an entertaining little man, especially when he voices his opinions about most other detectives. He has no admiration for those who search the vicinity of a crime for clues and calls them "human foxhounds." He even amuses himself by planting clues where they will be pounced on by the detectives from Paris whom he compares to a "good retriever dog." But he, after his quick eye has roved over the scene and he has observed the living persons who may have been near it, is content to use his brain cells on its problems.

The story is told in the first person by Captain Hastings, friend of M. Poirot, who shares lodgings in London with the detective and accompanies him when he is called to investigate a case. The crime which together they study in this tale is a mysterious murder at a little town on the French coast. A man of great wealth who spends his summers there is found dead on the golf links with a dagger plunged in his back. His wife, who is discovered bound and gagged in her bedroom, tells a tale of two strange bearded men who had broken in the night before and forced her husband to go with them. The plot has peculiar complications and the reader will have to be very astute indeed if he guesses who the criminal is until the last complexity has been unraveled. The author is notably ingenious in the construction and unraveling of the mystery, which develops fresh interests at every turn. She deserves commendation for the care with which the story is worked out and the good craftsmanship with which it is written.

M. Poirot is an ingenious and interesting addition to the gallery of fictional detectives. But she does not allow him, as sometimes happens in fiction, to dwarf the story. It is his habit when at work to remain in the background as much as possible and allow what he calls "the foxhound detectives" to monopolize the limelight. And so here the reader's chief interest is the story and its bewildering developments, although he is aware at all times of M. Poirot, hovering on the borders, observing, thinking, discussing, insisting on his theory of the personal touch in crime.

The Night Agatha Christie Vanished

IT WAS LIKE A PLOT FROM ONE OF HER
own novels: On the evening of December 4, 1926, Agatha Christie, carrying nothing but an attaché case, kissed her daughter good night and sped away from the home in England that she shared with her husband, Col. Archibald Christie. (He was having an affair with a younger woman; the public did not know this, but his wife definitely did.) No one knew where Christie was for almost two weeks.

Her disappearance was news the world over, making the front page of The Times on December 6 with the headline "Mrs. Agatha Christie, Novelist, Disappears in Strange Way From Her Home in England."

"The novelist's car was found abandoned near Guildford on the edge of a chalk pit, the front wheels actually overhanging the edge," the paper reported. "The car evidently had run away, and only a thick hedge-growth prevented it from plunging into the pit."

Police discovered an attaché case stuffed with papers and a few items of clothing in the car, but the novelist was nowhere to be found. Her husband told reporters that his wife was having a nervous breakdown, but a friend described Christie as "particularly happy in her home life and devoted to her only child."

After three days of searching for her, the police called it off. They said Christie's brother-in-law had received a letter from her, saying she was going to a Yorkshire spa "for rest and treatment." Case closed, right? Not quite. The police, apparently unconvinced by the letter, expanded their search, even bringing one of Christie's pets to the scene to see if he could track his owner's scent. (The dog just "whined pitifully.")

Detectives "are now said to be of the opinion that it is a case of suicide," The Times reported. The search seemed to center on a pond called

500 POLICE AND PLANES HUNT FOR MRS. CHRISTIE

Her Favorite Terrier Also Enlisted in Search for Missing British Novelist.

Copyright, 1926, by The New York Times Company.
Special Cable to THE NEW YORK TIMES.

LONDON, Dec. 9.—More than 500 police aided by airplanes continued the search today for the missing novelist, Mrs. Christie. They thoroughly combed the downs for a radius of two miles from the spot where her abandoned car was found, using motor tractors to break down thickets.

"the Silent Pool," which, according to local legend, was bottomless.

There was an especially tantalizing detail near the end of the story: Christie, the paper claimed, had been spooked by her own house. "It stands in a lonely lane, unlit at night, which has a reputation of being haunted. The lane has been the scene of a murder of a woman and the suicide of a man. . . . 'If I do not leave Sunningdale soon, Sunningdale will be the end of me,' she once said to a friend."

A week after Christie's disappearance, the police were flummoxed. "No reliable witness has seen her since the night she left her house in Sunningdale a week ago," The Times reported. But there was one important development. Christie had left three letters behind: one to her secretary, another to her brother-in-law and a third to her husband, who refused to divulge

Christie in the early 1920s.

The police, scrambling for clues, turned to Christie's manuscripts, examining what they thought was her work in progress, The Blue Train. However, this did not yield any information, and the police prepared to once again begin searching for the novelist, this time with the help of thousands of volunteers. Deputy Chief Constable Kenward of Surrey told the paper he believed the key to her disappearance lay near the chalk pit. "My sergeants are on duty there day and night and I expect developments," he said.

On December 13, between 10,000 and 15,000 people took part in the search for Mrs. Christie, aided by "six trained bloodhounds, a crate load of Airedale terriers, many retrievers and Alsatian police dogs, and even the services of common mongrels."

That same day, the police speculated that Christie could possibly be in London, "disguised and probably in male attire." And rumors began flying that she had left behind a sealed envelope that was only to be opened in the event her body was discovered.

Spiritualists even held a séance at the chalk pit. The Times reported, "It is understood the medium expressed the opinion that Mrs. Christie had met with foul play."

On December 14, the paper reported that the police had found some important clues nearby, including "a bottle labeled poison lead and opium, fragments of a torn-up postcard, a woman's fur-lined coat, a box of face powder, the end of a loaf of bread, a cardboard box and two children's books."

Perhaps more ominous was the detectives' new theory: "The police have information which they refuse to divulge and which leads them to the view that Mrs. Christie had no intention of returning when she left home."

On December 15, the paper reported that Christie had been found in a Yorkshire spa, Harrogate, nine days after she vanished. Christie had checked in to the Harrogate spa under the name "Mrs. Tressa Neele." When asked, Col. Christie insisted he had no idea what the meaning of that particular name was—nor, he

what she had written. Detectives appealed for help from motorists and amateur sleuths: "Without telling why, the police still believe she is somewhere on the downs . . . not far from the spot where her missing automobile was found."

In the same article, her personal secretary angrily denied that the whole thing was a publicity stunt: "It is ridiculous. Mrs. Christie is quite too much a lady for that." The secretary also handed over the note Christie had left for her, saying it contained only scheduling details. "At first I thought it was unimportant," the secretary told The Times. "It merely told me to cancel an appointment she had at Beverley, in Yorkshire, because, as she was feeling queer, she would not go there for the weekend. She wrote that she was going for a run in her car and would let me know Saturday by telegram or telephone where she was."

added, did his wife. Years later, it was revealed that Agatha Christie had, in fact, used the name of her husband's girlfriend.

When Col. Christie showed up in Harrogate to collect his wife, he was "welcomed by her with a stony stare." Later, hundreds of people showed up at a London train station as the couple made their way home, hoping to catch a glimpse. In the same piece, the paper noted that "hundreds of amateur detectives were today putting away their lynx eyes, gum shoes, and Sherlock Holmes pea jackets and resting from their weary trampings over the Surrey Downs."

In the days and months that followed, demand for her books soared.

The next chapter in the saga took place about 15 months later, when Agatha Christie sued her husband for divorce. Two years after that, Christie married again.

Over 90 years later, biographers and historians are still debating what happened during those days in 1926. Was it revenge, depression or amnesia? Biographies, like one by Laura Thompson, shed little light on the episode. ("It was the unspoken subject. Agatha refused to talk about it. To anyone. It was a real no-go," one of Christie's friends told Thompson.)

Christie herself discussed the incident publicly only once, in a 1928 interview she gave to *The Daily Mail.* She told them she had been driving past a quarry on December 3, 1926, when:

> [T]here came into my mind the thought of driving into it. However, as my daughter was with me in the car, I dismissed the idea at once. That night I felt terribly miserable. I felt that I could go on no longer. I left home that night in a state of high nervous strain with the intention of doing something desperate. . . . When I reached a point on the road which I thought was near the quarry, I turned the car off the road down the hill toward it. I left the wheel and let the car run. The car struck something with a jerk and pulled up suddenly. I was flung against the steering wheel, and my head hit something. Up to this moment I was Mrs. Christie.

She did not talk about what happened in *Agatha Christie: An Autobiography,* either, dismissing the end of her marriage in a few terse words: "There is no need to dwell on it."

MESSAGE ENDS HUNT FOR MRS. CHRISTIE

Writer Explains Disappearance in England by Saying She Went to Health Resort.

GUILDFORD, Surrey, England, Dec. ┆ (P) —There was an unexpected new turn to the mystery of the disappearance of the American writer of detective stories, Agatha Clarissa Christie, for whom the police and most of the country people have been searching for the past three days

Sarah Bernhardt's Library

The celebrated French actress died in March 1923, and a few months later the Book Review took note of her remarkable library when it was auctioned. Many of her literary contemporaries had signed copies of their books and plays for her. On the title page of his only book of verse, Guy de Maupassant scrawled, "To Mlle. Sarah Bernhardt, homage of an admirer, Guy de Maupassant." After she appeared in his play *Ruy Blas*, Victor Hugo sent her a copy and inscribed it, "At the feet of Sarah Bernhardt, Victor Hugo." There were signed works from Oscar Wilde, Émile Zola and the younger Alexandre Dumas.

Bernhardt photographed by Nadar in Paris, circa 1864.

1922 ——————————
T. S. Eliot publishes "The Waste Land." The Book Review pays no attention.

1923 ——————————
In a September 2 op-ed, the Book Review opines that "most modern novels produced in the United States are written without charm about stupid people."

1923 ——————————→
William Butler Yeats wins the Nobel and tells The Times, "If it [the award] is small we will spend it and be rich. If it is large we will invest it and be substantial."

Interesting Volumes From Sarah Bernhardt's Library

The library of Sarah Bernhardt has recently been sold at auction. Aside from the intrinsic value of the books, there is attached to this collection a historic interest in the dedications written by Mme. Bernhardt's literary contemporaries.

RUY BLAS

Victor Hugo—Sarah Bernhardt played the Queen in Victor Hugo's "Ruy Blas" in February, 1872. As a souvenir he sent her a copy of the play inscribed: "At the feet of Madame Sarah Bernhardt, Victor Hugo."

Alexander Dumas, Fils—The dedication the younger Dumas wrote on Bernhardt's copy of "L'Étrangère" represents the close of an incident of 1876 that nearly became open war between the author and the actress. From this came his inscription: "To Mlle. Sarah Bernhardt, with the infinite excuses, gratitude and compliments of the author, A. Dumas, Fils."

Pierre Loti, who was one of the habitués of Sarah Bernhardt's salon, inscribed a copy of his "Les Derniers Jours de Pékin"; "To Madame Sarah Bernhardt, who, of course, not only will not read this book, but will, besides, have the impudence to claim that I never sent her anything—her old friend, who nevertheless loves her tenderly. Pierre Loti."

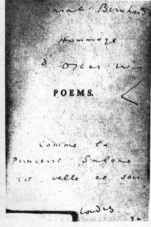

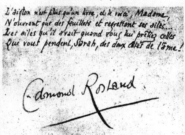

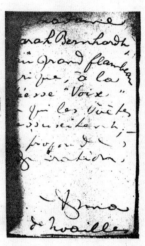

Oscar Wilde, whose "Salome" Bernhardt created, sent her from London a volume of his poems, dedicated: "To Sarah Bernhardt, homage from Oscar Wilde. How beautiful Princess Salome is tonight."

Edmond Rostand had printed for Mme. Bernhardt a special copy of "L'Aiglon," the title role of which she created in her own theatre in 1900. A free translation of his verse of dedication is: "And once more 'L'Aiglon' is a mere book! Here it is, Madame; it has only leaves now, and must regret its wings—the wings it had when you, Sarah, lent it those of your soul. Edmond Rostand."

Comtesse Anna de Noailles, member of the Belgian Academy, and the foremost woman poet of modern France, signed a copy of her "Eblouissements" as follows: "To Madame Sarah Bernhardt, whose lyric fire and divine voice give life to the poets—in profound admiration, Anna de Noailles."

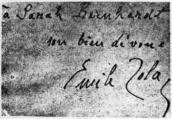

Guy de Maupassant was one of the first to proclaim the young Bernhardt a genius. He sent her, in 1860, his first and only book of verse, with the words: "To Mlle. Sarah Bernhardt, homage of an admirer, Guy de Maupassant."

Emile Zola sent Mme. Bernhardt his "Nana" with the simple dedication: "To Sarah Bernhardt—her devoted Emile Zola."

Gabriel D'Annunzio—On a copy of his "Vièrges aux Rochers," Gabriel d'Annunzio quoted a passage from Theocritus. Here the lips of Bernhardt are hailed as a touchstone of literary art.

Facsimiles from Seven Arts Syndicate, authorized by Maurice Bernhardt.

Willa Cather: "Don't Confuse Reading with Culture or Art"

During the 1920s, the Book Review began running longer, more in-depth author interviews than ever before.

TEA WITH WILLA SIBERT CATHER IS A RANK failure. The fault is entirely hers. You get so highly interested in what she has to say and how she says it that you ask for cream when you prefer lemon and let the butter on your cold toast grow cold and smeary. It is vastly more important to you to watch her eyes and lip, which betray her when she seems to be giving voice to a serious concept, but is really poking fun at the world—or at your own foolish question. For Willa Sibert Cather has a rare good sense, homespun sense, if you will, which she drives home with a well-wrought mallet of humor.

It started with the question of books and the overwhelming quantities which the American public of today is buying. What exactly was the explanation of that? Did it mean we were becoming a more cultured people, a more artistic people? Miss Cather was suffering from neuritis that day. It was difficult to understand whether the twinge that crossed her face was caused by the pain we gave her or that of her illness.

"Don't confuse reading with culture or art," she said, when her face cleared. There was laughter in her blue eyes. "Not in this country, at least. So many books are sold today because of the economic condition of this country, not the cultural. You might with equal reason ask whether we are becoming a more cultured people because so many more of us are buying chiffoniers and bureaus and toilet sets. Forty or 50 years ago these things were not to be found in the average home. Forty or 50 years ago we couldn't afford them and today we can. But, carrying the thought further, every home has not increased in beauty.

"Because of this vast amount of reading and writing, there are many among us who make the mistake of thinking we are an artistic people. Talking about it won't make us that. We can build excellent bridges, we can put up beautiful office buildings, factories; in time, it may be, we shall be known for the architecture which our peculiar industrial progress has fostered here, but literary art, painting, sculpture, no. We haven't yet acquired the good sense of discrimination possessed by the French, for instance. France is sensitive, we are not. It may be that our youth has something to do with it and yet I don't know whether that is it.

"Yet it isn't always a question of one country being artistic and another not. The world goes through periods or waves of art. Between these periods come great resting places. We may be resting right now. Other countries have their wealth of former years to fall back upon. We haven't."

Miss Cather poured some tea into a cup and diluted it with the cream we asked for but didn't want. We let it stand on the arm of the chair and proceeded with a question that her words had awakened.

"If we have no tradition of years behind us, the people who come to live here have. Are they contributing to the artistic expression of the country?"

Again that twinge crossed her face. This time it was plain that the question had started it.

"Contribute? What shall they contribute? If they were let alone, their lives might turn into the beautiful ways of their homeland. But they are not let alone. Social workers, missionaries—call them what you will—go after that, hound them, pursue them and devote their days and nights toward the great task of turning them into stupid replicas of smug American citizens. This passion for Americanizing everything and everybody is a deadly disease with us. We do it the way we build houses. Speed, uniformity, dispatch, nothing else matters."

We spoke about *My Antonia*, Miss Cather's story about the immigrant family of Czechs.

"Is *My Antonia* a good book because it is a story of the soil?" we asked. She shook her head.

"No, no, decidedly no. There is no formula, there is no reason. It was a story of people I knew. I expressed a mood, the core of which was like a folk song, a thing Grieg could have written. That it was powerfully tied to the soil had nothing to do with it. I might have written the tale of a Czech baker in Chicago and it would have been the same. It would have been smearier, joltier, noisier, less sugar and more sand, but still a story that had as its purpose the desire to express the quality of these people. No, the country has nothing to do

Cather in the 1920s.

with it, the city has nothing to do with it. The thing worthwhile is always unplanned. Any art that is a result of preconcerted plans is a dead baby."

Miss Cather is now writing a new novel which will come out next autumn. "There will be no theories, no panaceas, no generalizations. It will be a story about people in a prosperous provincial city in the Middle West. Nothing new or strange, you see." —*Rose C. Feld*

1923

Jean Toomer's *Cane* is published. The Book Review refers to it several years later as "a bravely beautiful collection of short stories."

1925

On August 9, a banner headline on the cover of the Book Review proclaims that "Little Hope Remains for Men: Women Are Becoming the Dominant Sex."

1925

Ernest Hemingway and F. Scott Fitzgerald meet in Paris, though perhaps not in the Dingo Bar as Hemingway recounted in *A Moveable Feast*.

The Fitzgerald family—Scott, Zelda and Scottie—dance in front of the Christmas tree, circa mid-1920s.

F. Scott Fitzgerald, *The Great Gatsby*

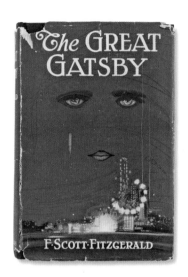

At the release of this American classic, our reviewer named Fitzgerald "the philosopher of the flapper" and called the book "a mystical, glamorous story of today."

OF THE MANY NEW WRITERS THAT SPRANG into notice with the advent of the post-war period, Scott Fitzgerald has remained the steadiest performer and the most entertaining. Short stories, novels and a play have followed with consistent regularity since he became the philosopher of the flapper with *This Side of Paradise*. With shrewd observation and humor he reflected the Jazz Age. Now he has said farewell to his flappers— perhaps because they have grown up—and is writing of the other sisters that have married. But marriage has not changed their world, only the locale of their parties. To use a phrase of Burton Rascoe's—his hurt romantics are still seeking that other side of paradise. And it might almost be said that *The Great Gatsby* is the last stage of illusion in this absurd chase. For middle age is certainly creeping up on Mr. Fitzgerald's flappers.

In all great arid spots nature provides an oasis. So when the Atlantic seaboard was hermetically sealed by law, nature provided an outlet, or inlet rather, in Long Island. A place of innate natural charm, it became lush and luxurious under the stress of this excessive attention, a seat of festive activities. It expresses one phase of the great grotesque spectacle of our American scene.

The story of Jay Gatsby of West Egg is told by Nick Carraway, who is one of the legion from the Middle West who have moved on to New York to win from its restless indifference—well, the aspiration that arises in the Middle West—and finds in Long Island a fascinating but dangerous

1926 ———————————————
A. A. Milne publishes *Winnie the Pooh.* His 6-year-old son, Christopher Robin, tells The Times, "Wait and see how Father likes the poems I write about him."

1927 ———————————————
Arthur Conan Doyle attends a séance and encounters a spirit who died in 1809 when he was pushed into a moat.

1928 ———————————————→
An American book dealer outbids the British Museum and buys the original manuscript of Lewis Carroll's *Alice in Wonderland.*

1921–1946

playground. In the method of telling, *The Great Gatsby* is reminiscent of Henry James's *Turn of the Screw*. You will recall that the evil of that mysterious tale which so endangered the two children was never exactly stated beyond a suggested generalization. Gatsby's fortune, business, even his connection with underworld figures, remain vague generalizations. He is wealthy, powerful, a man who knows how to get things done. He has no friends, only business associates, and the throngs who come to his Saturday night parties. Of his uncompromising love—his love for Daisy Buchanan—his effort to recapture the past romance—we are explicitly informed. This patient romantic hopefulness against existing conditions, symbolizes Gatsby. And like the *Turn of the Screw, The Great Gatsby* is more a long short story than a novel.

Nick Carraway had known Tom Buchanan at New Haven. Daisy, his wife, was a distant cousin. When he came East Nick was asked to call at their place at East Egg. The post-war reactions were at their height—everyone was restless—everyone was looking for a substitute for the

"Middle age is certainly creeping up on Mr. Fitzgerald's flappers."

excitement of the war years. Buchanan had acquired another woman. Daisy was bored, broken in spirit and neglected. Gatsby, his parties and his mysterious wealth were the gossip of the hour. At the Buchanans' Nick met Jordan Baker; through them both Daisy again meets Gatsby, to whom she had been engaged before she married Buchanan. The inevitable consequence that follows, in which violence takes its toll, is almost incidental, for in the overtones—and this is a book of potent overtones—the decay of souls is more tragic. With sensitive insight and keen psychological observation, Fitzgerald discloses in these people a meanness of spirit, carelessness and absence of loyalties. He cannot hate them, for they are dumb in their insensate selfishness, and only to be pitied. The philosopher of the flapper has escaped the mordant, but he has turned grave. A curious book, a mystical, glamourous story of today. It takes a deeper cut at life than hitherto has been essayed by Mr. Fitzgerald.

He writes well—he always has—for he writes naturally, and his sense of form is becoming perfected. —*Edwin Clark*

1928 ——————
H. G. Wells and George Bernard Shaw come out in support of *The Well of Loneliness,* the "sex novel" by Radclyffe Hall that had been banned in England.

1928 ——————
Margaret Mead publishes *Coming of Age in Samoa,* which the Book Review calls "a remarkable contribution to our knowledge of humanity."

1928 ——————→
When Claude McKay's *Home to Harlem* is published, the Book Review describes it as "a book that is beaten through with the rhythm of life that is a jazz rhythm."

Oh, Mother!

In a news item on September 18, 1933, Scottie Fitzgerald, Scott and Zelda's daughter, talked about the ways her parents' generation had failed their children.

THE 12-YEAR-OLD DAUGHTER OF F. SCOTT Fitzgerald, whose novel, *This Side of Paradise,* dealt with the American flapper some years ago, thinks that most of the girls and boys about whom her father wrote are rather incompetent parents today.

Mr. Fitzgerald is inclined to agree with that opinion.

"Maybe I'm getting old-fashioned," he said. "You know the type—old man Fitzgerald telling what's wrong with the world. But in most sections of the country my crowd aren't doing so well in the mother and father role."

"They don't seem to think a lot about their children," said Frances Scott Fitzgerald, the daughter. "They think the kids are going to be taught everything at school."

"Exactly," put in Fitzgerald. "They sit on their fat hams and leave their own jobs to teachers."

"How about the fathers?" Frances was asked.

"They don't see them very often, except when they come home from business and say go upstairs and be quiet or run around the other side of the house to play."

"Do children your age respect their parents?"

"Oh yes, they respect them, I guess. It's just that they don't know them so well. The parents are interested in their children, I think, but—well—they seem to want to do something for them but don't know how."

"I think one thing she was driving at," said the author later, "is that my own contemporaries have found their own lack of religious and moral convictions makes them incompetent to train their children."

HOLDS 'FLAPPERS' FAIL AS PARENTS

Daughter of Fitzgerald, Aged 12, Criticizes Heroines of 'This Side of Paradise.'

FATHER AGREES WITH HER

Novelist Says 'Kids of Ex-Flappers' Are Having a Sorry Time, Blaming Mothers.

Perched on the rail of the porch surrounding his rambling old country home, near Baltimore, the novelist continued:

"On the whole, the flappers turned out better than the boys of their age. They are the ones who missed the war but blame everything that's wrong with them on the war. It's an unhappy generation.

"Right now Zelda and I are more interested in the next crop of prom girls than in those of today, or of our day. They are the kids with ex-flappers for mothers and they are having the most sorry treatment over most of this country. Their mothers will let them do anything as long as it does not interfere with their own pleasures.

"Perhaps in the morning they'll give some attention to the children, but that afternoon they'll hunch themselves over a bridge table and pack the kids off to the movies where they'll get a two-hour dose of *Sins of Susie.*"

Virginia Woolf, *Mrs. Dalloway*

This slim, modernist novel has had an enduring impact on literature. At its publication, our reviewer recognized Woolf's accomplishment: "Virginia Woolf is almost alone . . . in the intricate yet clear art of her composition."

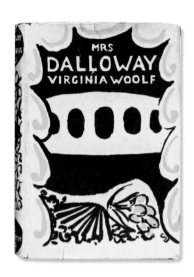

ONE DAY IN THE LIFE OF CLARISSA DALLOWAY, a June day in London, punctuated accurately, impersonally, unfeelingly, by the chimes of Big Ben and a fashionable party to end it, is the complete story of Mrs. Woolf's new novel, yet she contrives to enmesh all the inflections of Mrs. Dalloway's personality, and many of the implications of modern civilization, in the account of those twenty-four hours. Mrs. Dalloway in her own home is "the perfect hostess," even to her servants, to her daughter, her husband and her rejected suitor of long ago, who cannot free his mind of her. It is almost a perfect being that Mrs. Dalloway enjoys, but there is a resentfulness in her, some paucity of spiritual graces, or rather some positive hideousness.

Among Mrs. Woolf's contemporaries, there are not a few who have brought to the traditional forms of fiction, and the stated modes of writing, idioms which cannot but enlarge the resources of speech and the uses of narrative. Virginia Woolf is almost alone, however, in the intricate yet clear art of her composition. Clarissa's day, the impressions she gives and receives, the memories and recognitions which stir in her, the events which are initiated remotely and engineered almost to touching distance of the impervious Clarissa, capture in a definitive matrix the drift of thought and feeling in a period, the point of view of a class, and seem almost to indicate the strength and weakness of an entire civilization.

It is not only that Clarissa is giving, in fact does give, one of those parties at which the successful, the titled and the important pay a tacit homage to the political prestige of her husband, a member of Parliament, and an overt tribute to the fascinations of Clarissa herself. It is not alone that Clarissa's snobberies and exclusions, her hatred of ugliness and excess, her dainty wrapping of herself in cotton wool and her "tender superfluous probing into all that pollutes" are unerringly depicted. The whole progress of the circumstances of Clarissa's day, from the passing of a "somebody" in a closed motor car to the ignoring of a nobody at her party, make for a vivid interaction. —*John W. Crawford*

The Art of Woo

In this remarkable ad for the Pocket Classical Library, a young man—trying to impress his date—says "he was glad he could tell her that he had read the noteworthy classics. Glad he could discuss with her the masterpieces of Hawthorne, Carlyle, Kipling, Poe."

"What do you read?" she asked him

HE was glad he could tell her that he had read the noteworthy classics. Glad he could discuss with her the masterpieces of Hawthorne, Carlyle, Kipling, Poe.

"I don't read very much, you know," he said, presently. "I'm so busy making a career for myself that I haven't half the time for books I'd like to have."

"But you seem so well-read....!"

He smiled. "That is because I never waste any of my reading time. I read only worthwhile things that enrich my mind--the finer things--"

"You must have read all the classics."

"No," he admitted. "I don't even own complete sets of all the classics. I wish I could afford them."

"But you are familiar with all the masters--you discuss them all so easily! Surely you *must* have read them!"

Again he smiled. "I own the Pocket Classical Library," he said. "It's my complete library. And it *is* complete. It gives me all I need--all I want. The *best* in literature. I get all the 'high lights' of the classics, without taking the time to go through all of them. These 12 volumes which comprise the Pocket Classical Library represent the essence of a broad general education."

"You must tell me more about it!" she cried, intrigued.

And he told her, as best he could, about the Pocket Classical Library. How the idea had been conceived--how carried out. How the best authorities available had cooperated to make it the most interesting and informative set of books ever published.

THE POCKET CLASSICAL LIBRARY

The Essence of a University Education in 12 Splendid Volumes.

There is no better way to acquire knowledge, a cultural background, a familiarity with the finer things in life--than through books. But desultory reading, while interesting, is comparatively valueless. Haphazard reading gets you nowhere.

The important thing is a *definite plan of reading*--taking in only the high lights, the essentials, and omitting the non-essentials.

And that, precisely, is what the Pocket Classical Library now makes possible. The 12 volumes that comprise this Library contain the essence of all fine literature taught at college. They include the *best reading in the world*. They provide a lifelong source of cultural reading, of which no one can possibly tire.

Here, in 12 uniformly bound volumes, are Shelley's exquisite verse, Emerson's sound philosophies, Franklin's common sense, Mark Twain's inimitable humor, Kipling, Carlyle, Hawthorne, Spenser, Dickens, Conrad--all through the long list of immortals! Not too much. Just enough of each to give the reader a knowledge and understanding of the great men of literature.

Most important of all, with the Pocket Classical Library goes a remarkable READING GUIDE which makes it possible for you to map out a profitable course of reading for yourself. Here is your opportunity to *read with a purpose*

--the best in literature--the most fascinating--the most informative!

5 Days' Free Examination

The Pocket Classical Library is unquestionably one of the finest sets of books you could add to your library. It *is* a library, complete in itself! "I am inspired anew every time I pick up a volume of my Pocket Classical Library," writes one man who owns these books. You, too, will find endless hours of enjoyment and profit in these 12 carefully selected volumes.

Please examine them *at our expense*. Just use the convenient coupon below. Clip and mail it today, and the complete 12-volume Pocket Classical Library, with reading guide, will go forward to you at once. Within 5 days you have the privilege of returning the books --or keeping them as your own and sending only $1.85 as a first payment. Thereafter you send only $2 a month for 4 months, until the amazingly low price of only $9.85 has been paid.

You are the judge! Send off this coupon NOW. Nelson Doubleday, Inc., Dept. P-38, Garden City, New York.

Emma Goldman, *Living My Life*

An activist who fought for workers' rights, birth control and socialism in the early 20th century, Emma Goldman was born to a Jewish family in the Russian Empire and emigrated to the United States at 16. Her radical philosophy was forged in the anarchist organizing circles of New York's Lower East Side, where she moved in the wake of the 1886 Haymarket Riot in Chicago. She quickly became known as a fierce and prominent feminist, anarchist writer and speaker, but gained broader notoriety for her involvement in the attempted assassination of the tycoon Henry Clay Frick. In 1919, she was deported. Her memoir was published to great skepticism here, but the reviewer, R. L. Duffus, beseeched subscribers to read it, calling it a "great human narrative."

NO ONE WHO DESIRES TO UNDERSTAND radical psychology from the date of the hanging of the Chicago anarchists, in 1887, to the October revolution in Russia in 1919 should fail to read Emma Goldman's narrative of her own life, as here given. Nor should anyone who wishes to know how the Bolshevist régime in Russia looks to an observer who is not a Communist, yet who is certainly not imbued with the slightest faith in the so-called capitalistic system. But the reader who undertakes to consider her story as a great human narrative, which it is, should prepare himself by finding out first what anarchism is.

In the minds of many thousands of persons, probably the word suggests only one thing—hatred and violence. In this country it has been given that connotation by a series of events, the most notable of which were the Haymarket explosion in Chicago and the assassination of President McKinley. That murder has been committed by a few anarchists and either justified or condoned by many more, including Miss Goldman. Miss Goldman was an accessory before the fact in Alexander Berkman's attempt on the life of Henry Frick in 1892, and it was no fault of hers that Frick was not killed. Her sympathy went out to the assassin of McKinley, to Moyer, Pettibone and Haywood when they were on trial for the murder of ex-Governor Steunenberg, and to the McNamara brothers when they were charged, correctly, as it turned out, with the dynamiting of

1928 ———————
Bambi, by Felix Salten, comes out; the Book Review says "his deer, his screech owls, his butterflies" are "far more exciting to read about than hundreds of human beings who crowd the pages of our novels."

1929 ———————
Thomas Mann wins the Nobel "principally for his great novel, *Buddenbrooks,*" which the Book Review had called "immature."

1929 ———————→
Erich Maria Remarque publishes *All Quiet on the Western Front.*

<blockquote>
"One is pretty well convinced in the end that it actually was sympathy and not hatred that animated her."
</blockquote>

Goldman, circa 1915.

the *Los Angeles Times* building. But one is pretty well convinced in the end that it actually was sympathy and not hatred that animated her, even in her younger and more violent days. When she encountered hatred and violence masquerading as a holy cause in Russia during the early days of the Bolshevist régime she instinctively revolted against them. Confronted with a vicious disregard for human life she risked everything to proclaim her belief in its sanctity. Often carried away by wild impulses, she is fundamentally humane. Even those who differ most radically with her conclusions will find that they are dealing with a woman whose emotional reactions, once those conclusions are taken for granted, are as normal as their next-door neighbor's. Her heart is all right, whatever may be said of her dogma.

Having cleared the boards in some such fashion as this the reader may be prepared to follow the story as a human document of the most absorbing interest. Its dogmas become of lesser importance as one considers its characters. It would be easy enough for a psychologist of Dr. Watson's school—or perhaps of Dr. Freud's—to take them one by one and explain why they were anarchists rather than doctors, lawyers, generals or successful business men. Miss Goldman herself was plainly "conditioned" by an unhappy

home life dominated by an unhappy and tyrannical father. Johann Most was turned against society by a disfigured face which exposed him to the ridicule of his schoolmates. Berkman had a favorite uncle who had been condemned to death in Russia for his nihilist activities, and he had himself been expelled from schools for an anti-religious essay. All of them, perhaps, hated authority because authority as they had known it had been neither kind nor just to them. In Berkman this revolt took a form easily recognizable as a species of puritanism. In Emma Goldman, who had a passionate nature and the love of beauty which often goes with such a nature, no such narrowness was possible. She had an intelligent love of music and she became an excellent critic of the drama.

Her story thus falls into two parts—a long struggle to inculcate certain beliefs and a series of emotional experiences which might have come to her even had she been entirely devoid of intellectual interests. Her love life, as she relates it, might easily entitle her to be called a feminine Casanova, though she consistently gave even more abundantly than she received. Another writer telling the same incidents might have easily made them dull, absurd or indecent, but as Emma Goldman relates them they contain no trace of dullness, absurdity or indecency. Ironically enough, the men who had most power over her affections were often the weakest when measured by the stern requirements of her revolutionary faith. Such was "Fedya" and such, too, was the ineffable Ben Reitma, who probably did as much as any one in the middle years of Miss Goldman's life to get her into disfavor with her friends and into greater disfavor with the general public. Berkman, the most influential of all upon the course of her life, very early ceased to be a lover and became, as Miss Goldman constantly refers to him in her second volume, a pal.

Like every good novel, biography or autobiography the book reveals development and change. It is in the Russian sections of her narrative, indeed, that Miss Goldman rises to her full stature. One sees in them that her dream of revolution, whatever one may think of its practicality, its justice or its wisdom, did not originate in sadism or lust for power. When those elements entered into revolution in Russia she found herself in a quandary which shook the faith on which she had built her life. In her world of anarchists, Communists and Socialists she faced a decision as important, from that world's point of view, as Ramsay MacDonald's decision to form a coalition government was from his.

Quarrels among anarchists in this present generation are perhaps tempests in a teapot. If violent revolution again upsets the conservative apple cart in any country it is likely to be the violence of communism, not of anarchism. The anarchist is nowhere at home and his numbers are dwindling. Perhaps he will return in the gentler form of peaceful cooperation after the world has learned the painful lesson—if it ever does—that neither assassination nor war nor political executions nor the dragooning of opinion contribute to the general welfare. But this is all the more reason for reading Emma Goldman objectively and calmly. She belongs to a species which is at least temporarily vanishing and she is in her own right something which is rarely found, in palaces or hovels, in factories or offices or on the barricades—an original and picturesque personality. Her autobiography is one of the great books of its kind. —*R. L. Duffus*

1930 ————————————

Dorothy Parker's *Lament for the Living* is published; the Book Review praises her "well-known scalpel."

1930 ————————————

Sinclair Lewis becomes the first American to win the Nobel Prize for Literature. Theodore Dreiser is widely considered to have been a runner-up.

1931 ————————————→

Scandal! Theodore Dreiser repeatedly slaps Sinclair Lewis in the "softly plushed rooms" of New York's ritzy Metropolitan Club.

Early News Stories

News of authors has always been featured in The New York Times, but in its early years, the paper took a particular interest in what we might now deem trivial updates, such as the scandal caused by Colette's bare legs or the plundering of Upton Sinclair's kitchen.

COLETTE, AUTHOR, ON SHIP

French Woman Writer Wears Sandals and No Stockings.

Son, 6, Plans Revenge Poems On Milne When He Grows Up

Copyright, 1928, by The New York Times Co.
Special Cable to THE NEW YORK TIMES.

LONDON, March 18.—Christopher Robin, the boy immortalized by his father, A. A. Milne, for children the world over in "When We Were Very Young" and kindred volumes, plans, when he grows up, to take revenge upon his dad by writing poems about him.

DIVORCES BETTE DAVIS

Husband, H. O. Nelson, Testifies She Read Books Too Much

Upton Sinclair's Larder Raided

PASADENA, Calif., Dec. 17 (U.P.) —A bare larder and a mud-tracked kitchen greeted Upton Sinclair today on his return after a few days' absence. Uninvited "picnickers" had eaten his food, smoked his cigarettes and used his kitchen for a bath house after swimming in his swimming pool. "I don't think," he said, "that they read any of my books."

WOULD EMULATE ROOSEVELT.

Boy Reads His Book on Ranch Life and Runs Away.

TWAIN STARTLES LONDON.

Strolls In Bathrobe and Bare Legs from Hotel for a Plunge.

TWAIN'S MERRY CHRISTMAS.

Humorist Says He Would Not Think of Dying at His Time of Life.

LONDON AT A DOG DINNER.

"Call of the Wild's" Author Attends Birthday Party of Fluffy Ruffles.

Cullen on June 15, 1941.

Countee Cullen, *One Way to Heaven*

Cullen, a fixture of the Harlem Renaissance, may have been best known as a poet, but this novel made a splash when it was published. Our critic wrote that it was not just a vivid depiction of Harlem life but "an entertaining account of a very different section of Harlem society—the intellectuals, doctors and teachers, writers and musicians."

THOSE WHO ALREADY KNOW AND APPRECIATE Mr. Countee Cullen as a poet are not the only ones who will be interested in this first novel, *One Way to Heaven*. It must always be a difficult task to interpret one's own race to another; and though a novelist's work is written as a novel and not as an interpretation, yet it is almost unavoidable that a white reader, knowing Mr. Cullen's reputation, should look at it from that point of view. Most of us have not yet reached the stage where we can appreciate any story about colored people at its face value without always straining to find in it some sort of presentation of "Negro life." It is, therefore, from one who frankly knows little about the subject, an impertinence to say that Mr. Cullen paints a convincing picture of life in Harlem; but one can at least say that the picture is sometimes amusing, sometimes very moving, and at all times interesting.

One Way to Heaven is, essentially, the story of Sam Lucas, who was a wanderer and lived by his wits. Among other tricks he made a habit of attending revival meetings, and advancing at the crucial moment to fling down his pack of cards and his razor—thus assuring himself of generous treatment by the faithful until he chose to move on. One New Year's Eve he arrived in Harlem and proceeded to work his "conversion" as usual; and the evangelist who recognized the fraud could not bring himself to expose it because he felt that, in bringing souls to God, it had accomplished more than his inspired and impassioned preaching. Among those who saw God's power over sinners authentically displayed in Sam's sacrifice of the implements of sin was the beautiful Mattie, who simultaneously fell in love with him and acquired a genuine religious devotion. The story of their life together is commonplace in incident but admirable in treatment—his amiability, recklessness and complete lack of faith, in contrast with her fervent religion. Their great moment came when an errant Sam was brought back dying to the flat. In the depths of her misery his young wife let slip that she could be content if only she were assured that his soul was safe—and in describing the last kind, if facile, subterfuge of the unbeliever, Mr. Cullen has written a most effective and beautiful passage.

The book also contains an entertaining account of a very different section of Harlem society—the intellectuals, doctors and teachers, writers and musicians. Mr. Cullen's thumbnail sketches of these varied people, whether they are intelligent or whether they are pretentious, are all alike amusing and brilliant; and taken in conjunction with the more earnest and simple lives of Mattie and Sam they form an excellent and highly readable book which should not be missed.
—*Elizabeth Brown*

William Faulkner, *Light in August*

Coming on the heels of *The Sound and the Fury* and *As I Lay Dying*, *Light in August* was one of Faulkner's first attempts to grapple with racial strife in the South.

WITH THIS NEW NOVEL, MR. FAULKNER HAS taken a tremendous stride forward. To say that *Light in August* is an astonishing performance is not to use the word lightly. That somewhat crude and altogether brutal power which thrust itself through his previous work is in this book disciplined to a greater effectiveness than one would have believed possible in so short a time. There are still moments when Mr. Faulkner seems to write of what is horrible purely from a desire to shock his readers or else because it holds for him a fascination from which he cannot altogether escape. There are still moments when his furious contempt for the human species seems a little callow.

But no reader who has followed his work can fail to be enormously impressed by the transformation which has been worked upon it. Not only does Faulkner emerge from his book a stylist of striking strength and beauty; he permits some of his people, if not his chief protagonist, to act sometimes out of motives which are human in their decency; indeed, he permits the Rev. Gail Hightower to live his life by them. In a word, Faulkner has admitted justice and compassion to his scheme of things. There was a hint of this to come in the treatment of Benbow in *Sanctuary*. The gifts which he had to begin with are strengthened—the gifts for vivid narrative and the fresh-minted phrase. His eye for the ignoble in human nature is more keen than ever, but his vision is also less restricted.

There are two or three scenes in this book more searing than anything Faulkner has heretofore written, but they are also better integrated. Although the pattern of *Light in August* is streaked with red, there is a blending here with colors both more subdued and more luminous than were customary to his palette. The locale is again the "deep South"; and the characters include the white trash of which he has drawn such relentless portraits, plain folk of a better strain, whites of a higher order, Negroes, and for the subject of his most detailed attention a poor white with a probable mixture of Negro blood.

Light in August is a powerful novel, a book which secures Mr. Faulkner's place in the very front rank of American writers of fiction. He definitely has removed the objection made against him that he cannot lift his eyes above the dunghill. There are times when Mr. Faulkner is not unaware of the stars. One hesitates to make conjectures as to the inner lives of those who write about the lives of others, but Mr. Faulkner's work has seemed to be that of a man who has, at some time, been desperately hurt; a man whom life has at some point badly cheated. There are indications that he has regained his balance.

—*J. Donald Adams*

Faulkner during a visit to
West Point on April 20, 1962.

Copyright, 1933, by
The New York Times Company.

SUNDAY, JULY 9, 1933.

TWENTY PAGES

ONE HUNDRED YEARS OF FEMINISM

Two Books That Tell the Story of the Woman's Movement

ANGELS AND AMAZONS. A Hundred Years of American Women. By Inez Haynes Irwin. 531 pp. New York: Doubleday, Doran & Co., Inc. $2.50.

WOMEN IN THE TWENTIETH CENTURY. A Study of Their Political, Social and Economic Activities. By Sophonisba P. Breckinridge. (A new volume in the Recent Social Trends Monographs). New York: McGraw-Hill Book Company, Inc. $4.

By J. DONALD ADAMS

THAT was an auspicious day—"a climax," Mrs. Irwin calls it, in the history of feminism, when Elizabeth Cady Stanton and Lucretia Mott, American women delegates to the World's Anti-Slavery Conference held at London in 1840, walked out from the convention hall seething with indignation because the conference had ruled that women delegates might not take active part in the proceedings, but could sit decorously behind a screen in the gallery and listen to the men. William Lloyd Garrison had been expected to make the great speech of the occasion, but in protest at the meeting's action he took his seat beside Lucretia Mott and Elizabeth Stanton and did not speak at all. It was, as Mrs. Irwin describes it, "a beautiful gesture." As for the two women, they dedicated their lives to the woman's movement, and that very night planned the battle for woman suffrage.

It is the purpose of Mrs. Irwin's book to trace the entire history of that movement from its first feeble stirrings down to these Amazonian days. That too, is in part the purpose of Professor Breckinridge's "Women in the Twentieth Century," though most of her volume is given over to a statistical analysis of women's activities during the present century. "Women in the Twentieth Century" is frankly a source book, hardly intended for popular consumption. Mrs. Irwin's "Angels and Amazons" aims at being more colorful and interpretative, but its interest remains chiefly factual. There is a much better, a more vivid and penetrating book to be written about the woman's movement than Mrs. Irwin has succeeded in writing. But her book does bring together the facts in convenient form, and both books will be valuable to the future historian.

The actual beginnings of the woman's movement in America were not so dramatic as that far-reaching incident at the London conference of 1840. Mostly, the first steps along the rough and tortuous road the emancipators were to follow were taken in small, obscure places, among purely local groups. The movement was sporadic, slow-paced, halting. The world knows what it has since become—a rushing torrent in which women are caught up and borne, perhaps unavoidably now, to a destination that promises to alter the whole aspect of modern society. Beginning as an effort to ameliorate woman's lot, the current, or so it seems to some of us, has turned back upon woman herself, a force of incalculable power. To that aspect of the woman's movement we shall return later, pausing now to

mark the sources from which the stream arose.

Mrs. Irwin assures us, and with the support of ample evidence, that her confinement of the bounds of the woman's movement in America within the exact space of a century was not arbitrarily done. The year 1833 did mark a definite turning point in the history of American feminism. In that year the first permanent woman's club in the United States had its inception at Jacksonville, Ill. Later in the same year was formed the first woman's club with a political object—the Philadelphia Female Anti-Slavery Society. It was in 1833 that Lydia Maria Francis, a popular author of the period, whose previous writings had been confined to

such innocuous publications as "The Mother's Book," "The Girl's Book" and "A Biography of Good Wives," startled the country by publishing an anti-slavery tract, which she named "An Appeal on Behalf of That Class of Americans Called Africans." And finally, it was in 1833 that an American institution of higher learning (that quaint phrase which still survives) first opened its doors to women students. Oberlin College in Ohio established a "female department." The announcement is worth recording. The innovation was to effect "the elevation of female character by bringing within the reach of the misguided and neglected sex all the instruction privileges which have hitherto unreasonably distinguished

the leading sex from theirs." Little wonder, in the light of such language, that spirited women were in revolt!

But a still more significant and a vastly more dynamic development than any of these was already setting the pattern of the future when the events of 1833 transpired. Mrs. Irwin does well to emphasize the enormous potentialities which underlay Eli Whitney's invention of the cotton gin. It was a woman, incidentally, she reminds us—Catherine Littlefield Greene, the widow of General Nathanael Greene of Revolutionary fame—who conceived the idea that some one might invent a machine to separate cotton seeds from the fiber, suggested to Whitney that he work upon it, and

supported him with funds and encouragement. Later, she shared in his royalties. The results of that invention are historical commonplace. Not only was the institution of slavery, then showing marked signs of decline, sharply revived; a revolution was begun in the economic status of women. With large-scale production of cotton, the function of the home as an independent factory was destined to disappear. By 1822, as Mrs. Irwin notes, Lowell, Mass., had been created as a factory town, with its spindles and looms manned mostly by women. "By the 1820s, woman was coming out of the home, never to return on the same old terms."

To discover just where, in terms of numbers, that revolutionary change has led, we had best turn to the statistical tables contained in Professor Breckinridge's "Women in the Twentieth Century." Taking only the number of women 10 years of age and over classified as operatives in manufacturing industries, we find by the Bureau of Census figures that the total in 1930 was 1,658,799, or 37.3 per cent of the total number of persons so employed in the United States. Nearly 2,000,000 women were employed in that year in clerical occupations, or almost exactly half the total number of persons so employed. Remembering the great difficulty with which women forced their way into professional occupations—it was not, for instance, until 1848 that an institution was available in which women could study medicine (the Female Medical College in Boston, with a course which covered merely scientific midwifery)—there is even greater significance in the figures for professional occupations. There were 1,526,234 women professionally engaged in 1930, though of this large number by far the bulk is composed of 880,409 teachers and 228,737 trained nurses. The proportion of women to men in the professions was 46.9 per cent, but in the medical profession women numbered only 5.2 per cent and only 2.1 per cent in the law. Even so, there were 8,388 women physicians, surgeons and osteopaths in the United States in 1930 and 3,383 lawyers and judges. There were also 3,276 women clergymen. Professor Breckinridge offers us no comprehensive table for the field of women's latest conquest—that of public office—but she does include an interesting one showing the number of women holding such office in the four selected States of Connecticut, Michigan, Minnesota and Wisconsin. In Connecticut the number rose from 134 in 1925 to 652 in 1929; in Michigan, from 367 in 1927 to 793 in 1929; in Minnesota, from 227 in 1926 to 348 in 1930; in Wisconsin, from 62 in 1926 to 171 in 1929.

There is no need to rehearse here the gradual steps by which the woman's movement advanced its now far-flung lines, fighting hard for every inch of the way. The details are in Mrs. Irwin's book for those who wish to read them—and nearly all the names. "Angels and Amazons" is in large part a roster of those who have worked for "the cause." Indeed, one could wish sometimes that fewer names were

The "Modern Girl" Bursts Upon the World.

From a Drawing in The London Graphic.

(Continued on Page 14)

Inez Haynes Irwin, *Angels and Amazons,* and Sophonisba P. Breckinridge, *Women in the Twentieth Century*

In this review of two feminist histories, the critic—the editor of the Book Review—let his personal views of suffrage color his assessment: "If the anti-feminists are right," he wrote, "the success of the woman's movement . . . may be justly regarded as one of the major tragedies in the history of mankind."

THAT WAS AN AUSPICIOUS DAY—"A CLIMAX," Mrs. Irwin calls it, in the history of feminism, when Elizabeth Cady Stanton and Lucretia Mott, American women delegates to the World's Anti-Slavery Conference held at London in 1840, walked out from the convention hall seething with indignation because the conference had ruled that women delegates might not take active part in the proceedings, but could sit decorously behind a screen in the gallery and listen to the men. William Lloyd Garrison had been expected to make the great speech of the occasion, but in protest he took his seat beside Lucretia Mott and Elizabeth Stanton and did not speak at all. It was, as Mrs. Irwin describes it, "a beautiful gesture." As for the two women, they dedicated their lives to the woman's movement, and that very night planned the battle for woman suffrage.

It is the purpose of Mrs. Irwin's book to trace the entire history of that movement from its first feeble stirrings down to these Amazonian days. That too, is in part the purpose of Professor Breckinridge's *Women in the Twentieth Century,* though most of her volume is given over to a statistical analysis of women's activities during the present century. *Women in the Twentieth Century* is frankly a source book, hardly intended for popular consumption. Mrs. Irwin's *Angels and Amazons* aims at being more colorful, but its interest remains chiefly factual.

There is no speed to rehearse here the gradual steps by which the woman's movement advanced its now far-flung lines, fighting hard for every inch of the way. The details are in Mrs. Irwin's book for those who wish to read them—and nearly all the names. *Angels and Amazons* is in large part a roster of those who have worked for "the cause."

It was perhaps unkind to collect and publish. No intelligent man today questions the right of

1931 ——————————
Margaret Sanger publishes *My Fight for Birth Control.* The Book Review notes, "Verily, the way of the crusader is hard!"

1932 ——————————
Aldous Huxley publishes *Brave New World,* which the Book Review hails as a "knockabout farce."

1932 ——————————→
The Book Review finds *Little House in the Big Woods*, by Laura Ingalls Wilder, to be "refreshingly genuine and lifelike."

1921–1946

women to vote and to hold office if they so desire, but there are intelligent women who have begun to wonder if anticipation is not, in the terms of the old theme for debate, a greater good than realization.

There is no doubt that the emancipation of women and the mental attitudes which it has developed have helped in the creation of feminine leaders whose capacity for public service or for professional endeavor is better than that of many men. But the question remains, at what cost to themselves and to the race as a whole has this fitness been obtained?

The feminists have been intent upon making women able to do everything that a man can do, without reckoning the psychological and psychic cost to women of their effort. There is a cost, modern psychologists argue, because there are fundamental differences between the mental and emotional functioning of men and women. The feminine mentality is mutually bound up with feeling, whereas that of man rests more directly upon reason. Women's mental processes cling to what is concrete; men's venture much more readily into the abstract. If anybody doubts the truth of that distinction, let him search his memory for the name of one woman who has achieved fame in the field of metaphysics! The point is not that woman's brain is inferior to man's; merely that it works in a different way.

Now, the psychologist who holds this view will tell you that when women take upon themselves the functions normally assigned to men they set up in themselves a conflict between their conscious and subconscious selves which makes for anything but inner harmony and happiness. And he would be a rash philosopher who would maintain that the American woman of today is a happier person than her grandmother was at the same age, or her great-grandmother, in spite of the fact that the earlier woman had frequently a hard lot. There is something of an answer in the serene old faces that look out from the daguerreotypes of those who survived the rigors of plentiful child-bearing and the endless tasks of the household.

Nor is it simply in the effort to be as men that women, from the point of view of the anti-feminist, have sold their birthright for a mess of pottage. They are destroying themselves and endangering the race, he believes, by their acceptance of the ideal of self-realization, which is, of course, closely linked with their entrance into hitherto masculine fields. The abandonment of the idea of love, its reduction, as manifested between persons of opposite sex, to the level of a mere physical appetite, has its contributory effect. It is to ignore the old natural law of compensation, of complementary forces in nature, and it leads into the waste land.

If the anti-feminists are right, the success of the woman's movement, fostered as it has been by the economic trend, may be justly regarded as one of the major tragedies in the history of mankind. And if it is a tragedy, only the women themselves can avert its consequences.

—J. Donald Adams

1932 — President Herbert Hoover, addicted to mystery novels, buys them five at a time.

1934 — The Times reports that Jane Austen's *Pride and Prejudice* is the most-taught novel in American colleges.

1935 — The novelist Edna Ferber covers the Bruno Hauptmann trial for The Times and finds it "horrible and sickening and depressing and wonderful."

Margaret Mitchell, *Gone With the Wind*

The saga of Scarlett O'Hara was published on June 30. By the end of July, the Book Review was calling it "perhaps the fastest-selling book in recent publishing history." By Christmas, Macmillan had almost a million copies in print. Today, of course, many of the novel's themes—and its romanticization of slavery—are regarded as deeply problematic.

THIS IS BEYOND A DOUBT ONE OF THE MOST remarkable first novels produced by an American writer. It is also one of the best. *Gone With the Wind* is by no means a great novel. But it is a long while since the reading public has been offered such a bounteous feast of story telling.

The story opens in Georgia, immediately before the war. Most of the action takes place in and about Atlanta, the sprawling new city of the South, a crossroads planted in the red mud and soon a hustling town, rising as the railroads come and cross it east and west and north and south.

But Miss Mitchell's real triumph is Scarlett O'Hara, a heroine lacking in many virtues—in nearly all, one might say, but courage. She is a vital creature, this Scarlett, alive in every inch, selfish, unprincipled, ruthless, greedy and dominating, but with a backbone of supple, springing steel. Daughter of an immigrant Irishman who by force of character and personal charm fought his way into the ranks of the plantation nabobs and married a belle of aristocratic family, she was earthily Irish, with but little trace of her mother's gentle strain, and a complete rebel against the standards of the society in which she was reared. She is a memorable figure in American fiction. But she lives in her own right, completely, and will, I suspect, for a long time to come.

An almost equally vital figure is Rhett Butler, scapegrace son of a Charleston family, cynical and hard-bitten realist (but no more realist than Scarlett herself), who saw the hopelessness of the South's position from the first, and who, as a blockade runner, lined his pockets during the war. The remarkable thing about Miss Mitchell's portrait of him is that she has taken a stock figure of melodrama, even to the black mustache, the piercing eyes and the irresistible way with women, and made him credible and alive.

The battle of wills between these two, set against the cross-current of Scarlett's self-deceiving love for Ashley Wilkes, makes an uncommonly absorbing love story, and one that Miss Mitchell manages to tell with rarely a false note, and which she carries to a logical and unforced conclusion. Melanie, whom Ashley Wilkes married, and Ashley himself, are foils for these two. These are only Miss Mitchell's most fully drawn characters, the central figures of her story. She has a host of others, excellently if sketchily done. She draws on the whole social fabric of the antebellum, war time and Reconstruction South for her people.

He would be a rash critic who would make any prophecies as to Miss Mitchell's future. She has set herself a hard mark to match with a second book, and I hope only that she will not set too soon about it. —*J. Donald Adams*

Idaho: A Guide in Word and Picture

Released by the Federal Writers' Project of the Works Progress Administration, this was one of many such guides produced during the Great Depression. Writers like Ralph Ellison and John Steinbeck found gainful employment in this New Deal initiative at a time when there was little work elsewhere. The *American Guides* series remains the only project of its kind in the country's history, a comprehensive look at the nation's then 48 states, in addition to major cities and regional explorations.

FASCINATING PHOTOGRAPHS COME TO US, every now and then, of a great herd of antelope in a swift passage across the jungle-girt plains of farthest Africa. But the two herds of American antelope in Idaho are said to be the largest in the world. They are the fastest animals on this continent. And one of the many striking photographs that illustrate this new "guide" to Idaho pictures one of these herds in flight: the interesting, and indeed arresting, quality of this photograph is typical of the whole content of this excellent book.

The word "guide" is far too modest a term to describe a book with such readable text, such beautiful and broadly illustrative pictures as this. The history of the State, the Idaho Indians in their past and their present, the trees and flowers and birds and animals, the unusual and greatly varied features of the state's topography, Idaho's commercial resources, curious legends—even its ghost towns—are presented to readers in a great deal of detail, and always interestingly. Sight-seeing tours are planned for visitors. And a number of maps indicate several factors of the State's life and history, as well as its geographical make-up.

Although the people of Idaho should welcome this book with gratification, it has its greatest importance, in giving the rest of the country a new knowledge of one of our States. This is a fine example of the Federal Writers Projects' activity, and it will have a permanent value.

1936 ———————————
Dale Carnegie's *How to Win Friends and Influence People* is published, and the Book Review praises its "simple, sound, practical advice."

1937 ———————————
Ernest Hemingway and Max Eastman get into a fistfight at the Scribner offices.

1938 ———————————→
When *Rebecca* is published, the Book Review says that Daphne du Maurier is "almost in a class by herself."

John Steinbeck,
The Grapes of Wrath

Steinbeck's Depression-era tale, which captured the desperate plight of migrant farm workers, won both the Pulitzer Prize and the National Book Award. "Californians are not going to like this angry novel," our reviewer wrote. "The beauty and fertility of California conceal human fear, hatred and violence."

THERE ARE FEW NOVELISTS WRITING AS WELL as Steinbeck and perhaps a very few who write better; but it is interesting to note how very much alike they are in writing—Hemingway, Caldwell, Faulkner, Dos Passos. Each is writing stories and scenarios of America with a curious and sudden intensity, almost as if they had never seen or understood it before. They are looking at it again with revolutionary eyes. *The Grapes of Wrath* is as pitiful and angry a novel ever to be written about America.

It is a very long novel, the longest that Steinbeck has written, and yet it reads as if it had been composed in a flash, ripped off the typewriter and delivered to the public as an ultimatum. It is a long and thoughtful novel as one thinks about it. It is a short and vivid scene as one feels it.

The journey across is done in superb style, one marvellous short story after another, and all melting into this long novel of the great trek.

Californians are not going to like this angry novel. The beauty and fertility of California conceal human fear, hatred and violence. "Scairt" is a Western farmer's word for the inhabitants, frightened of the influx of workers eager for jobs, and when they are frightened they become vicious and cruel. This part of the story reads like the news from Nazi Germany. Families from Oklahoma are known as "Okies." While they work they live in what might as well be called concentration camps. Only a few hundred are given jobs out of the thousands who traveled West. Their pay is cut from 30 cents an hour to 25, to 20. If any one objects he is a Red, an agitator, a trouble maker who had better get out of the country. Deputy sheriffs are around with guns, legally shooting or clubbing any one from the rest of the Union who questions the law of California. The Joad family find only one place of order and decency in this country of fear and violence, in a government camp, and it is a pleasure to follow

Other Great 1930s Novels

MISS LONELYHEARTS,
BY NATHANAEL WEST
1933

West's novel about the male reporter picked to write a newspaper's advice column "is ostensibly a piece of humorous fiction," the Book Review said. "But do not class it with the clever wisecracking little volumes that emerge seasonally from the presses to carry on the tradition of bald American exaggeration. It is ostensibly satiric. But its irony has roots to it."

NIGHTWOOD,
BY DJUNA BARNES
1936

This novel is now a lauded queer classic—but you'd never know what it was about from the review: "People move in a kind of angry stupor, without love, without trust, and never without some inhuman fear that all the pin points of their own making will fuse into a spear and stab the life out of the consciousness that alone sustains them."

THE BIG SLEEP,
BY RAYMOND CHANDLER
1939

After this hard-boiled crime novel was published, our reviewer said, "His talents are so obvious that it does seem to me biased and blind to ticket him and similarly able talents in the mystery field as no more than light entertainment."

"It reads as if it had been composed in a flash, ripped off the typewriter and delivered to the public as an ultimatum."

the family as they take a shower bath and go to the Saturday night dances. But even here the deputy sheriffs, hired by the banks who run the Farmers Association, are poking in their guns, on the pretext of inciting to riot and the necessity of protective custody. The Joad family moves on through California, hunted by anonymous guns while they are picking peaches for 2 cents a box, hoping only for a little land free of guns and dust on which they might settle and work as they were accustomed to. The promised grapes of California have turned into grapes of wrath that might come to fruition at any moment.

How true this may be no reviewer can say. It is easy to add that the novel comes to no conclusion, that the preacher is killed because he is a strikebreaker, that Tom disappears as a fugitive from California justice, that the novel ends on a minor and sentimental note; that the story stops after 600 pages merely because a story has to stop somewhere. All this is true enough but the real truth is that Steinbeck has written a novel from the depths of his heart with a sincerity seldom equaled. It may be an exaggeration, but it is the exaggeration of an honest and splendid writer. —*Peter Monro Jack*

THE NEW YORK TIMES BOOK REVIEW

Richard Wright, *Native Son*

"The day *Native Son* appeared, American culture was changed forever," Irving Howe once wrote. The novel was a massive commercial success, selling 215,000 copies within three weeks of its publication. As the novelist Ayana Mathis wrote in The Times in 2015, this meant that "a great many people received a swift and unsparing education in the conditions in which blacks lived in ghettos all over America. Of course, black people already knew about all of that, so it is safe to conclude that Wright's intended audience was white."

A READY WAY TO SHOW THE IMPORTANCE OF this novel is to call it the Negro "American Tragedy" and to compare it roughly with Dreiser's masterpiece. Both deal seriously and powerfully with the problem of social maladjustment, with environment and individual behavior, and subsequently with crime and punishment. Both are tragedies and Dreiser's white boy and Wright's black boy are equally killed in the electric chair not for being criminals—since the crime in each case was unpremeditated—but for being social misfits. The pattern in both books is similar: the family, the adolescent, the lure of money and sex, fortuitous events, murder, trial and death. The conclusion in both is that society is to blame, that the environment into which each was born forced upon them their crimes, that they were the particular victims of a general injustice.

The startling difference in Mr. Wright's *Native Son* is that the injustice is a racial, not merely a social one. Dreiser's Clyde Griffiths represents a social "complex" that could be reasonably taken care of. Mr. Wright's Bigger Thomas is far beyond and outside of helpful social agencies. He represents an impasse rather than a complex, and his tragedy is to be born into a black and immutable minority race, literally, in his own words, "whipped before you born." Mr. Wright allows Bigger a brief moment of illumination into his hopeless condition before he is finally whipped out of the world.

The narrative of Bigger's life begins with a symbolic incident worth remarking on. He is 20 years old, living in a one-room tenement apartment in Chicago's South Side Black Belt, with his mother, his young sister, Vera, and younger brother, Buddy; they pay $8 rent a week; they are on relief. Bigger's first job when he wakes on the morning of his story is to kill a huge black rat that has got into the room. His intent destruction of the rat is a characteristic act.

It is later in the day when Bigger turns up to the job where the relief people have sent him, as chauffeur to one of Chicago's big executive types of the benevolent kind. This Mr. Dalton has given millions for social welfare, earmarked particularly for the Negro cause, for the National Association for the Advancement of Colored People, although most of it has dribbled into ping-pong tables in exemplary social clubs and the like. Bigger knows nothing about this, nor does he know that a good part of Mr. Dalton's money for charity comes from the exorbitant rents Dalton charges the Negroes

Wright, circa 1945.

to live in the overcrowded, rat-infested tenements that he owns in the Black Belt—in part, from the very room Bigger had left that morning.

On the night of the first day Bigger is to drive the daughter Mary to a university lecture. Mary has gone a little farther than her parents in practical sociology and directs Bigger to drive to Communist headquarters instead of the university. There she meets a practically perfect Communist, who shakes Bigger's hand and wants to be called by his first name, Jan.

How Bigger inadvertently murdered Mary that same night can be told only in the words that Mr. Wright uses. The necessary point is that he found he had killed her out of fear, out of his certain knowledge that he would be suspected (unjustly) of having raped the girl. When her mother, who is blind, comes to the bedroom to which Bigger has just carried her, Bigger puts a pillow over the girl's face to prevent her speaking of his presence there. Unconsciously he exerts more strength than he realizes. Mary is dead when Mrs. Dalton, believing that her daughter is merely drunk, leaves the bedroom without having discovered Bigger.

This is the beginning and end of Bigger's fatal history. The body he burns in the furnace, the head cut off with a hatchet because he cannot force it in, the exhaust fan switched on to clear the air of the basement of the smell of burning flesh. Bigger's mind reaches a rapid solution. As a Negro he will be the first suspect. But Jan, the Communist, he considers, is almost an equal object of mob hatred. He has been told by the politicians that the Reds are the dirtiest kind of criminals; he can easily throw the blame on Jan by asserting that Jan went home with the girl, he can even collect kidnapping money on

the pretense that Mary is still alive. This, one might say, is a typically criminal mind, but it is Mr. Wright's purpose to show it as a typical kind of social and racial conditioning. Bigger's crime is discovered. He commits another crime (this time merely the murder of his Negro mistress) to cover his tracks, but it is only now a matter of time between his flight and his fate. A Jewish Communist lawyer makes a brilliant speech in his defense, but there is nothing to be done save an attempt at explanation.

It will be argued, and I think with truth, that his character, Bigger, is made far too articulate, that he explains much too glibly in the latter part of the story how he came to meet his fate: "Seems sort of natural-like, me being here facing that death chair. Now I come to think of it, it seems like something like this just had to be." Later he has romanticized and rationalized himself into the declaration that "What I killed for must've been good! . . . It must have been good! When a man kills, it's for something . . . I didn't know I was really alive in this world until I felt things hard enough to kill for 'em." This, I believe, is so much romantic nonsense. Dreiser was wiser in allowing the reader to think out Clyde Griffiths in his own realistic terms: he did not interfere too much in the interpretation of his character. Mr. Wright does spoil his story at the end by insisting on Bigger's fate as representative of the whole Negro race and making Bigger himself say so. But this is a minor fault in a good cause. The story is a strong and powerful one and it alone will force the Negro issue into our attention. Certainly, *Native Son* declares Richard Wright's importance, not merely as the best Negro writer, but as an American author as distinctive as any of those now writing. —*Peter Monro Jack*

Carson McCullers, *The Heart Is a Lonely Hunter*

McCullers, now considered a master of the Southern Gothic, garnered instant praise with her debut: "She writes with a sweep and certainty that are overwhelming. *The Heart Is a Lonely Hunter* is a first novel. One anticipates the second with something like fear."

NO MATTER WHAT THE AGE OF ITS AUTHOR, *The Heart Is a Lonely Hunter* would be a remarkable book. When one reads that Carson McCullers is a girl of 22 it becomes more than that. Maturity does not cover the quality of her work. It is something beyond that, something more akin to the vocabulary of pain to which a great poet is born. Reading her one feels this girl is wrapped in knowledge which has roots beyond the span of her life and experience. How else can she so surely plumb the hearts of characters as strange and, under the force of her creative shaping, as real as she presents—two deaf mutes, a ranting, rebellious drunkard, a Negro torn from his faith and lost in his frustrated dream of equality, a restaurant owner bewildered by his emotions, a girl of 13 caught in the world of people and the world of shadows.

From its opening page, brilliant in its establishment of mood, character and suspense, the book takes hold of the reader. "In the town there were two mutes, and they were always together," Miss McCullers begins, and at once this unique novel swings into action. One of these mutes was the fat, greasy, ungainly Greek, Spiros Antonapoulos, who worked in his cousin's fruit store and made candy for him; the other was John Singer, who was employed as an engraver in a jewelry store. They lived together in two rooms, bound to each other by the physical handicap which made them alien in a world of normal people.

With a touch reminiscent of Faulkner but peculiarly her own, Miss McCullers describes their strange relationship, the fat Greek, greedy for food, petulant, mentally irresponsible, dominating the slender, gentle Singer. When the public habits of Antonapoulos become such that he is a menace to public decency, his cousin has him put away in an institution for the insane and John Singer is left alone, lost and stranded among people who talk.

Exiled from the home he and the Greek had made for each other, Singer takes a room in

THE NEW YORK TIMES BOOK REVIEW

1938
One of the year's biggest publishing successes is *The Yearling*, by Marjorie Kinnan Rawlings, which sells more than 250,000 copies.

1939
Ludwig Bemelmans publishes *Madeline,* introducing American children to the plucky little boarding-school student who lived "in an old house in Paris that was covered in vines."

1939
James Joyce's *Finnegans Wake* presents a real challenge for the paper's reviewer, who says "there is much in the book that he is still seeking explanation for."

McCullers in 1955.

the Kellys' boarding house and arranges to have all his meals in Biff Brannon's New York Café. The few things he needs to get over to other people he writes in careful script on cards he carries with him. Accustomed to living in a world of silence, he neither expects nor wants companionship of those who live in a world of sounds. Deepest in his heart is the yearning for the departed Antonapoulos.

With stinging subtlety, Miss McCullers builds up the growing importance of Singer in the lives of the people who come to know him. In developing Singer as the fountainhead of understanding and wisdom, she plunges into the heart of human desolation, into the pain of the ineffectuality of words as a bridge between people. Sitting silently in Biff Brannon's restaurant, lost in his dreams of the two rooms where Antonapoulos had cooked, smiling vaguely as he plans his vacation visit to the incarcerated Greek, Singer becomes a symbol of godliness. Saying nothing, it is assumed he knows everything. His smile is gentle, built of his own loneliness and because he cannot defend himself against the spate of words forced upon him, he listens with eyes fixed sympathetically upon moving lips.

"Reading her one feels this girl is wrapped in knowledge which has roots beyond the span of her life and experience."

With powerful strokes Miss McCullers paints the details of the lives of these people and those they touch. She is squeamish neither of word nor incident and her canvas is alive with the realities of their existence, more often savage and violent than tender. Her imagination is rich and fearless; she has an astounding perception of humanity which goes with equal certainty into the daily life of a drunken social rebel like Jake Blount and into the dreams of the music-hungry, lonely Mick Kelly. The effect is strangely that of a Van Gogh painting peopled by Faulkner figures. That it is the greedy Spiros Antonapoulos, greedy for sweets and vicious in an infantile way, who actually dominates the lives of the characters through his influence on John Singer, serves to heighten the terrific force of her story.

Carson McCullers is a full-fledged novelist whatever her age. She writes with a sweep and certainty that are overwhelming. *The Heart Is a Lonely Hunter* is a first novel. One anticipates the second with something like fear, so high is the standard she set. It doesn't seem possible that she can reach it again. —*Rose Feld*

1940 ——————

The British humorist P. G. Wodehouse is taken into custody by German troops at his home in Le Touquet, France, on June 6.

1941 ——————

Six months after her suicide, the British novelist Virginia Woolf is featured on the cover of the Book Review for the last time for *Between the Acts.*

1942 ——————→

Anne Frank makes the first entry in her diary on June 12.

THE NEW YORK TIMES BOOK REVIEW

114

Ernest Hemingway, *For Whom the Bell Tolls*

The New York Times weighed in on every book that Hemingway wrote. At least in the beginning, reviewers grudgingly praised his lean, sinewy style while making clear they did not approve of his subject matter or characters. In 1926, after the review of *The Sun Also Rises,* Hemingway wrote to his editor, Maxwell Perkins: "The Times review I had to read to the end before I found whether they really liked it or not. . . . It's funny to write a book that seems as tragic as that and have them take it for a jazz superficial story. If you went any deeper inside they couldn't read it because they would be crying all the time." But by 1940, Hemingway was such a towering cultural figure that the paper turned any scrap of news about him—his brawls and fistfights, his vacations, his car accidents—into a story, often on the front page. When *For Whom the Bell Tolls* arrived, J. Donald Adams, the editor of the Book Review, delivered an unqualified rave. (Four years later he would write, "Hemingway has still to prove himself as a novelist.")

THIS IS THE BEST BOOK ERNEST HEMINGWAY has written, the fullest, the deepest, the truest. It will, I think, be one of the major novels in American literature.

There were those of us who felt, when *To Have and Have Not* was published, that Hemingway was through as a creative writer. That is always a dangerous assumption to make regarding any writer of much innate ability, but it did seem that Hemingway was blocked off from further development. We were badly mistaken. Technical skill he had long ago acquired; the doubt lay in where and how he could apply it, and that doubt he has now sweepingly erased. The skill is even further sharpened than it was, but with it has come an inner growth, a deeper and surer feeling for life, than he has previously displayed. Whatever brought about this growth—whether his experience of the Spanish war, out of which this novel was made, or something else, it is plainly to be seen in this book, from beginning to end. There are no traces of adolescence in the Hemingway of *For Whom the Bell Tolls.* This is the work of a mature artist, of a mature mind.

The title derives from John Donne. The passage from which it comes faces the book's first page:

"No man is an *Iland,* intire of it selfe; every man is a peece of the *Continent,* a part of the *maine;* if a *Clod* bee washed away by the Sea, *Europe* is the lesse, as well as if a *Promontorie* were, as well as if a *Mannor* of thy *friends* or of *thine owne* were; any mans *death* diminishes *me,* because I am involved in *Mankinde;* And therefore never send to know for whom the *bell* tolls; it tolls for *thee.*"

It is a fine title, and an apt one, for this is a book filled with the imminence of death, and the manner of man's meeting it. That is as it should

The New York Times
OCTOBER 20
1 9 4 0

Book Review

Section

6

Copyright, 1940, by The New York Times Company.

THE NEW NOVEL BY HEMINGWAY

"For Whom the Bell Tolls" Is the Best Book He Has Written

FOR WHOM THE BELL TOLLS. By
Ernest Hemingway. 471 pp. New York:
Charles Scribner's Sons. $2.75.

By J. DONALD ADAMS

THIS is the best book Ernest Hemingway has written, the fullest, the deepest, the truest. It will, I think, be one of the major novels in American literature.

There were those of us who felt, when "To Have and Have Not" was published, that Hemingway was through as a creative writer. That is always a dangerous assumption to make regarding any writer of much innate ability, but it did seem that Hemingway was blocked off from further development. We were badly mistaken. Technical skill he had long ago acquired; the doubt lay in where and how he could apply it, and that doubt he has now sweepingly erased. The skill is even further sharpened than it was, but with it has come an inner growth, a deeper and surer feeling for life, than he has previously displayed. Whatever brought about this growth— whether his experience of the Spanish war, out of which this novel was made, or something else, it is plainly to be seen in this book, from beginning to end. There are no traces of adolescence in the Hemingway of "For Whom the Bell Tolls." This is the work of a mature artist, of a mature mind.

The title derives from John Donne. The passage from which it comes faces the book's first page:

No man is an *Iland*, intire of it selfe; every man is a *peece of the Continent*, a part of the *maine*; if a *Clod* bee washed away by the *Sea*, *Europe* is the lesse, as well as if a *Promontorie* were, as well as if a *Mannor* of thy *friends* or of *thine owne* were; any mans *death* diminishes *me*, because I am involved in *Mankinde*; And therefore never send to know for whom the *bell* tolls; it tolls for *thee*.

It is a fine title, and an apt one, for this is a book filled with the imminence of death, and the manner of man's meeting it. That is as it should be; this is a story of the Spanish war. But in it Hemingway has struck universal chords, and he has struck them vibrantly. Perhaps it conveys something of the measure of "For Whom the Bell Tolls" 'to say that with that theme, it is not a depressing but an uplifting book. It has the purging quality that lies in the presenting of tragic but profound truth. Hemingway has freed himself from the negation that held him in his other novels. As Robert Jordan lay facing death he looked down the hill slope and thought: "I have fought for what I believed in for a year now. If we win here we will win everywhere. The world is a fine place and worth the fighting

for and I hate very much to leave it."

The frame of the story is a minor incident in the horror that was the war in Spain. Robert Jordan is a young American in the Loyalist ranks who has been detailed to the blowing up of a bridge which the General Staff wants destroyed

Ernest Hemingway.

to prevent the bringing up of enemy reinforcements. His mission carried him into hill country where he must seek the aid of guerrilla bands. Jordan destroys the bridge, but while he is escaping with his companions his horse is knocked from under him by an exploding shell, and we leave him lying on the hillside, his leg crushed by the animal's fall. He sends his companions on and waits, with a submachine gun beside him, for the enemy's approach.

Those who leave him are, with Jordan,

the main figures in the story. Among them is the girl Maria, whom Jordan, in the four-day span of the story's action, has met and loved. And as "For Whom the Bell Tolls" is a better story of action than "A Farewell to Arms," so too is this a finer love story than that of Lieutenant Henry and Catherine Barkley. That is saying a good deal, but it is true. I know of no love scenes in American fiction and few in any other to compare with those of "For Whom the Bell Tolls" in depth and sincerity of feeling. They are unerringly right, and as much beyond those of "A Farewell to Arms" as the latter were beyond the casual couplings of "The Sun Also Rises."

The book holds, I think, the best character drawing that Hemingway has done. Robert Jordan is a fine portrait of a fighting idealist, and the Spanish figures are superbly done, in particular the woman Pilar, who should take her place among the memorable women of fiction—earthy and strong, tender, hard, wise, a woman who, as she said of herself, would have been a good man, and yet was a woman made for men. The brutal, unstable Pablo, in whom strength and evil were combined, the good and brave old man Anselmo— these and others are warmly living in this heroic story.

I wrote once that Ernest Hemingway can see and describe with a precision and a vividness unmatched since Kipling first displayed his great visual gift. There are scenes in this book finer than any he has done. The telling of how the Civil Guard was shot in Pablo's town and how the fascists were beaten to death between rows of men armed with flails and hurled over a cliff into the river 300 feet below, how the fascists walked out one by one from their prayers in the City Hall and severally met their deaths, has the thrust and power of one of the more terrible of Goya's pictures.

In all that goes to make a good novel "For Whom the Bell Tolls" is an advance beyond Hemingway's previous work. It is much more full-bodied in its drawing of character, visually more brilliant, and incomparably richer in content. Hemingway's style, too, has changed for the better. It was extraordinarily effective at times before, but it is shed now of the artificialities that clung to it. There is nothing obtrusive about the manner in which this book is written; the style is a part of the whole; there is no artifice to halt the eye. It has simplicity and power, delicacy and strength.

This is Hemingway's longest novel, and it could be, I think, as most books can, a little shorter, and with benefit. It seems to me that some of the long passages in which Robert Jordan's mind turns back to his days in Madrid retard the narrative unnecessarily and could well have been omitted. If there are other flaws in this fine performance, I have not yet found them. A very good novel it unquestionably is, and I am not at all sure that it may not prove to be a great one. That is not something to determine on a first reading. But this much more is certain: that Hemingway is now a writer of real stature, not merely a writer of abundant talents whose work does not measure up to his equipment. "For Whom the Bell Tolls" is the book of a man who knows what life is about, and who can convey his knowledge. Hemingway has found bigger game than the kudu and the lion. The hunter is home from the hill.

be; this is a story of the Spanish war. But in it Hemingway has struck universal chords, and he has struck them vibrantly. Perhaps it conveys something of the measure of *For Whom the Bell Tolls* to say that with that theme, it is not a depressing but an uplifting book. It has the purging quality that lies in the presenting of tragic but profound truth. Hemingway has freed himself from the negation that held him in his other novels. As Robert Jordan lay facing death he looked down the hill slope and thought: "I have fought for what I believed in for a year now. If we win here we will win everywhere. The world is a fine place and worth the fighting for and I hate very much to leave it."

The frame of the story is a minor incident in the horror that was the war in Spain. Robert Jordan is a young American in the Loyalist ranks who has been detailed to the blowing up of a bridge which the General Staff wants destroyed to prevent the bringing up of enemy reinforcements. His mission carried him into hill country where he must seek the aid of guerrilla bands. Jordan destroys the bridge, but while he is escaping with his companions his horse is knocked from under him by an exploding shell, and we leave him lying on the hillside, his leg crushed by the animal's fall. He sends his companions on and waits, with a submachine gun beside him, for the enemy's approach.

Those who leave him are, with Jordan, the main figures in the story. Among them is the girl Maria, whom Jordan, in the four-day span of the story's action, has met and loved. And as *For Whom the Bell Tolls* is a better story of action than *A Farewell to Arms,* so too is this a finer love story than that of Lieutenant Henry and Catherine Barkley. That is saying a good deal, but it is true. I know of no love scenes in American fiction and few in any other to compare with those of *For Whom the Bell Tolls* in depth and sincerity of feeling.

They are unerringly right, and as much beyond those of *A Farewell to Arms* as the latter were beyond the casual couplings of *The Sun Also Rises.*

The book holds, I think, the best character drawing that Hemingway has done. Robert Jordan is a fine portrait of a fighting idealist, and the Spanish figures are superbly done, in particular the woman Pilar, who should take her place among the memorable women of fiction—earthy and strong, tender, hard, wise, a woman who, as she said of herself, would have been a good man, and yet was a woman made for men. The brutal, unstable Pablo, in whom strength and evil were combined, the good and brave old man Anselmo—these and others are warmly living in this heroic story.

I wrote once that Ernest Hemingway can see and describe with a precision and a vividness unmatched since Kipling first displayed his great visual gift. There are scenes in this book finer than any he has done. The telling of how the Civil Guard was shot in Pablo's town and how the fascists were beaten to death between rows of men armed with flails and hurled over a cliff into the river 300 feet below, how the fascists walked out one by one from their prayers in the City Hall and severally met their deaths, has the thrust and power of one of the more terrible of Goya's pictures.

In all that goes to make a good novel *For Whom the Bell Tolls* is an advance beyond Hemingway's previous work. It is much more full-bodied in its drawing of character, visually more brilliant, and incomparably richer in content. Hemingway's style, too, has changed for the better. It was extraordinarily effective at times before, but it is shed now of the artificialities that clung to it. There is nothing obtrusive about the manner in which this book is written; the style is a part of the whole; there is no artifice to halt the eye. It has simplicity and power, delicacy and strength. —*J. Donald Adams*

The First Best-Seller List

Long before the Book Review was born, the newspaper was interested in what books were selling, often sending a reporter around the city to find out what was popular at individual stores. On October 31, 1896—in its third issue—the Book Review reprinted the best-seller lists collected by a literary journal called *The Bookman*. "*The Bookman*'s reports of the best-selling books," the Book Review assured its readers, came from "'trustworthy' sources in the towns named."

In 1897, the Book Review began what would be the first of many year-end roundups of best-selling titles. It noted that although it was quite clear that its own coverage was propelling some books to best-sellerdom, "we must seek elsewhere for causes which have carried into a 35th edition Mr. Ford's political novel, *Peter Stirling,* and into a 42nd Mr. Hope's historical piece of fiction, *The Prisoner of Zenda.*"

The Book Review soon began covering book sales in more creative ways. During the December holidays it regularly reported on sales at local department stores; not long after that, it did the same for summer vacation reading. For a time it printed the books most checked-out at the New York Public Library. And by 1901 it had created a regular column called "Books in Demand: Reports from Shops and Libraries as to Those Which Lead." These books, "which have sold best in the cities named and which have been most called for at public libraries during the month . . . have been received from regular correspondents of The New York Times who have made personal inquiries for the information they give." At a later date the Book Review began publishing the best-seller list curated by the trade magazine *Publishers Weekly* and, later still, one supplied by the book wholesaler Baker & Taylor.

Here's how the paper's official best-seller list looked when it first appeared on August 9, 1942.

The Best Selling Books, Here and Elsewhere

Fiction

Title	NEW YORK	BOSTON	PHILADELPHIA	WASHINGTON	BALTIMORE	ATLANTA	CLEVELAND	DETROIT	CHICAGO	ST. LOUIS	NEW ORLEANS	DALLAS	SAN FRANCISCO	LOS ANGELES
And Now Tomorrow, by Rachel Field	2	1	2	2	5	1	3	2	2	1		1		1
The Song of Bernadette, by Franz Werfel	1		4	1	4	2	1		3	2	4	2	5	2
Drivin' Woman, by Elizabeth Chevalier	4	3	1	3	1			4	1			3	3	3
The Moon Is Down, by John Steinbeck			3			4	3	4	3	2	4			5
Kings Row, by Henry Bellamann					2	5	2	1		4		5		
Until the Day Break, by Louis Bromfield	5	5	5	4		4								
Assignment in Brittany, by Helen MacInnes	3	2		3		5						2		
The Hour Before the Dawn, by Somerset Maugham				5						5	5			
The Sea-Gull Cry, by Robert Nathan		4												
Tap Roots, by James Street						3								
Mud on the Stars, by William B. Huie									5					
The Commandos, by Elliott Arnold									5					
Islandia, by Austin Wright												1		
The Sun Is My Undoing, by Marguerite Steen												3		
The Uninvited, by Dorothy MacArdle													1	
The Just and the Unjust, by James Gould Cozzens													4	
The Floods of Spring, by Henry Bellamann														4

Non-Fiction

Title	NEW YORK	BOSTON	PHILADELPHIA	WASHINGTON	BALTIMORE	ATLANTA	CLEVELAND	DETROIT	CHICAGO	ST. LOUIS	NEW ORLEANS	DALLAS	SAN FRANCISCO	LOS ANGELES
The Last Time I saw Paris, by Elliott Paul	1	4	2		4			4	4	2	1	2	3	4
Victory Through Air Power, by Alexander de Seversky	2		1	2	5	2	1	2	5	3	4	1	4	2
Washington Is Like That, by W. M. Kiplinger	4	3	3	1	1	3		1	1	5		3	2	
The Problems of Lasting Peace, by Hoover and Gibson	3	2	4	4			3	3	3	4			1	
Only the Stars Are Neutral, by Quentin Reynolds	5	5				2		2	1					3
Paul Revere, by Esther Forbes		1		3	3	4								
Assignment to Berlin, by Harry Flannery					2	4								1
Past Imperfect, by Ilka Chase								5				5	4	
Cross Creek, by Marjorie Kinnan Rawlings			5									2		
Private Breger, by Dave Breger					5									
The Long Ships Passing, by Walter Havighurst									5					
Flight to Arras, by Antoine de St. Exupery												3		
The Making of Tomorrow, by Roussy de Sales													5	
Prelude to Victory, by James B. Reston														5
Fighting Fleets, by Critchell Rimington													5	
Georgia: Unfinished State, by Hal Steed						1								

Betty Smith, *A Tree Grows in Brooklyn*

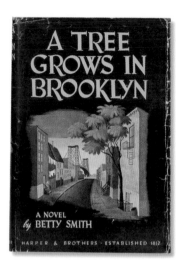

Readers loved 11-year-old Francie Nolan—the plucky girl at the heart of Smith's novel about growing up in the tenements of Brooklyn—and, from the beginning, saw her as a symbol of tenacity, courage and hope. Shortly after its publication, *A Tree Grows in Brooklyn* was released in a paperback Armed Services Edition. A 20-year-old Marine wrote Smith about his experience reading the book: "I went through hell in two years of combat overseas. . . . I just wanted you to understand that despite my youth I have seen a little bit of suffering. I can't explain the emotional reaction that took place, I only know that it happened and that this heart of mine turned over and became alive again. A surge of confidence has swept through me and I feel that maybe a fellow has a fighting chance in this world after all."

I USED TO THINK THAT SOMEDAY, WHEN THE mood came on me and there was time for it, I might sit down and tell the story of my old block in Williamsburg in Brooklyn. The story would be about rather strange kids and strange grown-ups, about Dorney Rogers who spent all his pennies for kerosene and blew the kerosene from his mouth at lighted matches held far out in front of him, just to exult over the flare. About the fat butcher who was a sadist and dragged his 95-pound wife across the floor by her hair until she screamed so the whole block could hear it. Crazy George would be in it, and Blubber Green, who always fell into alcoholic slumber on the crosstown trolley-car tracks. Diamond Julia would thread in and out of my story, flame-faced

---

1942 ——————————

Zora Neale Hurston publishes *Dust Tracks on a Road,* which the Book Review calls "a thumping story . . . live and vivid."

1943 ——————————

The Book Review's critic finds that *The Fountainhead*, by Ayn Rand, is "the only novel of ideas written by an American woman that I can recall."

1944 ——————————→

Kathleen Winsor's *Forever Amber,* the Book Review sniffs, is the story of "a happy harlot, and nothing more."

and never sober, awkwardly pitching rocks at the kids who followed and tormented her. Jaggers would be in it, too; Jaggers who went to the death house for killing a Pole in a barroom brawl but who came back to the block and sat for years in a second-floor window staring at nothing until he died in that position.

Betty Smith, though, has done the job in this delightful volume about Williamsburg as she knew it over 30 years ago. With incredible memory for detail she has brought in Gimpy, the sly old candy-store man who waylaid little girls in the back of his store. She has pinned to paper in three-dimensional writing Cheap Charlie, who cheated little boys and girls with the prize board that never really had the number in it for the roller skates or the big doll. She gives us an excellent portrait of the junk dealer to whose untidy shop little boys and girls would bring their treasures of tinfoil, brass, copper and lead pipe. She has reproduced the cries, the odors and the squalor of old Graham Avenue and its tenements; the hot-eyed old pickle peddlers, overstuffed mothers, breastfeeding their babies with disregard for the stares of passing little boys and girls.

The publishers choose to call this a novel, yet it is hardly that. There is little story, or plot, as the reader encounters it in an average novel. This is rather a stringing together of memory's beads and the workmanship is extraordinarily good. This is autobiography. Above all, it is a faithful picture of a part of Brooklyn that was mostly slums and misery. The picture is softened by almost poetic handling. It is old Williamsburg done, more or less, as James Farrell did the Chicago slums, but the writing is more subtle and the gentler woman's viewpoint gives it clear advantages.

The same people are in it, and they use the same language, but Miss Smith gives her story strength without using the words that little boys like to scrawl on red-brick walls and subway pillars.

The portraits of pitiful John Nolan, Uncle Willie Flittman and his enemy, the milk-wagon horse; poor Flossie Gaddis, who hides a withered arm from the beaux she hungrily seeks; Sissy, who draws her beaux too easily and slips from one "marriage" to another—all these are unforgettable. The book swarms with living people. When these characters sing, Betty Smith puts in their mouths, whether they be drunk or sober, the words of their songs—"Molly Malone," "Walter, Walter, Wildflower" and the songs that little girls shrilled under the stars on hot summer nights when the stoops were heavy with neighbors.

The book tells about the changes in the street with the coming of the first World War. Francie Nolan, the central figure in the book, has moved out of the dream world that was bounded, more or less, by the awesome atmosphere of the local public library, by the streets that lead to the neighborhood stores and by the view from the fire escape. The tree in the book's title is the evil-scented weedlike ailanthus, which grows out of old cellars, in dirty corner lots—anywhere in the sun-baked Williamsburg streets that the wind has blown dust into little heaps.

"It grew lushly, but only in tenement districts," the author tells you. "You took a walk on a Sunday afternoon and came to a nice neighborhood. You saw one of those trees through the iron gate leading to someone's yard and you knew that soon that section of Brooklyn would get to be a tenement district. That was the kind of tree it was. It liked poor people." —*Meyer Berger*

Adolf Hitler,
Mein Kampf

The full horror of what was transpiring in Europe—the knowledge that Hitler's genocidal vision was being fully realized—exists only between the lines of this review. Three days before it ran, there was an uprising at the Sobibor extermination camp where at least 170,000 Jews had already been killed in gas chambers. A day after the review, a thousand Jews were rounded up in Rome and began their train journey to Auschwitz. William S. Schlamm, an Austrian-American journalist, could not yet know of these events when he reviewed this translation by Ralph Manheim. But he did know that the Book Review was taking on the Nazis with the only weapon it has ever had in its arsenal: the interrogation of language.

THOUGH WE HAVE BEEN WARNED, ON HIGHEST authority, to go easy on the heads of foreign states, professional integrity compels this reviewer to inform you that Adolf Hitler is a poor writer. Such literary criticism will give but little comfort to the children of Warsaw. Still, what has been printed black on white, put between covers and copyrighted in Washington, constitutes a book, even if it is *Mein Kampf.*

For even if the Germans were to get away with a lenient peace this coagulated stench will stick to them for the rest of their national history—a fate truly worse than death. One should think that any intelligent post-Hitler government of the Reich would offer a medium-size German province for every copy of *Mein Kampf* available abroad, and still get a bargain. Yet, strangely enough, even Hitler's opponents among the Germans fail to realize that it would be much safer for them to be policed for a couple of centuries by Abyssinians than to be reminded that his book has been originally written in Goethe's language. So it seems that, after all, every nation has the best-seller it deserves.

To be sure, Hitler's language is not exactly Goethe's. In fact, one might be seriously worried about the competent author of this new translation of *Mein Kampf*. Ralph Manheim, who must have spent torturing months in the sewers of semantics, may have emerged with considerably duller senses for the rhymes and the rhythm of *Faust*. If this is the case he should be put on the honor list of war casualties. For he has served his country, and served it well, by producing the first English Hitler translation which does justice to the author. Here, for the first time, you get Hitler's prose almost as unreadable in English as it is in German.

Mr. Manheim's sacrifice must not be underrated. Up to now, every self-respecting translator (and they are a proud lot) dependably stumbled into the pitfall: He rendered the Hitler text in such a way that it made sense. The reason, of course, was the translator's respect not for the strange subject but for his own language. And indeed, to make Hitler sound in English (or in any other non-German language, for that matter) as he does in German is more than one can expect from a translator who expects to stay in the business. Confronted with a faithful translation of Hitler prose, any publisher or editor would ask, in disgust, if the young man was kidding. The result was that this reviewer, for instance, who is haunted by an incurable knowledge of German, never recognized a translated Hitler text and always had to dig up the original to find out who was talking. It was as if beauty-loving photographers, assigned to take a picture of Dillinger for the F.B.I. files, had first lifted his face.

There is little face-lifting in Manheim's new translation of *Mein Kampf*. He tells, in a thrifty foreword, of his predicament, successfully defending his literary honor against conceivable accusations that he doesn't know English. "Where Hitler's formulations challenge the reader's credulity I have quoted the German original in the notes. Seeing is believing," says Mr. Manheim, somewhat optimistically. But even he confesses that he has occasionally cut down sentences, deloused the text of innumerable particles (without which a Hitler manuscript is as naked as a Jimmy Durante spiel without a few "furthermores"), and abandoned an undisclosed number of verbal nouns. Obviously, even an audacious translator's courage has limits, which is regrettable. For one can be pretty sure that Manheim's is going to be the last English translation of *Mein Kampf*, and that future Anglo-Saxon generations will be allowed to assume that Germany's greatest political genius could actually articulate.

Without a personal stake in the profession of translating I feel free to show explicitly what I mean. On September 16, 1934, Adolf Hitler read a speech to an audience of a few thousand professors, writers and artists at a Kulturtagung in

"This is the Moronic Evil, so shapeless and pre-spiritual that it defies articulation."

Nuremberg. The following, on my word of honor, is a literal translation of two paragraphs, based on the official text:

"The picture of the human culture can build itself upon the entirely unconscious, because purely intuitive, realization of an internally, bloodily conditioned longing and its command. But moreover, it also can be influenced and formed by an external infection in a national body, coming there to an indisputable importance without being internally related with it as to essence."

In German, so help me, it sounds exactly as it does in this faithful translation. In German, too, there is not the faintest similarity to a thought and barely a trace of language, though a few thousand German university professors, writers and artists inhaled the German original as few "Hit Parade" girls could inhale Sinatra. The sum total of the academic degrees of this particular Hitler audience must have exceeded anything Harvard can display, even if you threw in Yale. If they were able to understand what Hitler wanted to say (as indeed they were), they must have developed unique organs of perception. For it simply can't be understood via the mind.

Thusly (to use the terminology of the author under discussion), the problem is not Hitler but his audience. When you have read Manheim's translation of *Mein Kampf*, the next worst thing to the original, you'll comprehend less than ever what has happened to the Germans, but you'll understand better what was bound to happen to the rest of Europe. This is not just bad style, not even its absence. This is the Moronic Evil, so shapeless and pre-spiritual that it defies articulation. If infusoria spoke they could probably use Hitler's language, but they would have to bark.

There is a fashionable debate in progress whether are not the Germans are paranoic. I wouldn't know. If a man asserts that he is the emperor of China you are fully entitled to think him mad. But what if he really becomes the Emperor of China? Stubborn psychiatrists may even then insist that the man is mad. But they'll be put in the bughouse. On literary and intellectual grounds there can be no difference of opinion concerning *Mein Kampf,* not even among reviewers whose business, as you know, is to disagree. But the only writing that counts in this particular case are General Eisenhower's communiqués.
—*William S. Schlamm*

Wartime Reading

IN 1942, THE BOOK REVIEW REPORTED that *Mein Kampf* was one of the most in-demand books at Army Red Cross hospital libraries. In an essay about her experience volunteering at one such library, Margaret Farrand Thorp wrote that "the soldier is most eager for books that will help him understand this war he is fighting," and there was a "steadily increasing demand for books about the Germans, the Japanese, the Chinese, the South Americans and particularly the Russians." Thorp added that novels were popular too, "not only with a purpose but for pleasure, and there tastes range from Thomas Mann to Zane Grey," and she also pointed out that "a good many men, we find, who are not habitual poetry readers now grope toward poetry for possible succor."

Red Cross libraries depended on donated books. "We are flooded with second-rate novels from the first quarter of the century, the sort of thing that has been preserved in the guest-room bookcase because someone enjoyed it back in 1912," Thorp noted tartly. "Those old novels, too, are usually bound in faded brown and cracked at the seams. They look dreary, and the external appearance of a book is more important in a military hospital than most civilians would suppose. When your world is almost solidly khaki-colored a red and green and yellow book is a pleasant thing to contemplate, regardless of his contents. The men always pick up first from the book cart the new book, and especially those with picture jackets. When a book goes into the Army, we have found, all of it goes to work. Its power is nearly double what it was before."

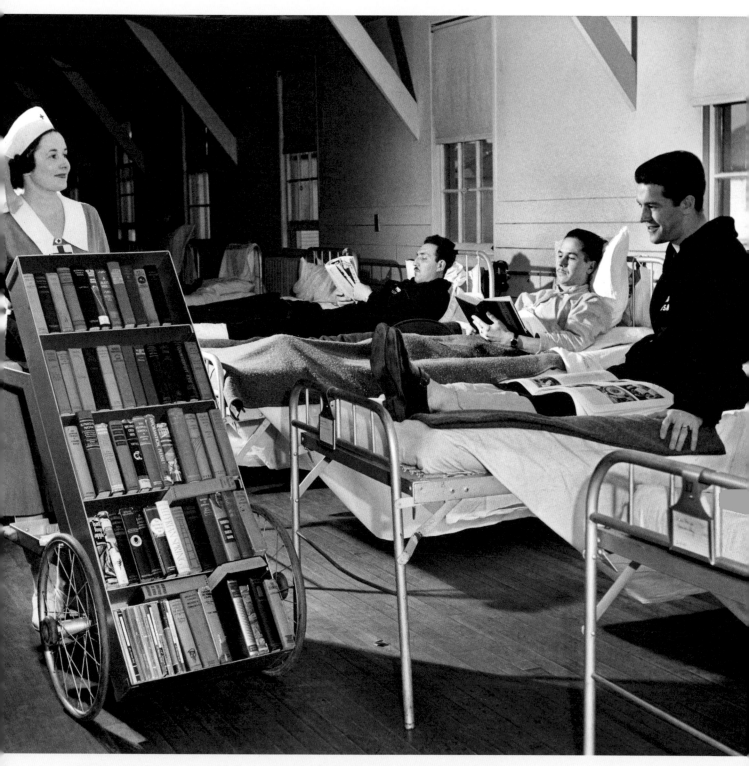

In 1942, a portable library is wheeled to patients of the Post Hospital at Fort Jay on Governor's Island.

Petry on November 12, 1948.

Ann Petry,
The Street

The first novel by a Black woman to sell over one million copies, *The Street* was both a literary thriller and a complex exploration of race, gender and class. While its protagonist, Lutie Johnson, labors in pursuit of the American dream, her efforts are stymied by the individuals and systems that do not wish her to succeed.

ANN PETRY HAS CHOSEN TO TELL A STORY about one aspect of Negro life in America, and she has created as vivid, as spiritually and emotionally effective a novel as that rich and important theme has yet produced. *The Street* is a work of close documentation and intimate perception. It is also a gripping tale peopled with utterly believable United States citizens, and overflowing with the classic pity and terror of good imaginative writing.

To Lutie Johnson, the attractive protagonist, her enemy is poverty. If the white man's rules are largely responsible for that poverty (and she feels they are), then very well, she fears and distrusts white people. But her personal epic of struggle—to provide a safe, free, comfortable home for herself and her charming little son, Bub—manifests itself more often than not against those of her own race and neighborhood in Harlem, New York City.

Lutie has had to struggle against the atmosphere of her father's home. He is an old man, whose crippled sense of dignity can express itself only in boozy orgies (but it was he who had forced Lutie to finish high school). She has also had to fight with her husband. Borne down by his own inability to find work, he has allowed Lutie to take a job as a housemaid in remote Connecticut; ultimately, he took in another woman to live with him on the money his wife sent home. Lutie and little Bub have left him now; she has taken a low-paid Civil Service job, and is trying to make ends meet in their tiny apartment on "The Street," which is 116th, in Harlem's heart. Above all, her struggle is now directed against this Street—the filth and litter, the torn papers, chicken bones, corset stays, tin cans that swirl on its sidewalks.

The people of the Street live with Trouble as with a member of the family. Trouble is disease, hunger, violence, the police. Trouble is the Street. Lutie Johnson wants to get out of it—she wants Bub out of it. She makes a valiant try—and she fails.

For the whole story, in its memorable simplicity and power, the reader is directed to the book itself. Few novels of the last several years have been so alive with the understanding of character as exemplified in Lutie herself; in the 8-year-old Bub; in the crazy super of the tenement house; in Min, the woman who lives with him; in Boots, the orchestra leader; and Junto, the one white man who enters the tragedy directly. It is a rare day when a novel based on a social issue exhibits the literary quality of *The Street.* —*Alfred Butterfield*

Christopher Isherwood, *The Berlin Stories*

BY ALFRED KAZIN

This collection is perhaps best known for the novella *Goodbye to Berlin* and the character of Sally Bowles, both of which inspired the musical and movie *Cabaret*. Our reviewer offered mixed praise for the author's gifts: "Isherwood is a real novelist, a real minor novelist."

RECENTLY, WHILE TALKING WITH A MAN JUST returned from Hollywood, I asked him what Isherwood was doing. "Oh, he's left the monastery and is writing movie scripts." The reply interested me, among other reasons, because it was said and received without mockery; it would have been funny enough of anyone else. For there is something about Christopher Isherwood's work that inspires respect and steady affection for the man, even when he chooses to cross the California bridge of sighs between a swami like Gerald Heard and the word factories of Culver City. I have not followed his excursions into Vedanta, but I trust him to seek the truth in his own way, knowing that he seeks it for me, too. I believe in him, though I may never believe his gospel. He inspires the same good faith in his readers that is so much the secret, in himself, of his gift for creating character; of looking at the human problem with love and openness.

Isherwood is a real novelist, a real minor novelist. How minor he can be is seen in *Prater Violet*, which is a charming encore to his best work, notable for the loving portrait of Friedrich Bergmann, but slight and essentially retrospective—in its own way, I suspect, a way of postponing the integration of his creative gifts with his religious search. How good a novelist he has been can be seen in *The Berlin Stories*, which is the welcome reissue of his two most famous novels—*The Last of Mr. Norris* and that little diamond among modern narratives, *Goodbye to Berlin*.

It is a great distinction to be a minor novelist today; it is much more difficult than to imitate the great novelists. We have many excellent minor poets; we have almost no novelists—only great armies of people who have taken advantage of the deceptive looseness of the novel to write political tracts, memories of battle, romances, biographies and apocalyptic visions. To be a real minor novelist is to do the undisguisable work of fiction—which is to create a real human scene whose meanings follow from what has been freshly demonstrated—without the imperative world-meaning, the search for basic control, which has marked the crisis of modern thought.

Isherwood is such a minor novelist, successful and delightful within his realm; but obviously only part of him gets into his fiction. He is interesting, among other reasons, because he is so fine-fibered an offshoot of the English genius. He writes his language—it is not always our language—with the tonal exactitude and humorous economy of a man who can be conventional, so distinct is his verbal inheritance. Isherwood's

"Isherwood's writing has the music of the old English fineness in it."

Isherwood on October 18, 1983.

writing has the music of the old English fineness in it. It never presses or stammers; its correctness is implicit in its wit and it is always headed for the comic; he is a man who touches his language with affectionate brush strokes in exile.

In a prefatory note Isherwood explains that the main character called "Christopher Isherwood" is only a "ventriloquist's dummy," not to be identified as a matter of course with himself. His landlady, Fraulein Schroder, calls him "Herr Issyvoo." That suits him better. He is not really Christopher Isherwood; he is an impersonation of the author, tougher in some respects than the real Isherwood and more tender in others. Yet he is not someone else than Isherwood, or even his mask. He is the man who wrote the story as he lived it and is now teaching, replenishing the "real" Isherwood to put it down. He is the hero of the author's literary and moral imagination, as each of us has a hero, bearing our name and attired in our flesh, who is the negotiable self-portrait we have of ourselves. Our literary self-portraits are not necessarily better than we are; only easier to live with in our own minds; and for purposes of artistic production, more fertile. They are ourselves, as genial and exact observers.

Clockwise from top Left: Amiri Baraka and Maya Angelou, 1991; Adrienne Rich, 1969; Langston Hughes, circa 1942; William Butler Yeats, 1917; Paul Laurence Dunbar; Robert Frost, 1958; Nikki Giovanni, 1972; Miguel Algarín, Lucky Cienfuegos and Miguel Piñero, 1976; W. H. Auden, 1962; Marianne Moore with Kenneth Koch, Alan Dugan, Robert Lowell and Stanley Kunitz, 1962; Edna St. Vincent Millay, 1914; Edith Sitwell; E. E. Cummings.

1921–1946

131

The New York Times Book Review

OCTOBER 6, 1946 — Copyright, 1946, by The New York Times Company. — SECTION 7

The New-York Times.

SATURDAY BOOK REVIEW SUPPLEMENT.

8 PAGES.

SATURDAY, OCTOBER 10, 1896.

COPYRIGHTED.

BOOKSELLERS IN CONCLAVE

Steps to be Taken to Combat the Department Stores.

The National Association of Booksellers, Newsdealers, and Stationers held their fourteenth annual convention in Boston on Tuesday and Wednesday of this week. Nearly one hundred delegates were present on Tuesday. Eighty-six of them represented eight unions. Fourteen States were represented.

A committee, which had been appointed to consider the subjects, presented a long list of resolutions advocating that all dealers friendly to the order be admitted; that the publishers of all ten-cent periodicals be asked to furnish their publications to dealers at a uniform rate of 7 cents; that the organization request Harper & Brothers to print the selling price of their magazine, 35 cents, on its cover; that the cause of the abuse and unfair treatment that has until now been accorded to book publishers should cease. All booksellers, stationers, &c., were earnestly requested to join in order that an appreciable force might be felt to emanate from them. Women engaged in the book and news trade also were requested to join in separate unions in the different cities and towns.

Before the evening session closed, the Committee on Nominations brought in the following list of officers, recommending them for the ensuing year: President—J. F. Martin, New-York; First Vice President—F. A. Salisbury, Providence, R. I.; Second Vice President—J. E. Gray, Everett; Secretary—J. H. Riley, Providence; Treasurer—J. H. Nolan, Providence; Sergeant at Arms—B. Lewis, Boston; Executive Committee—M. Moy of Pawtucket, H. N. Borden of Boston, F. J. Hayden of Providence, F. R. Sampson of New-York, W. D. Madigan of Lancaster.

At the afternoon session about 150 delegates were present, and later 175. The election of the officers recommended by the Nomination Committee in the morning session was first acted upon. The list as given was carried through, with the exception of T. F. Martin, who was the candidate for President favored by the fifteen New-York delegates. Against him the Eastern delegates arrayed Mr. Michael F. Moy, who twice before had been elected, and on a vote being taken he was elected.

At the session on Wednesday the relations existing between publishers and dealers were fully discussed. It was decided to acquaint the publishers with the competition that dealers are meeting with and to seek their aid in lessening the evil.

An extended discussion was then entered upon as to the best means to adopt to do away with the competition dealers are meeting with from department stores. It was decided to appeal to the dealers throughout the country and organize for the purpose of endeavoring to secure legislation which will exact a tax from department stores for every department which they conduct outside of the principal line of business in which the department stores are engaged. The dealers in Illinois are making strenuous efforts to obtain such legislation. It was decided, on motion of Mr. J. Daley, that the Secretary be authorized to send circulars to the trade, requesting a boycott on all publishers who do not treat the trade justly. The decision whether or not to send the circulars was left to the discretion of the Advisory Board.

OSCAR WILDE'S FORLORN STATE

Punishments He Undergoes—His Release Not Far Off.

What appears to be the best kind of information concerning the present condition of Oscar Wilde is given in the October number of The Bookman. Its authority is "an English official whose position is made him personally cognizant of the actual facts." The Bookman says:

"From this source we learn that Mr. Wilde's physical state is very distressing. He is unable to assimilate food, and an enteric disorder which has become chronic has reduced him to a condition of great weakness. He is rigidly enforced, and much so that he has several times been punished for half involuntarily turning his head in chapel to get a glimpse of the person seated beside him.

"We were inquisitive enough to ask the nature of his punishment on these occasions. 'Well,' was the reply, 'taken from him, having his cell—a strip of rag carpet rug in question is a strip of rag carpet which serves as a substitute for a mattress being spread upon the surface of a bare door which is his only bed; so that, when under punishment, he sleeps upon the bare planks.

"The gentleman who made these statements is persuaded that Wilde will lose either his life or his reason as the result of his imprisonment; but he probably underrates the extent of human endurance. The sentence, under the English system of commutation, has only some six months more to run, and it is generally understood that at its expiration Mrs. Wilde will rejoin her husband. As she has in her own right a settled income of £800 a year, they will probably make their future home in some obscure Continental town."

TO STEAL BANCROFT PLATES.

A Burglar's Attempt at the History Building in San Francisco.

Last week Wednesday an attempt was made in San Francisco to steal some of the plates of H. H. Bancroft's "History of the Pacific Coast," valued at $10,000. The story followed of accomplishing his purpose, but the cake possesses some interesting features. He began his work shortly after 6 o'clock in the evening and at 4:15 o'clock a

[text continues...]

ARDITI'S REMINISCENCES.

His Career as Operatic Conductor in London and New-York.

Signor Luigi Arditi, of whom Lumley said that, "taking all qualities into account, a more able conductor never reigned in this country," has just published in London a volume of reminiscences, which have been edited by the Baroness von Zedlitz. An advance notice of the work, in The London Daily News, contains the following:

Politics is does not touch upon although as Signor Arditi is known to have been the friend of Mazzini and other Italian patriots of his period, and later on was a more or less intimate acquaintance of Garibaldi, his reminiscences of political personages would, we think, be equal interest. The book, however, deals with Arditi's career from the time when he sailed vessel from Genoa two months on a sailing vessel from Genoa to Cuba, down to the present day; and, despite some pricing, it is crammed with good things concerning the musical celebrities whom the veteran conductor has met. It was, for example, thanks to Alboni, that Arditi still shows a bold blemish. His hair came off after a boyish illness; but Alboni had a superstition against it, threw, and clutching it off Arditi's head, threw it to the other end in New York; but Arditi afterward wore the wig.

IN THE PUBLIC EYE.

In some comments on Harold Frederic's dispatch to THE TIMES explaining how William Morris declined the Poet Laureateship, The Rochester Union adds that Morris was a friend of Lord Rosebery, in whose gift the appointment was, and who was said to be inclined to make him Poet Laureate. Lord Rosebery's inclinations in this respect, it is said, are so well known that Morris intimated to him through a friend that he could not accept the post if it were offered. The result was that Rosebery went out of office without making an appointment.

If Victor Hugo had not been a great writer he would have been a notable artist, but who ever knew that Robert Louis Stevenson was a draughtsman? And yet he was. He never wrote a better book than "Travels With a Donkey in the Cevennes," and he originally made a series of illustrations for it. The London Studio will reproduce these sketches, and, besides, some humorous cuts of Stevenson's, engraved by him, which he made while spending a Winter at Davos.

Two eccentric French journalists, MM. Leroy and Papillaud, started from Paris, in January, 1895, and without a sou in their pockets, depending on writing alone, reached Hongkong. They went through Italy, Greece, and Egypt. These literary tramps insist that they lived entirely by means of copy. M. Leroy, besides using his pen, made a "pencil serve him. The French Journal "En Route" describes their journey so far. Our fearless scribes, when last heard of, were making for Japan.

There is a proof reader's tale about the late H. C. Bunner. When his delightful "Love in Old Clothes" was set up quite nonplused an aged and worthy proof reader. The matter was written in a perfect Elizabethan style, whose words have additional letters, and some balance is kept up of clipping pronouns. The proof reader could not be made to understand it, and so he corrected every variation in his proof from Victorian

Fiftieth Anniversary Issue

Part One — Books of a Half Century   *Part Two — Books of the Week*

PAUL ORBAN.

The Book Review Turns 50

For this anniversary, the editors nodded at their history—but they also looked ahead, speculating how the postwar climate would affect the course of American literature, "the coming uses of energized plutonium permitting interested survivors."

THE FIRST ISSUE OF THE NEW YORK TIMES Book Review, published 50 years ago this week, looks appropriately quaint: No doubt today's anniversary issue will have certain aspects of antiquity 50 years from today—the coming uses of energized plutonium permitting interested survivors.

In plucking straws from the winds that have stirred the past half century, it will probably be prudent to remember that no age ever looks quite the same to any other age, or to different people, for that matter. You are not apt to get precisely the same view of the past from an old-timer nourishing his illusions as from a young explorer taking a new stand. It may be just as well to keep in mind the wry maxim which suggests that all generalizations are false, including this one.

As writers face today's weighty complexities there is a natural tendency to look back at the Nineties as rather good old days indeed, in a kind of retroactive search for tranquility. And the legend of the Gay Nineties gives color to the view. As a matter of fact, writers of the Nineties sometimes regarded their time in that way. A critic in the first issue of this review, for example, ignoring the historic sound of industrial and political strife that must have hummed at least faintly beneath his windows, was finding judicious fault with a new novel from France. "There are two young persons in this story," he said, "who would be mightily scorned by the American young person, the latter demanding healthy and unsentimental heroines to please this pleasant day and generation."

With the Civil War already three decades past, the Middle Nineties could be considered a comparably peaceful era, though the country's enormous commercial and industrial expansion was decidedly dynamic, and the fracas with Spain was to come soon enough. Nevertheless, things must have seemed a shade more settled and predictable to writers of the day than they do now, when we begin to talk about wars in all tenses at the breakfast table, get deep into the strike situation by noon and continue discussing both far into the atom-haunted night.

Mr. Cleveland was still president in 1896. Queen Victoria, whose name was to become a

1944 ———————————————
During the Battle of the Bulge, Kurt Vonnegut is captured by German troops.

1945 ———————————————
The Book Review begins a regular mystery column.

1946 ———————————————→
Dr. Benjamin Spock publishes *The Commonsense Book of Baby and Child Care.*

1921–1946

byword with the later generation of writers who took Victorianism as a symbol of the tune when things had seemed unnecessarily formal (not to say prudish and repressed), was being congratulated because on an early autumn day she had reigned for 59 years, 3 months and 5 days, thus breaking the record of George III. She was still going strong, too.

While contemporary writers have been liberated from some of the "opinions"—what a mild word!—of the iron-handed Genteel Tradition, they are by no means permanently free. The heirs of Crane and Howells and Norris and Garland have had need of the badge of courage as they have hazarded their fortunes on roads that were sometimes the main-traveled ones, sometimes not.

Probably the most widely quoted words of 1896 did not come from a novel or even verse; they came from a speech about a cross of gold and crown of thorns made by an orator from the Platte in Chicago, insisting that man's monetary standards were obsolete. But one of the best sellers of that year was by a young recent captain of Syracuse University's baseball team, Stephen Crane. The novel was *The Red Badge of Courage*, and if the 1946 lists hold books as good as that, literary historians of 1996 need not think too badly of us.

"No doubt today's anniversary issue will have certain aspects of antiquity 50 years from today."

The 10 most popular novels of 1896 were:

Tom Grogan,
by F. Hopkinson Smith

A Lady of Quality,
by Frances Hodgson Burnett

The Seats of the Mighty,
by Gilbert Parker

A Singular Life,
by Elizabeth Stuart Phelps Ward

The Damnation of Theron Ware,
by Harold Frederic

A Houseboat on the Styx,
by John Kendrick Bangs

Kate Carnegie,
by Ian Maclaren

The Red Badge of Courage,
by Stephen Crane

Sentimental Tommy,
by J. M. Barrie

Beside the Bonnie Brier Bush,
by Ian Maclaren

On the whole, then, not exactly the all-time list for a desert-island library. The critic of our day looking back from 1996 will find more lengthening trends where we could not see the glimmer of a tendency. He may wonder why we carried around so many cumbersome books (even our pocket-size books may look the size of live penguins to him) while he can hold in his hand a watch-size microfilm gadget that can reel off whole national literatures and even the first 200 volumes of Upton Sinclair's Lanny Budd series through its eyepiece. That's all very well. But wait till the critic of 2046 gets around to his day. —*Charles Poore*

LIFE IN 1896: A Rousing Game of Lawn Tennis on Staten Island.

Tzigane Music and Tokay Wine in "Bohemia"

FIFTY YEARS OF BEST SELLERS

1896
"Tom Grogan," by F. Hopkinson Smith.
"A Lady of Quality," by Frances Hodgson Burnett.

1897
"Quo Vadis," by Henry Sienkiewicz.
"The Choir Invisible," by James Lane Allen.

1898
"Caleb West," by F. Hopkinson Smith.
"Hugh Wynne," by S. Weir Mitchell.

1899
"David Harum," by Edward Noyes Westcott.
"When Knighthood Was in Flower," by Charles Major.

1900
"To Have and To Hold," by Mary Johnston.
"Red Pottage," by Mary Cholmondeley.

1901
"The Crisis," by Winston Churchill.
"Alice of Old Vincennes," by Maurice Thompson.

1902
"The Virginian," by Owen Wister.
"Mrs. Wiggs of the Cabbage Patch," by Alice Hegan Rice.

1903
"Lady Rose's Daughter," by Mrs. Humphry Ward.
"Gordon Keith," by Thomas Nelson Page.

1904
"The Crossing," by Winston Churchill.
"The Deliverance," by Ellen Glasgow.

1905
"The Marriage of William Ashe," by Mrs. Humphry Ward.
"Sandy," by Alice Hegan Rice.

1906
"Coniston," by Winston Churchill.
"Lady Baltimore," by Owen Wister.

1907
"The Lady of the Decoration," by Frances Little.
"The Weavers," by Gilbert Parker.

1908
"Mr. Crewe's Career," by Winston Churchill.
"The Barrier," by Rex Beach.

1909
"The Inner Shrine." Anonymous (Basil King).
"Katrine," by Elinor Macartney Lane.

1910
"The Rosary," by Florence Barclay.
"A Modern Chronicle," by Winston Churchill.

1911
"The Broad Highway," by Jeffery Farnol.
"The Prodigal Judge," by Vaughan Kester.

1912
"The Harvester," by Gene Stratton Porter.
"The Street Called Straight," by Basil King.

1913
"The Inside of the Cup," by Winston Churchill.
"V. V.'s Eyes," by Henry Sydnor Harrison.

1914
"The Eyes of the World," by Harold Bell Wright.
"Pollyanna," by Eleanor H. Porter.

1915
"The Turmoil," by Booth Tarkington.
"A Far Country," by Winston Churchill.

1916
"Seventeen," by Booth Tarkington.
"When a Man's a Man," by Harold Bell Wright.

1917
"Mr. Britling Sees It Through," by H. G. Wells.
"The First Hundred Thousand," by Ian Hay.

1918
"The U. P. Trail," by Zane Grey.
"My Four Years in Germany," by James W. Gerard.

1919
"The Four Horsemen of the Apocalypse," by V. Blasco Ibanez.
"The Education of Henry Adams," by Henry Adams.

1920
"The Man of the Forest," by Zane Grey.
"Now It Can Be Told," by Philip Gibbs.

1921
"Main Street," by Sinclair Lewis.
"The Outline of History," by H. G. Wells.

1922
"If Winter Comes," by A. S. M. Hutchinson.
"The Outline of History," by H. G. Wells.

1923
"Black Oxen," by Gertrude Atherton.
"Etiquette," by Emily Post.

1924
"So Big," by Edna Ferber.
"Diet and Health," by Lulu Hunt Peters.

1925
"Soundings," by A. Hamilton Gibbs.
"Diet and Health," by Lulu Hunt Peters.

1926
"The Private Life of Helen of Troy," by John Erskine.
"The Man Nobody Knows," by Bruce Barton.

1927
"Elmer Gantry," by Sinclair Lewis.
"The Story of Philosophy," by Will Durant.

1928
"The Bridge of San Luis Rey," by Thornton Wilder.
"Disraeli," by Andre Maurois.

1929
"All Quiet on the Western Front," by Erich Maria Remarque.
"The Art of Thinking," by Ernest Dimnet.

1930
"Cimarron," by Edna Ferber.
"The Story of San Michele," by Axel Munthe.

1931
"The Good Earth," by Pearl S. Buck.
"Education of a Princess," by Grand Duchess Marie.

1932
"The Good Earth," by Pearl S. Buck.
"The Epic of America," by James Truslow Adams.

1933
"Anthony Adverse," by Hervey Allen.
"Life Begins at Forty," by Walter B. Pitkin.

1934
"Anthony Adverse," by Hervey Allen.
"While Rome Burns," by Alexander Woollcott.

1935
"Green Light," by Lloyd C. Douglas.
"North to the Orient," by Anne Morrow Lindbergh.

1936
"Gone With the Wind," by Margaret Mitchell.
"Man the Unknown," by Alexis Carrel.

1937
"Gone With the Wind," by Margaret Mitchell.
"How to Win Friends and Influence People," by Dale Carnegie.

1938
"The Yearling," by Marjorie Kinnan Rawlings.
"The Importance of Living," by Lin Yutang.

1939
"The Grapes of Wrath," by John Steinbeck.
"Days of Our Years," by Pierre Van Paassen.

1940
"How Green Was My Valley," by Richard Llewellyn.
"I Married Adventure," by Osa Johnson.

1941
"The Keys of the Kingdom," by A. J. Cronin.
"Berlin Diary," by William L. Shirer.

1942
"The Song of Bernadette," by Franz Werfel.
"See Here, Private Hargrove," by Marion Hargrove.

1943
"The Robe," by Lloyd C. Douglas.
"Under Cover," by John Roy Carlson.

1944
"Strange Fruit," by Lillian Smith.
"I Never Left Home," by Bob Hope.

1945
"Forever Amber," by Kathleen Winsor.
"Brave Men," by Ernie Pyle.

(An Analysis of This List, by Alice P. Hackett, Will Be Found on Page 42.)

This is Gigi the merry-go-round horse

Gigi once belonged to a far away Prince

Gigi has traveled in Austria, France, England, and America

A young girl reads on a former carousel horse at the Coney Island branch of the Brooklyn Public Library, February 29, 1956.

1946

1971

CHAPTER THREE

The New York Times Book Review — JANUARY 1, 1956 — SECTION 7

MEN WHO DARED TO STAND ALONE

Political Integrity and the Price Paid For It Is Discussed by Senator Kennedy

By CABELL PHILLIPS

Senator John F. Kennedy

The New York Times Book Review — FEBRUARY 18, 1956 — SECTION 7

TRAGEDY BEHIND A TRAGIC MASQUE

The Play Eugene O'Neill Left Behind Is in Fact a Revealing Autobiography

By BROOKS ATKINSON

Eugene O'Neill

The New York Times Book Review — JANUARY 5, — SECTION 7

UNWORKED VEINS OF THE CIVIL WAR

There's Still Pay Dirt in Its History If Writers Are Willing to Dig for It

By EARL SCHENCK MIERS

The New York Times Book Review — SEPTEMBER 23, 1962 — SECTION 7

THERE'S POISON ALL AROUND US NOW

The Dangers in the Use of Pesticides Are Vividly Pictured by Rachel Carson

The New York Times Book Review — JULY 28, 1963 — SECTION 7

OUR PAST ISN'T WHAT IT USED TO BE

By C. VANN WOODWARD

The New York Times Book Review — JULY 26, 1964 — SECTION 7

TO LIFT THE SIEGE OF DENIAL

By SAUNDERS REDDING

The Rev. Martin Luther King, Jr., in Washington, August, 1963.

The New York Times Book Review — MARCH 20, 1966 — SECTION 7

DON'T TAKE IT TOO SERIOUSLY

The New York Times Book Review — SECTION 7 — April 19, 1970

Hard Times

An Oral History of the Great Depression by Studs Terkel.

By RICHARD RHODES

The New York Times Book Review — DECEMBER 6, 1970 — SECTION 1

Christmas Issue

Twelve Books Of 1970

The Nativity. Ivory book cover, 10th–11th century, probably Byzantine.

As the postwar literary boom began, "we think that a supplement like The New York Times Book Review has a unique, an exacting and at times unrewarding role to play out," Harvey Breit, a Book Review editor, wrote. "This is no more and no less than to establish communication between the popular artist and the serious reader, between the serious artist and the popular reader; it is to help bring all of our literature before all of our public and to help them make choices." During this period, however, the Book Review came under fire from some in the literary community, who called it—not without some justification—dutiful, old-fashioned and dull. That changed when John Leonard, who became the editor in December 1970, upended coverage by asking hard questions about what books were reviewed (and why), and by bringing in many new reviewers, many of them women and people of color.

John Hersey, *Hiroshima*

Originally published in *The New Yorker,* this chronicle of the United States' bombing of Hiroshima and its immediate aftermath helped to shape American understanding of the atomic bomb and the moral implications of its use.

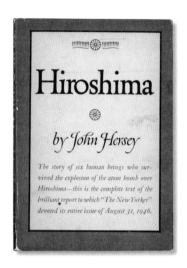

IN THE WANING DAYS OF LAST AUGUST PEOPLE all over the United States who read *The New Yorker* suddenly began to discuss the harrowing experiences of a clerk in the personnel department of a tin works, a doctor in a private hospital, a tailor's widow, a priest, a young member of a surgical staff and the pastor of a church. The six were, of course, the principals in John Hersey's *Hiroshima,* which Alfred A. Knopf has just published in book form—the quietest, and the best, of all the stories that have been written about the most spectacular explosion in the time of man.

Others, trying to bring home to us the millennial meaning silhouetted against that enormous flash of light, had bellowed at us, and exhorted at us, and thundered. Well they might. We needed all the warnings we could get. We needed them particularly after the first Bikini returns were in, when a certain lulling note of familiarity ("it's just another weapon") had begun to creep into our contemplation of the bomb that could scrawl finis across placid lands.

Hiroshima penetrated the tissue of complacency we had built up. It penetrated it all the more inexorably because it told its story not in terms of graphs and charts but in terms of ordinary human beings, Miss Sasaki, Dr. Fujii, Mrs. Nakamara, Father Kleinsorge, Dr. Sasaki, the Reverend Tanimoto, aliens and enemies though they were. Their stories had been taken down directly by Mr. Hersey, who brought to his interrogations and investigations the gifts he had already conspicuously shown as the Pulitzer-Prize-winning author of *A Bell for Adano* and as an outstanding war correspondent.

Hiroshima seems destined to become about the most widely read article and book of our generation. What effect will it have on the thinking of our time, particularly the thinking of our own people?

The overwhelming response to Mr. Hersey's story would seem to provide one overwhelming answer. It is simply that millions of people have wanted to hear what he has to say and to have others hear it, too. Among the stacks of letters that have been written to *The New Yorker,* perhaps one in ten objected to the magazine's having printed *Hiroshima,* and the dissenters were generally people who thought the magazine had strayed grievously out of its field. Most thought the Japs had the bomb coming to them.

A very small minority believes that we should never have used the bomb at all; this is balanced by the lunatic fringe which has already picked targets on which it would like us to use it again. And among minorities there is considerable difference of opinion. When someone who thinks we should never have used the bomb at all encounters people whose brothers were in the Death March on Bataan or whose sons were among the immense forces poised for the final invasion of Japan's home islands that General Marshall outlined in his report, there must be a profound cleavage.

In the subtly contrapuntal text of *Hiroshima* opinion is divided. "It was war," Mrs. Nakamura says, "and we had to expect it," though Dr. Sasaki has a more violent view, while a priest writes in his report: "It seems logical that he who supports total war in principle cannot complain of a war against civilians."

As for those who, for various and somewhat disparate reasons, say that we did not need to use the bomb because the Japanese would have collapsed pretty soon anyway, various things are said in rebuttal. One is the example of the fanatic resistance at Okinawa and the knowledge that similar installations had been prepared in the home islands (at Hiroshima, for one place) but on a much vaster scale. Another is the very gruesomeness of arriving at the equation of American lives it would be proposed to offer in the gamble of saving a Japanese city.

There is abundant evidence that most Americans took the bomb as the epitome of all the instruments of war that maim and blast and burn and kill, and that *Hiroshima* has stirred thousands to a new awareness of the necessity for world action to stop using them all—not excepting the even more lethal instruments that may now be germinating in the strange mind of man.
—*Charles Poore*

"*Hiroshima* seems destined to become about the most widely read article and book of our generation."

1947 — Margaret Wise Brown publishes *Goodnight Moon,* the book that will act as a soporific for generations of American children.

1949 — The poet Pablo Neruda flees Chile for Argentina after a warrant is issued for his arrest.

1949 — The novelist Rex Stout—whose most beloved character, Nero Wolfe, is a gourmand—begins reviewing cookbooks for the Book Review.

1946–1971

Paul Bowles, *The Sheltering Sky*

BY TENNESSEE WILLIAMS

Tennessee Williams, who had won a Pulitzer Prize in 1948 for his play *A Streetcar Named Desire,* reviewed this debut novel by Bowles, which went on to be acclaimed as one of the best of the 20th century.

AFTER SEVERAL LITERARY SEASONS GIVEN over, mostly, to the frisky antics of kids, precociously knowing and singularly charming, but not to be counted on for those gifts that arrive by no other way than the experience and contemplation of a truly adult mind, now is obviously a perfect time for a writer with such a mind to engage our attention. That is precisely the event to be celebrated in the appearance of *The Sheltering Sky,* Paul Bowles's first novel.

It has been a good while since first novels in America have come from men in their middle or late thirties (Paul Bowles is 38). Even in past decades the first novel has usually been written during the writers' first years out of college. Moreover, because success and public attention operate as a sort of pressure cooker or freezer, there has been a discouraging tendency for the talent to bake or congeal at a premature level of inner development.

In America the career almost invariably becomes an obsession. The "get-ahead" principle, carried to such extreme, inspires our writers to enormous efforts. A new book must come out every year. Otherwise they get panicky, and the first thing you know they belong to Alcoholics Anonymous or have embraced religion or plunged headlong into some political activity with nothing but an inchoate emotionalism to bring to it or to be derived from it.

Paul Bowles has deliberately rejected that kind of rabid professionalism. Better known as a composer than a writer, he has not allowed his passion for either form of expression to interfere with his growth into completeness of personality. Now this book has come at the meridian of the man and artist. And, to me very thrillingly, it brings the reader into sudden, startling communion with a talent of true maturity and sophistication of a sort that I had begun to fear was to be found nowadays only among the insurgent novelists of France, such as Jean Genet and Albert Camus and Jean-Paul Sartre.

There is a curiously double level to this novel. The surface is enthralling as narrative. It is impressive as writing. But above that surface is the aura that I spoke of, intangible and powerful, bringing to mind one of those clouds that you have seen in summer, close to the horizon and dark in color and now and then silently pulsing with interior flashes of fire. And that is the surface of the novel that has filled me with such excitement.

The story itself is a chronicle of startling adventure against a background of the Sahara and the Arab-populated regions of the African Continent, a portion of the world seldom dealt with by first-rate writers who actually know it. Paul Bowles does know it, and much better, for instance, than it was known by André Gide. He

THE NEW YORK TIMES BOOK REVIEW

probably knows it even better than Albert Camus. For Paul Bowles has been going to Africa, off and on, since about 1930. It thrills him, but for some reason it does not upset his nervous equilibrium. He does not remain in the coastal cities. At frequent intervals he takes journeys into the most mysterious recesses of the desert and mountain country of North Africa, involving not only hardship but peril.

The Sheltering Sky is the chronicle of such a journey. Were it not for the fact that the chief male character, Port Moresby, succumbs to an epidemic fever during the course of the story, it would not be hard to identify him with Mr. Bowles himself. Like Mr. Bowles, he is a member of the New York intelligentsia who became weary of being such a member and set out to escape it in remote places. Escape it he certainly does. He escapes practically all the appurtenances of civilized modern life. Balanced between fascination and dread, he goes deeper and deeper into this dreamlike "awayness."

From then on the story is focused upon the continuing and continually more astonishing adventures of his wife, Kit, who wanders on like a body in which the rational mechanism is gradually upset and destroyed. The liberation is too intense, too extreme, for a nature conditioned by and for a state of civilized confinement. Her primitive nature, divested one by one of its artificial reserves and diffidences, eventually overwhelms her, and the end of this novel is as wildly beautiful and terrifying as the whole panorama that its protagonists have crossed.

In this external aspect the novel is, therefore, an account of startling adventure. In its interior aspect, *The Sheltering Sky* is an allegory of the spiritual adventure of the fully conscious person

Bowles in Tangier, Morocco, circa 1967.

into modern experience. This is not an enticing way to describe it. It is a way that might suggest the very opposite kind of a novel from the one that Paul Bowles has written. Actually this superior motive does not intrude in explicit form upon the story, certainly not in any form that will need to distract you from the great pleasure of being told a first-rate story of adventure by a really first-rate writer.

I suspect that a good many people will read this book and be enthralled by it without once suspecting that it contains a mirror of what is most terrifying and cryptic within the Sahara of moral nihilism, into which the race of man now seems to be wandering blindly.

E. H. Gombrich, *The Story of Art*

Gombrich's survey is now one of the most popular books on art ever written, and at the time of its publication our reviewer recognized its potential for greatness, writing that it was as "thoughtfully conceived as a sensitive work of art."

OBJECTING TO ATTEMPTED EXPLANATIONS of things which words cannot properly explain, Picasso asks, "Why not try to understand the song of a bird?" Nevertheless, as E. H. Gombrich, a lecturer at the Warburg Institute in London, notes in the last chapter of this thoroughly readable art history, words are useful to clear away misunderstandings.

The average individual will be the first to admit his lack of understanding about the nature of modern art. What he usually doesn't realize, however, is that more often than not he lacks a full understanding of art in general, which results in an actual misunderstanding of the role which art plays in society.

To recount the long story of art and remove the misunderstanding is, in part, the task taken on by the author, who believes that no art is truly intelligible without some knowledge of the events which inspired it. I have always been strangely fascinated by this capacity for comprehensiveness, for the ability to bite the whole apple, so to speak, and to manage swallowing it without choking. Mr. Gombrich does not choke; nor, what is more important, does the reader.

The book was written for young people. Simple writing and lucid organization recommend it. Because of these qualities, the adult will find ideas juxtaposed which he may not have had occasion to think about.

Architecture, painting and sculpture are presented as part of the fabric of history rather than as separately embroidered elements. The chapter headings accent the historical flow: "Art for Eternity," "The Great Awakening," "The Realm of Beauty," describe the transition in social thought from Egypt to Hellenistic Greece; "The Church Triumphant," "Courtiers and Burghers," "The Conquest of Reality," deal with the emergence of the worldly scientist from the miraculous faith of the Middle Ages; "The Age of Reason" and "The Break in Tradition" point up the connection between the social outlook of Pope, Hogarth and Voltaire and departures from the Baroque tradition, represented by the self-confident independence of Jefferson, the mocking invention of Goya and the individual mysticism of Blake.

In fact, with so many topics so nearly arrayed, the book acquires an air of completeness, of finality. The author's enlightened introduction warns of this danger of half-knowledge, however, and a concluding note on art books guides the reader to further inquiry. Finally, as a nicety not to be overlooked, each chapter is concluded with a tailpiece illustrating the contemporary view of the artist at work in the particular period under discussion. We are pictorially reminded that the artist is a functioning member of society today, as well as yesterday. This small touch, when you think of it, is modest evidence that the book is thoughtfully conceived as a sensitive work of art. —*Bartlett H. Hayes Jr.*

AUGUST 6, 1950 | ESSAY

A Moveable Feast

BY ALICE B. TOKLAS

Toklas, the famed partner of Gertrude Stein, offered the Book Review her own recollections of the many writers the pair encountered in Paris.

FRESH FROM THE BOAT TRAIN THE FIRST person I met in Paris was the American writer Gertrude Stein. She so often wrote of her work, her friends and herself with intimacy and precision that one hesitates to add to the choice she considered appropriate to tell.

After the liberation in '44 she commenced to see quantities of GIs and some American officers. To a soldier who said to her, It is all very well for you to sit comfortably in your nice flat and pioneer in some new field. Advice from an armchair isn't convincing. I think, she answered him, I have given proof of having accepted the pioneer's hardships. That struggle was the natural way of living to her. Is temptation tempting, she used to ask. Americans were surprised, some of them shocked by her remaining so typically American, by her not having taken advantage of the foreign culture about her. Culture never did interest her.

In those early days there were in Paris several American women who wrote novels who looked down upon those who wrote on art who in turn looked down upon fashion writers.

Then one summer—it must have been '12—we met Carl Van Vechten. It was on all sides love at first sight and the beginning of a long rare friendship, indescribable loyalty on his side, complete dependence on G.S.'s. Had she not said to him when it was proposed to her who had a horror of heights that she should fly to Chicago, to hear her opera, I'll go if you come along. We saw Carl a year later with lovely Fania Marinoff, his wife. And from then on there was an uninterrupted correspondence.

It was he who found her first and years later was her last publisher. It was Carl who persuaded Donald Evans to publish "Tender Buttons." By then he had written "Peter Whiffle," the first of those novels of the epoch he had created. Then one day he suddenly gave up the greatest of the arts for photography. When G.S. deplored the too frequent divorces and remarriages of one of their friends he said, you must remember with her that marriage is but a stepping-stone to a higher life.

Then the '14-'18 war came. The American lady novelists, poetesses and fashion writers had gone home and after the peace were replaced by a younger generation of Americans who came to Paris to write, many of them believing that in the city of boulevard bars (Prohibition was at its height in the U.S.) and Baudelaire, writing was a contagious craft.

Sherwood Anderson came to see G.S. on his first visit to Paris and frequently on his second. He had a winning brusquerie, a mordant wit and an all-inclusive heart—the combination was irresistible. He spoke no French but got on amazingly well with the Parisians, particularly with the working people. He told us that when he had been for some time going about the country lecturing, one day he discovered that he held his audience in his hand the way an opera singer does, and naturally he broke his contract at once and stopped lecturing.

1946–1971

Scott Fitzgerald, the first of the lost generation, as G.S. called them, was the only one at the time of their descent on Paris to have already given proof of a gift—and ample proof it was. He was distinguished, highly intelligent and completely attaching. He came to see G.S. on his 30th birthday and said that it was unbearable for him to have to face the fact that his youth was over. But you've been writing like a man of 30, she said with insistence. Have I, he said questioningly. He never believed what she told him about his work. It was too comforting to be true. He had a cynical wit. It's easy to falter the old, he said apropos of the clumsiness of one of his contemporaries when they came to see us.

Then there was Dos Passos with his Latin charm and Glenway Wescott with his Canadian accent and Hemingway whose dark luminous eyes—they were that then—and flashing smile and the *guiches* he affected made him look like an Italian. He once told us he had Italian blood. Hemingway in speaking of a rich American and his wife who had come to Paris to become writers said that he had known them before they could read or write. And in a kind of way I feel that about Hemingway, that is that neither reading nor writing is a natural inevitable necessity for him.

Ezra Pound, whom we met a few times in the 1920s, had a great interest in Japanese prints, political economy and Oriental music. He reminded me of Queen Victoria's remark after someone had most unfortunately been selected to sing to the Queen "The Wearing of the Green," so sad and so very mistaken.

T. S. Eliot was brought to call upon G.S. once. He was a sober, almost solemn, not so young man who, refusing to give up his umbrella, sat clasping its handle while his eyes burned brightly in a non-committal face.

It wasn't until 1934 that G.S. met Thornton Wilder. They immediately formed a warm

friendship. Endless were their discussions, on walks in the country, on crowded city streets, in her home. Some of the solutions went into her work. Thornton's varied interests and activities fascinated her, they seemed to concentrate his qualities, not to disperse them. *Heaven's My Destination* she said was the American novel; she wanted him to write more of them. Of his plays she preferred the one-act play *Queens of France*.

Of the young American writers in Paris today there are the G.I.'s with their Bill of Rights and their second novel on the way who are taking a course at the Sorbonne called French Civilization, for which at the end of the year they will be given a certificate of attendance. And there are the more serious Fulbright scholars who are writing tomes for their doctorate. There is a young, a very young man named Otto Friedrich who is now working on his fourth novel and who may easily become the most important young man of the future. And young George John, whose early poetic achievement so greatly impressed G.S. and whose present development she foresaw.

It would be well if one could end on this encouraging note but one can not completely ignore the highly colorful group in and about the cafés of Place Saint-Germain-des-Prés. They publish and contribute their writings to at least one little review. They may be gently dismissed with an "unpredictable future."

The New York Times Book Review

AUGUST 6, 1950   Copyright, 1950, by The New York Times Company.   SECTION 7

THEY WHO CAME TO PARIS TO WRITE

For nearly a half century, Alice B. Toklas, the long-time companion-secretary of Gertrude Stein, has known and watched the Americans who found in Paris the best place to write and dream their dreams. In the following article she recalls some of the best known and pays her respects to the new generation that is seeking in Paris the same sort of fame won by those who have gone before.

By ALICE B. TOKLAS

PARIS.

BEFORE I came to Paris Henry James had already gone to live in England. When we went there in 1902 it had been arranged that we should spend a day with him at Rye, but to my bitter disappointment we received word that he was too indisposed to receive us on the appointed day, would we come some day on the following week? Alas, we had to return to Paris before then. It is my unique lost opportunity. The influence of the years Henry James spent in France is abundantly to be found in what he wrote in England. Could "The Spoils of Poynton," though placed in England, have been so poignantly described without his having had intimate French experience? Did the foreign experience, first in Italy and then in France, finally in England, even his eventually becoming a British subject, did these make him less an American? Was his nationality not strengthened by his exterior conformity to the ways and habits of another country?

Fresh from the boat train the first person I met in Paris was the American writer Gertrude Stein. She so often wrote of her work, her friends and herself with intimacy and precision that one hesitates to add to the choice she considered appropriate to tell.

AFTER the liberation in '44 she commenced to see quantities of G. I.'s and some American officers. Among the first who came to see her was Joseph Barry now of THE NEW YORK TIMES, with whom she formed a lively friendship. She met four or five major generals and was surprised to find how much she enjoyed them. One of them asked her as he was leaving after a first visit, May I come again, Miss Stein. You have not hestitated to tell me of your preference for the G. I.'s. Alas that I should be a general. To which she answered, Yes, do. Evidently generals are not works of art. You see, in pictures I do not care for the end of a series. I like the pictures that are painted while the struggle to express something new is still going on. But the finished product of you generals has interested me. So do come again.

To a soldier who said to her, It is all very well for you to sit comfortably in your nice flat and advise us to go home and pioneer in some new field. Advice from an armchair isn't con-

Impressions, Observations and Asides By Gertrude Stein's Closest Companion

Alice B. Toklas (left) and Gertrude Stein in Culoz, France, in 1944.

vincing. I think, she answered him, I have given proof of having accepted the pioneer's hardships. That struggle was the natural way of living to her. Is temptation tempting she used to ask. Americans were surprised, some of them shocked by her remaining so typically American, by her not having taken advantage of the foreign culture about her. Culture never did interest her.

The next American writer I met was Mildred Aldrich whose "Hilltop on the Marne" was a best seller in '15. She had been the dramatic critic on The Boston Transcript and called every one by their Christian names. In introducing two new friends to us she said, May I present Henry and Roger. Mildred, asked G. S., what may their family names be. Yes, Yes, said Mildred turning to the two men, what may your family names be. The taller an American answered MacBride and the dark-eyed Englishman murmured Fry.

In those early days there were in Paris several American women who wrote novels who looked down upon those who wrote on art who in turn looked down upon fashion writers.

Then one summer—it must have been '12, we met Carl Van Vechten briefly. It was on all sides love at first sight and the beginning of a long rare friendship, indescribable loyalty on his side, complete dependence on G. S.'s. Had she not said to him when it was proposed to her who had a horror of heights that she should fly to Chicago to hear her opera, I'll go if you come along. We saw Carl a year later with lovely Fania Marinoff, his wife. And from then on there was an uninterrupted correspondence.

IT was he who found her first and years later her last publisher. It was Carl who persuaded Donald Evans to publish "Tender Buttons." By then he had written "Peter Whiffle," the first of those novels of the epoch he had created. And then one day he suddenly gave up the greatest of the arts for photography. When G. S. deplored the too frequent divorces and remarriages of one of their friends he said, you must remember that with her marriage is but a stepping-stone to a higher life.

Then the '14-'18 war came. The American lady novelists, poetesses and fashion writers had gone home and after the peace were replaced by a younger generation of Americans who came to Paris to write, many of them believing that in the city of boulevard bars (prohibition was at its height in U. S.) and Baudelaire, writing was a contagious craft.

Sherwood Anderson came to see G. S. on his first visit to Paris and frequently on his second. He had a winning brusquerie, a mordant wit and an all-inclusive heart — the combination was irresistible. He spoke no French but got on amazing well with the Parisians, particularly with the working people. He told us that when he had been for some time going about the country lecturing, one day he discovered that he held his audience in his hand the way an opera singer does, naturally he broke his contract at once and stopped lecturing. He was very handsome and incredibly charming and the story teller.

SCOTT FITZGERALD, the first of the lost generation as G. S. called them, was the only one at the time of their descent on Paris to have already given proof of a gift—and ample proof it was. He was distinguished, highly intelligent and completely attaching. He came to see G. S. on his thirtieth birthday and said that it was unbearable for him to have to face the fact that his youth was over. But you've been writing like a man of 30, she said with insistence. Have I, he said questioningly. He never believed what she told him about his work. It was too comforting to (Continued on Page 25)

Salinger with a copy of *The Catcher in the Rye* on November 20, 1952, in Brooklyn.

J. D. Salinger, *The Catcher in the Rye*

Salinger's classic tale of adolescent angst and alienation was greeted with enthusiasm by James Stern, who wrote his review in the voice of the novel's protagonist.

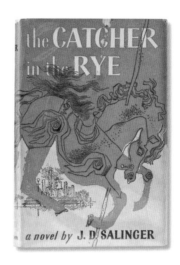

THIS GIRL HELGA, SHE KILLS ME. SHE READS just about everything I bring into the house, and a lot of crumby stuff besides. She's crazy about kids. I mean stories about kids. But Hel, she says there's hardly a writer alive can write about children. Only these English guys Richard Hughes and Walter de la Mare, she says. The rest is all corny guy or a phony book quick as a dog smells a rat. This phoniness, it gives old Hel a pain if you want to know the truth. That's why she came hollering to me one day, her hair falling over her face and all, and said I had to read some damn story in *The New Yorker*. Who's the author? I said. Salinger, she told me, J. D. Salinger.

"For Esmé—with Love and Squalor" was this story's crumby title. But *boy,* was that a story. Hel, I said when I was through, just you wait till this guy writes a novel. Novel, my elbow, she said. This Salinger, he won't write no crumby novel. He's a short story guy—Girls, they kill me. They really do.

But I was right, if you want to know the truth. You should've seen how old Hel hit the ceiling when I told her this Salinger, he has not only written a novel, it's a Book-of-the-Month Club selection, too. For crying out loud, she said, what's

it about? About this Holden Caulfield, I told her, about the time he ran away to New York from this Pencey Prep School in Agerstown, Pa. Why'd he run away, asked old Hel. Because it was a terrible school, I told her, no matter how you looked at it. And there were no girls.

Away she went with this crazy book, *The Catcher in the Rye*. What did I tell ya, she said the next day. This Salinger, he's a short story guy. And he knows how to write about kids. This book though, it's too long. Gets kind of monotonous. And he should've cut out a lot about these jerks and all that crumby school. They depress me. They really do. Salinger, he's best with real children. I mean young ones like old Phoebe, his kid sister. She's a personality. Holden and little old Phoebe, Hel said, they kill me.

Know what? This Holden, he finds the whole world's full of people who say one thing and mean another and he doesn't like it; and he hates movies and phony slobs and snobs and crumby books and war. Boy, how he hates war. Just like you, Hel, I said. But old Hel, she was already reading this crazy *Catcher* book all over again. That's always a good sign with Hel. —*James Stern*

Salinger Speaks

When the notoriously reclusive author spoke to a reporter in 1974, it was front-page news.

GOADED BY THE PUBLICATION OF unauthorized editions of his early, previously uncollected works, the reclusive author J. D. Salinger broke a public silence of more than 20 years last week, issuing a denunciation and revealing he is hard at work on writings that may never be published in his lifetime.

Speaking by telephone from Cornish, N.H., where he makes his home, the 55-year-old author whose most recent published work, *Raise High the Roof Beam, Carpenters* and *Seymour, an Introduction*, appeared in 1962, said: "There is a marvelous peace in not publishing. It's peaceful. Still. Publishing is a terrible invasion of my privacy. I like to write. I love to write. But I write just for myself and my own pleasure."

For nearly half an hour after saying he intended to talk "only for a minute," the author, who achieved literary fame and cultish devotion enhanced by his inaccessibility following publication of *The Catcher in the Rye i*n 1951, spoke of it, work, his obsession with privacy and his uncertain thoughts about publication.

The interview with Mr. Salinger, who was at times warm and charming, at times wary and skittish, is believed to be his first since 1953, when he granted one to a 16-year-old representative of the high school newspaper in Cornish.

What prompted Mr. Salinger to speak now on what he said was a cold, rainy, windswept night in Cornish was what he regards as the latest and most severe of all invasions of his private world: the publication of *The Complete Uncollected Short Stories of J. D. Salinger,* Vols. 1 and 2.

During the last two months, about 25,000 copies of these books, priced at $3 to $5 for each volume, have been sold first here in San Francisco, then in New York, Chicago and elsewhere, according to Salinger, his lawyers and book dealers around the country.

"Some stories, my property, have been stolen," Mr. Salinger said. "Someone's appropriated them. It's an illicit act. It's unfair. Suppose you had a coat you liked and somebody went into your closet and stole it. That's how I feel."

"They're selling like hotcakes," said one San Francisco book dealer. "Everybody wants one."

"It's amazing some sort of law and order agency can't do something about this," Mr. Salinger said. "Why, if a dirty old mattress is stolen from your attic, they'll find it. But they're not even looking for this man."

Discussing his opposition to republication of his early works, Mr. Salinger said they were the fruit of a time when he was first beginning to commit himself to being a writer. He spoke of writing feverishly, of being "intent on placing [his works] in magazines."

Suddenly he interrupted himself. "I'm still trying to protect what privacy I have left," he said.

Did he expect to publish another work soon?

There was a pause.

"I really don't know how soon," he said. There was another pause, and then Mr. Salinger began to talk rapidly about how much he was writing, long hours, every day, and he said he was under contract to no one for another book.

"I don't necessarily intend to publish posthumously," he said, "but I do like to write for myself."

"I pay for this kind of attitude. I'm known as a strange, aloof kind of man. But all I'm doing is trying to protect myself and my work."

"I just want all this to stop. It's intrusive. I've survived a lot of things," he said in what was to be the end of the conversation, "and I'll probably survive this." —*Lacey Fosburgh*

William F. Buckley Jr., *God and Man at Yale*

Buckley, perhaps the most widely known conservative intellectual of the 20th century, first came to public attention for this treatise on what he regarded as the failures of his alma mater. The book was published to mixed notices, with McGeorge Bundy writing in *The Atlantic,* "I find the book is dishonest in its use of facts, false in its theory and a discredit to its author." Our reviewer offered a more generous assessment of the text.

WILLIAM BUCKLEY, YALE '50 AND AS A SENIOR the able editor of *The Yale Daily News,* has written a book that challenges political, religious and educational liberalism. Nominally his book is about education at Yale. Actually it is about American politics.

How right he is (and likewise John Chamberlain in his well-written preface) to insist that man has a moral nature, that statism threatens it, that freedom depends on the traditional value-code of the West and that unmoral materialism results in a suicidal tolerance debunking all values as equally "relative." Specifically, Buckley attacks "statism and atheism" on the Yale campus. Yet what is his alternative? Nothing more inspiring than the most sterile Old Guard brand of Republicanism, far to the right of Taft.

Is there no "selfish materialism" at all among the National Association of Manufacturers as well as among the "New Deal collectivists" here denounced? Is it not humorless, or else blasphemous, for this eloquent advocate of Christianity, an unworldly and anti-economic religion, to enshrine jointly as equally sacrosanct: "Adam Smith and Ricardo, Jesus and Saint Paul?" And why is this veritable Eagle Scout of moral sternness silent on the moral implications of McCarthyism in his own camp?

In this urgent crisis, when our survival against Soviet aggression depends on cooperating with both conservatives and anti-Red heroes like the socialist Reuter in Europe, the author irresponsibly treats not only mild social democracy but even most social reform as almost crypto-Communism. He damns Communism, our main enemy, not half so violently as lesser enemies like the income tax and inheritance tax. Words will really fail you when you reach the book's final "message": Trustees and alumni should violate the legally established academic freedom to "banish from the

---

1950 ————

Patricia Highsmith publishes *Strangers on a Train,* which the Book Review's crime columnist calls "a tense, well-written, hare-and-hounds thriller."

1950 ————

Poet Gwendolyn Brooks becomes the first African-American writer to win a Pulitzer Prize.

1950 ————→

L. Ron Hubbard publishes *Dianetics,* and the Book Review is not a fan: "Books like this do harm by their grandiose promises to troubled persons."

classroom" not merely Communists but all professors deviating far from Adam Smith!

Has a young Saint Paul emerged from the Yale class of 1950 to bring us the good tidings of a new conservatism and old morality? The trumpets of advance publicity imply it. However, this Paul-in-a-hurry skips the prerequisite of first being a rebel Saul. The difference between a shallow and profound conservatism is the difference between the easy, booster affirmation that precedes the dark night of the soul and the hard-won tragic affirmations that follow it. True: We need, as Buckley argues, more conservatism and traditional morality. Still, they must be earned by suffering and a change of heart, not by glibly being "his class's Bright Young Man" (to quote the Yale Class History on Buckley).

Great conservatives—immortals like Burke, Alexander Hamilton, Disraeli, Churchill, Pope and Swift—earned the right to be sunnily conservative by their long dark nights. You can earn it by being a tortured romantic Irishman like Burke. You can earn it by Churchill's bitter decade before his great hour in 1940. You do not earn a heartfelt and conviction-carrying conservatism by the shortcut of popular campus clubman, without the inspiring agony of lonely, unrespectable soul-searching.

As gadfly against the smug Comrade Blimps of the left, this important, symptomatic and widely hailed book is a necessary counterbalance. However, its outworn Old Guard antithesis to the outworn Marxist thesis is not the liberty security synthesis the future cries for. Some day, being intelligent and earnest, Buckley may give us the hard-won wisdom of synthesis. For that, he will first need to add, to his existing virtues, three new ones: sensitivity, compassion, and an inkling of the tragic paradoxes of *la condition humaine*.
—*Peter Viereck*

Ralph Ellison, *Invisible Man*

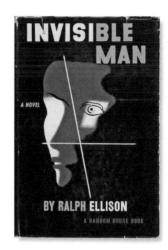

In his acceptance speech for the 1953 National Book Award, Ellison said: "To see America with an awareness of its rich diversity and its almost magical fluidity and freedom I was forced to conceive of a novel unburdened by the narrow naturalism which has led after so many triumphs to the final and unrelieved despair which marks so much of our current fiction."

THE GEOGRAPHY OF HELL IS STILL IN THE PROcess of being mapped. The borders shift, the shore lines erode, coral islands appear complete with new sirens, but all the men who have been there speak with a similar voice. These reports are seldom mistaken as coming from anywhere else. As varied as the life might be on the surface, the life underground has a good deal in common—the stamp of hell, the signature of pain, is on all of the inhabitants. Here, if anywhere, is the real brotherhood of man. Fleeing toward hell, Dante beheld a man whose voice seemed weak from a long silence, and he cried to him, saying, "Have pity on me, whoever thou art, shade or real man!"

Shade or real man? Visible or invisible? The Invisible Man would have smiled in recognition if hailed like that. He lives, he tells us, in an underground hole. To fill this dark hole with light, he burns 1,369 bulbs. He burns them free. A fine Dostoevskyan touch. In his *Notes From the Underground* Dostoevsky says: "We are discussing things seriously; but if you won't deign to give me your attention, I will drop your acquaintance. I can retreat into my underground hole."

The Invisible Man is also discussing things seriously. His report in this novel might be subtitled, "Notes From Underground America," or "The Invisible Black Man in the Visible White Man's World." That is part of his story, but the deeper layer, revealed, perhaps, in spite of himself, is the invisible man becoming visible. The word, against all of the odds, becoming the flesh. Neither black nor white flesh, however, for where the color line is drawn with profundity, as it is here, it also vanishes. There is not much to choose, under the skin, between being black and invisible, and being white, currently fashionable and opaque.

"Let us descend into the blind world here below," Virgil says, and the Invisible Man descends through the ivy-covered college doors. His report begins the day that rich men from the North, white philanthropists, appear on the campus of a Negro college in the South. They are there for the ceremony of Founders Day. The Invisible Man, a student at the college, is chosen to act as the chauffeur for one of them. He shows him, inadvertently, the underground

Ellison in 1966.

Ralph Ellison,
Dancing and Writing

When Anatole Broyard, a critic and editor at The Times, saw Ralph Ellison at a New Year's party, it gave him the idea for this essay, published in 1982. "Ralph dances the way he writes, both with the beat and against it," he wrote.

WATCHING PEOPLE DANCE AT A PARTY on New Year's Eve, I found myself wondering about the uses of tradition in art. It seemed to me that many of the people in the room danced awkwardly, even sheepishly. Their dancing vacillated, in a rather clumsy pastiche, between folk, jazz and musical comedy idioms.

It occurred to me that here was a metaphor for one of the difficulties of American art, the problem of its relation to the artist's history and to the history of his country. In painting and music, American artists have often borrowed their sense of orientation from European sources, but literature, by definition, has to find its own voice. In fact, the search for a natural, or native, voice is a recurrent theme in American literature.

Writers who draw on ethnic sources have an advantage. For several generations many Jewish writers have used their ethnic background as a contrapuntal device, although this practice seems to be thinning out now into little more than irony, a fundamentally ironic stance or dance.

Writers make all sorts of desperate gestures in their search for a frame of reference. A few years ago, feeling that my own coordinates or structures were becoming stale, I enrolled in The School for Creative Movement in the Arts, an institution in New York City that approaches the body as a paradigm for the self. My instructor there said that, like most people, I had greatly limited my possibilities of movement. According to him, I tended to play it safe, to feel more comfortable conjugating simple structures than risking more complex ones. Almost everything he said about moving seemed to apply equally to writing, and I wondered whether a giving in to impulse, to movement for its own sake, wasn't one of the ways in which American writers compensate for their ambiguous cultural heritage.

There was one person at the New Year's Eve party who did not dance awkwardly or ambivalently, and who has always made it clear that he has no doubts about his orientation. This was Ralph Ellison, the black novelist who wrote *Invisible Man.* Ellison often talks about the black cultural tradition, which he uses much as a jazz musician uses melody as a basis for improvisations. For him, rhythm is one aspect of the black writer's irony.

Ralph dances the way he writes, both with the beat and against it. He does more different steps than other people, more figures, you might say, as in figures of speech. Though he works in a traditional framework of the Lindy, the two-step and the rumba, he achieves more variety, expression and spontaneity than those people who conceive of dancing as an entirely uninhibited or improvised activity.

You can see the same esthetic on another level in this passage from *Invisible Man:* "He was standing and he fell. He fell and he kneeled. He kneeled and he bled. He bled and he died. He fell in a heap like any man and his blood spilled like any blood; red as any blood, wet as any blood and reflecting the sky and the buildings and birds and trees, or your face if you'd looked into its dulling mirror." The first four short sentences are like gospel or blues. The rhythms of the next long sentence draw on jazz, bop and high rhetoric, though that red is a perfect blue note.

Like Jewish writers, some black writers are beginning to move away from their tradition, to thin it out toward irony, anger and even deracination. Because he knows what he can do with the black idiom, Ralph Ellison tends to resist certain revisions of it. "When the word changed from 'Negro' to 'black,'" he once said to me, "an element of mysticism slipped in that I've never felt comfortable with."

Some black writers might argue that Ellison's dancing and writing might benefit from an element of mysticism, that it might make him a more contemporary or universal performer. And he might answer that a writer who dilutes his tradition or his idiom may find himself lost in the limbo between his own history and the history of literature. In doing such a tricky dance, an author may also get out of step with his partner, the reader.

Though the black writer's response to his history may be changing, it is still his principal frame of reference. In the work of most non-black novelists, their relation to their culture remains ambiguous. For example, at the end of *Zuckerman Unbound,* Philip Roth's long struggle with his Jewishness approaches something like a metaphysics of deracination, a rejection that feels like an inverted embrace, an eternal kiss goodbye. Still, there are some signs of a revival of traditional values in Saul Bellow's increasingly acerbic protests against their disappearance and in John Updike's Whitmanesque evocation of American grass roots in *Rabbit Is Rich.*

Perhaps the writer can only "dance" with his tradition because the music keeps changing. As American life, black and white, moves from melody, or the feeling of continuity, toward harmonics, which is a more elliptical kind of relationship, all we can do is cast about for appropriate chords. —*Anatole Broyard*

black world that should not be seen. Before the day is over, both the millionaire and the student have been disillusioned, and the student, expelled from the college, leaves for New York. In the city he becomes increasingly invisible. Hearing him rouse the crowd at the scene of a Harlem eviction, a key party bigwig sees a bright future for him in the brotherhood. The mysteries of the Order, revealed and unrevealed, as they fall to the lot of the Invisible Man, have the authentic air of unreality that must have bemused so many honest, tormented men.

Perhaps it is the nature of the pilgrim in hell to see the visible world and its inhabitants in allegorical terms. They do not exist, so much as they represent. They appear to be forces, figures of good and evil, in a large symbolical frame, which makes for order, but diminishes our interest in their predicament as people. This may well be the price of living underground. We are deprived of uniqueness, no light illuminates our individuality.

The reader who is familiar with the traumatic phase of the black man's rage in America will find something more in Mr. Ellison's report. He will find the long anguished step toward its mastery. The author sells no phony forgiveness. He asks none himself. It is a resolutely honest, tormented, profoundly American book.

"Being invisible and without substance, a disembodied voice, as it were, what else could I do?" the Invisible Man asks us in closing. "What else but try to tell you what was really happening when your eyes were looking through! And it is this which frightens me: Who knows but that, on the lower frequencies, I speak for you?"

But this is not another journey to the end of the night. With this book the author maps a course from the underground world into the light. *Invisible Man* belongs on the shelf with the classical efforts man has made to chart the river Lethe from its mouth to its source. —*Wright Morris*

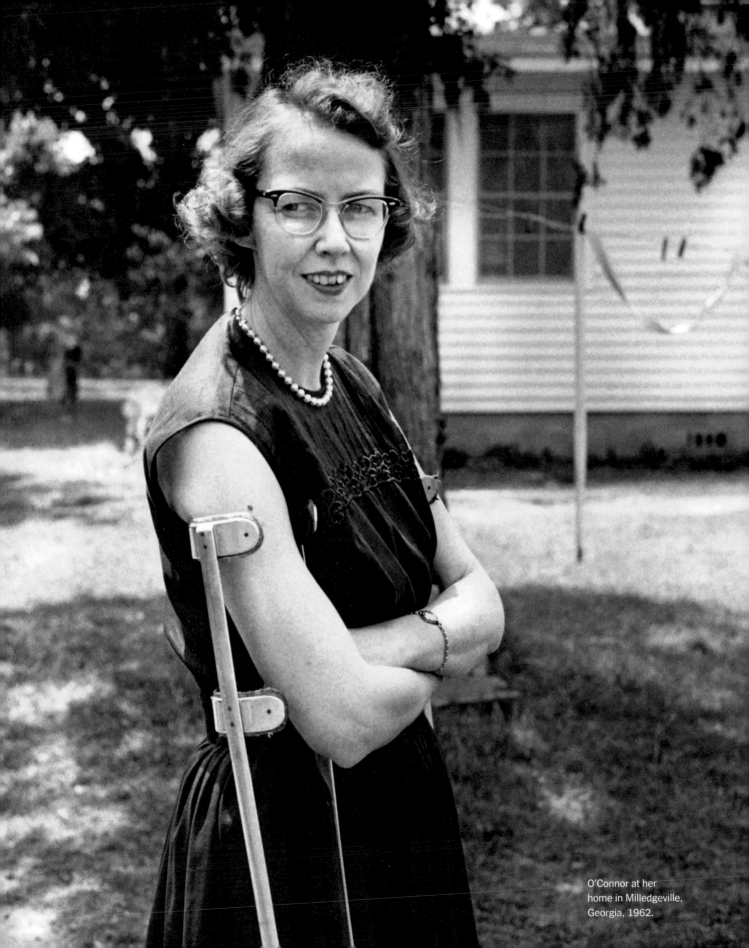

O'Connor at her home in Milledgeville, Georgia, 1962.

Flannery O'Connor, *Wise Blood*

BY WILLIAM GOYEN

Although she would later be better known for her short stories, including the classroom staple "A Good Man Is Hard to Find," O'Connor's debut novel established the Southern writer as a powerful young voice.

THIS FIRST NOVEL, WHOSE LANGUAGE IS Tennessee-Georgia dialect expertly wrought into a clipped, elliptic and blunt style, introduces its author as a writer of power. There is in Flannery O'Connor a fierceness of literary gesture, an angriness of observation, a facility for catching, as an animal eye in a wilderness, cunningly and at one sharp glance, the shape and detail and animal intention of enemy and foe. The world of *Wise Blood* is one of clashing in a wilderness.

When Hazel Motes, from Eastrod, Tenn., is released from the Army at the age of 22, he comes to a Southern city near his birthplace. He falls under the spell of Asa Hawks, a "blind" street preacher who shambles through the city with his degenerate daughter, Lily, age 15. The story of this novel, darting through rapid, brute, bare episodes told with power and keenness, develops the disintegration and final destruction of Hazel who physically and psychologically becomes Hawks and parrot-preaches (in vain) to the city crowds from the hood of his second-hand Essex.

In Taulkinham, U.S.A., the city of Fiendish Evangelists, one is brought into a world not so much of accursed or victimized human beings as into the company of an ill-tempered and driven collection of one-dimensional creatures of sheer meanness and orneriness, scheming landladies, cursing waitresses, haunted-house people, prostitutes, fake blind men who take on, as they increase in number, the nature and small size of downright skulduggery and alum-mouthed contrariness. One is never convinced of any genuine evil in these people, only of a sourness; they seem not to belong to the human race at all, they are what the geneticist calls a race of "sports."

The stark dramatic power of the scenes is percussive and stabbing, but Miss O'Connor seems to tell her story through clenched teeth in a kind of Tomboy, Mean-Moll glee, and a few times she writes herself into episodes that have to contrive themselves to deliver her out of them, and then she is compelled to go on too far beyond or in the direction of sensationalism.

Miss O'Connor's style is tight to choking and as direct and uncompounded as the order to a firing squad to shoot a man against a wall. One cannot take this book lightly or lightly turn away from it, because it is inflicted upon one in the same way its people take their lives—like an indefensible blow delivered in the dark. Perhaps this sense of being physically struck and wounded is only the beginning of an arousal of one's questioning of the credibility of such a world of horror. In such a world, all living things have vanished and what remains exists in a redemptionless clashing of unending vengeance, alienated from any source of understanding, the absence of which does not even define a world of darkness, not even that—for there has been no light to take away.

1946–1971

Anne Frank, *The Diary of a Young Girl*

Written by a young Jewish girl during the German occupation of the Netherlands during World War II, this journal was translated by B. M. Mooyaart-Doubleday and published in the United States with an introduction by Eleanor Roosevelt.

ANNE FRANK'S DIARY IS TOO TENDERLY intimate a book to be frozen with the label "classic," and yet no lesser designation serves. But her book is not a classic to be left on the library shelf. It is a warm and stirring confession, to be read over and over from insight and enjoyment.

Anne Frank lived in astonishing circumstances: she was hidden with seven other people in a secret nest of rooms behind her father's place of business in Amsterdam. Thus, the diary tells the life of a group of Jews waiting in fear of being taken by the Nazis. It is, in reality, the kind of document that John Hersey invented for *The Wall.*

There is no lugubrious ghetto tale, no compilation of horrors. Reality can prove surprisingly different from invented reality, and Anne Frank's diary simply bubbles with amusement, love, discovery. It has its share of disgust, its moments of hatred, but it is so wondrously alive, so near, that one feels overwhelmingly the universalities of human nature. These people might be living

next door. Because the diary was not written in retrospect, it contains the trembling life of every moment—Anne Frank's voice becomes the voice of six million vanished Jewish souls.

Anne's father had already brought the family out of Germany in 1933. In June, 1942, a few weeks after the diary begins, the S.S. sends a call-up for Anne's sister, Margot, and the family goes into hiding. The Van Daans, with their 16-year-old son Peter, join the Franks. Later, because "Daddy says we must save another person if we can," an elderly dentist named Dussel is squeezed into the Secret Annex.

Two years passed in disciplined activities. The hidden ones kept busy with smuggled correspondence courses in speed shorthand, in Latin, in nursing; Dussel even attempted dental operations, hilariously described by Anne. She records the family disputes and the comic moments, as when her father lies on the floor trying to overhear an important business conference downstairs; Anne flattens herself beside him, lending a sharp ear. But business is so dull, she falls asleep.

Most wondrous of all is her love affair with Peter. It is this unfolding psychological drama of a girl's growth, mingled with the physical danger of the group, that frees Anne's book from the horizontal effect of most diaries. Hers rises continuously, with the tension of a well-constructed novel.

"I want to go on living even after my death," Anne wrote. "I am grateful to God for giving me this gift, this possibility of developing myself and of writing, of expressing all that is in me." Hers was probably one of the bodies seen in the mass grave at Bergen-Belsen, for in August 1944, the knock came on that hidden door in Amsterdam. After the people had been taken away, Dutch friends found Anne's diary in the debris, and saved it.

THE CHILD BEHIND THE SECRET DOOR

ANNE FRANK: The Diary of a Young Girl. Translated from the Dutch by B. M. Mooyaart-Doubleday. Introduction by Eleanor Roosevelt. 285 pp. New York: Doubleday & Co. $3.

By MEYER LEVIN

An Adolescent Girl's Own Story of How She Hid for Two Years During the Nazi Terror

ANNE FRANK'S diary is too tenderly intimate a book to be frozen with the label "classic," and yet no lesser designation serves. For little Anne Frank, spirited, moody, witty, self-doubting, succeeded in communicating in virtually perfect, or classic, form the drama of puberty. But her book is not a classic to be left on the library shelf. It is a warm and stirring confession, to be read over and over for insight and enjoyment.

The diary is a classic on another level, too. It happened that during the two years that mark the most extraordinary changes in a girl's life, Anne Frank lived in astonishing circumstances: she was hidden with seven other people in a secret nest of rooms behind her father's place of business, in Amsterdam. Thus, the diary tells the life of a group of Jews waiting in fear of being taken by the Nazis. It is, in reality, the kind of document that John Hersey invented for "The Wall."

This is no lugubrious ghetto tale, no compilation of horrors. Reality can prove surprisingly different from invented reality, and Anne Frank's diary simply bubbles with amusement, love, discovery. It has its share of disgust, its moments of hatred, but it is so wondrously alive, so near, that one feels overwhelmingly the universalities of human nature. These people might be living next door; their within-the-family emotions, their tensions and satisfactions are those of human character and growth, anywhere.

BECAUSE the diary was not written in retrospect, it contains the trembling life of every moment—Anne Frank's voice becomes the voice of six million vanished Jewish souls. It is difficult to say in which respect her book is more "important," but one forgets the double significance of this document in experiencing it as an intimate whole, for one feels the presence of this child-becoming-woman as though she was snuggled on a near-by sofa.

We meet Anne on her thirteenth birthday, "Quicksilver Anne" to her adored father, but "Miss Chatterbox" and "Miss Quack-Quack," she tells us, to her teacher—for the family is still at liberty. Indeed, her teacher makes her write a self-curing essay on chattering; she turns in a poem that convulses teacher and class, and is allowed to remain her talkative self without further reprimand.

Yet, with the moodiness of adoles-

A journalist and novelist, Mr. Levin recently wrote "In Search: An Autobiography," an examination of the Jewish psyche in the modern world.

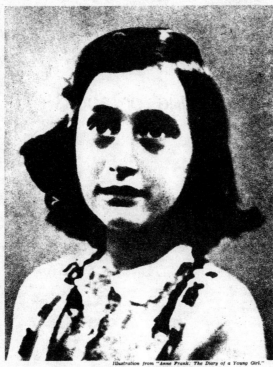

Illustration from "Anne Frank: The Diary of a Young Girl."
Anne Frank: A photograph found in her diary.

cence, she feels lonesome. "Let me put it more clearly, since no one will believe that a girl of 13 feels herself quite alone in the world, nor is it so. I have darling parents and a sister of 16. I know about thirty people whom one might call friends—I have strings of boy friends, anxious to catch a glimpse of me, who * * * peep at me through mirrors in class. I have relations, aunts, uncles, who are darlings too, a good home, no—I don't seem to lack anything. But it's the same with all my friends, just fun and nothing more. We don't seem to be able to get any closer, that is the root of the whole trouble. Hence, this diary. I want this diary itself to be my friend, and shall call my friend Kitty."

What child of 13 hasn't had these feelings, and resolved to confide in a diary? Anne carried it through, never shrinking from revealing the ugly things about herself.

Her father had already brought the family out of Germany in 1933. In June, 1942, a few weeks after the diary begins, the SS sends a call-up for Anne's sister, Margot, and the family goes into hiding. "I began to pack some of our most vital belongings into a school satchel * * * this diary, then hair curlers, handkerchiefs, schoolbooks, a comb, old letters." The Van Daans, with their 16-year-old son Peter, join the Franks. Later, because "Daddy says we must save another person if we can," an elderly dentist named Dussel is squeezed into the Secret Annex. He gets Anne's bed; she sleeps on a settee lengthened by chairs.

A born writer, Anne zestfully portrays the Annex inhabitants, with all their flaws and virtues. The common life effect which Mr. Hersey sought to suggest in "The Wall" here flowers with utter spontaneity. But Anne Frank's diary probes far deeper than "The Wall" into the core of human relations, and succeeds better than "The Wall" in bringing us an understanding of life under threat.

And this quality brings it home to any family in the world today. Just as the Franks lived in momentary fear of the Gestapo's knock on their hidden door, so every family today lives in fear of the knock of war. Anne's diary is a great affirmative answer to the life-question of today, for she shows how ordinary people, within this ordeal, consistently hold to the greater human values.

The Frank's Dutch friends in the office on the other side of the secret door sustained them to the end. "Never have we heard *one* word of the burden which we certainly must be to them. * * * They put on the brightest possible faces, bring flowers and presents for birthdays, risking their own lives to help others." These Dutch friends, Miep, Elli, Kraler, Koophuis, even managed to smuggle in Chanukah gifts, and shyly offered their Christmas remembrances to the hidden Jews.

TWO years passed in disciplined activities. The hidden ones kept busy with smuggled correspondence courses in speed shorthand, in Latin, in nursing; Dussel even attempted dental operations, hilariously described by Anne. She herself studied mythology, ballet, "family trees," while keeping up her schoolwork. She records the family disputes—Mrs. Van Daan violently resisting the sale of her fur coat, only to see it smoked up in black market tobacco! And the comic moments, as when her father lies on the floor trying to overhear an important business conference downstairs; Anne flattens herself beside him, lending a sharp ear. But business is so dull, she falls asleep.

Most wondrous of all is her love affair. Like a flower under a stone fulfilling itself, she came to her first love in her allotted time. "I give myself completely. But one thing. He may touch my face, but no more." All is told, from her potato-fetching devices for going up to Peter's attic lair, to the first misplaced kiss, on her ear. And the parents worrying about the youngsters trysting up there in the dusk, sitting by the window over the canal. And her fears that her older sister is lonely and jealous, leading to an amazing exchange of letters between the two girls, in those hidden rooms. Finally, there is even the tender disillusionment with Peter, as Anne reaches toward maturity, and a character understanding replaces the first tug of love. In all this there are perceptions in depth, striv- *(Continued on Page 22)*

There is anguish in the thought of how much creative power, how much sheer beauty of living, was cut off through genocide. But through her diary Anne goes on living. From Holland to France, to Italy, Spain. The Germans too have published her book. And now she comes to America. Surely she will be widely loved, for this wise and wonderful young girl brings back a poignant delight in the infinite human spirit.

—*Meyer Levin*

Clockwise from top left: Lorraine Hansberry, 1959;
Ntozake Shange, 1977; Lillian Hellman, 1966;
Arthur Miller, 1952; Suzan-Lori Parks, 2014; Oscar
Wilde, circa 1882; Tennessee Williams, 1965; Noël
Coward, 1949; Tom Stoppard, 1972.

E. B. White, *Charlotte's Web*

BY EUDORA WELTY

When this children's classic was published in 1952, it was reviewed by Eudora Welty, who distilled its simplicity and sweetness in her celebrated review. "What the book is about is friendship on earth, affection and protection, adventure and miracle, life and death, trust and treachery, pleasure and pain, and the passing of time," she wrote. "As a piece of work it is just about perfect, and just about magical in the way it is done." Some pig, indeed.

E. B. WHITE HAS WRITTEN A BOOK FOR children, which is nice for us older ones as it calls for big type. The book has liveliness and felicity, tenderness and unexpectedness, grace and humor and praise of life, and the good backbone of succinctness that only the most highly imaginative stories seem to grow.

Wilbur is of sweet nature—he is a spring pig—affectionate, responsive to moods of the weather and the song of the crickets, has long eyelashes, is hopeful, partially willing to try anything, brave, subject to faints from bashfulness, is loyal to friends, enjoys a good appetite and a soft bed, and is a little likely to be overwhelmed by the sudden chance for complete freedom. He changes the subject when the conversation gets painful, and a buttermilk bath brings out his beauty. When he was a baby he was a runt, but the sun shone pink through his ears, endearing him to a little girl named Fern. She is his protector, and he is the hero.

Charlotte A. Cavatica ("but just call me Charlotte") is the heroine, a large gray spider "about the size of a gumdrop." She has eight legs and can wave them in friendly greeting. When her friends wake up in the morning she says "Salutations!"—in spite of sometimes having been

1953 — Lawrence Ferlinghetti and Peter Martin open San Francisco's City Lights Bookstore.

1954 — Ernest Hemingway and his fourth wife, Mary, are reported safe after their small chartered plane crashes in East Africa.

1955 — *Bonjour Tristesse,* the smash European hit novel by the 18-year-old French novelist Françoise Sagan, is translated into English.

White with his dachshund, Minnie, at *The New Yorker* in the late 1940s.

up all night herself, working. She tells Wilbur right away that she drinks blood, and Wilbur on first acquaintance begs her not to say that.

Another good character is Templeton, the rat. "Talking with Templeton was not the most interesting occupation in the world," Wilbur finds, "but it was better than nothing." Templeton grudges his help to others, then brags about it, can fold his hands behind his head and sometimes acts like a spoiled child. There is the goose, who can't be surprised by barnyard ways. "It's the old pail-trick, Wilbur. . . . He's trying to lure you into captivity-ivity. He's appealing to your stomach." The goose always repeats everything. "It is my idio-idio-idiosyncrasy."

What the book is about is friendship on earth, affection and protection, adventure and miracle,

life and death, trust and treachery, pleasure and pain, and the passing of time. As a piece of work it is just about perfect, and just about magical in the way it is done. What it all proves—in the words of the minister in the story which he hands down to his congregation after Charlotte writes "Some Pig" in her web—is "that human beings must always be on the watch for the coming of wonders." Dr. Dorian says in another place, "Oh no, I don't understand it. But for that matter I don't understand how a spider learned to spin a web in the first place. When the words appeared, everyone said they were a miracle. But nobody pointed out that the web itself is a miracle." The author will only say, "Charlotte was in a class by herself."

"At-at-at, at the risk of repeating myself," as the goose says, *Charlotte's Web* is an adorable book.

Welty at the Algonquin Hotel prior to receiving a National Book Award on May 1, 1980.

Eudora Welty, Book Review Editor

EUDORA WELTY SPENT THE SUMMER of 1944 working at the Book Review at the invitation of its editor Robert Van Gelder, who had admired her first book. Tasked with finding new critics, she recommended an old friend, Nash K. Burger, who went on not only to write for the Book Review but to work there as well. Of Welty's time there, Burger later wrote that "although the only battlefields Eudora had probably ever seen were at Vicksburg and Shiloh, she turned out splendid reviews of World War II battlefield reports from North Africa, Europe and the South Pacific. When a churlish Times Sunday editor suggested that a lady reviewer from the Deep South might not be the most authoritative critic for the accounts of World War II's far-flung campaigns, she switched to a pseudonym, Michael Ravenna."

As Ravenna, she reviewed *Artist at War* by George Biddle, an artist hired by the war department who spent time on the front lines in Tunis and Italy. "In drawing and text Mr. Biddle has honestly tried to omit nothing for us," she wrote. "His equable humor and usually sanguine spirit contribute to the validity of what he tells, as does the use of his diary form, for all this gives a matter-of-fact, believable character to his notations." She added, "The time when he sketched some Italian prisoners only to find that they, from their corner, were sketching him, remarking, "He who laughs best laughs last," is the telling kind of entertainment he finds and passes on to us."

Between 1943 and 1984, Welty wrote 59 book reviews for The New York Times.

Ryunosuke Akutagawa, *Rashomon and Other Stories*

Twenty-five years after Akutagawa's death, the Book Review examined the collection—translated by Takashi Kojima—that inspired Akira Kurosawa's acclaimed 1950 film of the same name.

Akutagawa in the 1920s.

ONE THING IS CERTAIN. AKUTAGAWA DOES not belong to the jade-and-peonies school of Oriental writing. In the spare, textured prose of these six short stories, he brings us cleareyed glimpses of human behavior in the extremities of poverty, stupidity, greed, vanity. If lotus blossoms appear at all, they are firmly rooted in the background vegetation.

A muscular moralist, working in a small framework, Akutagawa believes that Man is a poor thing who almost always reacts badly. A satirical writer with a delicate, Chaplinesque quality (in which illusion and reality are blended in a kind of fairy-tale surrealism), he is drawn first to the fictional possibilities of pretense and hypocrisy. To find a comparison the reader must go to the paintings of his countryman Kuniyoshi, in which the colors are somber, the palette limited, and the detached social comment unmistakable.

Here is storytelling of an unconventional sort, with most of the substance beneath the shining, enameled surface. For some, it will seem too superficial, too artful and "clever." Few will deny the tension or psychological focus of the themes.

Consider the range and play of subjects. "In a Grove," the most explicit and formally plotted of the six, recounts three versions of an incident involving murder, rape and suicide. In the conflicting testimony of the three principals, Akutagawa finds dramatic expression of his views on human deceit, treachery and heartlessness. Less complex but more revealing in its directness, "Kesa and Morito" tells of a man and his mistress groveling helplessly in the ashes of dead romance. He has agreed to murder the innocent husband while she secretly plans to use the crime as the key to her own redemption.

One wonders whether Akutagawa, misanthrope that he must have been, would be entirely happy to know that his stories provide special pleasure 25 years later. —*James Kelly*

1946–1971

169

De Beauvoir at Les Deux Magots in Paris, circa 1944.

Simone de Beauvoir, *The Second Sex*

This foundational feminist text, which influenced and inspired many voices of the women's movement, was originally published in France in 1949 and was translated into English a few years later by H. M. Parshley. Our reviewer—a man—found it to be "a truly magnificent book, even if sometimes irritating to a mere male."

"ONE WONDERS IF WOMEN STILL EXIST, IF they will always exist, whether or not it is desirable that they should, what place they occupy in this world, what their place should be." The questions are radical enough, comprehensive enough, searching enough. And Simone de Beauvoir's answers are subtle and profound. This is no piece of flamboyant journalism and certainly not a petulant defense of her sex. Nor is it merely an extended essay, although it is indeed literature in the grand sense.

Essentially this is a treatise which integrates the most variegated strands of history, philosophy, economics, biology, belles-lettres, sociology and anthropology. I cannot think of a single American scholar, man or woman, who controls such a vast body of knowledge as this French writer.

It is a truly magnificent book, even if sometimes irritating to a mere male. It should be a required companion volume to all who read the forthcoming report of Kinsey and his associates.

For Mlle. de Beauvoir says much about sexuality that is important which we are not likely to get from the Indiana group. Statistical tables of the incidence of various types of sexual acts need to be balanced by the historical depth, philosophical sophistication and exquisite psychological sensibilities of a Simone de Beauvoir.

My reservations are on a host of specific matters and two general issues. Of the former category I can mention only a few by way of example. If one presses some of the author's statements to their logical extremes, it would seem that she wanted and thought it possible that all women should become artists or intellectuals. We know that neither all men nor all women have such potentialities. Nor do they want to have them.

I think that perhaps there is too much about sexuality in *The Second Sex* and relatively little said (though well) about economic, political and social factors. In spite of her careful and precise attention to the facts of biology she seems at times to be saying, "Oh, but women can transcend all this." One is reminded occasionally of the one-line book review of another famous book by a woman. "Does she really know any culture in which the men have the babies?"

This reviewer was left with the conviction that Mlle. de Beauvoir was most reluctant to accept any genuine determination of woman's psyche by her biological nature.

Enough of this cavilling. "The Second Sex" has what Plutarch said of the buildings on the Acropolis: "There is such a certain flourishing freshness in it." It is a threadbare cliché to speak of not doing justice to a book, but in this case I must resort to the cliché, for I have never been so acutely conscious of incomplete justice.
—*Clyde Kluckhohn*

Ray Bradbury,
Fahrenheit 451

The science fiction editor J. Francis McComas was not entirely won over by this dystopian novel, which went on to become Bradbury's most famous work.

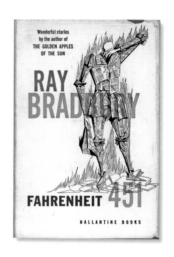

WHILE IT SHOULD BE NOTED THAT THIS volume contains two short fantasies, our chief concern is with the third and title piece. Reading Ray Bradbury's first full-scale novel is an unsettling experience. All his customary hypnotic eloquence, his remarkable virtuosity cannot hide the distressing fact that this is no precisely designed work of fiction but a polemic; moving and convincing at times, this glum portrayal of a distant future makes its appeal exclusively to the emotions.

Mr. Bradbury seems to have developed a virulent hatred for many aspects of present-day culture, namely, such monstrosities as radio, TV, most movies, amateur and professional sports, automobiles and other similar aberrations which he feels debase the bright simplicity of the thinking man's existence. He has projected a grisly world in which citizens seemingly do nothing but watch television screens whose screens cover the walls of the living room; occasionally they careen about the streets in vehicles called "beetles" whose average speed is 100 miles per hour. Naturally, any strolling pedestrian is promptly jailed as a subversive.

Even more despicable (and dangerous to the established order) is the pariah who insists on *reading*. For the time has come when owning books, even the possession of a single volume of nursery rhymes, is a heinous offense. Enforcers of this popular prohibition are the firemen, those one-time guardians of life and property whose sole responsibility is the immediate destruction of any written word.

The intriguing idea might well serve as a foundation on which to build a worst of all possible worlds. And to a certain extent it does seem implausible. Unfortunately, Bradbury goes little further than his basic hypothesis. The rest of his equation is jerry-built. He makes the book's climax an all-out atomic war, without even hinting at the war's causes, or the rival political systems waging it. While there are scenes told with that heart-wrenching detail of which Ray Bradbury is an acknowledged master, the characters remain spare symbols whose imagined lives are curiously inconsistent with established fact.

—*J. Francis McComas*

Other Controversial Novels

BRAVE NEW WORLD, BY ALDOUS HUXLEY 1932

Huxley's portrayal of a "Satirical Model T World" raised eyebrows for its depictions of sexuality, but our reviewer was more concerned with his grim predictions for the future: "If Mr. Huxley is unduly bothered about the impending static world, let him go back to his biology and meditate on the possibility that even in laboratory-created children mutations might be inevitable."

ANIMAL FARM, BY GEORGE ORWELL 1946

Orwell's now-famous allegory of the Russian Revolution and the Soviet Union under Stalin has been banned in many countries, but Arthur M. Schlesinger Jr. offered high praise in the Book Review: "The steadiness and lucidity of Orwell's merciless wit are reminiscent of Anatole France and even of Swift."

LOLITA, BY VLADIMIR NABOKOV 1958

Even before its U.S. publication, Nabokov's novel about a man named Humbert Humbert and his obsession with a young girl had already caused a stir. As Elizabeth Janeway wrote in her review, "*Lolita is* one of those occasional books which arrive swishing behind them a long tail of opinion and reputation which can knock the unwary reader off his feet."

THE BELL JAR, BY SYLVIA PLATH 1971

Of Sylvia Plath's semi-autobiographical work—which would later be banned in places for its profanity and depiction of birth control—the Book Review had nothing but praise: "It is a fine novel, as bitter and remorseless, as her last poems—the kind of book Salinger's Franny might have written about herself 10 years later, if she had spent those 10 years in Hell."

THE SATANIC VERSES, BY SALMAN RUSHDIE 1989

Many Muslim countries banned this novel because of its controversial portrayal of the faith's key figures, but A. G. Mojtabai offered a glowing review: "Rushdie is a storyteller of prodigious powers, able to conjure up whole geographies, causalities, climates, creatures, customs, out of thin air."

AMERICAN PSYCHO, BY BRET EASTON ELLIS 1991

Some people thought this controversial novel about a Harvard-educated yuppie slashing and murdering his way through Manhattan was sharp social satire; others declared it to be nothing but sensationalist garbage.

J. R. R. Tolkien, *The Fellowship of the Ring*

BY W. H. AUDEN

None other than Auden, the poet, reviewed the first volume of Tolkien's Lord of the Rings trilogy.

SEVENTEEN YEARS AGO THERE APPEARED, without any fanfare, a book called *The Hobbit* which, in my opinion, is one of the best children's stories of this century. In *The Fellowship of the Ring,* which is the first volume of a trilogy, J. R. R. Tolkien continues the imaginative history of the imaginary world to which he introduced us in his earlier book but in a manner suited to adults, to those, that is, between the ages of 12 and 70. For anyone who likes the genre to which it belongs, the Heroic Quest, I cannot imagine a more wonderful Christmas present. All Quests are concerned with some numinous Object, the Waters of Life, the Grail, buried treasure etc.; normally this is a good Object which it is the Hero's task to find or to rescue from the Enemy, but the Ring of Mr. Tolkien's story was made by the Enemy and is so dangerous that even the good cannot use it without being corrupted.

The hero, Frodo Baggins, belongs to a race of beings called hobbits, who may be only three feet high, have hairy feet and prefer to live in underground houses, but in their thinking and sensibility resemble very closely those arcadian rustics who inhabit so many British detective stories. For over a thousand years the hobbits have been living a peaceful existence in a fertile district called the Shire, incurious about the world outside. Actually, the latter is rather sinister; towns have fallen into ruins, roads into disrepair, fertile fields have returned to wilderness, wild beasts and evil beings on the prowl, and travel is difficult and dangerous. In addition to the Hobbits, there are Elves who are wise and good, Dwarves who are skillful and good on the whole, and Men, some warriors, some wizards, who are good or bad. The present incarnation of the Enemy is Sauron, Lord of Barad-Dur, the Dark Tower in the Land of Mordor. Assisting him are Orcs, wolves and other horrid creatures and, of course, such men as his power attracts or overawes.

Of any imaginary world the reader demands that it seem real, and the standard of realism demanded today is much stricter than in the time, say, of Malory. Mr. Tolkien is fortunate in possessing an amazing gift for naming and a wonderfully exact eye for description; by the time one has finished his book one knows the histories of Hobbits, Elves, Dwarves and the landscape they inhabit as well as one knows one's own childhood.

If one is to take a tale of this kind seriously, one must feel that, however superficially unlike the world we live in its characters and events may be, it nevertheless holds up the mirror to the only nature we know, our own; in this, too, Mr. Tolkien has succeeded superbly, and what happened in the year of the Shire 1418 in the Third Age of Middle Earth is not only fascinating in A.D. 1954 but also a warning and an inspiration. No fiction I have read in the last five years has given me more joy than *The Fellowship of the Ring.*

Eugene O'Neill, *Long Day's Journey Into Night*

The Nobel-winning playwright requested that *Long Day's Journey Into Night* be released 25 years after his death, but his widow waited only three years before publishing it. The semi-autobiographical play is considered to be one of the finest dramatic works of the 20th century.

AMONG THE PAPERS EUGENE O'NEILL LEFT when he died in 1953 was the manuscript of an autobiography. Not an autobiography in the usual sense, however. For *Long Day's Journey Into Night* is in the form of a play—a true O'Neill tragedy, set in 1912 in the summer home of a theatrical family that is isolated from the community by a kind of ingrown misery and a sense of doom.

The play is solely occupied with the private anguish of an overwrought family held together by incurable afflictions. In the affectionate inscription to his wife, O'Neill characterizes the work as "a play of old sorrow, written in tears and blood," but "with deep pity and understanding and forgiveness for all the haunted Tyrones."

Essentially, *Long Day's Journey Into Night* is not so much a tale as O'Neill's remorseless attempt to tell the blunt truth about his family as a matter of artistic conscience. The truth is ugly. For the father has a peasant-like parsimony about his domestic affairs that embitters the family and alienates the sons. Ensnared in the meshes of a narcotic habit, the mother disintegrates as a human being while the family looks on in helpless horror. The older brother, drunken, crude, cynical, is pure evil. O'Neill does not forgive him for his malice.

But he analyzes the character of his mother and father with a kind of austere understanding that ultimately spares them. Life has worn them down. The father has risen out of grinding poverty to a place in public life that he is incapable of mastering. Fear of returning to poverty poisons his instincts and judgment. And the mother's addiction to narcotics is a vice for which she is not responsible.

Although the character of the younger son is the focal point of the drama, he is the least developed or analyzed. Perhaps O'Neill felt inhibited here. Perhaps he was willing to let the long shelf of his published works stand as his own record. More likely, he felt shy about dramatizing himself or reluctant to take advantage of his authorship of an autobiographical drama to distinguish himself from his family.

Long Day's Journey Into Night is no more devastating than other stories O'Neill told. But it seems more devastating because it is as personal and literal as drama can be. This was the environment, respectably middle class on the surface, obsessed and tortured inside, out of which our most gigantic writer of tragedy emerged.

—*Brooks Atkinson*

James Baldwin, *Notes of a Native Son,* and Langston Hughes, *The Selected Poems of Langston Hughes*

Authors aren't allowed mutual reviews in the Book Review anymore, but in the 1950s there was a moment of kismet. In our February 26, 1956, issue, Hughes considered Baldwin's *Notes of a Native Son,* and on March 29, 1959, Baldwin returned the volley with a review of Hughes's *Selected Poems of Langston Hughes.* The writers were harsh but also perceptive about and alive to each other's creative genius.

Langston Hughes on
Notes of a Native Son

I THINK THAT ONE DEFINITION OF THE great artist might be the creator who projects the biggest dream in terms of the least person. There is something in Cervantes or Shakespeare, Beethoven or Rembrandt or Louis Armstrong that millions can understand. The American native son who signs his name James Baldwin is quite a ways off from fitting such a definition of a great artist in writing, but he is not as far off as many another writer who deals in picture captions of journalese in the hope of capturing and retaining a wide public. James Baldwin writes down to nobody, and he is trying very hard to write up to himself. As an essayist he is thought-provoking, tantalizing, irritating, abusing and amusing. And he uses words as the sea uses waves, to flow and beat, advance and retreat, rise and take a bow in disappearing.

In *Notes of a Native Son,* James Baldwin surveys in pungent commentary certain phases of the contemporary scene as they relate to the citizenry of the United States, particularly Negroes. Harlem, the protest novel, bigoted religion, the Negro press and the student milieu of Paris are all examined in black and white, with alternate shutters clicking, for hours of reading interest. When the young man who wrote this book comes to a

---

1956 — When Grace Metalious's racy novel, *Peyton Place,* is published, the Book Review headlines its assessment "Small Town Peep Show."

1956 — Sylvia Plath and Ted Hughes meet at a party in Cambridge, England.

1956 — The 38-year-old senator from Massachusetts, John F. Kennedy—whose *Profiles in Courage* tops the best-seller list—hosts the National Book Awards.

Baldwin at the Plaza Hotel on June 27, 1973.

point where he can look at life purely as himself, and for himself, the color of his skin mattering not at all, when, as in his own words, he finds "his birthright as a man no less than his birthright as a black man," America and the world might as well have a major contemporary commentator.

Few American writers handle words more effectively in the essay form than James Baldwin. To my way of thinking, he is much better at provoking thought in the essay than he is arousing emotion in fiction. I much prefer *Notes of a Native Son* to his novel, *Go Tell It on the Mountain*, where the surface excellence and poetry of his writing did not seem to me to suit the earthiness of his subject matter. In his essays, words and material suit each other. The thought becomes poetry, and the poetry illuminates the thought.

That Baldwin's viewpoints are half American, half Afro-American, incompletely fused, is a hurdle which Baldwin himself realizes he still has to surmount. When he does, there will be a straight-from-the-shoulder writer, writing about the troubled problems of this troubled earth with an illuminating intensity that should influence for the better all who ponder on the things books say.

1946–1971

Hughes in 1958.

James Baldwin on
The Selected Poems of Langston Hughes

EVERY TIME I READ LANGSTON HUGHES I AM amazed all over again by his genuine gifts—and depressed that he has done so little with them. A real discussion of his work demands more space than I have here, but this book contains a great deal which a more disciplined poet would have thrown into the waste-basket (almost all of the last section, for example).

There are the poems which almost succeed but which do not succeed, poems which take refuge, finally, in a fake simplicity in order to avoid the very difficult simplicity of the experience! And one sometimes has the impression, as in a poem like "Third Degree"—which is about the beating up of a Negro boy in a police station—that Hughes has had to hold the experience outside him in order to write at all. And certainly this is understandable. Nevertheless, the poetic trick, so to speak, is to be within the experience and outside it at the same time—and the poem fails.

I do not like all of "The Weary Blues," which copies, rather than exploits, the cadence of the blues, but it comes to a remarkable end. And I am also very fond of "Island," which begins "Wave of sorrow/Do not drown me now."

Hughes, in his sermons, blues and prayers, has working for him the power and the beat of Negro speech and Negro music. Negro speech is vivid largely because it is private. It is a kind of emotional shorthand—or sleight-of-hand—by means of which Negroes express, not only their relationship to each other, but their judgment of the white world. And, as the white world takes over this vocabulary—without the faintest notion of what it really means—the vocabulary is forced to change. The same thing is true of Negro music, which has had to become more and more complex in order to continue to express any of the private or collective experience.

Hughes knows the bitter truth behind these hieroglyphics: what they are designed to protect, what they are designed to convey. But he has not forced them into the realm of art where their meaning would become clear and overwhelming. "Hey, pop!/ Re-bop!/ Mop!" conveys much more on Lenox Avenue than it does in this book, which is not the way it ought to be.

Hughes is an American Negro poet and has no choice but to be acutely aware of it. He is not the first American Negro to find the war between his social and artistic responsibilities all but irreconcilable.

1957 — Gabriel García Márquez encounters his idol Ernest Hemingway on a Paris street. Decades later he will write an essay about it for the Book Review.

1957 — Dorothy Parker reviews S. J. Perelman's *The Road to Miltown*.

1957 — Publisher, poet and bookseller Lawrence Ferlinghetti is arrested for publishing and selling Allen Ginsberg's *Howl and Other Poems,* which had been seized by custom officials for obscenity.

Shirley Jackson, *The Haunting of Hill House*

Nearly 60 years after it was first published, the novelist Neil Gaiman told the Book Review that this tale of Gothic horror was the scariest book he'd ever read: "A maleficent house, real human protagonists, everything half-seen or happening in the dark. It scared me as a teenager and it haunts me still."

THIS REVIEW OF SHIRLEY JACKSON'S NEW novel properly begins with the confession that I am not sure of anything about it except its almost unflagging interest. The obliqueness, the tangential dartings of Miss Jackson's uniquely imaginative mind occasionally conflict with the forward movement of her narrative, but they do not undo her spell. In *The Haunting of Hill House* she has produced caviar for connoisseurs of the cryptic, the bizarre, the eerie, guiding us along the frontiers between commonplace reality and some strange "absolute reality" of her own.

Hill House stands near Hillsdale in a region that smacks of back-country New England. The house has an evil reputation and has long been shunned. Dr. Montague, investigator of psychic phenomena, wishes to live in it for a summer with three companions: Luke, a nephew of the owner, and two young women, Eleanor and Theodora.

They are strangers to each other. The invitations to the two girls had come because Eleanor as a child had been close to poltergeist phenomena and Theodora has a record of marked extrasensory perception.

Eleanor is the focal figure of the book. The events in which the house asserts its peculiar properties increasingly close upon and isolate her. She feels, with horror, that "it knows my name." Meantime a disquieting doubt in sown in the reader's mind. Is Eleanor at Hill House or not? To compound the riddle, in whatever sense she is there at all, it seems certain that she stays there. If this perplexes you, it is by intent. The story must not be told here. It's enough to say that at certain moments, quietly, in quick, subtle transitions of tone, Miss Jackson can summon up stark terror, make your blood chill and your scalp prickle.

Who can understand Hill House? The walls are imperceptibly out of plumb, the halls are labyrinthine, there is an inexplicable cold area at its nursery door. Its enigma is unpenetrated and even what happens there is shadowy. Dr. Montague says: "The concept of certain houses as unclean or forbidden—perhaps sacred—is as old as the mind of man. Hill House, whatever the cause, has been unfit for human habitation for upwards of 20 years." It is "disturbed, perhaps. Leprous. Sick. Any of the popular euphemisms for insanity; a deranged house is a pretty conceit."

With her "conceit" of Hill House, whether pretty be the word for it or not, Shirley Jackson proves again that she is the finest master currently practicing in the genre of the cryptic, haunted tale. To all the classic paraphernalia of the spook story, she adds a touch of Freud to make the whole world kin. —*Edmund Fuller*

"It's enough to say that at certain moments,
quietly, in quick, subtle transitions of tone,
Miss Jackson can summon up stark terror,
make your blood chill and your scalp prickle."

Jackson in 1956.

Harper Lee, *To Kill a Mockingbird*

The story of Scout Finch and her growing understanding of racial injustice was an instant success at the time of its publication. Until 2015, when an earlier version of the novel, *Go Set a Watchman,* was released, it was Lee's only published book.

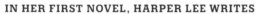

IN HER FIRST NOVEL, HARPER LEE WRITES with gentle affection, rich humor and deep understanding of small-town family life in Alabama. The setting is Maycomb, a one-taxi village, "awkwardly inland," where "a day was 24 hours long but seemed longer," and nobody hurried because there was nowhere to go; where a snowstorm was a big event, and in the scorching summer heat ladies "bathed before noon, after their three o'clock naps, and by nightfall were like soft tea-cakes with frostings of sweat and sweet talcum."

It is an easy-going but narrow-minded community, whose foot-washing Baptists feel perfectly free to denounce Miss Maudie Atkinson, a passionate garden-lover, because "anything that's pleasure is a sin." At the other extreme stand men like Atticus Finch, a highly esteemed lawyer and the embodiment of fearless integrity, magnanimity and common sense. In the novel's chief public event, he defends a worthy young Negro falsely accused of raping a girl from the town's most disreputable white family.

Maycomb has its share of eccentrics and evil-doers, but Miss Lee has not tried to satisfy the current lust for morbid tales of Southern depravity. Her central characters, the Finches, are a thoroughly decent and happy family. Besides Atticus, a widower of 50, there are two engaging children: Jean Marie, a tomboy better known as Scout, and Jeremy, or Jem, four years her senior. When the novel ends, Scout is only 8; but she is a lively lass, into everything. In the episodes that mold Scout's character, Miss Lee develops the importance of developing an open, unprejudiced, well-furnished mind of one's own.

The praise Miss Lee deserves must be qualified somewhat by noting that oftentimes Scout's expository style has a processed, homogenized, impersonal flatness quite out of keeping with the narrator's gay, impulsive approach to life in youth. Also, some of the scenes suggest that Miss Lee is cocking at least one eye toward Hollywood. Moviegoing readers will be able to cast most of the roles very quickly, but it is no disparagement of Miss Lee's winning book to say that it could be the basis for an excellent film. —*Frank Lyell*

Joseph Heller, *Catch-22*

It may be one of the most significant novels of the 20th century, but the Book Review was not a fan of *Catch-22*.

CATCH-22 **HAS MUCH PASSION, COMIC AND** fervent, but it gasps for want of craft and sensibility. A portrait gallery, a collection of anecdotes, some of them wonderful, a parade of scenes, some of them finely assembled, a series of descriptions, yes, but the book is no novel. One can say that it is much too long because its material—the cavortings and miseries of an American bomber squadron stationed in late World War II Italy—is repetitive and monotonous. Or one can say that it is too short because none of its many interesting characters and actions is given enough play to become a controlling interest. Its author, Joseph Heller, is like a brilliant painter who decides to throw all the ideas in his sketchbooks onto one canvas, relying on their charm and shock to compensate for the lack of design.

If *Catch-22* were intended as a commentary novel, such sideswiping of character and action might be taken care of by thematic control. It fails here because half its incidents are farcical and fantastic. The book is an emotional hodgepodge; no mood is sustained long enough to register for more than a chapter.

As satire *Catch-22* makes too many formal concessions to the standard novels of our day. There is a certain amount of progress: The decent get killed off, the self-seekers prosper, and there is even a last minute turnabout as the war draws to an end. One feels the author should have gone all the way and burlesqued not only the passions and incidents of war, but the traditions of representing them as well. It might have saved him from some of the emotional pretzels which twist the sharpness of his talent. —*Richard G. Stern*

"Joseph Heller is like a brilliant painter who decides to throw all the ideas in his sketchbooks onto one canvas."

1958
The Soviet authorities force Boris Pasternak to decline the Nobel Prize for Literature.

1961
The Book Review is not a fan of *The Carpetbaggers,* by Harold Robbins, saying it was "not quite proper to have printed" it between covers of a book: "It should have been inscribed on the walls of a public lavatory."

1962
On May 19, William Faulkner R.S.V.P.'s no to a White House dinner for Nobel laureates, saying, "That's a long way to go just to eat."

1946–1971

Joseph Heller at a rehearsal of his play
We Bombed in New Haven in 1968.

Turn On, Tune In, Read a Book

Other literary counterculture hits.

ON THE ROAD,
BY JACK KEROUAC
1957

Though David Dempsey wrote in his review that Kerouac's novel was an "affectionate lark" and "enormously readable," he also added that "one reads it in the same mood that they might visit a sideshow—the freaks are fascinating although they are hardly part of our lives."

ONE FLEW OVER THE
CUCKOO'S NEST,
BY KEN KESEY
1962

"What Mr. Kesey has done in his unusual novel is to transform the plight of a ward of inmates in a mental institution into a glittering parable of good and evil."

THE ELECTRIC KOOL-AID
ACID TEST,
BY TOM WOLFE
1968

Hell's Angels, Timothy Leary, the Grateful Dead and Allen Ginsberg all have cameos in Wolfe's acid-soaked "celebration of psychedelia," a nonfiction account of Ken Kesey and the Merry Pranksters that, our reviewer said, "is to the hippie movement what Norman Mailer's *The Armies of the Night* was to the Vietnam protest movement."

SLAUGHTERHOUSE-FIVE,
BY KURT VONNEGUT
1969

Vonnegut's epic about the World War II firebombing of Dresden—which he survived as a prisoner of war—was "extraordinary," the Book Review said, adding, "The best writers of our time have been telling us with all their imaginative power that our problems are not in our institutions but in ourselves."

FEAR AND LOATHING IN LAS VEGAS,
BY HUNTER S. THOMPSON
1971

Calling it "by far the best book yet written on the decade of dope gone by," our critic said that its "highest art is to be the drug it is about, whether chemical or political. To read it is to swim through the highs and lows of the smokes and fluids that shatter the mind."

STEAL THIS BOOK,
BY ABBIE HOFFMAN
1971

"If you are a teenage runaway on the lam, or a 50-year-old executive finally gone bananas and about to drop out, then what you should probably read is *Steal This Book* . . . a hip Boy Scout handbook, a manual for survival in the counterculture."

Rachel Carson, *Silent Spring*

Carson's investigation into the use of pesticides awakened readers to their insidious and destructive effects and helped spur the modern environmental movement.

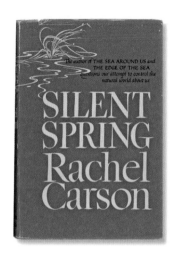

POISONING PEOPLE IS WRONG. YET, FOR THE sake of "controlling" all kinds of insects, fungi and weed plants, people today are being poisoned on a scale that the infamous Borgias never dreamed of. Cancer-inducing chemicals remain as residues in virtually everything we eat or drink. A continuation of present programs that use poisonous chemicals will soon exterminate much of our wildlife and man as well. So claims Rachel Carson in her provocative new book, *Silent Spring.*

Her book is a cry to the reading public to help curb private and public programs which by use of poisons will end by destroying life on earth.

Know the facts and do something about the situation, she urges. To make sure that the facts are known, she recounts them and documents them with 55 pages of references. She intends to shock and hopes for action. She fears the insidious poisons, spread as sprays and dust or put in foods, far more than the radioactive debris from a nuclear war. Miss Carson, with the fervor of an Ezekiel, is trying to save nature and mankind from chemical biocides.

Her account is dismal. It is not hopeless—at least not yet. But she demands a quick change in "our distorted sense of proportion." How can intelligent beings seek to control a few unwanted species by a method that contaminates the entire environment and brings the threat of disease and death even to our own kind? "For the first time in the history of the world," she writes, "every human being is now subjected to contact with dangerous chemicals from the moment of conception until death."

Albert Schweitzer has said, "Man can hardly recognize the devils of his own creation." Yet *Silent Spring* will remind some people that a few years ago they went without cranberry sauce at Thanksgiving rather than risk eating berries contaminated with a cancer-inducing chemical used improperly by some growers as a weed-killer in the cranberry bogs.

"If the Bill of Rights contains no guarantee that a citizen shall be secure against lethal poisons distributed either by private individuals or by public officials, it is surely only because our forefathers, despite their considerable wisdom and foresights, could conceive of no such problem," she says. *—Lorus and Margery Milne*

The New York Times Book Review

SEPTEMBER 23, 1962 · © 1962, by The New York Times Company · SECTION 7

THERE'S POISON ALL AROUND US NOW

SILENT SPRING. By Rachel Carson. Drawings by Lois and Louis Darling. 368 pp. Boston: Houghton Mifflin Company. $5.

By LORUS and MARGERY MILNE

The Dangers in the Use of Pesticides Are Vividly Pictured by Rachel Carson

POISONING people is wrong. Yet, for the sake of "controlling" all kinds of insects, fungi and weed plants, people today are being poisoned on a scale that the infamous Borgias never dreamed of. Cancer-inducing chemicals remain as residues in virtually everything we eat or drink. A continuation of present programs that use poisonous chemicals will soon exterminate much of our wild life and man as well. So claims Rachel Carson in her provocative new book, "Silent Spring."

"Silent Spring" is similar in only one regard to Miss Carson's earlier books ("Under the Sea Wind," "The Sea Around Us," "The Edge of the Sea"): in it she deals once more, in an accurate, yet popularly written narrative, with the relation of life to environment. Her book is a cry to the reading public to help curb private and public programs which by use of poisons will end by destroying life on earth.

Know the facts and do something about the situation, she urges. To make sure that the facts are known, she recounts them and documents them with 55 pages of references. She intends to shock and hopes for action. She fears the insidious poisons, spread as sprays and dust or put in foods, far more than the radioactive debris from a nuclear war. Miss Carson, with the fervor of an Ezekiel, is trying to save nature and mankind from chemical biocides that John H. Baker (then President of the National Audubon Society) identified in 1958 as "The greatest threat to life on earth."

HER account of the present is dismal. It is not hopeless—at least not yet. But she demands a quick change in "our distorted sense of proportion." How can intelligent beings seek to control a few unwanted species by a method that contaminates the entire environment and brings the threat of disease and death even to our own kind? "For the first time in the history of the world," she writes, "every human being is now subjected to contact with dangerous chemicals from the moment of conception until death. * * * These chemicals are now stored in the bodies of the vast majority of human beings, regardless of age. They occur in the mother's milk, and probably in the tissues of the unborn child."

Albert Schweitzer has said, "Man can hardly even recognize the devils of his own creation." Yet "Silent

Mr. and Mrs. Milne, educators and biologists, are authors of "The Senses of Animals and Men," "The Balance of Nature" and other books.

Painting by Alex Colville. Collection Art Gallery of Toronto. Courtesy Robert Isaacson Gallery.
"The present is dismal but not hopeless."

Spring" will remind some people that a few years ago they went without cranberry sauce at Thanksgiving rather than risk eating berries contaminated with a cancer-inducing chemical used improperly by some growers as a weed-killer in the cranberry bogs. A few others may recall that tax money was paid not only to growers of cranberries, but also (a year or so earlier) to poultry raisers whose chickens retained dangerous amounts of a chemical included in poultry feed upon Government recommendation and had to be condemned.

Miss Carson adds many other instances to the list, and points to programs that cost many millions of tax dollars, yet were doomed at the outset to failure. She gives details about the gypsy-moth campaigns that killed fish, crabs and birds as well as some gypsy moths; about the fire-ant program that killed cows, wiped out pheasants, but not fire ants; and dozens of others that led to *more* of the pest (or of new pests) by destroying the natural means of control.

Miss Carson gives most of her attention to insecticides, herbicides and fungicides, since these are the most dangerous poisons. She shows the futility of relying on them or any new substitutes offered to counteract the swift evolution of immunity to chemical control shown by more and more insects and fungus diseases. She quotes an authority on cancer, Dr. W. C. Hueper of the National Cancer Institute, who has given "DDT the definite rating of a 'chemical carcinogen'"—a cancer inducer. She notes that "storage of DDT [in the body] begins with the smallest conceivable intake of the chemical (which is present as residues on most foodstuffs) and continues until quite high levels are reached. The fatty storage depots act as biological magnifiers, so that an intake of as little as one-tenth of 1 part per million in the diet results in storage of about 10 to 15 parts per million, an increase of one hundredfold or more. * * * In animal experiments, 3 parts per million has been found to inhibit an essential enzyme in heart muscle; only 5 parts per million has brought about necrosis or disintegration of liver cells; only 2.5 parts per million of the closely related chemicals dieldrin and chlordane did the same." Other modern insecticides are still more deadly. Nor did the discovery of their poisonous character "come by chance: insects were widely used [during World War II] to test chemicals as agents of death for man."

IN some of the chapters, Miss Carson does approve of alternatives to the widespread use of poisonous chemicals. She points to the successful controlling of scale insects with ladybird beetles, and Japanese beetles with the "milky disease." So often, harmful species, new to a given area, have ceased to be much of a problem as soon as their natural enemies or their equivalents appear or are introduced. The natural struggle for survival can then keep the numbers of the pests at a fairly low level. This approach, as Miss Carson emphasizes, rarely creates new pests, whereas extermination campaigns often do so.

Those who grow and store food and other products that can be hurt by pests will surely accuse "Silent Spring" of telling only part of the story. They will claim that today efficiency in raising and distributing food and wood depend upon the use of poisons. The traces of chemical compounds left in and on these materials are the price we must pay for such efficiency. If biological control methods were relied upon or hand labor required, the yield would be smaller and the market price higher. They might ask, "Do you want wormy apples and buggy flour, or traces of pesticides that by themselves have not yet been proved harmful?"

Miss Carson can also count on vociferous rebuttal (Continued on Page 26)

Books That Changed
How We Lived

ETIQUETTE IN SOCIETY, IN BUSINESS, IN POLITICS, AND AT HOME,
BY EMILY POST
1922

Post wrote her guide to manners, she told The Times, after "it became my mission to tell people who did not know the rules what they were."

THE COMMONSENSE BOOK OF BABY AND CHILD CARE,
BY DR. BENJAMIN SPOCK
1946

By the time Spock died in 1998, his "homey handbook on child care," which coached parents to trust their instincts, had become one of the best-selling books of all time.

THE DEATH AND LIFE OF GREAT AMERICAN CITIES,
BY JANE JACOBS
1961

In her "crisp, pungent and engaging book," Jacobs—who believed endless blocks of high-rise housing dehumanized big cities—offered a blueprint to fix them.

THE FEMININE MYSTIQUE,
BY BETTY FRIEDAN
1963

Challenging the widely accepted notion that a woman's sole possible fulfillment was in the role of house-wife, Friedan's critique drew legions of white middle-class women to the feminist movement.

UNSAFE AT ANY SPEED,
BY RALPH NADER
1965

The Book Review called this a "ringing indictment" of the auto industry and its "laxity over minimum safety standards and its collusion in preventing safety legislation."

ON DEATH AND DYING,
BY ELISABETH KÜBLER-ROSS
1969

This best-seller introduced the "five stages of grief" and sparked a public investment in dignified end-of-life care. "Too often," she said in an interview with The Times, "modern medical institutions crush a patient's dignity even while trying to save his life."

DIET FOR A SMALL PLANET,
BY FRANCES MOORE LAPPE
1971

Lappe's ethical concerns about eating meat—and about the environmental damage caused by animal farming—turned her book into a best-seller. A few years after it came out, The Times wrote that "it remains the definitive work on the modern scientific underpinnings of vegetarianism."

Hannah Arendt, *Eichmann in Jerusalem*

This report on the trial of Adolf Eichmann by the German-born political theorist Hannah Arendt remains controversial to this day, yet the concept it introduced—"the banality of evil"—is widely recognized as an influential contribution to ethical and political thought.

ADOLF EICHMANN, ONE OF HITLER'S principal instruments in the Nazi program to exterminate the Jews of Europe, was hanged on May 31, 1962, but in this book he is very much alive. We see him energetically striding from page to page, we observe him in shining, black-leather boots stamping into governmental, military and diplomatic offices in all parts of Europe. We follow him, his ornamented cap at a sharp angle, storming into hotels, concentration camps, railroad trains, human abattoirs and emerging with neither a dirty spot on his immaculate uniform, nor—according to Eichmann, with Hannah Arendt apparently supporting his boast—a dirty spot on his conscience.

That is what this book is principally about: Adolf Eichmann's conscience. The author covered the trial of Eichmann in Jerusalem for *The New Yorker,* and the series of articles in that magazine, which form the bulk of this book, stirred controversy as a strong wind agitates the waters of a lake. The book, which follows the articles as a gale succeeds a rising wind, will probably evoke a great deal of pensive reflection; Eichmann was no ordinary criminal, and his deeds were not the subject of the ordinary court of assizes.

Miss Arendt devotes considerable space to Eichmann's conscience and informs us that one of Eichmann's points in his own defense was "that there were no voices from the outside to arouse his conscience." How abysmally asleep is a conscience when it must be aroused to be told there is something morally wrong about pressing candy upon a little boy to induce him to enter a gas chamber of death?

The author believes that Eichmann was misjudged in Jerusalem and quotes, with astounding credulity, his statement: "I myself had no hatred for the Jews." Sympathizing with Eichmann, she laments, "Alas, nobody believed him." Should anyone be blamed for lifting an eyebrow to the suggestion that Eichmann loved the Jews? At the end of the war he exclaimed: "I shall laugh when I jump into the grave, because of the feeling that I killed five million Jews. This gives me a lot of satisfaction and pleasure."

1962
Muriel Spark publishes *The Prime of Miss Jean Brodie,* which the Book Review says is written "with cool exactness . . . and compassionate wit."

1963
In a story about women authors, the Book Review notes that "the hand that rocks the cradle also has a certain competence in rocking the typewriter."

1964
When *Candy* is published in the United States, the Book Review says that "Terry Southern holds nothing sacred, not even pornography."

1946–1971

Arendt at the New School in 1969.

"The disparity between what Miss Arendt states, and what the ascertained facts are, occurs with such disturbing frequency in her book that it can hardly be accepted as an authoritative historical work."

If, in recalling the period, one could shut one's eyes to the scenes of brutal massacre and stop one's ears to the screams of horror-stricken women and terrorized children as they saw the tornado of death sweeping toward them, one could almost assume that in some parts of the book the author is being whimsical. For instance, she says that Eichmann was a Zionist and helped Jews to get to Palestine. The facts, as set forth in the judgment handed down by the District Court of Jerusalem, are entirely to the contrary. As far back as November, 1937, after an espionage trip into the Middle East he reported that the plan for emigration of Jews to Palestine "was out of the question," it being "the policy of the Reich to avoid the creation of an independent Jewish State in Palestine."

Miss Arendt says that the only time Eichmann gave an "order to kill" was in the autumn of 1941 when he "proposed killing by shooting" of 8,000 Serbian Jews. This is quibbling. While heading the "Eichmann Special Operation Unit" in Hungary, he shipped, in less than two months, 434,351 Jews in 147 trains of sealed freight cars to Auschwitz where the gas chambers had to work at full capacity to kill the human cargoes. These 434,351 Jews died as the result of Eichmann's orders as much as if he had personally directed the gassing and the cremating crews.

The disparity between what Miss Arendt states, and what the ascertained facts are, occurs with such disturbing frequency in her book that it can hardly be accepted as an authoritative historical work. She says Eichmann never "actually attended a mass execution by shooting" or watched a "gassing process." Eichmann himself spoke of attending a mass shooting and described seeing "marksmen . . . shooting into the pit." The pit was "full of corpses." The Court, in its final judgment, described Eichmann at Treblinka, one of the death camps in the East, watching "the naked Jews being led to the gas chambers along paths surrounded by barbed wire."

According to Miss Arendt, Eichmann never saw "the killing installations" at Auschwitz, although she admits he went to this charnel house "repeatedly." Her observation is like saying that one repeatedly sojourned at Niagara Falls but never noticed the falling water. Eichmann dispatched over two million Jews into the Auschwitz "destruction machinery" of which, Miss Arendt admits, he saw "enough to be fully informed."

Miss Arendt says that Eichmann, "to a truly extraordinary degree," received the "cooperation" of the Jews in their own destruction. This astonishing conclusion is predicated on statements of others that some Jewish leaders dealt with Eichmann, and that, in certain instances, Jews took part in police work. The fact that Eichmann with threats of death coerced occasional Quislings and Lavals into "cooperation" only adds to the horror of his crimes. —*Michael A. Musmanno*

1964 ———————————————————
Gloria Vanderbilt reviews Louise Fitzhugh's first novel, *Harriet the Spy.*

1964 ———————————————————
Hubert Selby Jr.'s *Last Exit to Brooklyn* is published. "Simply repulsive," the Book Review opines.

1966 ———————————————————→
The Book Review says that readers who purchase Pauline Réage's *Story of O* looking for "the titillation it affords will pay again in another coin before they put the book down."

1946–1971

SUMMER READING THROUGH TIME

JUNE 25, 1898

JUNE 11, 1911

MAY 19, 1918

JUNE 19, 1949

JUNE 11, 1950

JUNE 6, 1954

JUNE 7, 1964

JUNE 2, 1968

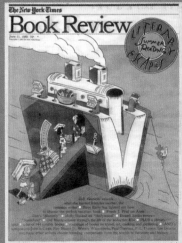

The World in Vogue, compiled by the Viking Press and Vogue

BY DAWN POWELL

Dawn Powell, a satirical novelist, playwright and essayist, was largely forgotten after her death in 1965. She penned only one book review for The Times—but what a review!

CALL IT ANTHOLOGY, CALL IT MAGAZINE history, call it family album, this mighty work is better classified as an architectural wonder along with the Triborough Bridge, the Holland Tunnel, the Thruways. Supplied with the foundation by 70 years' worth of *Vogue,* editors Jessica Daves, Alexander Liberman, Bryan Holme and Katharine Tweed have constructed a bridge over the peak spots in the "arts, society, literature, theatre, fashion, sports and world affairs of these seven momentous decades."

If you have regarded *Vogue* strictly as an ephemeral fashion magazine where strange wondrous creatures parade clothes never to be seen on human hide, where the word "everyone" does not mean you or me or even the *Vogue* reporter but a glittering shadow, a Tinker Bell glimpsed over your shoulder, then you are bound to be astonished at the solid values that have survived the editorial sieve. Fashions, in the garment sense, have been heaved into the closet except for documentary reports on the making of fashion. The editors, instead, wish to present a chronicle of changing customs, and with their photographs, art reproductions, key pieces on passing fads, they do perform an invaluable service.

Say this for *Vogue:* It has never surrendered the honest satisfactions of snobbery; it has never conceded that the velvet rope is pure licorice and the Diners' Card a guarantee of social success. Its function has always been solemnly medicinal—to provide delicious discontent. Here is what other people have and you haven't; here is where some go but never you. Here is the lovely land of never, and you may dream of it, but that's all—there is no play-now-pay-later way to visit it.

The best piece of writing is Frank Crowninshield's report of "Ten Thousand Nights in a Dinner Coat." He declared that the smart thing, under Mrs. William Astor and Ward McAllister's reign, was "to be dull, to be opulent, to be stuffed, to be bored."

If you had fun, then it was clear you weren't "in." Then Mrs. Stuyvesant Fish took over the reins, and laughter became smart; rules were broken; pranks were admired. I have a conviction that no matter how much Mrs. Fish herself loved laughter, it could never replace the solid, feather-bed anaesthesia of boredom and boring, the birthright of the Four Hundred.

Ballooning in the 90s, or skirt dancing, the flying machine, the San Francisco earthquake, the Armory Show, lady clam-diggers in bustles, hats and high button shoes—these are the bright glimpses along *Vogue*'s bridge of memory. If you missed the reality and never did "what everyone is doing," then remember that *Vogue*'s bridge has never pretended to be more than the Rainbow.

Tom Wolfe, *The Kandy-Kolored Tangerine-Flake Streamline Baby*

BY KURT VONNEGUT

Wolfe burst onto the literary scene with this zeitgeisty collection of essays that captured the people and pop culture of the early 1960s.

NOTE TO THE PEOPLE OF MEDICINE HAT, Alberta, who may not know it: Tom Wolfe is the most exciting—or, at least, the most jangling—journalist to appear in some time. He writes mainly for *Esquire* and *The Herald Tribune.* Everybody talks about him. He is no shrinking violet, neither is he a gentleman. He is a superb reporter who hates the East and the looks of old people. He is a dandy and a reverse snob.

The temptation when reviewing his works, of course, is to imitate him cunningly. Holy animals! Sebaceous sleepers! Oxymorons and serpentae carminael! Tabescent! Infarcted! Stretchpants netherworld! Schlock! A parodist might get the words right, but never the bitchy melody. Interestingly: the most tender piece in this collection depends upon a poem by Kipling for depth, and has G. Huntington Hartford 2d. for its hero.

The frightful, public gastrectomies Wolfe performed on Norman Mailer and William Shawn so recently, without anesthetics or rubber gloves, came too late for this book, will no doubt lead off the next. What we have here are 22 of the exercises that built up to such violence: Cassius Clay, Las Vegas, Baby Jane Holzer, automobile collisions as entertainment, automobile customizing, automobile racing, nannies, Howard Rushmore, weak, dumb, rich divorcées, fag interior decorators, and on and on. Fame has come quickly for Wolfe, and should have, for he is almost certainly the fastest brilliant writer around. Will he blow up? Some people must hope so. Who is a complete stranger to envy and Schadenfreude?

Wolfe comes on like a barbarian (as Mark Twain did), like a sixth Beatle (Murray the K being the fifth), but he is entitled to call himself "Doctor Wolfe," if he wants to. He has a Ph.D. in American studies from Yale, and he knows everything. I do not mean he thinks he knows everything. He knows all the stuff that Arthur Schlesinger Jr. knows, keeps picking up brand new, ultra-contemporary stuff that nobody else knows, and arrives at zonky conclusions couched

---

1968 ——————————
Charlayne Hunter, who reviews Eldridge Cleaver's *Soul on Ice,* writes that "it is not a book about the prison life of a black man" but "about the imprisonment of men's souls by society."

1969 ——————————
Isaac Asimov publishes his 100th book, titled, appropriately enough, *Opus 100.*

1969 —————————→
N. Scott Momaday becomes the first Native American to win a Pulitzer, with his novel *House Made of Dawn.*

1946–1971

Wolfe on 58th Street, New York City, on July 30, 1968.

in scholarly terms. I wish he had headed the Warren Commission. We might then have caught a glimpse of our nation.

He is also loaded with facile junk, as all personal journalists have to be—otherwise, how can they write so amusingly and fast? His language is admired, but a Wolfe chrestomathy would drive one nuts with repetitions, with glissandi and tin drummings that don't help much. The words "tabescent" and "infarcted" appear again and again, and, upon investigation, turn out to be not especially useful or piquant. Young breasts ("Mary Poppins") point upward again and again like anti aircraft batteries, and women's eyes are very often like decals, and transistors are very often plugged into skulls, and feet very often wear winkle-picker shoes.

Then again, America is like that. And maybe the only sort of person who can tell us the truth about it any more is a Ph.D. who barks and struts himself like Murray the K, the most offensive of all disk jockeys, while feeding us information. Advanced persons in religion have been trying this approach for some time. Who can complain if journalists follow?

Wolfe is a Southerner, and he is electric with regional animosity. He feels buoyant in the South and Far West, speaks loathingly of "the big amoeba god of Anglo-European sophistication that gets you in the East." There are some unpleasant pen-and-ink drawings he has made of New York in this book, by the way, caricatured Ashcan School. No girls are pretty, and nobody smiles. (The best drawing by Wolfe that I have seen so far is a Beerbohmish self-portrait that appeared in *Newsweek* a while back. The artist sees himself as an Edwardian fop with a plowboy's three-by-eight wrists, and loves him.)

"The frightful, public gastrectomies Wolfe performed on Norman Mailer and William Shawn so recently, without anesthetics or rubber gloves, came too late for this book."

His particular delight in his New York pieces is to show up the art establishment and its friends as intellectual and moral tinhorns. It's a mild, funny little establishment to bop so hard. For all Wolfe's passion and exclamation points, most of the people he bops are essentially harmless. They make the mistake of having something like an amusing time in New York, or of being no longer young anywhere. There is a built-in joke, I know: Wolfe has proved to himself and to some others that teen-age culture is becoming dominant, so he casts himself as a teen-ager, a razzer of old folks and old establishments, the better to describe that culture. But he sounds hooked to me.

I have been trying to identify the key that winds up his mainspring so tight, and, though he is 33 years of age, I think this might be it: He is, like all teen-agers, terribly embarrassed or annoyed by almost anything an American grownup not associated with automobiles may wear or say or do.

Verdict: Excellent book by a genius who will do anything to get attention.

Other Great Reviews
by Kurt Vonnegut

THE RANDOM HOUSE DICTIONARY OF THE ENGLISH LANGUAGE
1966

"I wonder now what Ernest Hemingway's dictionary looked like, since he got along so well with dinky words that everybody can spell and truly understand."

PRIZE STORIES 1966: THE O. HENRY AWARDS
1966

"Still and all, the book might as well be dated 1937 as 1966. The people who have written these stories so well are gentlefolk, and the best American short-story writers, the ones most violently responsive to their times, have always been barbarians."

ANY GOD WILL DO, BY RICHARD CONDON
1966

"The book is an honorable failure—a failure because it is boring. Condon has not solved a technical problem which may well be insoluble: how to write interestingly about a man who is truly empty. . . . Too bad."

THE BOSS, BY GOFFREDO PARISE
1966

"Years ago, when I worked as a public-relations man for General Electric, I was rated by three of my co-workers every six months— anonymously. Then I had to go over the comments with my boss, promising to improve. One comment about myself that sticks in my mind for some reason: 'No personality.' This may be why I am now being sent so many novels about depersonalized people for comment and review."

A TIME TO DIE, BY TOM WICKER
1975

"The book is designed like a shish kebab, with novelistic scenes from Wicker's childhood and youth alternating with hard-edged episodes from Attica, and with Tom Wicker himself as the skewer. The materials placed shoulder-to-shoulder on the skewer are as unlike as ripe peaches and hand grenades."

Opposite: Vonnegut photographed at his home in Barnstable, Cape Cod, on March 15, 1969.

Truman Capote: "Murder Was a Theme Not Likely to Darken and Yellow With Time"

In Cold Blood, Capote's famous non-fiction novel about the murder of the Clutter family, appeared as a four-part series in *The New Yorker* in 1965, and was published as a book in January 1966. George Plimpton, a founding editor of *The Paris Review,* spoke with Capote about his process, and how, exactly, the author of *Breakfast at Tiffany's* came to offer insight into the minds of murderers.

Q. Why did you select this particular subject matter of murder; had you previously been interested in crime?

A. Not really, no. During the last years I've learned a good deal about crime, and the origins of the homicidal mentality. Still, it is a layman's knowledge and I don't pretend to anything deeper. The motivating factor in my choice of material—that is, choosing to write a true account of an actual murder case—was altogether literary. The decision was based on a theory I've harbored since I first began to write professionally, which is well over 20 years ago. It seemed to me that journalism, reportage, could be forced to yield a serious new art form: the "nonfiction novel," as I thought of it.

Q. What is the first step in producing a "non-fiction novel"?

A. The difficulty was to choose a promising subject. If you intend to spend three or four or five years with a book, as I planned to do, then you want to be reasonably certain that the material will not soon "date." The content of much journalism so swiftly does, which is another of the medium's deterrents. A number of ideas occurred, but one after the other, and for one reason or another, each was eventually discarded, often after I'd done considerable preliminary work. Then one morning in November, 1959, while flicking through The New York Times, I encountered on a deep-inside page, this headline: Wealthy Farmer, 3 of Family Slain.

Q. Why did you decide it was the subject you had been looking for?

A. I didn't. Not immediately. But after reading the story it suddenly struck me that a crime, the study of one such, might provide the broad scope I needed to write the kind of book I wanted to write. Moreover, the human heart being what it is, murder was a theme not likely to darken and yellow with time.

I thought about it all that November day, and part of the next; and then I said to myself: Well, why not this crime? The Clutter case. Why not pack up and go to Kansas and see what happens? Of course it was a rather frightening thought!— to arrive alone in a small, strange town, a town in the grip of an unsolved mass murder. Still, the circumstances of the place being altogether unfamiliar, geographically and atmospherically, made it that much more tempting. Everything would seem freshly minted—the people, their accents and attitudes, the landscape, its contours,

Capote working on *Answered Prayers*, the novel he never finished, on June 5, 1971.

the weather. All this, it seemed to me, could only sharpen my eye and quicken my ear.

In the end, I did not go alone. I went with a lifelong friend, Harper Lee. She is a gifted woman, courageous, and with a warmth that instantly kindles most people, however suspicious or dour. She had recently completed a first novel (*To Kill a Mockingbird*), and, feeling at loose ends, she said she would accompany me in the role of assistant researchist.

We traveled by train to St. Louis, changed trains and went to Manhattan, Kan., where we got off to consult Dr. James McClain, president of Mr. Clutter's alma mater, Kansas State University. Dr. McClain, a gracious man, seemed a little nonplussed by our interest in the case; but he

gave us letters of introduction to several people in western Kansas. We rented a car and drove some 400 miles to Garden City. It was twilight when we arrived. I remember the car-radio was playing, and we heard: "Police authorities, continuing their investigation of the tragic Clutter slayings, have requested that anyone with pertinent information please contact the Sheriff's office."

If I had realized then what the future held, I never would have stopped in Garden City. I would have driven straight on. Like a bat out of hell.

Q. What was Harper Lee's contribution to your work?
A. She kept me company when I was based out there. I suppose she was with me about two

months altogether. She went on a number of interviews; she typed her own notes, and I had these and could refer to them. She was extremely helpful in the beginning, when we weren't making much headway with the townspeople, by making friends with the wives of the people I wanted to meet. She became friendly with all the church-goers. A Kansas paper said the other day that everyone out there was so wonderfully coopera-tive because I was a famous writer. The fact of the matter is that not one single person in the town had ever heard of me.

Q. How did the two murderers—Perry and Dick—accept being used as subjects for a book?
A. They had no idea what I was going to do. Well, of course, at the end they did. Perry was always asking me: Why are you writing this book? What is it supposed to mean? I don't understand why you're doing it. Tell me in one sentence why you want to do it. So I would say that it didn't have anything to do with changing the readers' opinion about anything, nor did I have any moral reasons worthy of calling them such—it was just that I had a strictly aesthetic theory about creating a book which could result in a work of art.

"That's really the truth, Perry," I'd tell him, and Perry would say, "A work of art, a work of art," and then he'd laugh and say, "What an irony, what an irony." I'd ask what he meant, and he'd tell me that all he ever wanted to do in his life was to produce a work of art. "That's all I ever wanted in my whole life," he said. "And now, what has happened? An incredible situation where I kill four people, and *you're* going to produce a work of art." Well, I'd have to agree with him. It was a pretty ironic situation.

Q. Do you think Perry and Dick were surprised by what they were doing when they began the killings?

A. Perry never meant to kill the Clutters at all. He had a brain explosion. I don't think Dick was surprised, although later on he pretended he was. He knew, even if Perry didn't, that Perry would do it, and he was right. It showed an awfully shrewd instinct on Dick's part. Perry was bothered by it to a certain extent because he'd actually done it. He was always trying to find out in his own mind why he did it. He was amazed he'd done it. Dick, on the other hand, *wasn't* amazed, *didn't* want to talk about it, and simply wanted to forget the whole thing: he wanted to get on with life.

Q. After their conviction, you spent years cor-responding and visiting with the prisoners. What was the relationship between the two of them?
A. When they were taken to Death Row, they were right next door to each other. But they didn't talk much. Perry was intensely secretive and wouldn't ever talk because he didn't want the other prison-ers to hear anything that he had to say. He would write Dick notes on "kites" as he called them. He would reach out his hand and zip the "kite" into Dick's cell. Dick didn't much enjoy receiving these communications because they were always one form or another of recrimination—nothing to do with the Clutter crime, but just general dissatisfac-tion with things there in prison and . . . the people, very often Dick himself. Perry'd send Dick a note: "If I hear you tell another of those filthy jokes again I'll kill you when we go to the shower!" He was quite a little moralist, Perry, as I've said.

Q. How often did the two correspond with you?
A. Except for occasional fallings-out, they'd write twice a week. I wrote them both twice a week all those years. One letter to the both of them didn't work. I had to write them both, and I had to be careful not to be repetitious, because they were very jealous of each other. Or rather, Perry was terribly jealous of Dick, and if Dick got one more

letter than he did, that would create a great crisis. I wrote them about what I was doing, and where I was living, describing everything in the most careful detail. Perry was interested in my dog, and I would always write about him, and send along pictures. I often wrote them about their legal problems.

Q. You once said that emotionality made you lose writing control—that you had to exhaust emotion before you could get to work. Was there a problem with *In Cold Blood,* **considering your involvement with the case and its principals?**

A. Yes, it was a problem. Nevertheless, I felt in control throughout. However, I had great difficulty writing the last six or seven pages. This even took a physical form: hand paralysis. I finally used a typewriter—very awkward as I always write in longhand.

Q. Did you see the prisoners on their final day? Perry wrote you a 100-page letter that you received after the execution. Did he mention that he had written it?

A. Yes, I was with them the last hour before execution. No, Perry did not mention the letter. He only kissed me on the cheek, and said, "Adios, amigo."

Q. What was the letter about?

A. It was a rambling letter, often intensely personal, often setting forth his various philosophies. He had been reading Santayana. Somewhere he had read *The Last Puritan,* and had been very impressed by it. What I really think impressed him about me was that I had once visited Santayana at the Convent of the Blue Nuns in Rome. He always wanted me to go into great detail about that visit, what Santayana had looked like, and the nuns, and all the physical details. Also, he had been reading Thoreau. Narratives didn't interest him at all. So in his letter he would

write: "As Santayana says"—and then there'd be five pages of what Santayana *did* say. Or he'd write: "I agree with Thoreau about this. Do you?"—then he'd write that he didn't *care* what I thought, and he'd add five or ten pages of what he agreed with Thoreau about.

Q. The case must have left you with an extraordinary collection of memorabilia.

A. My files would almost fill a whole small room, right up to the ceiling. All my research. Hundreds of letters. Newspaper clippings. Court records—the court records almost fill two trunks. There were so many Federal hearings on the case. One Federal hearing was twice as long as the original court trial. A huge assemblage of stuff. I have some of their personal belongings—all of Perry's because he left me everything he owned; it was miserably little, his books, written in and annotated; the letters he received while in prison . . . not very many . . . his paintings and drawings. Rather a heartbreaking assemblage that arrived about a month after the execution. I simply couldn't bear to look at it for a long time. I finally sorted everything. Then, also, after the execution, that 100-page letter from Perry got to me. The last line of the letter—it's Thoreau, I think, a paraphrase, goes "And suddenly I realize life is the father and death is the mother." The last line. Extraordinary.

Q. What will you do with this collection?

A. I think I may burn it all. You think I'm kidding? I'm not. The book is what is important. It exists in its own right. The rest of the material is extraneous, and it's personal. What's more, I don't really want people poking around in the material of six years of work and research. The book is the end result of all that, and it's exactly what I wanted to do from it.

Frantz Fanon,
Black Skin, White Masks

Fanon's writing inspired and informed several liberation movements, from the Black Power movement to the Palestinian struggle. Six years after his death, following the translation of his first book into English by Charles Lam Markmann, the Book Review examined his contributions.

ABOUT TWO YEARS AGO FRANTZ FANON'S *The Wretched of the Earth* appeared in America, and since then a growing number of both Negroes and whites have found this direct, personal message on the problems of race the most convincing and appealing one around. In that book, written toward the end of his short life (he died of cancer at 36), he tried to show what colonialism does to both victim and oppressor—a subject he was certainly in a position to understand. He had come to France from Martinique, another black man from an overseas "protectorate" in search of an education and some "freedom." He went to medical school, became a psychiatrist and during the Algerian rebellion was sent to Africa, where he soon lost interest in treating French soldiers who were trying to keep one more nation in bondage.

In 1952, when he was 27—before he was to join the Algerian rebels—his first book, *Black Skin, White Masks,* was published in France; at that time he commented that it "should have been written three years ago. . . . But these truths were a

fire in me then. Now I can tell them without being burned." As some of his colleagues might put it: he obviously had his "problems" for a long time.

His "problems" started at birth, and would not have cleared up with a lifetime of "therapy"; nor in his estimate will white doctors everywhere escape the "problems" that plague them as members of racist, exploitative societies. If the Negro can never get around the psychological consequences of his condition, the white man, particularly the one who fancies himself sensitive and compassionate, will forever squirm as he tries to rationalize or forget the elementary fact that black skin is all that is necessary to keep citizens of the world's leading democracies from money, power and self-respect.

Fanon took up the mentality of the oppressor in his later books; in this first one he has on his mind himself and millions of other Negroes. He wants to make his own people more self-conscious, in the best sense of that word, so that perhaps they, rather than he as a psychiatrist, will bring the white man to his sense; that is, make him do something about his guilts and the economic or political facts that continue to justify those guilts.

To achieve his purposes, Fanon draws from a number of sources—his own life, his observations in the Antilles and in France, and the writings of social scientists, novelists and poets. However, since he is writing to awaken people, to inform them so that they will act, he makes no effort to be systematic, comprehensive, or even orderly. Quite the contrary, one feels a brilliant, vivid and hurt mind, walking the thin line that separates effective outrage from despair.

Right off, the reader is told not to expect still another psychological analysis of the Negro "mind" or "personality." The meaning of being black is what the author wants to spell out, but the social facts that make for that "meaning" have to be stated again and again, particularly by a psychiatrist, who knows how many of his colleagues are quite ready to forget what a hungry stomach, a scornful look, or the butt of a rifle can do to a man's unconscious, to his "inner" life of dreams and fantasies, to his sense of "reality." Fanon leaves nothing undone to make his point that the black man, no matter how ingenious, adaptive or even deluded he becomes, cannot escape the history of his people.

As a psychiatrist he summons what every clinician knows about the child's early susceptibility to the fears and anxieties of his parents, and relates that knowledge to Negroes, who are predominantly poor and kept apart—as their children eventually discover and never forget. As a philosopher he calls upon men like Sartre, who have written about "the other" (be he Jew, Hun, Bolshevik or next-door neighbor) and insists that the problem of color is much more complicated than even they say. ("Jean-Paul Sartre had forgotten that the Negro suffers in his body quite differently than the white man. . . . The white man is not only 'the other' but also the master, whether real or imaginary.") As a writer he demonstrates what others have before him, how insidiously the problem of race, of color, connects with a whole range of words and images; so that black becomes associated with the dark and the shadowy, with evil, sadness and corruption, while white merges into what is light, hopeful, clean and pure.

Yet it is Fanon the man, rather than the medical specialist or intellectual, who makes this book so hard to put down. His ideas and feelings fairly pour out, and often he makes no effort to tone down his language, to sound like a detached

Fanon.

raisonneur, that image so many American psychiatrists cultivate. He clearly had every chance to deceive himself, to become a prosperous doctor very much "accepted" by liberal and even doting white friends. Instead he became a fighter and a voice for the oppressed, whom he also had the courage to warn: no religious or mystical attitude, no psychological "defense" will enable the Negro to feel "secure" or "himself" until he is no longer the white man's social and economic prey; and when that moment comes—he died believing it was not near at hand—the Negro will be able to demonstrate the same wonderful and awful possibilities that every other man does. To have known that at 27, Frantz Fanon must have liberated himself not only from racism, but a good number of other dead-end streets that continue to attract the rest of us, no matter what our color. —*Robert Coles*

1946–1971

Toomer in 1934.

Jean Toomer, *Cane*

Decades after it was first published,
a Black classic was rediscovered.

FOR THE FIRST TIME IN NEARLY HALF A
century, a major effort of the Negro literary
imagination is available to the general reader.
First published in 1923, *Cane* was a commercial
failure, selling about 500 copies before it disappeared from public view. For years the book has
been a collector's item, and even library copies
have been difficult to find. Now, with the appearance of a paperback edition from Harper & Row,
Cane will take its place among the classics of
American letters.

Toomer's literary career began in the 1920s,
with the publication of stories and poems in such
magazines as *Broom, Secession, Double Dealer,
Dial* and *Little Review.* The decisive factor in
his life and art was his ambivalence toward his
blackness. At times he found it convenient or
adventuresome to live as a white man. Moreover,
from a philosophic or religious point of view, he
frequently regarded his blackness as a category
to transcend, a limitation to overcome. But it
is equally true that at other times, and notably
during the composition of *Cane,* he was inspired
to make a passionate affirmation of his blackness.
The book is in fact a poetic celebration of his black
identity, all the more poignant for the complicated
tensions with which the subject was surrounded.

Toomer's symbol for his blackness is the
Southern cane: "Oracular./Redolent of fermenting
syrup,/Purple of the dusk,/Deep-rooted cane."
Cane represents the sweetness of life. It is connected with sex, with a fullness of emotion, with a
sense of soil, of rootedness, of the pain and beauty
of the Negro past. It is expressive, moreover, of a
deep yearning for the rural South. Down home is
still the bloody shrine of the black man's heart.

Part I of *Cane*, which is set in rural Georgia,
consists of a series of portraits of Southern
women who embody the values that Toomer
associates with "cane." Taken together, the stories
comprise a critique of Western rationalism. They
deal with such subjects as infanticide, hysteria,
mysticism, prophecy and lynching. In Part II, the
scene shifts to the black ghetto of Washington,
D.C. Following the trajectory of the Great
Migration, Toomer gives us images of urban
Negro life. We move from the value system of the
black peasantry to that of the black bourgeoisie.
The theme of the best stories is the liberation of
the Negro intellectual. Part III is concerned with
the black writer's quest for the past. It turns on a
dramatic contrast between two Northern intellectuals who find themselves in rural Georgia,
saturated as it is in pain.

Cane represents a pilgrimage to the soil of
one's ancestors. It is a spiritual journey that
every black American must undertake if he hopes
to discover his authentic self. Toomer confronts
the black man with the pain and beauty of his
Southern heritage. That pain, and the power to
transform it into beauty, is what the younger
generation means by "soul." It was Jean Toomer's
genius to discover and to celebrate the qualities
of "soul," and thereby to inaugurate the Negro
Renaissance. For this alone he will be enshrined
as a major figure in the canon of American letters.
—*Robert Bone*

1946–1971

Philip Roth: "He Is Obscene Because He Wants to Be Saved"

George Plimpton appeared in our pages several times—this time, talking to Roth in the wake of his sexually explicit novel *Portnoy's Complaint*.

Q. Would you say something about the genesis of *Portnoy's Complaint*? How long has the idea of the book been in mind?

A. Some of the ideas that went into the book have been in my mind ever since I began writing. I mean ideas about style and narration, about form and procedure.

Q. I was thinking more in terms of the character and his predicament when I asked how long you had in mind "the idea of the book."

A. I know you did. That's partly why I answered as I did.

Q. But surely you don't intend us to believe that this volatile novel of sexual confession, among other things, had its conception in purely literary motives?

A. No, I don't. But the conception is really nothing, you know, beside the delivery. My point is that until my "ideas," about sex, about guilt, about childhood, about Jewish men and Gentile women, were absorbed by an overall fictional strategy and goal, they were not ideas unlike everyone else's. Everybody has "ideas" for novels; the subway is jammed with people hanging from the straps, their heads full of "ideas" for novels they cannot begin to write. I am often one of them.

Q. Given the book's openness about intimate sexual matters, as well as its frank use of obscenity, do you think you would have embarked upon such a book in a climate unlike today's? Or is the book appropriate to these times?

A. As long ago as 1958, in *The Paris Review*, I published a story called "Epstein" that some people found very disgusting in its intimate sexual revelations; and my conversation, I have been told, has never been as refined as it should be. I think that many people in the arts have been living in "a climate like today's" for some time now; the mass media have just caught up, that's all, and with them, the general public. Obscenity as a usable and valuable vocabulary, and sexuality as a subject, have been available to us since Joyce, and I don't think there's a serious American writer in his thirties who has felt restricted by the times particularly, or suddenly now feels liberated because these have been advertised as "the swinging sixties." In my writing lifetime, the use of obscenity has by and large been governed by one's literary taste and tact and not by the mores of the audience.

Q. What about the audience? Don't you write for an audience? Don't you write to be read?

A. To write to be read and to write for "an audience" are two different matters. If you mean by "an audience" a particular readership which we can describe in terms of its education, or politics, or religion, or even by its literary tone, the answer is no. When I'm at work I don't really have any group of people in mind whom I want to

Roth at Princeton on January 20, 1964.

communicate with; rather, what I want is for the work to communicate itself as fully as it possibly can, in accordance with its own intentions. Precisely so that it *can be* read, *but on its own terms*. When one has an audience in mind, it is not any special interest group whose beliefs and demands one either accedes to or challenges, but a kind of ideal reader whose *sensibilities* have been totally given over to the writer, in exchange for his seriousness.

Chekhov makes a nice distinction, in discussing the purposes of his art, between "the solution of the problem and a correct presentation of the problem"—and adds, "only the latter is obligatory for the artist."

Q. Are you suggesting, then, that in *Portnoy's Complaint* "a correct presentation of the problem"

requires a frank revelation of intimate sexual matters, as well as an extensive use of obscenity? That this is a way of being "serious," as you put it, with the reader?

A. Yes, I am. Obscenity is not only a kind of language that is used in *Portnoy's Complaint*, it is very nearly the issue itself. The book isn't full of dirty words because "that's the way people talk," that's one of the lesser reasons for using obscenity in fiction. Very few people actually do talk the way Portnoy "talks" in this book—this is a man speaking out of an overwhelming obsession: he is obscene because he wants to be saved.

Q. Do you think there will be Jews who will be offended by this book?

A. I think there will even be Gentiles who will be offended by this book.

Laurence J. Peter and Raymond Hull, *The Peter Principle*

In this now-famous business classic, Peter and Hull posited that in hierarchical organizations, "every employee tends to rise to his level of incompetence."

IT USED TO BE A FAVORITE THEME OF CON-servative columnists and editorial writers: the monumental bungling of the Russian socialist system and the lean, brisk efficiency of "Yankee ingenuity and know-how." Then came World War II, and 11 million Americans (or was it 13 million?) put on military uniforms and learned how to organize a maximum number of people into a hierarchy to accomplish a minimal amount of useful work. There was even the boast—anticipating our present defense establishment—that for every man actually fighting, another 11 or 15 or some other figure were needed to back him up, which led inevitably to an act of identification of patriotism with inefficiency, especially in the minds of Congressional appropriations groups.

Today American society is murky with hierarchical struggles, and we are all indebted to Laurence J. Peter and his collaborator for developing this brilliant principle to explain modern civilization and even to suggest an escape for those who may be Fed Up.

The principle is very simple: "In a hierarchy every employee tends to rise to his level of incompetence." That is, if a man does well in one job, he is promoted to another higher up the ladder and so on till he reaches a job he can't do well. (The names of prominent public figures crowd the mind.) Obviously, the man's superiors will recommend no further promotions for him. He has reached his "level of incompetence," his "final placement" or, in everyday terms, "success." As the authors observe, "The cream rises until it sours."

Messrs. Peter and Hull omit nothing. They examine in excruciatingly familiar detail the operations of hierarchies—school systems, government agencies, sales organizations, industries, churches, political parties. They dismiss Marxist theory as the opiate of the masses and credit Einstein with the present vogue for long hair among young men. They enunciate subsidiary principles: the "attempt to relieve high-level incompetence." They identify medical and non-medical indicators of "success": peptic ulcers, sexual impotence, and so on to Tabulatory Gigantism: "an obsession with having a bigger desk than his colleagues."

This is a fine book, a beautiful, tonic book, full of the joy of recognition. Luckily it is humor. We don't have to take it seriously; we don't have to believe it. We are only obliged to take seriously things we don't really believe in—religion, morality, etc. —*Paul Showers*

"As the authors observe, 'The cream rises until it sours.'"

Books That Meant Business

MY YEARS WITH GENERAL MOTORS, BY ALFRED P. SLOAN 1964

"It should be said at once that this book is not the random (or complacent or apologetic) reflections of a successful man who also became rich in the process; nor is it a formal and full-dress history of General Motors," the paper's original reviewer wrote. "It is not a personal narrative; Sloan never mentions his own family, where he has lived, his tastes or pet hates. It is a broadly intelligent, in fact, subtle, account of the theory and strategy of business enterprise by one of its most skillful practitioners."

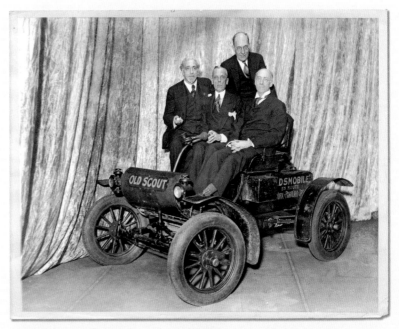

Sloan, along with three other "early motor enthusiasts," at a luncheon at New York's Waldorf-Astoria Hotel on January 9, 1933.

BUSINESS ADVENTURES, BY JOHN BROOKS 1969

Bill Gates has called this book—a collection of corporate profiles—"the best business book I've ever read." Back in 1969, the Book Review liked it, too, praising the author's "great curiosity" and noting with satisfaction that "Brooks has chosen to present these absorbing tales with no preface, no introduction, no effort at 'pulling them together.' . . . There is no pretense; these are 12 *New Yorker* magazine pieces, and that's that."

EMOTIONAL INTELLIGENCE, BY DANIEL GOLEMAN 1995

"There is nothing more American," wrote Eugene Kennedy in the Book Review, "than treating life as a multipart but curable illness." In identifying what he called emotional intelligence as the key to success, Goleman refused "to oversimplify our emotional lives or to provide painless ways to manage them." To do so, argued Kennedy, was not only "unpatriotic" but "original and persuasive."

1946–1971

211

Norman Mailer
rides the Cyclone
on Coney Island,
Brooklyn, in 1969.

A woman reads in the MoMA sculpture garden beside *Floating Figure* by Gaston Lachaise, New York City, May 1979.

Mario Puzo, *The Godfather*

BY DICK SCHAAP

Schaap, a sports journalist, proved to be the perfect reviewer for Puzo's pulpy Mafia classic.

THERE ARE STRONG SIMILARITIES BETWEEN Michael Corleone and Alexander Portnoy. Neither of them wishes to enter his father's line of work. Each of them falls for a White Anglo-Saxon Protestant girl. Of course, there are some differences, too. When Alexander Portnoy's father is frustrated, he gets constipated; when Michael Corleone's father is frustrated, he gets someone killed.

The Godfather is the coming of age of Michael Corleone in a world that Philip Roth never knew. It is the world of the Mafia in America, and the dialogue and the logic of *The Godfather* ring true enough to raise the suspicion that, at least by hearsay, Mario Puzo knows his subject well.

If Philip Roth has created a Jewish mother who can actually give you heartburn, Mario Puzo has created a Sicilian father who will make you shiver every time you stroll on Mulberry Street. And, with loving care and detail, what Roth has done for masturbation, Puzo has done for murder.

Yet it is unfair to carry the analogy too far. *The Godfather* is not written nearly so artfully as *Portnoy's Complaint.* Nor does it approach the humor of Roth's work. Yet *The Godfather* is such

a compelling story, a better-written Sicilian entry into the Irving sweepstakes, that any day now, I am certain the Portnoy family and the Corleone family will end up sharing the heady heights of best-sellerdom as comfortably as the Jews and the Italians have long shared the pleasures of salami.

To condense *The Godfather*, it is the account of the rise and fall and rise of the Corleone empire, ruled by the godfather himself, Don Vito Corleone. Puzo performs a neat trick; he makes Don Vito a sympathetic, rather appealing character, part robbing hood and part Robin Hood. Without sugarcoating Don Vito's sins, Puzo makes the man believable and, more important, understandable.

Don Vito's supporting cast includes his three sons, Santino, who is too tough; Frederico, who is too weak; and Michael, who is, by the Don's standards, just right. Tom Hagen, the Don's Irish-German-American counselor, weaves in and out of the story, and so does the Don's wayward godson, Johnny Fontane, a crooner whose voice goes sour, whose career nosedives after a disastrous showbiz marriage and whose career revives after he plays a dramatic role in a movie about soldiers. (If there is any justice at all, Frank Sinatra deserves a piece of the royalties on half the novels published in the last few years.)

The plot revolves around gang warfare, and the names of the antagonists might as well read Anastasia and Genovese and Gallo and Profaci because almost all of the incidents spring straight from the headlines on page 3 of *The Daily News* (or page 87 of The Times, for that matter). For the most part, they only kill each other; as far as I can recall, only two innocents get killed in the entire book, and one of them is a horse—a magnificent horse, to be sure. The incidents— from a gangland kidnapping in Manhattan to an

Puzo in 1969.

Apalachin-type sitdown to a murder on the Southern State Parkway— guarantee the pace of the narrative; the deeper strength of the narrative comes from examinations of the Mafia mind, a dedication to a peculiar kind of professionalism, a conviction that street justice is more equal and more honest than the justice practiced in the courts.

The Godfather is weakest when Puzo drags in dramatic scenes that advance neither his plot nor his characters. He has collected vivid vignettes, based partly or wholly on fact, that he could not resist throwing in. I can't particularly blame him; some of the extraneous Hollywood and Las Vegas scenes are wonderful little anecdotes that would brighten even the most blasé cocktail party; it

"What Roth has done for masturbation, Puzo has done for murder."

would have taken a very strong-willed man to keep them out of The Godfather. Puzo gave in. He also gave in to a scene in which Don Vito "coined a phrase that was to become as famous in its way as Churchill's Iron Curtain." At the big meet with the rival Mafioso, Vito Corleone says, "We will manage our world for ourselves because it is our world, cosa nostra." If the book were a cartoon strip, an electric bulb would have glowed above Don Vito's head.

Allow for a touch of corniness here. Allow for a bit of overdramatization there. Allow for an almost total absence of humor. Still Puzo has written a solid story that you can read without discomfort in one long sitting. Pick a night with nothing good on television, and you'll come out far ahead.

1946–1971

215

Jacqueline Susann, *The Love Machine*

BY NORA EPHRON

Susann's most famous novel, *Valley of the Dolls,* was dismissed in short, sniffy fashion when it was published in 1966: "At a tense moment, when a 'stomach lurched,' I think I felt a little something myself." But Nora Ephron instantly grasped—and loved—what Susann was doing, and it shows in this piece, which is part review, part feature.

ROBIN STONE IS THE LOVE MACHINE. MY goodness yes. Robin Stone, who drinks his vodka straight, who is positively insatiable in the kip, who runs the largest television network in the country, and who is not only a magnificent sadist but a weak, vulnerable one at that, is the love machine. "I think Robin Stone is divine," says Jacqueline Susann. "Don't you?"

Yes.

Robin Stone is, of course, the hero of Miss Susann's new novel, *The Love Machine,* and if he has brought happiness to almost none of Miss Susann's fictional heroines—who are, incidentally, the most willing group of masochists assembled outside the pages of de Sade—he is nevertheless on the verge of transporting the booksellers of America to unparalleled heights of ecstasy. Hot on the heels of Alexander Portnoy and his Complaint (Philip Roth's novel now has a staggering 450,000 copies in print) come Robin Stone and *The Love Machine* (with a first printing of 250,000 copies). And along with the book, as an added dividend, come Miss Susann and her husband, producer Irving Mansfield, who have already begun the first of a series of nationwide tours dedicated to knocking Roth off the top of the best-seller list.

"It's wild," said Michael Korda, editor-in-chief at Simon & Schuster, which is publishing Miss Susann's novel. "You have these two giant books out at the same time, and their merits aside, one of them is about masturbation and the other is about successful heterosexual love. If there's any justice in the world, *The Love Machine* ought to knock *Portnoy* off the top simply because it's a step in the right direction."

The publication of *The Love Machine* should not be confused with a literary event. Not at all. There is nothing literary about Miss Susann—a former actress who became somewhat successful in the fifties doing Schiffli embroidery commercials with her poodle Josephine—or her writing. She is a natural storyteller, but her characters' motivations leave much to be desired and their mental processes are often just plain silly.

As for her dialogue ("my forte," says Miss Susann), I have never met anyone who talks quite the way the characters do in Miss Susann's books. On the other hand, I have never met any of Jacqueline Susann's friends, who apparently do talk that way. For example, James Aubrey, former president of C.B.S., who was convinced that he was the prototype for Robin Stone, called Miss Susann one day, and according to her, said, "Jackie, make me mean. Make me a son of a bitch." Like that.

But if Jacqueline Susann is no literary figure, she is nevertheless an extraordinary publishing

Susann walks with her poodle, Josephine, through Central Park on April 18, 1969.

phenomenon. Seven years ago, she gave up acting to write a rather charming little book about her poodle. It was called *Every Night, Josephine!* It was published by Bernard Geis Associates, and it sold quite nicely. Then, in 1966 Geis published her first novel, *Valley of the Dolls.* The story of three young women who come to New York to find fame and fortune and end up hooked on pills, the book sold 350,000 copies in hardcover and, far more astonishing, eight million copies in paperback. It is now among the top all-time best sellers and has just gone into its 53rd Bantam softcover printing.

"When you think of all guys out there with pipes and tweed suits who've been waiting years to write the great American novel," said Miss Susann's husband Irving Mansfield, "and you think how the one who's done it is little Jackie who never went to college and lives on Central Park South, well, it's really fabulous, isn't it?"

Yes.

As it happens, though, Mansfield's analysis of his wife's triumph is not quite accurate. Jacqueline Susann has not beaten out all those guys with pipes and tweeds, whoever they are. She has beaten out all those people who work in big cities, see the wages of sin thriving around them, read best-selling dirty novels, and say, "I can write that." In fact, they cannot write that.

When *Valley of the Dolls* was published, it was not favorably received by the critics. When it succeeded, most observers gave the credit to Mansfield and Miss Susann for their frenetic promotional efforts. But a book that sells 10 million copies in all editions has more than just promotion going for it—and *Valley* had a good deal more. For one thing, it was the kind of book most of its readers (most of whom were women and a large number of whom were teen-agers) could not put down. I, for one, could not: I am an inveterate reader of gossip columns and an occasional reader of movie magazines, and for me reading *Valley of the Dolls* was like reading a very very long, absolutely delicious gossip column full of nothing but blind items; the fact that the names were changed and the characters disguised just made it more fun.

In addition, *Valley* had a message that had a magnetic appeal for women readers: It described the standard female fantasy—of going to the big city, striking it rich, meeting fabulous men—and went on to show every reader that she was far better off than the heroines in the book—who took pills, killed themselves and made general messes of their lives. It was, essentially, a morality tale. And despite its reputation, it was not really a dirty book. Most women, I think, do not want to read hard-core pornography. They do not even want to read anything terribly technical about the sex act. What they want to read about is lust. And Jacqueline Susann gave it to them—just as Grace Metalious did. Hot lust. Quivering lust. High-school lust. Sweaters are always being ripped open in Miss Susann's books. Pants are always being frantically unzipped. And everyone is always wanting everyone else.

The Love Machine is a far better book than *Valley*—better written, better plotted, better

structured. It is still, to be sure, not exactly a literary work. But in its own little sub-category of popularly-written *romans à clef,* it shines, like a rhinestone in a trash can. The novel deals primarily with the rise and fall of Robin Stone, who rises and falls from the network presidency. His psychological problems are straight out of Hitchcock (to be specific, *Marnie).* And he runs through the lives of a good half-dozen women in the course of the book, leaving all of them scarred and mutilated—a couple of them literally so. With the possible exception of *Cosmopolitan Magazine,* no one writes about sadism in modern man and masochism in modern woman quite as horribly and accurately as Jacqueline Susann.

Simon & Schuster paid $250,000 for the hardcover rights to *The Love Machine.* (Miss Susann signed with them after buying out her contract with Bernard Geis for $400,000 in an out-of-court settlement.) Bantam Books has advanced $250,000 for the paperback edition. A $1 million movie offer from Twentieth Century-Fox has been turned down by the Mansfields, who think it is inadequate. An initial advertising budget of $75,000 is planned—much of it to pay for full-page newspaper spreads of Miss Susann's face, false eyelashes, and a one-shoulder silver sequined dress—and it is a fraction of what will ultimately be spent promoting the book. Says Simon & Schuster's Korda: "You have to push this book beyond regular book buyers to people who probably haven't been in a bookstore since *Valley of the Dolls* was published in hardcover."

In the meantime, Miss Susann has already begun her third novel. It is tentatively titled *The Big Man.* The theme, said Miss Susann, "is a girl's search for the big man. Her father was a big man. I think most girls have a thing for their fathers, don't you?"

Yes.

Other Great Reviews
by Nora Ephron

DO YOU SLEEP IN THE NUDE?, BY REX REED 1968

"Rex Reed is a saucy, snoopy, bitchy man who sees with sharp eyes and writes with a mean pen and succeeds in making voyeurs of us all," Ephron wrote of the famous movie critic in her review of his memoir. "If any of this sounds as if I don't like Rex Reed, let me correct that impression. I love Rex Reed."

A STATE OF HEAT, BY SHEILAH GRAHAM 1972

Graham, a longtime Hollywood gossip columnist, "has written a sort of combination sex memoir and sex manual," Ephron wrote. "As the book unfolds, however, it becomes clear that sexual advice from Sheilah Graham is about as reliable as etiquette lessons from Attila the Hun."

DOG DAYS AT THE WHITE HOUSE, BY TRAPHES BRYANT 1975

Ephron clearly had a great time with this scandal-packed presidential tell-all by a onetime White House electrician. "There is a lot of gossip, of course. Naked blondes run through the White House while Mrs. Kennedy is away, and the staff complains bitterly about having to pick the blond bobby pins out of the President's bed. Lyndon Johnson parades nude before his staff. Nixon ignores his wife and spends all his time with Bebe Rebozo."

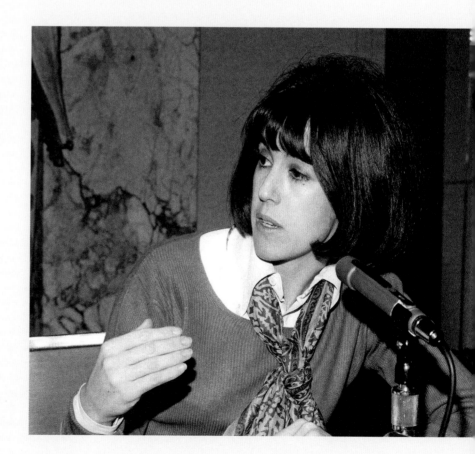

Ephron speaks on a panel discussion for a Women in Literature conference on April 12,1972.

Crichton sits
and smokes for
a portrait in 1970.

Michael Crichton: "Any Idiot Should Be Able to Write a Potboiler"

This profile of Crichton—then a fourth-year medical student as well as the most buzzed-about author of the moment—appeared next to the review of his novel *The Andromeda Strain.*

IF THERE IS A BIGGER LITERARY PROPERTY these days than Michael Crichton (rhymes with frighten), where will the money come from? Within the past six months, young Crichton (he is 26, stands 6 feet 9 inches and is in his fourth year at Harvard Medical School), has:

- Finished *The Andromeda Strain,* which is a Book of the Month Club co-selection for June and has been sold to Universal for $250,000;

- Written an original screenplay called *Morton's Run,* which has also been sold to Universal;

- Fulfilled two thirds of a contract for three original paperbacks;

- Written a prospectus for a TV series, and a two-hour script for a pilot show;

- Continued work on a nonfiction study of the Massachusetts General Hospital;

- Done magazine articles;

- Started four novels and two screenplays;

- Steeled himself to hear the worst about his seventh book, *The Venom Business,* to be published July 15.

Crichton writes summers, during Christmas vacations—and sometimes when he should be at class or clinic. "It's a bit like epileptic seizures," he said. "This spring I freed myself from classes and I wrote like a fiend."

Because of his height he is exempt from the draft. Since doctors, however, are drafted whatever their height, he will not become an intern. "Anyway," he says, "as you go on in medicine the conflict of interest grows between the demands of writing and commitment to your patients."

"At medical school a number of people find it intriguing that I write," said Crichton, "and have always been well disposed. The dean always reads my books. A few of the teachers feel I'm wasting my time, and that in some way I've wasted theirs. When I asked for a couple of days off to go to California about a movie sale, that raised an eyebrow.

"These months have been explosive, but I consider everything that happened as external to me. All I did was write a book, and the publishing bandwagon super-phenomenon has nothing to do with me. It's occasionally disturbing to meet people who can't see beyond this person who's at medical school, who's made a lot of bread writing novels, and who's famous.

"I'm not going to buy a yacht or a gold lamé suit or divorce my wife. She was working to put me through medical school, and every time the money was about to run out it was time to write another book."

It was after he graduated from Harvard College and began travelling in Europe on a fellowship that Crichton decided to write his first book. "I decided any idiot should be able to write a potboiler set in Cannes and Monaco," he said, "and it took me 11 days."

"The book was no good," he added. But NAL published it as *Scratch One,* giving the author's name as John Lange. Crichton decided on a pseudonym so that future patients would not believe he was interested in them for his plots instead of their pains. He became addicted to pseudonyms when he decided his output appeared too great for a single author. His fourth book—*A Case of Need*—boasted a new pseudonym: Jeffery Hudson. The name belonged to a dwarf in the court of Charles I who was served to his monarch in a pie and later captured by Barbary pirates.

"My feeling about the Lange books is that my competition is in-flight movies," said Crichton. "One can read the books in an hour and a half, and be more satisfactorily amused than watching Doris Day. I write them fast and the reader reads them fast, and I get things off my back."

For *The Andromeda Strain* he was willing to slow down. "The idea was in my mind for at least three years," he said, "and I was trying to write it for a year and a half, collecting newspapers clippings and research articles, and writing draft after draft. Every draft was awful. What I was up against was the very considerable absurdity of the idea of a plague from outer space. When I finally learned that a complicated quarantine procedure really existed for the U.S. moon program,

it was a considerable psychological boost, and then I knew I could do the book."

Crichton has even considered a third pseudonym—a woman's name—to see how amusing it would be to write from a woman's viewpoint. He may call herself Marie Antoinette (court of Louis XVI), whose goose was cooked by a cake and who was later captured by Bastille pirates.

Whether as Lange or Hudson or Antoinette or even the essential Crichton, he has become less indulgent about his facility for generating 10,000 words each 15-hour working day as he heats up potboilers that are never watched very long. He would like to write seriously about: euthanasia (he favors it), abortion on demand (ditto), marijuana (he wants it legalized), and the battered baby problem (he gropes for words to express his shock). He is already serious enough about reading (300 books a year) and seeing other people's movies (60 a year).

For a change of climate and scenery, he and his wife are moving to California after his graduation this month from medical school. One immediate project is a joint novel with his 19-year-old brother, Douglas, a junior at Harvard. "It's about youth and drugs," said the older Crichton. "I wrote it completely from beginning to end. Now he's rewriting it from beginning to end, and then I'll rewrite it completely. Eventually we'll have a book.

"Since Douglas is concerned about anonymity, we'll probably call the author *Time* Magazine."
—*Israel Shenker*

1970 ———————————

On November 4, Hunter S. Thompson, the self-proclaimed "freak power" candidate, loses his bid to become the sheriff of Pitkin County, Colorado.

1971 ———————————

The publication of Bob Dylan's poetry collection, *Tarantula,* "is not a literary event because Dylan is not a literary figure," the Book Review says. "Literature comes in books, and Dylan does not intend his most important work to be read."

1971 ———————————→

For the first time since 1964, no Pulitzer Prize for fiction is awarded.

1970s Touchstones

ARE YOU THERE, GOD? IT'S ME, MARGARET,
BY JUDY BLUME
1970

Ask any American woman where the rhyme "I must—I must—I must increase my bust!" comes from, and they'll tell you instantly that it's from this book, which has been passed around by generations of preadolescent girls drawn to Margaret's anxiety about breasts, menstruation and boys. The original Times review called it "funny, warm and loving" but warned, "Few males of any age will be interested in Margaret."

ZEN AND THE ART OF MOTORCYCLE MAINTENANCE,
BY ROBERT PIRSIG
1974

Not really about zen, and not really about motorcycles, either, this book—set on a father-son motorcycle trip—is nothing less than a dissertation on the meaning of life. "Is *Zen and the Art of Motorcycle Maintenance* a novel or an autobiography?" asked Edward Abbey in his review. "In this case the distinction is of no importance. Call the book, as Pirsig himself does, an *inquiry.* Therein lies its singular energy and force."

ROOTS,
BY ALEX HALEY
1976

This historical novel following a young African slave and his descendants was a blockbuster. In his review, James Baldwin wrote, "It suggests, with great power, how each of us, however unconsciously, can't but be the vehicle of the history which has produced us. Well, we can perish in this vehicle, children, or we can move on up the road."

THE WORLD ACCORDING TO GARP,
BY JOHN IRVING
1979

The mother-son novel raised a slew of questions for our reviewer: "What traumas suffered by John Irving elicited *The World According to Garp*? . . . The fact that such questions are not really answerable, except in imagination, does not make them less interesting and important."

KINDRED,
BY OCTAVIA BUTLER
1979

In Butler's hands, time travel—often schlocky and overdone—was an elegant, precise plot device, turning the story of a modern-day Black woman who travels back to Antebellum Maryland, where she saves the life of a white boy, into a blistering treatise on slavery.

James Dickey, *Deliverance*

BY EVAN S. CONNELL

"*Deliverance* is the kind of novel few serious writers attempt any longer," the paper's critic Dwight Garner wrote in his 2010 reappraisal.

DELIVERANCE IS JAMES DICKEY'S FIRST novel, and it is bad news for the competition.

Let us get this "first novel" tag out of the way. Dickey is not one of those precocious sophomores who miraculously emerge from a university cocoon but disappear forever at the first frost. He is middle aged. He was a night-fighter pilot during World War II. He has been a money-making advertising executive, a teacher, lecturer and poet. Four years ago he got the National Book Award for poetry. That is to say, he has already served his apprenticeship with words.

Now, about the story. The poet-in-residence at the University of South Carolina has written a novel that will curl your toes. Four suburban men take a three-day canoe trip down a wild stretch of river in the mountains and meet a couple of rednecks. Well, sir, by the time we hit page 222 we have been treated to sodomy, two bow-and-arrow murders, an accidental death by drowning, three burials, one broken leg, a spiraling fall from a cliff in the company of a corpse, and a do-it-yourself bit of surgery because the narrator has managed to get an arrow stuck in his own flank.

At about this point, if not sooner, you wonder how much more you can take without relaxing into laughter. Dickey's canoe rides to the limit of dramatic tension. Perhaps he crosses that elusive boundary; it is hard to judge. If he has, his book will not be remembered next year by discriminating readers. If there is an important weakness to the novel, this probably is it. But you keep turning pages, regardless, to find out what happens next. There are higher compliments for an author, though not many.

Stylistically, the prose has been combed, yet not so neatly that it can be arranged into blank verse; and, as you expect of an established poet, the images are clear.

Now and again some unbelievable dialogue extrudes; certain words are overused; motivation is not always convincing, particularly in the scene where three out of four sophisticated city dwellers decide they should conceal a murder; and there may be other points for quibbling. But all in a lump these do not weigh much because the story is absorbing, even when you are not quite persuaded Dickey has told the truth. He is effective and he is deft, with the fine hand of an archer. God knows what he might accomplish when he gets used to the form.

Robert Hayden, *Words in the Mourning Time*

Hayden released this poetry collection in the wake of the assassinations of Malcolm X, Martin Luther King Jr. and Robert Kennedy, and during the Vietnam War.

THE RECENT PUBLICATION OF ROBERT Hayden's new book of poems, *Words in the Mourning Time,* once again brings us the work of one of the most underrated and unrecognized poets in America. Until the publication of *Selected Poems* in 1966, Hayden was unrepresented by a book of his own poems, except for two small, privately printed books and a volume published in England. Now 57 years old, he has had to wait too long for the recognition that his work has merited for 20 years. But that is primarily because he is black.

If there was scarcely a market for black writers before the 1960s, black poets must have been regarded as something odd indeed, particularly a poet who refused to be pressed into anyone's preconceived mold of what a black poet should be. Yet, Hayden persevered—teaching, writing, publishing where he could and giving occasional readings.

When I read his poetry I know that I am in the presence of a man who honors language. His images give the reader a new experience of the world. In his *Selected Poems* are found such lines as: "Graveblack vultures encircle afternoon" "palm leaf knives of sunlight" "autumn hills/in blazonry of farewell scarlet." And in *Words in the Mourning Time* these lines appear: "His injured childhood bullied him" "God brooms had swept/the mist away." He chooses words with the care of a sculptor chipping into marble and, in his poem "El Hajj Malik El Shabazz," from *Words in the Mourning Time,* a vivid historical portrait of Malcolm X is presented in six short lines:

> *He X'd his name, became his people's anger,*
> *exhorted them to vengeance for their past;*
> *rebuked, admonished them, their scourger, who*
> *would shame them, drive them from the lush ice*
> *gardens of their servitude.*

Such a simple phrase—"He X'd his name"—but it sets up reverberations that extend back to August of 1619.

I left Nashville in 1961, and though I saw Mr. Hayden a few times afterwards, our relationship slowly diminished. I, his "son," had to find my own way, and he found new "sons" in succeeding classes. The last time I saw him was in May, 1966. I was working for the Student Non-Violent Coordinating Committee and had just come from the meeting in which Stokely Carmichael had been elected chairman. Black power was just a few weeks away, but Mr. Hayden had already felt the heat of its approaching flames. At a writers' conference held at Fisk a few weeks before, he had been severely attacked as an "Uncle Tom" by the students and other writers. When I walked into his house, his first words to me were a tirade against "the nationalists."

He had also just been awarded the Grand Prize for Poetry at the First World Festival of

Negro Arts at Dakar, Senegal. That honor was not enough, however, to offset being rejected and attacked by black students and black writers. He had always insisted on being known as a poet, not a black poet, and he could be belligerent about it. I listened to him again as he angrily maintained that there was "no such thing as black literature. There's good literature and there's bad. And that's all!" I couldn't wholly agree then (and I'm still not sure), nor could I understand why he was so vociferous in denying that he was a black poet. After all, he was the man who had written "Middle Passage," "Frederick Douglass" and "Runagate Runagate," three of the finest poems about the black experience in the English language. Why couldn't he admit that he was a black poet?

To be a black artist has always been difficult. The mere fact that he is black means that he is associated with a "cause." It is his birthright, whether he wants it to be or not. Yet, while no one expects Philip Roth, for example, to be a spokesman for Jews, it is the black writer's fate to have his work judged more on the basis of racial content than artistic merit. This is because whites only grant the right of individuality to whites. A black is not an individual; he is the representative of a "cause." Unfortunately, blacks concur in this evaluation. They see each other as "causes" and have little, if any, use for a black writer who does not concern himself with "the cause." Both races think the black writer is a priest, offering absolution to whites or leading Blacks to the holy wars.

To a black artist, like Mr. Hayden, who was not conceived or reborn in the womb of black power, such thinking is not only repugnant, it is a direct assault upon art itself. By its very nature, art is revolutionary, because it seeks to change the consciousness, perceptions and very beings of those who open themselves to it. Its revolutionary nature, however, can only be mortally wounded if it must meet political prescriptions. That, however, is now being demanded of the black artist.

Robert Hayden refuses to be defined by anything other than the demands of his craft. He does not want to be restricted solely to the black experience or have his work judged on the basis of its relevance to the black political struggle. First and foremost, he is not a pawn in some kind of neo-medieval morality play. His task is, in his words, merely that which has always been the poet's task: "to reflect and illuminate the truth of human experience."

Now, I know that his desire to be regarded as nothing more or less than a poet was not a denial of his blackness, but the only way he knew of saying that blackness was not big enough to contain him. He wanted to live in the universe.

In the ninth part of the title poem of *Words in the Mourning Time,* he writes:

We must not be frightened nor cajoled into accepting evil as deliverance from evil. We must go on struggling to be human, though monsters of abstractions police and threaten us. Reclaim now, now renew the vision of a human world where godliness is possible and man is neither gook nigger honkey wop nor kike but man permitted to be man.

If we ever reach that time when man is permitted to be man, one of the reasons will be men and women like this poet, Robert Hayden, who, when pressed into the most terrifying corners of loneliness, refused to capitulate to those, who in the screaming agony of their own pain and loneliness, could do nothing but return evil for evil.
—*Julius Lester*

Hayden, circa 1950.

Dee Brown, *Bury My Heart at Wounded Knee*, and Angie Debo, *A History of the Indians of the United States*

BY N. SCOTT MOMADAY

Momaday—the first Native American to win the Pulitzer Prize for fiction, for House Made of Dawn *— called Brown's book "extraordinary on several accounts."*

THE OLD MAN KIOWA GEORGE POOLAW, WHO lived not far from my grandmother's house on Rainy Mountain Creek, died without having learned to read or write. But among his effects there was found a ledger in which he had kept a pictographic calendar of events, a history of the Kiowa tribe, from 1832 to 1900. Kiowa George was a deliberate man, and his method was simple; he set down the one or two most important events of each year and let it go at that. Such was his concept of history.

Thus there are recorded the winter in which Little War Bonnet was killed in New Mexico (1844-45) and the summer of the chinaberry sun dance, in which Yellow Wolf was born (1850). These things mean nothing to us, of course, but to Kiowa George, and his contemporaries, they were moments in which the whole meaning of the past was concentrated. Referring to them his generation could know precisely where it was in time.

In the wake of much recent activity among those who have implemented programs in ethnic studies in our colleges and universities, there has developed an interest in what might be called the underside of American history. It seems to have occurred to us at last that there is a dimension to our national experience that remains relatively unknown—a dimension more richly documented than we could have guessed, and that is worth our while to consider and understand.

Here are two books that focus upon the place of the American Indian in our history. One purports to be a history of the Indians, the other an Indian history. This distinction is of some importance, I believe; for ultimately we must be concerned not only with conflicting interpretations of history but with different notions of what history is and ought to be as well. How are we to account for the Compromise of 1850 and the birth of Yellow Wolf, for example, in one and the same chronicle? Neither Angie Debo nor Dee Brown considers this question directly, but their methods seem to anticipate it.

Of the two books, *A History of the Indians of the United States* is easily the more conventional. It is a comprehensive survey, objective in style and chronological in organization. But here this combination of qualities results in a kind of prose dilemma; the compactness and continuity such a coverage required are never quite achieved. More often than not, the text seems too conscious of itself, inhibited, intimidated and confused by myriad facts and figures.

In a way, this is the historian's plight. It never ceases to confound us who are rooted in what

Momaday in October 1985.

is called Western civilization that the Indian, so richly diverse in his character and society, so prominent in the determination of American history, should invest himself in an oral tradition, to the exclusion of documents and deeds. In the early 400 pages of Miss Debo's book we see how the familiar patterns of invasion, conquest and diplomatic administration emerge upon the geography of Progress. And familiar is perhaps the key word here. One has the sense that nothing is so appropriate to this account of the subject as the maxim that history repeats itself.

Bury My Heart at Wounded Knee is a much better book than the title would indicate; it is, in fact, extraordinary on several accounts. It is first and foremost a compelling history of the American West, distinguished not because it is, as the dust jacket has it, an Indian history (it is

"It seems to have occurred to us at last that there is a dimension to our national experience that remains relatively unknown."

based largely upon the records of treaty councils and the words of such Indian leaders as Chief Joseph, Geronimo and Crazy Horse), but because it is so carefully documented and designed. The book covers only 30 years—1860 to 1890—but they are the years in which the West was won, as they say, and the culture and civilization of the Indians lost.

It will come as a surprise to many readers of this book (and I sincerely hope that there are many indeed) that so much of great drama and moment actually took place in the three decades of this remarkable story. And Mr. Brown's book is a story, a whole narrative of singular integrity and precise continuity; that is what makes the book so hard to put aside, even when one has come to the end.

Having read Mr. Brown, one has a better understanding of what it is that nags at the American conscience at times (to our everlasting credit) and of that morality which informs and fuses events so far apart in time and space as the massacres at Wounded Knee and My Lai.

1971

Pablo Neruda wins the Nobel "for a poetry that with the action of an elemental force brings alive a continent's destiny and dreams."

1971

Eight years after her death, Sylvia Plath's novel *The Bell Jar* is published in the U.S.

1971

Every member of the National Book Award's fiction committee, chaired by William Styron, threatens to quit rather than consider Erich Segal's *Love Story.* "It simply doesn't qualify as literature," Styron says.

Reading in the subway, 1981.

1971

CHAPTER FOUR

1996

The New York Times Book Review — JULY 23, 1972, SECTION 7

Papers on The War

So that what changed him would change America

The New York Times Book Review — June 4, 1972

In Search Of Nixon

The New York Times Book Review — MARCH 24, 1974, SECTION 7

Everybody who's nobody and the nobody who's everybody

Working

The New York Times Book Review — MARCH 6, 1977

Falconer

Talk With John Cheever

The New York Times — Book Review — February 9, 1986

Breeders, Wives and Unwomen

Poetry in Motion: The Video Muse

William Buckley: I Write Fast. So What?/3

The New York Times — Book Review — April 10, 1988

The Heart's Eternal Vow

Budapest Letter: New Themes, New Writers

The Unsparing Disease/3

The New York Times — Book Review — February 17, 1991

Behind the Black Lace Curtain

The Earliest Virginia Woolf/5

The New York Times — Book Review — August 22, 1993

Processed in Pleasantville

World War II: Children on the Home Front/9

The New York Times — Book Review — September 12, 1993

The Sword And the Savior

Robert Altman Reinvents Raymond Carver/3

After the bold, brash experimentation of the early 1970s under the editor John Leonard, the Book Review settled into a more predictable rhythm. Predictable, however, didn't mean dull; it continued to put fresh and surprising books on the cover and cajoled writers to take on weighty and unexpected topics. It continued to drive the cultural conversation—reviewing Art Spiegelman's comic "Maus" before it was issued in book form, printing a statement in support of Toni Morrison after *Beloved* failed to win the National Book Award and interviewing Randy Shilts when his investigation into the handling of the AIDs crisis was published.

Henry Bech Interviews John Updike

The Book Review was fortunate enough to persuade Henry Bech, the hero of John Updike's previous book, to interview Mr. Updike on the subject of his new novel, *Rabbit Redux*.

UPDIKE'S OFFICE IS CONCEALED IN A KIND OF false-bottomed drawer in the heart of downtown Ipswich (Mass.), but the drowsy locals, for a mere 30 pieces of silver, can be conned into betraying its location. A stuck-looking door is pulled open; an endless flight of stairs, lit by a team of dusty fireflies, is climbed. Within the sanctum, squalor reigns unchallenged. A lugubrious army-green metal desk rests in the center of a threadbare Oriental rug reticulate with mousepaths; the walls are camouflaged in the kind of cardboard walnut paneling used in newly graduated lawyers' offices or in those Los Angeles motels favored by the hand-held cameramen and quick-tongued directeurs of blue movies. On the bookshelves, evidently stained by a leopard in the process of shedding his spots, rest repellent books—garish schoolboy anthologies secreting some decaying

Updikean morsel, seven feet of James Buchanan's bound works adumbrating the next novel, some daffodil-yellow building-trade manual penumbrating *Couples;* and, most repellent of all, a jacketless row of the total oeuvre, spines naked as the chorus of *Hair,* revealing what only the most morbid have hitherto suspected, that since 1959 (*The Poorhouse Fair,* surely his masterpiece) Updike with Alfred A. Knopf's connivance has been perpetuating a uniform edition of himself. Beclouding all, the stink of nickel cigarillos, which the shifty, tremulous, asthmatic author puffs to sting the muse's eyes into watering ever since at the Surgeon-General's behest, he excised cigarettes from his armory of crutches.

Updike, at first sight, seems bigger than he is, perhaps because the dainty stitchwork of his prose style readies one for an apparition of elfin dimensions. An instant layer of cordial humorousness veneers a tough thickness of total opacity, which may in turn coat a center of heartfelt semi-liquid. Shamefacedly I confessed my errand—to fabricate an "interview" for one of those desperate publications that seek to make weekly "news" of remorselessly accumulating Gutenbergian silt. Shamefacedly, Updike submitted. Yet, throughout the interview that limped in the van of this consent, as the pumpkin-orange New England sun lowered above the chimney pots of a dry-cleaning establishment seen darkly through an unwashed window, Updike gave the

1971 ———————————————
In her rave review of *The Autobiography of Miss Jane Pittman,* Alice Walker says Ernest J. Gaines "revels in the rich heritage of Southern black people."

1974 ———————————————
Studs Terkel publishes *Working,* which the Book Review praises for its "electricity and emotional power."

1974 ———————————————
The Book Review finds Peter Benchley's *Jaws* to be "a mite malodorous."

impression of (and who wouldn't?) wanting to be elsewhere. He kept interjecting his desire to go "home" and "shingle" his "barn"; it occurred to this interviewer (the Interviewer, as Mailer would say), that the uniform books, varied in tint and size as subtly as cedar shakes, were themselves shingles, with which this shivering poor fellow hopes to keep his own skin dry in the soaking downpour of mortality.

Having neglected to read more than the first pages, which concern a middle-aged ex-athlete enjoying a beer with his elderly father, I was compelled to cast my interrogation in rather general terms. Viz.:

Q.: Are you happy?
A.: Yes, this is a happy limbo for me, this time. I haven't got the first finished copies yet, and haven't spotted the first typo. I haven't had to read any reviews.

Q.: How do you find reviews?
A.: Humiliating. It isn't merely that the reviewers are so much cleverer than I, and could write such superior fictions if they deigned to; it's that even the on-cheering ones have read a different book than the one you wrote. All the little congruences and arabesques you prepared with such delicate anticipatory pleasure are gobbled up as if by pigs at a pastry cart. Still, the ideal reader must—by the ontological argument—exist, and his invisibility therefore be a demonic illusion sustained to tempt us to despair.

Q.: Do you envision novels as pills, broadcasts, tapestries, explosions of self, cantilevered constructs, or what?

Updike at home on Martha's Vineyard on July 27, 1971.

A.: For me, they are crystallizations of visceral hopefulness extruded as a slow paste which in the glitter of print regains something of the original, absolute gaiety. I try to do my best and then walk away rapidly, so as not to be incriminated.

Q.: I'd like to talk about the new book, but the truth is I can't hold bound galley pages, my thumbs keep going to sleep, so I didn't get too far into this, what? *Rabbit Rerun.*
A.: *(eagerly, pluggingly):* Redux. Latin for led back. You know Latin: Apologia Pro Vita Sua. The next installment, 10 years from now, I expect to call *Rural Rabbit*—you'll notice at the end of this book Janice talks about them getting a farm. The fourth and last, to come out in 1991 if we all live, is tentatively titled *Rabbit Is Rich*. Nice, huh?

Q.: *(turning tape recorder down to pianissimo):* Not bad. *Pas mal.* Not bad.
A.: *(gratefully, his shingling hand itching):* Thanks. Thanks a lot.

Reviews of Updike's Work

PIGEON FEATHERS AND OTHER STORIES
1962

"John Updike is the most talented writer of his age in America (he is 30)."

—ARTHUR MIZENER

COUPLES
1968

"A few years ago, Norman Mailer the critic publicly advised John Updike to keep his foot in the whorehouse door and forget about his damn prose style."

—WILFRID SHEED

RABBIT IS RICH
1981

"In Rabbit's desire and ability to be happy Updike finds the yeast he seeks more often than finds, and he kneads his dough well as always, and the novel rises."

—ROGER SALE

THE WITCHES OF EASTWICK
1984

"Much of *The Witches of Eastwick* is satire, some of it literary playfulness and some plain bitchery. It could be that any attempt to analyze further would be like taking an elephant gun to a puff pastry."

—MARGARET ATWOOD

RABBIT AT REST
1990

"Its courageous theme—the blossoming and fruition of the seed of death we all carry inside us—is struck in the first sentence, as Harry Angstrom, Rabbit, now 55 years old, more than 40 pounds overweight, waits for the plane that is bringing his son, Nelson, and Nelson's family to visit him and his wife in their semi-retirement in Florida: He senses that it is his own death arriving, 'shaped vaguely like an airplane.'"

—JOYCE CAROL OATES

ODD JOBS
1991

"Mr. Updike, of course, is a psychotic Santa of volubility, emerging from one or another of his studies (he is said to have four of them) with his morning sackful of reviews, speeches, reminiscences, think pieces, forewords, prefaces, introductions, stories, playlets and poems. Preparing his cup of Sanka over the singing kettle, he wears his usual expression: that of a man beset by an embarrassment of delicious drolleries. The telephone starts ringing. A science magazine wants something pithy on the philosophy of subatomic thermodynamics; a fashion magazine wants 10,000 words on his favorite color. No problem—but can they hang on? Mr. Updike has to go upstairs again and blurt out a novel."

—MARTIN AMIS

Nikki Giovanni, *Gemini*

BY JUNE JORDAN

Giovanni was just 28 and known primarily as a poet when she published *Gemini,* which was reviewed by a more established peer in the Black Arts Movement. Although Jordan was less than impressed with this "extended autobiographical statement," Giovanni has gone on to enjoy a long and celebrated career.

WELL, THIS "EXTENDED AUTOBIOGRAPHICAL statement" by Nikki Giovanni is not an autobiography. It may therefore disappoint many among her plentiful followers who will buy a copy, hoping to find out about their poet. If you read through the 13 separate essays, you can conclude that Nikki Giovanni came from a middle-class background: Both parents were college graduates and pursued professional careers. She grew up in Knoxville, Tenn. She took her own undergraduate degree at Fisk University: She loved her grandmother, and her mother, especially, loves her son,

Thomas, loves her sister, Gary, and liked to fight for her, from when she was 4 years old. Her family has long regarded Miss Giovanni as a genius, and she has long regarded herself as a genius. More than that, of an autobiographical nature, her fans will not learn—not here.

The reader never hears of any real trouble in her life; she must have had some. There are no Giovanni word-dealings with personal pain, or anguish. And where are the men who have figured in her life? (Even her father and grandfather receive comparatively incidental mention, before disappearing from the page.) And who are the people who have helped her with her career? And who are her friends? And so forth.

That's enough about what's missing. What you do have is a collection of essays with titles such as "Spiritual View of Lena Horne," "On Being Asked What It's Like to Be Black," and "Don't Have a Baby Till You Read This." Compared to the autobiographical writings of Maya Angelou, or of Alice Walker in "To Hell With Dying," or of Julius Lester, in *Search for the New Land,* this is light stuff. Still, it is an entertaining collection of mostly high-spirited raps. Its interest is guaranteed by Miss Giovanni's status as a leading black poet and celebrity.

All the essays are first person. Some of them are enjoyable—jive pieces of pure jive. Witness "Revolutionary Tale," where the reader is promised the story of how and why Miss

---

1974
Erma Bombeck reviews *Free to Be . . . You and Me,* edited by Marlo Thomas: "I couldn't resist the temptation to grade myself on how many sexist sins I had committed in the name of tradition."

1976
In her review of Martin Amis's second novel, *Dead Babies,* Margaret Drabble writes, "This book in its way is memorable. One might want to forget it, but it won't be easy."

1976
Spiro Agnew publishes *The Canfield Decision,* which is about a vice president "destroyed by his own ambition," and *the Book Review* hires John Kenneth Galbraith to review it.

1971–1996

Giovanni photographed
at her apartment on
April 13, 1969.

Giovanni arrived "late," to join "The Movement." Instead, the reader is taken on a float among the laughing bubbles of a really tall tale.

"Black Poems, Poseurs and Power" offers the reader an engaging piece of self-criticism, in the sense that it questions where we, black folks, are heading, how we are handling the trip, and why. Miss Giovanni believes: "There is a tendency to look at the Black experience too narrowly." This can lead to a blacker-than-thou kind of non-think: Black may discriminate against black, for instance, if the brother or the sister is not wearing the "right" "Black" clothing of the moment.

One more essay must be mentioned, her last: "Gemini—A Prolonged Autobiographical Statement on Why." This will prove particularly interesting to everyone familiar with the author's poems. When you compare the poetry with the ambivalence and wants expressed in this essay, it becomes clear that a transition is taking place

> "All the essays are first person. Some of them are enjoyable— jive pieces of pure jive."

inside the artist. In this final essay she is a woman writing: "I don't want my son to be a warrior. I don't want my son to be a George or a Jonathan Jackson. I didn't have a baby to see him be cannon fodder." Whatever the depth of the transition, the uncertainties are real and plainly spoken: "Perhaps Black people don't want Revolution at all. That too must be considered. I used to think the world needs what I need. But perhaps it doesn't." And, the final, two lines of the book: "I really like to think a Black, beautiful, loving world is possible. I really do, I think."

To be sure, that is a puzzling conclusion. Is it the black part, or the beautiful, or the "loving world" part, that leaves her unsure—or all of them? Maybe that was the goal, to raise more questions about herself, at the age of 27, than she would or could answer. At 27, that might seem fair enough, and a lot less surprising than an honest-to-God autobiography.

1977

Colleen McCullough, the author of *The Thorn Birds,* abandons plans to attend nursing school, telling the Book Review, "I don't believe a patient would appreciate the idea of having a millionaire nurse carry the bedpan."

1977

The Book Review asks Allen Ginsberg what he likes best about his own poetry. "Cranky music," he replies.

1978

Isaac Bashevis Singer wins the Nobel for "for his impassioned narrative art which, with roots in a Polish-Jewish cultural tradition, brings universal human conditions to life."

1971–1996

241

Stephen King, *Carrie*

When Stephen King's first novel was published, it ended up, inexplicably, in the Book Review's crime fiction column.

MAYBE, STRICTLY SPEAKING, IT IS NOT A mystery book. But it does have action, suspense and, at the end, a holocaust. And it is exceedingly well-written. So don't miss *Carrie,* by Stephen King, a first novel and one guaranteed to give you a chill.

Carrie is about a telekinetic girl in a small town in Maine. She is an unhappy girl. Her mother is a horror, a religious fanatic eager to beat the goodness of Christ into sinners with a powerful right hand. No wonder Carrie grows up all but mute, unattractive, shy. She is the butt of jokes in school; she is poorly coordinated; she does not appear to be very bright. But she has strange gifts. Finally, pushed beyond what her emotional state can absorb, she runs psychically amok, unleashing all the latent powers in her. The result is sheer disaster for her and for all around her.

King does more than tell a story. He is a schoolteacher himself and he gets into Carrie's mind as well as into the minds of her classmates. He also knows a thing or two about symbolism—blood symbolism especially. That this is a first novel is amazing. King writes with the kind of surety normally associated only with veteran writers. This mixture of science fiction, the occult, secondary school sociology, kids good and bad and genetics turns out to be an extraordinary mixture. —*Newgate Callendar*

1978
The Book Review says that Christina Crawford's *Mommie Dearest* reveals Joan Crawford "as a woman who could have shown the Marquis de Sade a thing or two when it came to what she called 'disciplining' her children."

1980
More than a decade after John Kennedy Toole commits suicide, his novel, *A Confederacy of Dunces,* is published. It goes on to win the Pulitzer.

1982
Ntozake Shange dedicates her novel *Sassafras, Cypress and Indigo* to "all women in struggle."

Stephen King, Book Reviewer

King has been writing for the Book Review for decades.

GLITZ,
BY ELMORE LEONARD
1985

"How good is this novel? Probably the most convincing thing I can say on the subject is that it cost me money. After finishing *Glitz,* I went out to the bookstore at my local mall and bought everything by Elmore Leonard I could find—the stuff I didn't already own, that is."

A LONG FATAL LOVE CHASE,
BY LOUISA MAY ALCOTT
1995

When this 1866 suspense thriller was finally published more than 125 years after Alcott wrote it, King weighed in on it for the Book Review. He called it "a wonderful entertainment," adding, "it tends to confirm Alcott's position as the country's most articulate 19th-century feminist. But the novel . . . offers something perhaps even more valuable: a fascinating look into a divided mind that was both attracted to themes of violence and sexuality and ashamed by its own interest."

King in 1974.

HANNIBAL,
BY THOMAS HARRIS
1999

Of this long-awaited follow-up to *The Silence of the Lambs,* King wrote, "Harris is not for all these people, of course—I don't think many of the Danielle Steel crowd will be rushing out to buy a book in which one character is eaten from the inside out by a ravenous moray eel—but for those who like what Harris can do so brilliantly, no book report is required."

1971–1996

243

Carl Bernstein and Bob Woodward, *All the President's Men*

BY DORIS KEARNS

This book about the Watergate scandal, by two *Washington Post* reporters, helped take down President Nixon, who resigned two months after it was published.

AT FIRST READING, *ALL THE PRESIDENT'S Men,* the third-person narrative by the two *Washington Post* reporters whose investigative reporting earned their paper a Pulitzer Prize, is a detective story. It turns Watergate into a fast-moving mystery, a whodunit written with ease, if not elegance.

It begins, as mysteries do, with a crime—the burglary on June 17, 1972, of the Democratic National Committee headquarters. As the author-sleuths retrace the crime their investigation leads from a simple break-in to a massive strategy of spying and sabotage—from five petty criminals to all the President's men. Woodward and Bernstein have rigorously reduced their tale to essentials, stripped it of introspection, philosophizing and background detail.

But the narrative form imposed upon the material obscures important themes in a book whose subject is, after all, history not fiction. We urge the young detectives on, forgetting that the scene is not Perry Mason's courtroom where justice triumphs and order is restored, and that the sleuths are not Holmes and Watson, but two young reporters left by default to play the hero.

There is a second even more powerful story in the dramatic account of the inner workings of one newspaper: *The Washington Post.* The reporters' meetings with city editor Barry Sussman; metropolitan editor Harry Rosenfeld; managing editor Howard Simons, and executive editor Benjamin Bradlee—to decide which stories would go into print are the best parts of the book. The editors play the role of prosecutor and judge, demanding to know how the stories have been put together, how many sources had corroborated the information (at least two were necessary) and how reliable the sources were.

The editors' standards provided a coherence and direction for the reporters. The interrogatory procedure built a sense of shared responsibility with the executives of *The Post* which gave the reporters self-confidence, even courage. Moreover, the editors stood firm when the reporters stumbled. "We stand by our story," Bradlee wrote, at a time when the reporters themselves were in despair. Discussing the subpoenas the Committee to Re-elect the President issued for the reporters' notes, Bradlee said: "Of course we're going to fight this one all the way up."

The book is less satisfactory in dealing with conflicts which arose outside the editorial meetings. Several times the reporters had to make difficult ethical decisions. Sometimes the rules were clear: Woodward refused a bribe for an interview. Bernstein's decision, despite anxiety about the rights of privacy, to call friends in the telephone company and in a credit card company to obtain burglar Bernard Barker's phone

Bernstein and Woodward at *The Washington Post* in 1973.

records and dirty trickster Donald Segretti's travel and expense records was not so easily made. Woodward memorized the names of the grand jury members so that he and Bernstein could approach them for information even though it meant asking the jurors to break the law. Together the reporters decided to blow the cover of a confidential source and identify an F.B.I. agent to his superior.

How did they weigh the competing values in those decisions? The book does not say. The same dispassionate language which keeps the story moving keeps the reader at the threshold of moral choice; rarely does it permit looking at the decision-making process. Even in the incidents

which might be revealing—Bernstein's sleepless night after their story implicating Haldeman in the operation of the illegal fund, or Woodward's distress as Judge Sirica jailed a fellow reporter while letting the two *Post* reporters go free for unprofessional behavior—personal struggles of these heroes are merely mentioned.

This reservation aside, Woodward and Bernstein have written a remarkable book. I was particularly impressed by their portrait of the White House staff, of men who had no higher goal than re-electing the President. There are no values to weigh because there is but one value. It is voiced best through Hugh Sloan: "One breathed a rarefied air when one was in the President's service. The people in the White House believed they were entitled to do things differently, to suspend the rules, because they were fulfilling a mission. That was the only important thing—the mission. It was easy to lose perspective."

The suspense in *All the President's Men* is more pervasive and finally more terrifying than a suspense story which holds its readers shivering in the darkness of graveyards and gothic castles because the setting is sunny Washington, D.C., a familiar place suddenly made unfamiliar by the presence of overwhelming fear. Disaffected C.R.P. employees trembling in their doorways, wanting to be helpful but afraid of the consequences, plead with the sleuths never to call again. "Nobody knows what they'll do," one employee said. "They are desperate." Who are they?

The climate of fear is best illustrated in episodes involving Woodward's meetings with a confidential source—Deep Throat. (Anonymous even now—one man or possibly several—Deep Throat had access to information from the White House, the Justice Department, the F.B.I. and C.R.P.) Their 2 A.M. meetings in a cold, dark underground garage far from the center of town are superbly and suspensefully described. The reporters' 3 A.M. meeting with Bradlee held on his lawn because they were afraid of being bugged is melodramatic, but despite the cliché description not unreasonable paranoia.

Raymond Chandler said an unresolved detective story is like an unresolved chord in music. The end ties everything together by establishing the culprit's guilt and bringing him to justice. Punishment is part of the logic of the form. *All the President's Men* runs into structural difficulties because at the end of the book, McCord, Liddy, Hunt, Stans, Mitchell, Magruder, Dean, Haldeman and Ehrlichman are all indicted but the evidence leads to one more criminal, higher up than even the highest aide. The circle of involvement is completed when we learn Richard Nixon has bugged himself, thus setting the machinery of impeachment in motion. The book just stops.

"All the President's Men is . . . more terrifying than a suspense story which holds its readers shivering in the darkness of graveyards and gothic castles."

Vincent Bugliosi and Curt Gentry, *Helter Skelter*

This account of the Manson murders, by the deputy district attorney who prosecuted the case, went on to become one of the best-selling true-crime books ever.

"THIS INMATE WILL NO DOUBT BE IN SERIOUS difficulty soon," wrote the orientation officer at Terminal Island Prison in California, when, in 1956, 22-year-old Charles Manson entered the facility to begin a three-year sentence. "He is young, small, baby-faced, and unable to control himself," the officer observed. Manson had expressed one preference with regard to his work assignment, "a small detail where he is not with too many men. He states that he has a tendency to cut up and misbehave if around a gang. . . ." Manson, a decade later, found his ultimate gang—a pack of mindblown runaways, very young and mostly female, detritus of the psychedelic mid-sixties—and, with their unquestioning obedience, Manson managed his ultimate cut-ups: a spate of savage, mindless murders— some, almost certainly, as yet unsolved—that culminated in 1969, one hot August weekend in Los Angeles.

In less than 48 hours, three women and one man, all under Manson's command, variously shot, stabbed, beat and hung seven people, among them Roman Polanski's eight-months-pregnant wife, Sharon Tate, and a wealthy supermarket owner, Leno LaBianca, who was found with the word "WAR" carved in his abdomen and a knife still protruding from his throat. The Murder scenes were marked by blood writing, on a front door, on a refrigerator and on the walls.

The crimes led to the longest and most expensive murder trial in American criminal history. Vincent Bugliosi was the Deputy District Attorney in Los Angeles who successfully prosecuted the Tate-LaBianca killers. *Helter Skelter* is Bugliosi's account of the murders, their investigation and the trial itself, co-authored with Curt Gentry.

The previous major Manson text—Ed Sanders's *The Family*—was eccentrically written, with something of a counter-cultural sensibility. Bugliosi's and Gentry's telling is rendered, appropriately enough, in the language of a D.A.: methodical, tight, occasionally ironical and rising to emotional pitch only on rare occasion. And even when Bugliosi raises his voice, one still senses the calculated flavor of a closing argument to the jury.

Oddly, though, the manner of telling works, in this case of what will likely survive as the most repugnant and meaningless crime of our era. The nature of the case itself is awful enough that it needs nothing more than unspectacular language. It is quickly clear, as well, that Bugliosi's concern is at least as much with the intellectual process of investigation and prosecution as with the crime and the criminals themselves.

The first fifth of the book (at the end of which Manson and company are in custody) leaves one with two impressions: wonder, inevitably, at the horror of the murders themselves and the inhumanness of the Manson people—and wonder, as well, that the Los Angeles Police Department ever managed to solve the case in the first place.

The trial itself, however, is clearly the center of Bugliosi's interests. In *Helter Skelter,* Bugliosi emerges as the very apotheosis of the shrewd, tough, fair-minded prosecutor, fascinated and challenged by Manson's personality, repelled by the character of the other defendants. Manson, in the course of the trial, expressed respect for Bugliosi—as well as threatening to kill him. (The female defendants christened him "The Bug.")

Judging from the comedy of errors that Bugliosi depicts the investigation to have been, one might think that the prosecutor's own contribution was simply a bit of diligence. Bugliosi himself, however, clearly ranks as primary his reconstruction of motive. "The prosecution does not have the legal burden of proving motive," Bugliosi points out. "But motive is extremely important evidence. A jury wants to know why." And on the surface, the Manson murders appeared nearly as senseless and motiveless as one could imagine.

"Helter skelter," Bugliosi finally deduced, was the kernel of Manson philosophy. Helter skelter was Manson's phrase (borrowed from the Beatles' *White Album*) for the apocalyptic race war he hoped the murders might launch (a war that only Manson and his tribe, ensconced in Death Valley, would survive). Again within the context of the *White Album,* the blood-writing at the murder scenes was intended to suggest black perpetrators.

The entire notion—far more involved and obscure than the preceding suggests—is so quirky, inconsistent and psychotic that it seems a remarkable accomplishment on Manson's part that he managed to sell it to his unimaginative, middle-class band of runaways. And it's as much an accomplishment on Bugliosi's part that he unraveled the whole twisted ideological package. But most to the prosecutor's credit is that he managed to turn around and sell it himself to an unimaginative middle-class jury. In that courtroom feat, more than any other, Charles Manson truly met his match in Vincent Bugliosi.
—*Michael Rogers*

1982 ——————————

Sue Grafton publishes *A is for Alibi,* and the mystery columnist is not a fan, saying the book "lacks real flair."

1985 ——————————

Isabel Allende publishes *The House of the Spirits,* which the Book Review calls "spectacular."

1986 ——————————→

Rachel Ingalls's novel *Mrs. Caliban,* which all but disappeared after its 1982 publication, is re-released to acclaim.

Clockwise from top left: Midtown Manhattan, 1984; Greenpoint, 1994; Bryant Park, 1977; a New York bookstore, 1963.

1971–1996

Opposite: Central Park, 1979.
Clockwise from top: outside Parsons School of Design,
1979; Bryant Park, 1977; Penn Station, 1960.

Shere Hite, *The Hite Report*

BY ERICA JONG

A novelist known for her depictions of female sexuality reviewed a groundbreaking report on that very subject.

ONE OF THE FASCINATING THINGS ABOUT THE seemingly copious literature of sex is its glaring omissions: Although there are any number of books about female sexuality by men, there are virtually no books about male sexuality by women and relatively few books about male sexuality by men themselves. This would seem to indicate that women's sexuality is regarded as a "problem" whereas men's is not regarded at all (perhaps because it is seen as the norm). No woman I have ever met (or read about) would dare presume to tell a man what he feels during the sex act, how his orgasm is best obtained, whether he is feeling what he should be feeling—yet men have been telling women all those things about their sexuality for centuries. As one character in Doris Lessing's *The Golden Notebook* remarks: "Women of any sense know better, after all these centuries, than to interrupt when men start telling them how they feel about sex."

What Shere Hite has done seems very simple, but next to the inscrutable prose of Masters and Johnson, her simplicity is more than welcome. She sent questionnaires to 3,000 women of all ages, professions and geographical locations,

asking them everything about sex, orgasm, masturbation and she composed a book of their replies. The women speak in their own words and what they have to say is utterly fascinating and often surprising.

Though it may seem to many that sex is everywhere available and has become too free and too public, *The Hite Report* is quite another picture. As one woman says, "Being nonorgasmic, sex is often on my mind and takes a lot of my energy." It would also seem that a society obsessed with sex is starved for it rather than satiated. The explosion of porn, massage parlors and sexual guides is a symptom of puritanism, not its swan song.

We learn from *The Hite Report* just how much sexual starvation exists in the midst of this seeming plenty. We learn that 95 percent of women (even those who think themselves "frigid") always reach orgasm when they masturbate, even though no one taught them how and even though most of them feel guilty about it. We learn how they do it, how they hold their legs up for orgasm, what they think about, whether or not they make noise, move, lie still, what devices they use (from electric toothbrushes to water spouts!). We learn how they feel about intercourse, their anger at not reaching orgasm when their men do, their real pleasure in giving pleasure, their paradoxical tendency to suppress anger (and their own feelings) in an attempt to win love and approval.

In fact we learn many paradoxes about women from this book and one of the most moving realizations that emerges from it is the female tendency to tie the psyche into knots. Women, whether they love men or women, seem to be painfully divided about their sexuality. Their own needs and society's expectations for them are in conflict. Often it takes them years to admit what they like sexually and years longer to ask for it. The heritage of a patriarchy in which children were a man's wealth and ownership of women was the means of production has apparently left women confused about what role sex should play in life when society no longer needs them as baby machines.

Most of the respondents to Hite's questionnaires thought that the sexual revolution was a myth, that it had left them free to say yes (but not to say no), that the double standard was alive and well, that the quantity of sex had gone up, not the quality. Most of them labeled themselves "good girls" and told of family backgrounds in which their parents clearly communicated that sex for girls was bad and that girls who did "it" would be despised by boys. No wonder most of them grew up despising themselves. But it was also interesting to discover that despite the prevalence of sexual starvation (or, at least, anemia), the women came across, as a whole, as a very romantic group. They are still longing for the one perfect love, still desiring constancy rather than promiscuity.

Remember all those magazine articles of a few years ago about the sexual "revolution," the death of marriage, insatiable multi-orgasmic women and impotent men? Apparently none of them was true. The more sex changes, the more it stays the same. Read *The Hite Report* if you want to know how sex really is right now.

Hite on August 13, 1987.

John Cheever, *Falconer*

BY JOAN DIDION

In this review of John Cheever's fourth novel, Joan Didion opened with a lively defense of literary WASPs. "In a very real way," she wrote, "the white middle-class Protestant writer in America is in fact homeless"—a claim that ruffled feathers at the time, and would likely do so today. Didion's characteristic clarity and her capacity to convey the merits of Cheever's style shine in the review that follows.

SOME OF US ARE NOT JEWS. NEITHER ARE some of us Southerners, nor children of the Iroquois, nor the inheritors of any other notably dark and bloodied ground. Some of us are even Episcopalians. In the popular mind this absence of any particular claim on the conscience of the world is generally construed as a historical advantage, but in the small society of those who read and write it renders us "different," and a little suspect. We are not quite accredited for suffering, nor do we have tickets for the human comedy. We are believed to have known no poverty except that of our own life-force. We are seen by the tolerant as carriers merely of an exhausted culture, and by the less tolerant as carriers of some potentially demonic social virus. We are seen as

dealers in obscure manners and unwarranted pessimism. We are always "looking back." We are always lamenting the loss of our psychic home, a loss which is easy to dismiss—given our particular history in this particular country—as deficient in generality and even in credibility. Yet in a very real way the white middle-class Protestant writer in America is in fact homeless—as absent from the world of his fathers as he is "different" within the world of letters—and it is precisely this note of "homelessness" that John Cheever strikes with an almost liturgical intensity in his extraordinary new novel, *Falconer*.

Of course this note of exile and estrangement has always been present in Cheever's fiction, from the early stories on. But in the beginning Cheever characters appeared to be exiled merely by their own errors or passions or foolishness: lost wives and quixotic husbands, apparently golden individuals who conceived their children at the St. Regis Hotel and tumbled their card houses down for love of the grocery boy, love of the plumber, love of the neighbor who came to collect for Muscular Dystrophy and had six drinks and let her hair fall down. They tried to behave well and they drank too much. Their best light was that which dapples lawns on late summer afternoons, and their favorite note was "plaintive": everything they heard was "plaintive," and served to remind them that life and love were but fleeting shadows, to teach them to number their days and to call them home across those summer lawns. They yearned always after some abstraction symbolized by the word "home," after "tenderness," after "gentleness," after remembered houses where the fires were laid and the silver was polished and everything could be "decent" and "radiant" and "clear."

Such houses were hard to find in prime condition. To approach one was to hear the quarreling inside. To reach another was to find it boarded up, obscene with graffiti, lost for taxes. There was some gap between what these Cheever people searching for home had been led to expect and what they got, some error in expectations, and it became increasingly clear that Cheever did not locate the error entirely in the hearts of the searchers.

Alfred Kazin has described a Cheever story, one which opens with a non-fatal plane crash, this way: "The 'country husband' in this most brilliant of Cheever's stories returns home to find that his brush with death is not of the slightest interest to his family, so he falls in love with the babysitter. He does not get very far with the baby-sitter, so he goes to a therapist who prescribes woodworking. The story ends derisively on the brainwashed husband who will no longer stray from home. But who cares about this fellow?"

Actually this is not an accurate precis of "The Country Husband" (the story does not end "derisively," the husband is not "brainwashed," the story suggests not that the husband will "no longer stray from home" but rather that his "home" is a moral and economic illusion), nor does Kazin seem to have meant it to be; it is instead a deflationary reduction, the walker in the city giving a rhetorical raspberry to the kid down from Westchester in his Sunday School suit, and I

quote it only to illustrate the particular irritability that Cheever provokes among some readers.

Cheever is too "brilliant" for his own good, Cheever is too smooth by half. Cheever almost makes these readers "care" about his babysitters and brainwashed husbands and bewildered women with too much money and not a thought in their heads, but not quite. These readers see through Cheever's beautiful shams and glossy tricks, past his summer lawns and inherited pearls and what they see is this: a writer who seems to them to be working out, quite stubbornly and obsessively, allegorical variations on a single and profoundly unacceptable theme, that of "nostalgia," or the particular melancholia induced by long absence from one's country or home.

"Nostalgia" is in our time a pejorative word, and the emotion it represents is widely perceived as retrograde, sentimental and even "false." Yet Cheever has persisted throughout his career in telling us a story in which nostalgia is "real," and every time he tells this story he refines it more, gets closer to the bone, elides another summer lawn and pulls the rug from under another of his own successful performances. "The time for banal irony, the voice-over, is long gone," reflects Ezekiel Farragut, the entirely sentient protagonist of Cheever's new novel, *Falconer*. "Give me the unchanging profundity of nostalgia, love and death." In this sense of obsessive compression and abandoned artifice *Falconer* is a better book

1986 — The Nigerian playwright, poet and novelist Wole Soyinka wins the Nobel Prize in literature.

1989 — On February 14, the Ayatollah Ruhollah Khomeini says Salman Rushdie must die for writing *The Satanic Verses*.

1989 — The dissident and playwright Václav Havel becomes the president of Czechoslovakia.

1971–1996

Cheever at home in his office in Ossining, New York, on October 6, 1979.

than the Wapshot novels, a better book even than *Bullet Park*, for in *Falconer* those summer lawns are gone altogether, and the main narrative line is only a memory.

Falconer is the name of a prison (actually the name of the prison is "Daybreak House," but this "had never caught on"), and it is at Falconer that Farragut is serving time for the murder of his brother. "I thought that my life was one hundred per cent frustration," Farragut is advised by his wife, Marcia, when she visits Falconer for the first time. "But when you killed your brother I saw that I had underestimated my problems." Marcia, who is a truer lover of Italy and of one Maria Lippincott Hastings Guglielmi than she

is of Farragut, nonetheless would have visited sooner had she not been in Jamaica. "I," Marcia informs the guard who tells her the visitors' rules, "am a taxpayer. It costs me more to keep my husband in here than it costs me to send my son to a good school."

Cheever has a famous ear, but he is up to something more in *Falconer* than a comedy of prison manners. Events are peculiar. Farragut's beloved Jody, the one who knew how to save his face, escapes Falconer by masquerading as an acolyte when the Cardinal makes a helicopter visit. Farragut himself leaves Falconer, alive, in a body bag. On its surface *Falconer* seems at first to be a conventional novel of crime and punishment and redemption—a story about a man who kills his brother, goes to prison for it and escapes, chanced for the better—and yet the "crime" in this novel bears no more relation to the "punishment" than the punishment bears to the redemption. The surface here glitters and deceives. Causes and effects run deeper.

Of course Farragut has been, all his life, afflicted with nostalgia. Of course "home" has been hard to locate. Of course he has resorted to anodynes—in this case heroin—to dull his affliction. "There is a Degas painting of a woman with a bowl of chrysanthemums that had come to represent to Farragut the great serenity of 'mother.' The world kept urging him to match his own mother, a famous arsonist, snob, gas pumper and wing shot, against this image . . . why had the universe encouraged this gap?"

At Falconer there is no heroin to blur this question and Farragut must manage with methadone. "When do you think you'll be clean," Marcia asks. "I find it hard to imagine cleanliness," Farragut answers. "I can claim to imagine this, but it would be false. It would be as though I had claimed to reinstall myself in some afternoon of my youth." "That's why you're a lightweight," Marcia says. "Yes," Farragut says.

Yes and no. Of all those Cheever characters who have suffered nostalgia, Farragut is perhaps the first to apprehend that the home from which he has been gone too long is not necessarily on the map. He seems to be undergoing a Dark Night of the Soul, a purification, a period of suffering in order to re-enter the ceremonies of innocence, and in this context the question of when he will be "clean" has considerable poignance. As a matter of fact it is this question that Cheever has been asking all along—when will I be clean was the question on every summer lawn—but he has never before asked it outright, and with such transcendent arrogance of style Farragut is not

the first Cheever character to survive despite his father's attempt to abort him, but in the past it took core words. Farragut is not the first Cheever character to see freedom as the option to book a seat on the Tokyo plane, but in the past the option was open. Addiction has been common but not before to heroin. The spirit of fratricide has been general, but not until now the act. In this way *Falconer* is a kind of contemplation in shorthand, a meditation on the abstraction Cheever has always called "home" but has never before located so explicitly in the life of the spirit. I have every expectation that many people will read *Falconer* as another Cheever story about a brainwashed husband who lacked energy for the modern world, so he killed his brother and who cares, but let me tell you: it is not, and Cheever cares.

"Cheever has persisted throughout his career in telling us a story in which nostalgia is 'real,' and every time he tells this story he refines it more, gets closer to the bone, elides another summer lawn and pulls the rug from under another of his own successful performances."

An Exchange
with Alfred Kazin

TO THE EDITOR:

I am glad that Joan Didion admires John Cheever's *Falconer,* which is his best novel and has the force and subtlety of his marvelous short stories. But I am shocked by the self-pity and social venom with which she has constructed her review by isolating and enlarging on one sentence from my *Bright Book of Life* about Cheever's story "The Country Husband." I knew that Joan Didion was a true-blue American from the West and almost as much a traditionalist as I am. I had no idea that as a mere WASP she is "not quite accredited for suffering"; I have read all her books, and my impression is just the opposite.

Didion says that I misreported "The Country Husband." When I said that the hapless unloved husband was "brainwashed" at the end, I of course meant that he had been accommodated by his therapist to the life that robbed him of hope. When I said that he will "no longer stray from home," I meant just what Miss Didion means when she says "his 'home' is a moral and economic illusion."

It may not be my fault that Miss Didion finds it hard to read my writing. Her emotions are much too overloaded for book review. She virtually rings the whole piece around my next sentence—"But who cares about this fellow?"—but falsifies what I meant by this. I said that the husband of the story is not a very luminous or interesting human being; Miss Didion tacitly agrees. I added: ". . . there is no mastery in Cheever's story except Cheever's. It is Cheever one watches in the story, Cheever who moves us by the shape of his effort in every line by the cruel lucidity he brings to this most prosperous, equitable and accomplished world as a breaking of the heart." In this particular case Cheever plainly "cared" less about the husband than about his situation, his "illusion" that he had a "home."

None of this would matter if Miss Didion did not then proceed to a wild personal attack. She suggests that I did not wish to be honest in my reading of "The Country Husband."

This is worse than outrageous—it is stupid. I have devoted most of my working life to interpreting, and celebrating, a largely Protestant literature. I do not care to have my good faith as a critic impugned by someone who in order to praise John Cheever thinks it necessary to begin: "Some of us are not Jews. Some of us are even Episcopalians."

ALFRED KAZIN
New York City

JOAN DIDION REPLIES:

Oh, come off it, Alfred.

Joan Didion sits with her daughter, Quintana, and Abigail McCarthy, the writer and former wife of Senator Eugene McCarthy, on September 1, 1977. The two women were panelists for a discussion at the Kennedy Center titled "Literature and Politics: A Quest or Enduring Values?"

Michael Herr,
Dispatches

A major work of New Journalism, *Dispatches* chronicled Herr's experiences as the Vietnam correspondent for *Esquire*. Our reviewer offered high praise: "Quite simply, *Dispatches* is the best book to have been written about the Vietnam War."

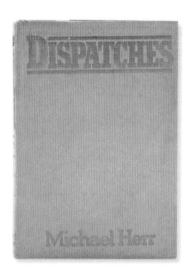

DURING THE PAST FEW YEARS I HAVE TRIED TO read most of the Vietnam books that have been published. I read them hoping to understand the war, to know what it was like to fight there, how it differed from all our other wars. Some already seem distant and dated. Others, like Daniel Lang's *Casualties of War* and Jonathan Schell's *Village of Ben Suc,* were chilling in their reflection of some of our servicemen's murderous detachment. I tried to finish Frances FitzGerald's *Fire in the Lake,* but although I was dazzled by the brilliance with which she illuminated Vietnam's political landscape, her book never quite penetrated my tangled emotions.

Certain books seemed to me to capture exactly the mood and madness of specific aspects of the war; Ron Kovic's mortification in *Born on the Fourth of July* and Ronald J. Glasser's burn ward memories in *365 Days* haunt and hurt. But now there is a book that seems to be making all the right sort of incoming noises that indicate a direct hit: Michael Herr's *Dispatches.*

Quite simply, *Dispatches* is the best book to have been written about the Vietnam War.

Dispatches must be read because, even if there already exists a surprisingly rich selection of writings on Vietnam, nothing else so far has even come close to conveying how different this war was from any we fought—or how utterly different were the methods and the men who fought for us.

Vietnam required not only new techniques of warfare, but new techniques in writing as well. News cameramen and photographers could show us sometimes what the war looked like, but an entirely new language, imagery and style were needed so that we could understand and feel. Until Michael Herr, no reporter or writer seemed to capture it. The previous books seem to have been trapped in styles left over from previous wars, and I read them feeling as dissatisfied with their attempts to explain the Vietnam experience as I have been with the astronauts' tedious responses to questions on what it was really like to orbit in space or walk on the moon. (Only Yuri Gagarin's thrilling "I am Eagle!" tells me anything at all.)

Herr's literary style derives from the era of acid rock, the Beatles' films, of that druggy, Hunter Thompson once-removed-from-reality appreciation of The Great Cosmic Joke. He was covering Vietnam for *Esquire*—"*Esquire*, wow, they got a guy over here?" a Marine asks him. "What . . . for? You tell 'em what we're wearin'?" Secondly, as Herr notes, he wasn't there to fight, he "was there to watch. . . . Talk about impersonating an identity, about locking into a role, about irony: I went to cover the war and the war covered me; an old story, unless of course you've never heard it." While the newspaper and news magazine correspondents were writing against daily or weekly deadlines, Herr's stories wouldn't appear in *Esquire* until five months after they'd been written. This lag gave him the opportunity to write thoughtful, polished, tough, compassionate pieces in which he could capture the image exactly: "Sitting in Saigon," he tells us, "was like sitting inside the petals of a poisoned flower."

To Michael Herr's everlasting credit he never ceased to feel deeply for the men with whom he served; he never became callous, always worried for them, agonized over them, on occasion even took up arms to defend them. His greatest service, I'm convinced, is this book. What more need one really say about our young who fought in Vietnam than this: "Along the road," Herr writes, "there is a two-dollar piece of issue. A poncho which has just been used to cover a dead Marine, a blood-puddled, mud-wet poncho going stiff in the wind. It has reared up there by the road in a horrible streaked ball. I'm walking along this road with two black grunts, and one of them gives the poncho a vicious, helpless kick. 'Go easy, man,' the other one says. 'That's the American flag you gettin' your foot into.'" —*C.D.B. Bryan*

Other Vietnam Classics

FIRE IN THE LAKE, BY FRANCES FITZGERALD 1972

This history of Vietnam—the country and the war—was published before the conflict had ended. The Book Review's assessment of the situation was bleak: "To any reader of this fine book the idea that we have some face left to save will seem a very sad joke, and one conclusion imposes itself."

A BRIGHT SHINING LIE, BY NEIL SHEEHAN 1988

The former New York Times reporter's famous account of John Paul Vann and American involvement in the war was called an essential work of "disillusion" in our pages. "If there is one book that captures the Vietnam War in the sheer Homeric scale of its passion and folly," wrote Ronald Steel, "this book is it."

THE THINGS THEY CARRIED, BY TIM O'BRIEN 1990

O'Brien's now-famous short story collection about a platoon of American soldiers—grunts—on the ground in Vietnam got a rave review calling it "high up on the list of best fiction about *any war.*"

THE SORROW OF WAR, BY BAO NINH 1995

Of this acclaimed novel by a Vietnamese author, the Book Review wrote, "Once again the reader learns that war is hell—even when your side is supposedly the winner."

JANUARY 9, 1983 | ESSAY

From the Poets in the Kitchen

BY PAULE MARSHALL

The novelist best known for her debut, Brown Girl, Brownstones, *a story of Barbadian immigrants living in Brooklyn, Marshall described her experience growing up within that community, and how the conversations of women gathered in her kitchen went on to inform her writing life.*

SOME YEARS AGO, WHEN I WAS TEACHING A graduate seminar in fiction at Columbia University, a well-known male novelist visited my class to speak on his development as a writer. In discussing his formative years, he seriously endangered his life by remarking that women writers are luckier than those of his sex because they usually spend so much time as children around their mothers and their mothers' friends in the kitchen.

My guest wasn't really being sexist or trying to be provocative. What he meant was that, given the way children are (or were) raised in our society, with little girls kept closer to home and their mothers, the woman writer stands a better chance of being exposed to the kind of talk that goes on among women, more often than not in the kitchen; and that this experience gives her an edge over her male counterpart by instilling in her an appreciation for ordinary speech.

"If you say what's on your mind in the language that comes to you from your parents and your street and friends you'll probably say something beautiful," Grace Paley tells her students. It's all a matter of exposure and a training of the ear for the would-be writer. And, according to my guest lecturer, this training often takes place in as unglamorous a setting as the kitchen.

He didn't know it, but he was essentially describing my experience as a little girl. I grew up among poets. Now they didn't look like poets—whatever that breed is supposed to look like. Nothing about them suggested that poetry was their calling. They were just a group of ordinary housewives and mothers, my mother included, who dressed in a way (shapeless housedresses, dowdy felt hats and long, dark, solemn coats) that made it impossible for me to imagine they had ever been young.

Nor did they do what poets were supposed to do—spend their days in an attic room writing verses. They never put pen to paper except to write occasionally to their relatives in Barbados. "I take my pen in hand hoping these few lines will find you in health as they leave me fair for the time being," was the way their letters invariably began. Rather, their day was spent "scrubbing floor," as they described the work they did.

Several mornings a week these unknown bards would put an apron and a pair of old house shoes in a shopping bag and take the train or streetcar from our section of Brooklyn out to Flatbush. There, those who didn't have steady jobs would wait on designated corners for the white housewives in the neighborhood to come along and bargain with them over pay for a day's work cleaning their houses. This was the ritual even in the winter. Later, armed with the few

THE NEW YORK TIMES BOOK REVIEW

dollars they had earned, which in their vocabulary became "a few raw-mouth pennies," they made their way back to our neighborhood, where they would sometimes stop off to have a cup of tea or cocoa together before going home to cook dinner for their husbands and children.

The basement kitchen of the brownstone house where my family lived was the usual gathering place. Once inside the warm safety of its walls the women threw off the drab coats and hats, seated themselves at the large center table, drank their cups of tea or cocoa, and talked. While my sister and I sat at a smaller table doing our homework, they talked—endlessly, passionately, poetically, and with impressive range. No subject was beyond them.

True, they would indulge in the usual gossip: whose husband was running with whom, whose daughter looked slightly "in the way" (pregnant) under her bridal gown as she walked down the aisle. But they also tackled the great issues of the time. They were always discussing the state of the economy. It was the mid and late 30s then, and the aftershock of the Depression, with its soup lines and suicides on Wall Street, was still being felt.

They talked politics. Roosevelt was their hero. He had come along and rescued the country, and in gratitude they christened their sons Franklin and Delano and hoped they would live up to the names.

If F.D.R. was their hero, Marcus Garvey was their God. The name of the fiery, Jamaican-born black nationalist of the 20s was constantly invoked around the table. For he had been their leader when they first came to the United States from the West Indies shortly after World War I. They had contributed to his organization, the United Negro Improvement Association, out of their meager salaries, bought shares in his

Marshall prepares a Barbadian dish in October 1969.

ill-fated Black Star Shipping Line, and at the height of the movement they had marched in Harlem during the great Garvey Day parades. Garvey: He lived on through the power of their memories.

And their talk was of war and rumors of wars. They raged against World War II when it broke out. If it was their sons, they swore they would keep them out of the Army by giving them soap to eat each day to make their hearts sound defective. Hitler? He was for them "the devil incarnate."

Then there was home. They reminisced often and at length about home. The old country. Barbados—or Bimshire, as they affectionately called it. The little Caribbean island in the sun they loved but had to leave.

America came in for both good and bad marks. They lashed out at it for the racism they encountered. They took to task some of the people they worked for, especially those who gave them only a hard-boiled egg and a few spoonfuls of cottage cheese for lunch. "As if anybody can scrub floor on an egg and some cheese that don't have no taste to it!"

Yet although they caught H in "this man country," as they called America, it was nonetheless a place where "you could at least see your way to make a dollar." They might even one day accumulate enough dollars, with both them and their husbands working, to buy the brownstone houses which, like my family, they were only leasing. This was their consuming ambition: to "buy house" and to see the children through.

The talk that filled the kitchen those afternoons was highly functional. Not only did it help them recover from the long wait on the corner that morning and the bargaining over their labor, it restored them to a sense of themselves and reaffirmed their self-worth. Through language they were able to overcome the humiliations of the work-day.

That freewheeling, wide-ranging, exuberant talk functioned as an outlet for their tremendous creative energy. They were women in whom the need for self-expression was strong, and since language was the only vehicle readily available to them they made of it an art form that—in keeping with the African tradition in which art and life are one—was an integral part of their lives.

Confronted by a world they could not encompass, and at the same time finding themselves permanently separated from the world they had known, they took refuge in language. "Language is the only homeland," Czesław Miłosz, the émigré Polish writer and Nobel laureate, has said. This is what it became for the women at the kitchen table.

My mother and her friends were after all the female counterpart of Ralph Ellison's invisible man. They suffered a triple invisibility, being black, female and foreigners. They really didn't count in American society except as a source of

cheap labor. They couldn't tolerate the fact of their invisibility, their powerlessness. And they fought back, using the only weapon at their command: the spoken word.

Those late afternoon conversations were a way for them to exercise some measure of control over their lives. "Soully-gal, talk yuh talk!" they were always exhorting each other. "In this man world you got to take yuh mouth and make a gun!" They were in control, if only verbally and if only for the two hours or so that they remained in our house.

They had taken the standard English taught them in the primary schools of Barbados and transformed it into an idiom, an instrument that more adequately described them—changing around the syntax and imposing their own rhythm and accent so that the sentences were more pleasing to their ears. They added the few African sounds and words that had survived, such as the derisive suck-teeth sound and the word "yam," meaning to eat. And to make it more vivid, they brought to bear a raft of metaphors, parables, Biblical quotations, sayings and the like:

Nothing, no matter how beautiful, was ever described as simply beautiful. It was always "beautiful-ugly": the beautiful-ugly dress, the beautiful-ugly house, the beautiful-ugly car. Why the word "ugly," I used to wonder, when the thing they were referring to was beautiful, and they knew it. Why the antonym, the contradiction, the linking of opposites? It used to puzzle me greatly as a child.

There is the theory in linguistics which states that the idiom of a people, the way they use language, reflects not only the most fundamental views they hold of themselves and the world but their very conception of reality. Perhaps in using the term "beautiful-ugly" to describe nearly everything, my mother and her friends were expressing what they believed to be a fundamental dualism in life: the idea that a thing is at the same time its opposite.

Using everyday speech, simple commonplace words—but always with imagination and skill—they gave voice to the most complex ideas. Flannery O'Connor would have approved how they made ordinary language work, as she put it, "double-time," stretching, shading, deepening its meaning. Like Joseph Conrad they were always trying to infuse new life in the "old old words worn thin . . . by . . . careless usage."

By the time I was 8 or 9, I graduated from the kitchen to the Macon Street branch of the Brooklyn Public Library, and thus from the spoken to the written word.

I was sheltered from the storm of adolescence in the library, reading voraciously, indiscriminately, from Jane Austen to Zane Grey, with a special passion for the long, full-blown, richly detailed 18th- and 19th-century picaresque tales: *Tom Jones. Great Expectations. Vanity Fair.*

But although I loved nearly everything I read, I sensed a lack. Something I couldn't quite define was missing. And then one day I came across a book by Paul Laurence Dunbar, and I found the photograph of a wistful, sad-eyed poet who to my surprise was black. I turned to a poem at random. "Little brown-baby wif spa'klin' / eyes / Come to yo' pappy an' set on his knee." Although I had a little difficulty at first with the words in dialect, the poem spoke to me as nothing I had read before of the closeness, the special relationship I had had with my father, who by then had become an ardent believer in Father Divine and gone to live in Father's "kingdom" in Harlem. Reading it helped to ease the tight knot of sorrow and longing I carried around in my chest that refused to go away. I read another poem. "Lias! "Lias! Bless de Lawd! / Don' you know de day's / erbroad? / Ef you don' get up, you scamp / Dey'll be trouble in dis camp." It reminded me of the way my mother sometimes yelled at my sister and me to get out of bed in the mornings.

I began to search for books and stories and poems about "The Race," about my people. While not abandoning Thackeray, Fielding, Dickens and the others, I started asking the reference librarian, who was white, for books by Negro writers, although I did so at first with a feeling of shame— the shame I and many others used to experience in those days whenever the word "Negro" or "colored" came up.

No grade school teacher of mine had ever mentioned Dunbar or James Weldon Johnson or Langston Hughes. I didn't know that Zora Neale Hurston existed. Nor was I aware of people like Frederick Douglass and Harriet Tubman—their spirit and example—or the great 19th-century abolitionist and feminist Sojourner Truth. There wasn't even Negro History Week when I attended P.S. 35 on Decatur Street!

It was around that time that I began harboring the dangerous thought of someday trying to write myself. Dunbar permitted me to dream that I might someday write, and with something of the power with words my mother and her friends possessed.

When people ask me who my major influences were, they are sometimes a little disappointed when I don't immediately name the usual literary giants. True, I am indebted to those writers, white and black, whom I read during my formative years and still read for instruction and pleasure. But they were preceded in my life by another set of giants whom I always acknowledge before all others: the group of women around the table long ago. They taught me my first lessons in the narrative art. They trained my ear. They set a standard of excellence. This is why the best of my work must be attributed to them; it stands as testimony to the rich legacy of language and culture they so freely passed on to me in the wordshop of the kitchen.

Hurston in 1950.

Zora Neale Hurston

BY HENRY LOUIS GATES JR.

The critic and historian Henry Louis Gates Jr. has contributed many reviews and essays to the Book Review. Here, he examined the legacy of Zora Neale Hurston, a prominent voice of the 1930s and 40s who, until recently, had faded into relative obscurity.

HOW WAS HURSTON—THE RECIPIENT OF TWO Guggenheim Fellowships and the author of four novels, a dozen short stories, two musicals, two books on black mythology, dozens of essays and a prizewinning autobiography—lost from all but her most loyal followers for two full decades? There is no easy answer to this question. It is clear, however, that the enthusiastic responses Hurston's work engenders today were not shared by several of her black male contemporaries. In reviews of *Mules and Men* (1935), *Their Eyes Were Watching God* (1937) and *Moses: Man of the Mountain* (1939), Sterling A. Brown, Richard Wright and Ralph Ellison condemned her work as "socially unconscious" and derided her "minstrel technique." Of *Moses,* Ellison concluded, "for Negro fiction, it did nothing." Hurston's mythic realism, lush and dense with a lyrical black idiom, was regarded as counterrevolutionary by the proponents of social realism, and she competed with Wright, Ellison and Brown for the right to determine the ideal fictional mode for representing

Negro life. She lost the battle but may yet win the war.

In a marvelous example of what Freud might call the return of the repressed, Hurston has been rediscovered in a manner unprecedented in the black literary tradition. Since 1975, when Walker published "Looking for Zora," a moving account of her search for and discovery of her own literary lineage and Hurston's grave, contemporary readers have been treated to a feast of the formerly forgotten writer's words in re-edited versions of her works and in two sustained literary biographies. Of these publications, none are more important to reassessing Hurston's standing than Robert Hemenway's new edition of *Dust Tracks on a Road* and Blyden Jackson's edition of her third novel, *Moses: Man of the Mountain.*

Mr. Hemenway, a professor of English at the University of Kentucky and the author of a superb Hurston biography, has restored three chapters that were either heavily revised for or deleted from the autobiography when it was first published. In these chapters Hurston gives us, among other things, her full critique of racial chauvinism, imperialism, neocolonialism and economic exploitation.

Even Hurston's most devoted readers have had difficulty understanding some conservative aspects of her politics—particularly her disapproval of the United States Supreme Court decision outlawing racial segregation in public schools. However, the restored version of the chapter entitled "Seeing the World as It Is" reveals that Hurston questioned "race consciousness"—"It is a deadly explosive on the tongues of men"—because she viewed it as being on a continuum with Nazism. She also argued that Hitler's transgression in subjugating neighboring countries was that he treated Europeans just as Europeans had treated their colonial subjects in Africa, Asia and Latin America. She devotes much of this chapter to a critique of neocolonialism: "One hand in somebody else's pocket and one on your gun, and you are highly civilized. Your heart is where it belongs—in your pocketbook. . . . Democracy, like religion, never was designed to make our profits less." Virtually overnight Hurston's politics have become so much more complex and curious. One wonders what Wright would have thought had he read this restored material.

Not only was Hurston more "political" than we believed, but—according to this edition—she was a decade older as well. When she enrolled in Howard University in 1918, she was not 17 years old; she was 27. And when she died broken in spirit and health in 1960, she not only looked to be a woman of 69, she was. These two facts are certain to generate all sorts of reconsiderations of Hurston's place in the black literary tradition, most, I would imagine, to her benefit.

Rereading Hurston, I was struck by how conscious her choices were. The explicit and the implicit, the background and the foreground, what she states and what she keeps to herself—these, it seems to me, reflect Hurston's reaction to traditional black male autobiographies (in which, "in the space where sex should be," as one critic says, we find white racism) and to a potentially hostile readership. As Lyndall Gordon says of Virginia Woolf, "the unlovable woman was always the woman who used words to effect. She was caricatured as a tattle, a scold, a shrew, a witch." Hurston, who had few peers as a wordsmith, was often caricatured by black male writers as frivolous, as the fool who "cut the monkey" for voyeurs and pandered to the rich white women who were her patrons. I believe that for protection, she made up significant parts of herself, like a masquerader putting on a disguise for the ball, like a character in her fictions. Hurston wrote herself just as she sought in her works to rewrite the "self" of "the race." She revealed her imagination as it sought to mold and interpret her environment. She censored all that her readership could draw upon to pigeonhole or define her life as a synecdoche of "the race problem."

Hurston's achievement in *Dust Tracks* is twofold. First, she gives us a writer's life—rather than an account of "the Negro problem"—in a language as "dazzling" as Mr. Hemenway says it is. So many events in the book were shaped by the author's growing mastery of books and language, but she employs both the linguistic rituals of the dominant culture and those of the black vernacular tradition. These two speech communities are the sources of inspiration for Hurston's novels and autobiography. This double voice unreconciled—a verbal analogue of her double experiences as a woman in a male-dominated world and as a black person in a nonblack world—strikes me as her second great achievement.

The unresolved tension between Hurston's two voices suggests that she fully understood the principles of modernism. Hers is a narrative strategy of self-division, the literary analogue of the hyphen in "Afro-American," the famous twoness W. E. B. Du Bois said was characteristic of the black experience. Hurston uses the two voices to celebrate both the psychological fragmentation of modernity and the black American. Hurston—the "real" Zora Neale Hurston whom we long to locate in this book—dwells in the silence that separates these two voices: she is both and neither, bilingual and mute. This brilliant strategy, I believe, helps explain why so many contemporary critics and writers can turn to her works again and again and be repeatedly startled at her artistry.

I wrote at the outset that Hurston's works have served as models that a new generation of black women writers have revised. Who in the black tradition did Hurston revise? Who were her formal influences? Blyden Jackson's insightful introduction to *Moses: Man of the Mountain* not only restores to us this important allegorical novel but helps us understand much about Hurston's influences.

The novel translates the Moses myth into the black tradition, creating a Moses who is an accomplished hoodoo man. Though allegorical, the novel is also a satire of, as Mr. Jackson writes, the "regrettably wide and deep division in loyalties among (the black) upper class, its black bourgeoisie, and the Negro masses from whom (Hurston's) folklore came." Mr. Jackson, a professor of English at the University of North Carolina, writes that *Moses* is unique in the black tradition because mythology not only informs the structure of the novel but assumes that structure as well. In other words, Hurston creates, or re-creates, a myth, the myth of a black Moses. She signifies on the Moses legends—she parodies and revises them, making them at once black and an allegory of black history in the West.

Ralph Ellison wrote of *Moses* that *Green Pastures,* the melodramatic, widely popular play that depicted an all-black heaven, had challenged Hurston to do for Moses what it had done for Jehovah. But Hurston did it artistically rather than melodramatically. Mr. Hemenway reminds us that Freud published two controversial essays on Moses' Egyptian origins a year before Hurston wrote her *Moses.* Perhaps these shaped her writing. I believe, however, that Hurston's ultimate source was another black woman writer, Frances E. W. Harper, who published her own account in *Moses: A Story of the Nile* in 1869. Both works are allegories, both stress Moses' identity as a conjurer, and both utilize multiple voices.

If a generation of splendid writers has turned to Hurston for their voices, it is fitting that she herself quite probably turned to a black female literary ancestor. But Hurston's lasting and most original contribution is that she always found, as she put it, "a Negro way of saying" a thing and appropriated the English language and Western literary forms to create the black and female perspectives that her texts so splendidly embody. The publication of Hurston's complete uncollected works is what we actually need. But with the republication of these two books, we will not lose Hurston again.

1990

J. K. Rowling dreams up Harry Potter while on a train ride from Manchester to London.

1990

Octavio Paz wins the Nobel for his "impassioned writing with wide horizons, characterized by sensuous intelligence and humanistic integrity."

1990

Days after Simon & Schuster cancels Bret Easton Ellis's serial-killer novel, *American Psycho,* Vintage Books snaps it up.

1971–1996

Art Spiegelman, "Maus"

BY KEN TUCKER

Spiegelman's comic strip had not yet been published in book form when Ken Tucker called attention to it in our pages.

SINCE 1980, A SELF-DESCRIBED "GRAPHIX magazine" called *Raw* has published six installments of "Maus," a comic strip written and drawn by Art Spiegelman. In "Maus," Mr. Spiegelman recreates the experiences of his parents, Polish Jews who were persecuted by the Nazis during World War II. A remarkable feat of documentary detail and novelistic vividness, the strip is also striking in another way: Its protagonists are drawn as mice; their Nazi captors are represented as cats.

Co-edited by Mr. Spiegelman and Francoise Mouly, *Raw* is usually published twice a year in New York. Its 12,000 copies are sold mainly in bookstores around the country. Perhaps because of *Raw*'s limited circulation, few people are aware of the unfolding literary event "Maus" represents. Bernard Riley, curator of popular and applied graphic art for the Library of Congress, says the strip's narrative structure and its social and political themes make it comparable to 19th-century literature. "It's good, serious work," Mr. Riley says. "'Maus' brings back an excitement that has been lost in comic art. You get the

feeling reading him that you're on the cutting edge of graphics, a field that has been stagnant for a long time now."

Mr. Spiegelman tells the story of his parents as he first heard it, through a series of conversations with his father. The artist himself appears in the strip as a laconic narrator-mouse in jeans and a rumpled shirt, perennially puffing on a cigarette. He and his father take aimless walks through the latter's Rego Park, Queens, neighborhood or sit around a small kitchen table while Art coaxes the stoic Vladek Spiegelman to tell the story of his life: Vladek's early career in Poland as a textile salesman; his courtship of and marriage to Art's mother, Anja, in 1937; the couple's internment in a Nazi concentration camp and their escape in 1945. Mr. Spiegelman explores the legacy of that period. Most of the Spiegelman family—grandparents, aunts, uncles, cousins—either died or disappeared. His mother eventually committed suicide and Vladek subsequently married Mala, a Polish concentration camp survivor. Running through the story is Vladek's unrelenting obsession with his experience at the hands of the Nazis. This is an epic story told in tiny pictures.

The drawing in "Maus" is blunt and unadorned. Characters are sketched with a few lines in black-and-white panels and shaded with the most elementary crosshatching. As art, Mr. Spiegelman says, "Maus" is intentionally simple: "seeing these small pages of doodle drawings—rough, quick drawings—makes it seem like we found somebody's diary and are publishing facsimiles of it."

Mr. Spiegelman's characters stand, dress and speak as humans; they just happen to have long, narrow, white, mouse faces. Why mice? "A few years ago I was looking at a lot of animated cartoons from the 1920s and 30s, and I was struck by the fact that, in many of them, there was virtually no difference between the way mice and black people were drawn. This got me thinking about drawing a comic strip that used mice in a metaphor for the black experience in America. Well, two minutes into it, I realized that I didn't know the first thing about being black, but I was Jewish, and I was very aware of the experiences of my parents in World War II, so that pushed me in that direction.

"What amazed me was that I have continued to find parallels, some of them painfully ironic, to this artistic metaphor. For example, in *Mein Kampf* Hitler refers to Jews as 'vermin.' I saw a Nazi propaganda film in which shots of crowds of Jews in a busy marketplace were contrasted with shots of scurrying rats. There is also a short story by Kafka called 'Josephine the Singer, or the Mouse Folk' which portrays Jews as mice.

"All of these things served as buttresses for what I was attempting," Mr. Spiegelman says. "Then too, I needed to deal with the characters as animals to have some distance from the materials—in an early version of the story I started out doing portraits of my parents, but it became too sentimental. Comics is a language of signs, and by using these masklike faces on top of what are real people, the metaphor remains useful, and adds to the story a resonance it wouldn't have otherwise."

This is Mr. Spiegelman's triumph in "Maus": He tempts sentimentality by suggesting a pop-culture cliché—wide-eyed mice menaced by hissing cats—and then thoroughly denies that sentimentality with the sharp, cutting lines of his drawing and the terse realism of his dialogue.

"This is an epic story told in tiny pictures."

Does it sound odd to speak of comic strips in such serious terms? Can a medium whose most pervasive representatives are the perennial best-sellers Snoopy the dog and Garfield the cat possibly interest serious readers? Only in America would these questions even arise. Comic strips—prized as a fresh, even radical variation on fine art throughout the world, particularly in Europe and Japan—are in America widely reviled as the lowest of the low arts, aimed, most adults assume, at young children or immature eccentrics. Few Americans who are otherwise well-informed and open-minded in cultural matters seem aware of the excellent, sometimes innovative work being done by a small but prolific number of comic-strip artists.

Comic strips with political or avant-garde esthetics, with intentions beyond mere entertainment, are not new. By the 1960s, however, the newspaper comic strip and its companion format, the comic book, had become so tediously familiar, so segregated as a diversion created solely for children, that a rebellion was almost inevitable. By the end of the decade, "underground comics" had appeared. They reveled in colorful tales of drug consumption and explicit sex, and unleashed at least one genius—the savagely misanthropic and witty Robert Crumb—and a whole generation of original artists. Mr. Feiffer notes that "'Maus' is not a 60s work—it's not countercultural at all. There is no reason why a much larger audience than the one that usually reads comics could not become engrossed in 'Maus.'"

Toni Morrison, *Beloved*

BY MARGARET ATWOOD

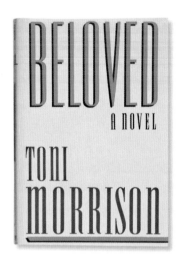

Sometimes a book that will become an undisputed classic is met at the moment of its publication with appropriate awe. Such was the case with Morrison's *Beloved,* a remarkable ghost story set in the years after the Civil War. The book won the Pulitzer Prize for fiction, and in 2006 was named the best novel of the previous 25 years by a group of prominent writers, critics and editors polled by the Book Review.

BELOVED IS TONI MORRISON'S FIFTH NOVEL, and another triumph. Indeed, Morrison's versatility and technical and emotional range appear to know no bounds. If there were any doubts about her stature as a pre-eminent American novelist, of her own or any other generation, *Beloved* will put them to rest. In three words or less, it's a hair-raiser.

In *Beloved,* Morrison turns away from the contemporary scene that has been her concern of late. This new novel is set after the end of the Civil War, during the period of so-called Reconstruction, when a great deal of random violence was let loose upon blacks, both the slaves freed by Emancipation and others who had been given or had bought their freedom

earlier. But there are flashbacks to a more distant period, when slavery was still a going concern in the South and the seeds for the bizarre and calamitous events of the novel were sown. The setting is similarly divided: the countryside near Cincinnati, where the central characters have ended up, and a slave-holding plantation in Kentucky, ironically named Sweet Home, from which they fled 18 years before the novel opens.

There are many stories and voices in this novel, but the central one belongs to Sethe, a woman in her mid-30s, who is living in an Ohio farmhouse with her daughter, Denver, and her mother-in-law Baby Suggs. *Beloved* is such a unified novel that it's difficult to discuss it without giving away the plot, but it must be said at the outset that it is, among other things, a ghost story, for the farmhouse is also home to a sad, malicious and angry ghost, the spirit of Sethe's baby daughter, who had her throat cut under appalling circumstances 18 years before, when she was 2. We never know this child's full name, but we—and Sethe—think of her as Beloved, because that is what is on her tombstone. Sethe wanted

Morrison photographed in Manhattan on November 17, 2008.

"Dearly Beloved," from the funeral service, but had only enough strength to pay for one word. Payment was 10 minutes of sex with the tombstone engraver. This act, which is recounted early in the novel, is a keynote for the whole book: in the world of slavery and poverty, where human beings are merchandise, everything has its price, and price is tyrannical.

"Who would have thought that a little old baby could harbor so much rage?," Sethe thinks, but it does; breaking mirrors, making tiny handprints in cake icing, smashing dishes and manifesting itself in pools of blood-red light. As the novel opens, the ghost is in full possession of the house, having driven away Sethe's two young sons. Old Baby Suggs, after a lifetime of slavery and a brief respite of freedom—purchased for her by the Sunday labor of her son Halle, Sethe's husband—has given up and died. Sethe lives with her memories, almost all of them bad. Denver, her teen-age daughter, courts the baby ghost because, since her family has been ostracized by the neighbors, she doesn't have anyone else to play with.

The supernatural element is treated, not in an *Amityville Horror,* watch-me-make-your-flesh-creep mode, but with magnificent practicality, like the ghost of Catherine Earnshaw in *Wuthering Heights.* All the main characters in the book believe in ghosts, so it's merely natural for this one to be there. As Baby Suggs says, "Not a house in the country ain't packed to its rafters with some dead Negro's grief. We lucky this ghost is a baby. My husband's spirit was to come back in here? or yours? Don't talk to me. You lucky." In fact, Sethe would rather have the ghost there than not there. It is, after all, her adored child, and any sign of it is better, for her, than nothing.

This grotesque domestic equilibrium is disturbed by the arrival of Paul D., one of the "Sweet Home men" from Sethe's past. The Sweet Home men were the male slaves of the establishment.

Their owner, Mr. Garner, is no Simon Legree; instead he's a best-case slave-holder, treating his "property" well, trusting them, allowing them choice in the running of his small plantation, and calling them "men" in defiance of the neighbors, who want all male blacks to be called "boys." But Mr. Garner dies, and weak, sickly Mrs. Garner brings in her handiest male relative, who is known as "the schoolteacher." This Goebbels-like paragon combines viciousness with intellectual pretensions; he's a sort of master-race proponent who measures the heads of the slaves and tabulates the results to demonstrate that they are more like animals than people. Accompanying him are his two sadistic and repulsive nephews. From there it's all downhill at Sweet Home, as the slaves try to escape, go crazy or are murdered. Sethe, in a trek that makes the ice-floe scene in *Uncle Tom's Cabin* look like a stroll around the block, gets out, just barely; her husband, Halle, doesn't. Paul D. does, but has some very unpleasant adventures along the way, including a literally nauseating sojourn in a 19th-century Georgia chain gang.

Through the different voices and memories of the book, including that of Sethe's mother, a survivor of the infamous slave-ship crossing, we experience American slavery as it was lived by those who were its objects of exchange, both at its best—which wasn't very good—and at its worst, which was as bad as can be imagined. Above all, it is seen as one of the most viciously antifamily institutions human beings have ever devised. The slaves are motherless, fatherless, deprived of their mates, their children, their kin. It is a world in which people suddenly vanish and are never seen again, not through accident or covert operation or terrorism, but as a matter of everyday legal policy.

Slavery is also presented to us as a paradigm of how most people behave when they are given absolute power over other people. The first effect, of course, is that they start believing in their own superiority and justifying their actions by it. The second effect is that they make a cult of the inferiority of those they subjugate. It's no coincidence that the first of the deadly sins, from which all the others were supposed to stem, is Pride, a sin of which Sethe is, incidentally, also accused.

Back in the present tense, in chapter one, Paul D. and Sethe make an attempt to establish a "real" family, whereupon the baby ghost, feeling excluded, goes berserk, but is driven out by Paul D.'s stronger will. So it appears. But then, along comes a strange, beautiful, real flesh-and-blood young woman, about 20 years old, who can't seem to remember where she comes from, who talks like a young child, who has an odd, raspy voice and no lines on her hands, who takes an intense, devouring interest in Sethe, and who says her name is Beloved.

Students of the supernatural will admire the way this twist is handled. Morrison blends a knowledge of folklore—for instance, in many traditions, the dead cannot return from the grave unless called, and it's the passions of the living that keep them alive—with a highly original treatment. The reader is kept guessing; there's a lot more to Beloved than any one character can see, and she manages to be many things to several people. She is a catalyst for revelations as well as self-revelations; through her we come to know not only how, but why, the original child Beloved was killed. And through her also Sethe achieves, finally, her own form of self-exorcism, her own self-accepting peace.

In this book, the other world exists and magic works, and the prose is up to it. If you can believe page one—and Morrison's verbal authority compels belief—you're hooked on the rest of the book. The epigraph to *Beloved* is from the Bible, Romans 9:25: "I will call them my people, which were not my people; and her beloved, which was not beloved." Taken by itself, this might seem to favor doubt about, for instance, the extent to which Beloved was really loved, or the extent to which Sethe herself was rejected by her own community. But there is more to it than that. The passage is from a chapter in which the Apostle Paul ponders, Job-like, the ways of God toward humanity, in particular the evils and inequities visible everywhere on the earth. Paul goes on to talk about the fact that the Gentiles, hitherto despised and outcast, have now been redefined as acceptable. The passage proclaims, not rejection, but reconciliation and hope. It continues: "And it shall come to pass, that in the place where it was said unto them, Ye are not my people; there shall they be called the children of the living God."

Morrison is too smart, and too much of a writer, not to have intended this context. Here, if anywhere, is her own comment on the goings-on in her novel, her final response to the measuring and dividing and excluding "schoolteachers" of this world. An epigraph to a book is like a key signature in music, and *Beloved* is written in major.

1991 —————————————

Naomi Wolf publishes *The Beauty Myth,* which the paper calls "sweeping, messy, vigorous, callow but stouthearted."

1993 ——————————————

The Book Review publishes in color for the first time.

1993 ——————————————→

Toni Morrison wins the Nobel Prize for "novels characterized by visionary force and poetic import."

1971–1996

275

Black Writers in Praise of Toni Morrison

After *Beloved* did not win the National Book Award, the Book Review published a statement in her defense signed by 48 writers.

DESPITE THE INTERNATIONAL STATURE OF Toni Morrison, she has yet to receive the national recognition that her five major works of fiction entirely deserve: she has yet to receive the keystone honors of the National Book Award or the Pulitzer Prize. We, the undersigned black critics and black writers, here assert ourselves against such oversight and harmful whimsy.

The legitimate need for our own critical voice in relation to our own literature can no longer be denied. We, therefore, urgently affirm our rightful and positive authority in the realm of American letters and, in this prideful context, we do raise this tribute to the author of *The Bluest Eye, Sula, Song of Solomon, Tar Baby* and *Beloved*.

Alive, we write this testament of thanks to you, dear Toni: alive, beloved and persevering, magical. Among the fecund intimacies of our hidden past, and among the coming days of dream or nightmares that will follow from the bidden knowledge of our conscious heart, we find your life work ever building to a monument of vision and discovery and trust. You have never turned away the searching eye, the listening ear attuned to horror or to histories providing for our faith. And freely you have given to us every word that you have found important to the forward movement of our literature, our life. For all of America, for all of American letters, you have advanced the moral and artistic standards by which we must measure the daring and the love of our national imagination and our collective intelligence as a people.

Your gifts to us have changed and made more gentle our real time together. And so we write, here, hoping not to delay, not to arrive, in any way, late with this, our simple tribute to the seismic character and beauty of your writing. And, furthermore, in grateful wonder at the advent of *Beloved*, your most recent gift to our community, our country, our conscience, our courage flourishing as it grows, we here record our pride, our respect and our appreciation for the treasury of your findings and invention.

Robert Allen, Maya Angelou, Houston A. Baker Jr., Toni Cade Bambara, Amina Baraka, Amiri Baraka, Jerome Brooks, Wesley Brown, Robert Chrisman, Barbara Christian, Lucille Clifton, J. California Cooper, Jayne Cortez, Angela Davis, Thulani Davis, Alexis De Veaux, Mari Evans, Nikky Finney, Ernest J. Gaines, Henry Louis Gates Jr., Paula Giddings, Vertamae Grosvenor, Cheryll Y. Greene, Rosa Guy, Calvin Hernton, Nathan Irvin Huggins, Gloria T. Hull, Gale Jackson, June Jordan, Paule Marshall, Nellie McKay, Louise Meriwether, Louise Patterson, Richard Perry, Arnold Rampersad, Eugene Redmond, Sonia Sanchez, Hortense Spillers, Luisah Teish, Joyce Carol Thomas, Eleanor Traylor, Quincy Troupe, Alice Walker, Mary Helen Washington, John Wideman, Margaret Wilkerson, John A. Williams, Sherley Anne Williams.

Morrison on December 23, 1985.

Randy Shilts: "It Was Happening to People I Cared About"

The investigative journalist spoke about researching—and writing—*And the Band Played On,* his blockbuster book about the paltry governmental response to the AIDS epidemic.

Shilts on November 11, 1987.

"ANY GOOD REPORTER COULD HAVE DONE THIS story," said Randy Shilts, explaining how a political reporter for *The San Francisco Chronicle* was drawn to covering AIDS full time. "But I think the reason I did it, and no one else did, is because I am gay. It was happening to people I cared about and loved."

In a telephone interview from a New York hotel where he was staying during a book tour, Mr. Shilts said his coverage of the AIDS story for the paper has been unusual, but not that extraordinary. He has essentially devoted the last five years of his life to writing about the AIDS epidemic. He took only a six-month leave from *The Chronicle* to work on *And the Band Played On.*

"If I were going to write a news story about my experiences covering AIDS for the past five years," Mr. Shilts said, "the lead would be: In November of 1983, when I was at the San Francisco Press Club getting my first award for AIDS coverage, Bill Kurtis, who was then an anchor for the *CBS Morning News,* delivered the keynote speech. . . .

"He started with a little joke. . . . In Nebraska the day before, he said he was going to San Francisco. Everybody started making AIDS jokes and he said, 'Well, what's the hardest part about having AIDS?' The punch line was, 'Trying to convince your wife that you're Haitian.'" The episode, Mr. Shilts remarked, "says everything about how the media had dealt with AIDS. Bill Kurtis felt that he could go in front of a journalists' group in San Francisco and make AIDS jokes. First of all, he could assume that nobody there would be gay and, if they were gay, they wouldn't talk about it and that nobody would take offense at that. To me, that summed up the whole problem of dealing with AIDS in the media. Obviously, the reason I covered AIDS from the start was that, to me, it was never something that happened to those other people." —*Gina Kolata*

Gabriel García Márquez, *Love in the Time of Cholera*

BY THOMAS PYNCHON

Three years after he was awarded the Nobel Prize, García Márquez published his great novel of love and passion. Pynchon, whose novels are of similarly vast and sprawling scope, reviewed this later translation by Edith Grossman.

LOVE, **AS MICKEY AND SYLVIA**, **IN THEIR 1956** hit single, remind us, love is strange. As we grow older it gets stranger, until at some point mortality has come well within the frame of our attention, and there we are, suddenly caught between terminal dates while still talking a game of eternity. It's about then that we may begin to regard love songs, romance novels, soap operas and any live teen-age pronouncements at all on the subject of love with an increasingly impatient, not to mention intolerant, ear.

At the same time, where would any of us be without all that romantic infrastructure, without, in fact, just that degree of adolescent, premortal hope? Pretty far out on life's limb, at least. Suppose, then, it were possible, not only to swear love "forever," but actually to follow through on it—to live a long, full and authentic life based on such a vow, to put one's allotted stake of precious time where one's heart is? This is the extraordinary premise of Gabriel García Márquez's new novel *Love in the Time of Cholera*, one on which he delivers, and triumphantly.

In the post-romantic ebb of the 70s and 80s, with everybody now so wised up and even growing paranoid about love, once the magical buzzword of a generation, it is a daring step for any writer to decide to work in love's vernacular, to take it, with all its folly, imprecision and lapses in taste, at all seriously—that is, as well worth those higher forms of play that we value in fiction. For García Márquez the step may also be revolutionary. "I think that a novel about love is as valid as any other," he once remarked in a conversation with his friend, the journalist Plinio Apuleyo Mendoza (published as *El Olor de la Guayaba*, 1982). "In reality the duty of a writer—the revolutionary duty, if you like—is that of writing well."

And—oh boy—does he write well. He writes with impassioned control, out of a maniacal serenity: the Garcimarquesian voice we have come to recognize from the other fiction has matured, found and developed new resources, been brought to a level where it can at once be classical and familiar, opalescent and pure, able to praise and curse, laugh and cry, fabulate and sing and when called upon, take off and soar, as in this description of a turn-of-the-century balloon trip:

"From the sky they could see, just as God saw them, the ruins of the very old and heroic city of Cartagena de Indias, the most beautiful in the world, abandoned by its inhabitants because of the sieges of the English and the atrocities of the buccaneers. They saw the walls, still intact, the brambles in the streets, the fortifications devoured by heartsease, the marble palaces and the golden altars and the viceroys rotting with plague inside their armor.

"They flew over the lake dwellings of the Trojas in Cataca, painted in lunatic colors, with pens holding iguanas raised for food and balsam apples and crepe myrtle hanging in the lacustrian gardens. Excited by everyone's shouting, hundreds of naked children plunged into the water, jumping out of windows, jumping from the roofs of the houses and from the canoes that they handled with astonishing skill, and diving like shad to recover the bundles of clothing, the bottles of cough syrup, the beneficent food that the beautiful lady with the feathered hat threw to them from the basket of the balloon."

This novel is also revolutionary in daring to suggest that vows of love made under a presumption of immortality—youthful idiocy, to some—may yet be honored, much later in life when we ought to know better, in the face of the undeniable. This is, effectively, to assert the resurrection of the body, today as throughout history an unavoidably revolutionary idea. Through the ever-subversive medium of fiction, García Márquez shows us how it could all plausibly come

about, even—wild hope —for somebody out here, outside a book, even as inevitably beaten at, bought and resold as we all must have become if only through years of simple residence in the injuring and corruptive world.

Here's what happens. The story takes place between about 1880 and 1930, in a Caribbean seaport city, unnamed but said to be a composite of Cartagena and Barranquilla—as well, perhaps, as cities of the spirit less officially mapped. Three major characters form a triangle whose hypotenuse is Florentino Ariza, a poet dedicated to love both carnal and transcendent, though his secular fate is with the River Company of the Caribbean and its small fleet of paddle-wheel steamboats. As a young apprentice telegrapher he meets and falls forever in love with Fermina Daza, a "beautiful adolescent with . . . almond-shaped eyes," who walks with a "natural haughtiness . . . her doe's gait making her seem immune to gravity." Though they exchange hardly a hundred words face to face, they carry on a passionate and secret affair entirely by way of letters and telegrams, even after the girl's father has found out and taken her away on an extended "journey of forgetting." But when she returns, Fermina rejects the lovesick young man after all, and eventually meets and marries instead Dr. Juvenal Urbino who, like the hero of a 19th-century novel, is well born, a sharp dresser, somewhat stuck on himself but a terrific catch nonetheless.

For Florentino, love's creature, this is an agonizing setback, though nothing fatal. Having sworn to love Fermina Daza forever, he settles in to wait for as long as he has to until she's free again. This turns out to be 51 years, 9 months and 4 days later, when suddenly, absurdly, on a Pentecost Sunday around 1930, Dr. Juvenal

Gárcia Márquez in 1976.

Urbino dies, chasing a parrot up a mango tree. After the funeral, when everyone else has left, Florentino steps forward with his hat over his heart. "Fermina," he declares, "I have waited for this opportunity for more than half a century, to repeat to you once again my vow of eternal fidelity and everlasting love." Shocked and furious, Fermina orders him out of the house. "And don't show your face again for the years of life that are left to you. . . . I hope there are very few of them."

The heart's eternal vow has run up against the world's finite terms. The confrontation occurs near the end of the first chapter, which recounts Dr. Urbino's last day on earth and Fermina's first night as a widow. We then flash back 50 years, into the time of cholera. The middle chapters follow the lives of the three characters through the years of the Urbinos' marriage and Florentino

Ariza's rise at the River Company, as one century ticks over into the next. The last chapter takes up again where the first left off, with Florentino, now, in the face of what many men would consider major rejection, resolutely setting about courting Fermina Daza all over again, doing what he must to win her love.

In their city, throughout a turbulent half-century, death has proliferated everywhere, both as *el cólera*, the fatal disease that sweeps through in terrible intermittent epidemics, and as *la cólera*, defined as choler or anger, which taken to its extreme becomes warfare. Victims of one, in this book, are more than once mistaken for victims of the other. War, "always the same war," is presented here not as the continuation by other means of any politics that can possibly matter, but as a negative force, a plague, whose only meaning is death on a massive scale. Against this dark ground, lives, so precarious, are often more and less conscious projects of resistance, even of sworn opposition, to death. Dr. Urbino, like his father before him, becomes a leader in the battle against the cholera, promoting public health measures obsessively, heroically. Fermina, more conventionally but with as much courage, soldiers on in her chosen role of wife, mother and household manager, maintaining a safe perimeter for her family. Florentino embraces Eros, death's well-known long-time enemy, setting off on a career of seductions that eventually add up to 622 "long-term liaisons, apart from . . . countless fleeting adventures," while maintaining, impervious to time, his deeper fidelity, his unquenchable hope for a life with Fermina. At the end he can tell her truthfully—though she doesn't believe it for a minute—that he has remained a virgin for her.

So far as this is Florentino's story, in a way his bildungsroman, we find ourselves, as he earns the suspension of our disbelief, cheering him on, wishing for the success of this stubborn warrior against age and death, and in the name of love. But like the best fictional characters, he insists on his autonomy, refusing to be anything less ambiguous than human. We must take him as he is, pursuing his tomcat destiny out among the streets and lovers' refuges of this city with which he lives on terms of such easy intimacy, carrying with him a potential for disasters from which he remains safe, immunized by a comical but dangerous indifference to consequences that often borders on criminal neglect. The widow Nazaret, one of many widows he is fated to make happy, seduces him during a night-long bombardment from the cannons of an attacking army outside the city. Ausencia Santander's exquisitely furnished home is burgled of every movable item while she and Florentino are frolicking in bed. A girl he picks up at Carnival time turns out to be a homicidal machete-wielding escapee from the local asylum. Olimpia Zuleta's husband murders her when he sees a vulgar endearment Florentino has been thoughtless enough to write on her body in red paint. His lover's amorality causes not only individual misfortune but ecological destruction as well: as he learns by the end of the book, his River Company's insatiable appetite for firewood to fuel its steamers has wiped out the great forests that once bordered the Magdalena river system, leaving a wasteland where nothing can live. "With his mind clouded by his passion for Fermina Daza he never took the trouble to think about it, and by the time he realized the truth, there was nothing anyone could do except bring in a new river."

In fact, dumb luck has as much to do with getting Florentino through as the intensity or purity of his dream. The author's great affection for this character does not entirely overcome a sly concurrent subversion of the ethic of machismo, of which García Márquez is not especially fond, having described it elsewhere simply as

usurpation of the rights of others. Indeed, as we've come to expect from his fiction, it's the women in this story who are stronger, more attuned to reality. When Florentino goes crazy with love, developing symptoms like those of cholera, it is his mother, Transito Ariza, who pulls him out of it. His innumerable lecheries are rewarded not so much for any traditional masculine selling points as for his obvious and aching need to be loved. Women go for it. "He is ugly and sad," Fermina Daza's cousin Hildebranda tells her, "but he is all love."

And García Márquez, straight-faced teller of tall tales, is his biographer. At the age of 19, as he has reported, the young writer underwent a literary epiphany on reading the famous opening lines of Kafka's *Metamorphosis,* in which a man wakes to find himself transformed into a giant insect. "Gosh," exclaimed García Márquez, using in Spanish a word we in English may not, "that's just the way my grandmother used to talk!" And that, he adds, is when novels began to interest him. Much of what came in his work to be called "magic realism" was, as he tells it, simply the presence of that grandmotherly voice.

Nevertheless, in this novel we have come a meaningful distance from Macondo, the magical village in *One Hundred Years of Solitude* where folks routinely sail through the air and the dead remain in everyday conversation with the living: we have descended, perhaps in some way down the same river, all the way downstream, into war and pestilence and urban confusions to the edge of a Caribbean haunted less by individual dead than by a history which has brought so appallingly many down, without ever having spoken, or having spoken gone unheard, or having been heard, left unrecorded. As revolutionary as writing well is the duty to redeem these silences, a duty García Márquez has here fulfilled with honor and compassion. It would be presumptuous to speak of moving "beyond" *One Hundred Years of Solitude* but clearly García Márquez has moved somewhere else, not least into deeper awareness of the ways in which, as Florentino comes to learn, "nobody teaches life anything." There are still delightful and stunning moments contrary to fact, still told with the same unblinking humor—presences at the foot of the bed, an anonymously delivered doll with a curse on it, the sinister parrot, almost a minor character, whose pursuit ends with the death of Dr. Juvenal Urbino.

But the predominant claim on the author's attention and energies comes from what is not so contrary to fact, a human consensus about "reality" in which love and the possibility of love's extinction are the indispensable driving forces, and varieties of magic have become, if not quite peripheral, then at least more thoughtfully deployed in the service of an expanded vision, matured, darker than before but no less clement.

It could be argued that this is the only honest way to write about love, that without the darkness and the finitude there might be romance, erotica, social comedy, soap opera—all genres, by the way, that are well represented in this novel—but not the Big L. What that seems to require, along with a certain vantage point, a certain level of understanding, is an author's ability to control his own love for his characters, to withhold from the reader the full extent of his caring, in other words not to lapse into drivel.

In translating *Love in the Time of Cholera*, Edith Grossman has been attentive to this element of discipline, among many nuances of the author's voice to which she is sensitively, imaginatively attuned. My Spanish isn't perfect, but I can tell

> "There is nothing I have read quite like this astonishing final chapter, symphonic, sure in its dynamics and tempo."

that she catches admirably and without apparent labor the swing and translucency of his writing, its slang and its classicism, the lyrical stretches and those end-of-sentence zingers he likes to hit us with. It is a faithful and beautiful piece of work.

There comes a moment, early in his career at the River Company of the Caribbean when Florentino Ariza, unable to write even a simple commercial letter without some kind of romantic poetry creeping in, is discussing the problem with his uncle Leo XII, who owns the company. It's no use, the young man protests—"Love is the only thing that interests me."

"The trouble," his uncle replies, "is that without river navigation, there is no love." For Florentino this happens to be literally true: the shape of his life is defined by two momentous river voyages, half a century apart. On the first he made his decision to return and live forever in the city of Fermina Daza, to persevere in his love for as long as it might take. On the second, through a desolate landscape, he journeys into love and against time, with Fermina, at last, by his side. There is nothing I have read quite like this astonishing final chapter, symphonic, sure in its dynamics and tempo, moving like a riverboat too, its author and pilot, with a lifetime's experience steering us unerringly among hazards of skepticism and mercy, on this river we all know, without whose navigation there is no love and against whose flow the effort to return is never worth a less honorable name than remembrance—at the very best it results in works that can even return our worn souls to us, among which most certainly belongs *Love in the Time of Cholera*, this shining and heartbreaking novel.

"This Book Was a Pleasure"

FOR GABRIEL GARCÍA MÁRQUEZ, the pleasure and turmoil of writing change from novel to novel. In the case of *One Hundred Years of Solitude,* he thought so long and hard about the story that when he finally sat down to commit it to paper, it came in a great burst. In Mexico City, his longtime home base, we talked about what writing the novel had been like. "This book was a pleasure," he said. "It could have been much longer, but I had to control it. There is so much to say about the life of two people who love each other. It's infinite."—*Marlise Simons*

Q: You wrote most of the book in Cartagena?

A: Yes, and those two years when I was writing it was a time when I was almost completely happy. Everything went well for me. People spend a lifetime thinking about how they would really like to live. I asked my friends and no one seems to know very clearly. To me it's very clear now. I wish my life could have been like the years when I was writing *Love in the Time of Cholera.*

I would get up at 5:30 or 6 in the morning. I need only six hours of sleep. Then I quickly listened to the news. I would read from 6 to 8, because if I don't read at that time I won't get around to it anymore. I lose my rhythm. Someone would arrive at the house with fresh fish or lobster or shrimp caught nearby. Then I would write from 8 till 1. After lunch I had a little siesta. And when the sun started going down I would go out on the street to look for places where my characters would go, to talk to people and pick up language and atmosphere. So the next morning I would have fresh material I had brought from the streets.

I also had one of the most curious and enjoyable literary experiences I've ever had. One of the characters was Fermina, an 18-year-old girl living in a Caribbean town in the late 19th century. She lived with her father, a Spanish immigrant, and with her mother, who I could not figure out. I could not see her: not the face, the name or anything about her. And then one day I woke up and realized what had happened. The mother had died while the girl was still young. And when I saw that the mother was dead, she became alive and real. She grew and had a great presence—in the house, in everyone's memory. It made me so happy to resolve this. I had been stretching the logic of the book. I had been trying to put a dead person among the living, and that was not possible.

Q: I know you get a lot of mail from your readers. What sort of things do they write to you?

A: The letters I find most interesting are from people who ask me where I got this theme or that passage or such and such a character. Because they feel it is about something or someone they know. They will say: So and so is just like my aunt. Or: I have an uncle just like him. And: that episode happened exactly like that in my village. How did you know about it? People from all over Latin America wrote such things, especially after *One Hundred Years of Solitude.* They felt it was part of their lives.

Q: That's why you still refuse to let the book be filmed? Because that identification will be lost?

A: It will be destroyed. Because film does not allow for that. The face of the actor, of Gregory Peck, becomes the face of the character. It cannot be your uncle, unless your uncle looks like Gregory Peck.

"Damn It to Hell, Mr. Auden"

To the Editor:

How sad that W. H. Auden chose to alter his own work, changing "We must love one another or die" to "We must love one another and die" (Noted With Pleasure, Nov. 19). Which shifts the whole meaning in the direction of the very Doomsters most of us would like to escape. Must I interpret Mr. Auden to himself? I chose to interpret Auden's original phrase as meaning if we do not love we die. In the midst of life, surrounded by death, if we do not love someone and are not loved in return, we are a shell. In the loving give-and-take there is vital life, there is purpose, there is joy. Without love we might as well be dead. To be in love doesn't mean we ignore the darkness that surrounds us. But being in love, we are a light to one another. Damn it to hell, Mr. Auden, put your words back the way that you wrote them in the first place!

RAY BRADBURY
Los Angeles

Bradbury in Los Angeles, circa 1980.

Peggy Noonan, *What I Saw at the Revolution*

BY WILFRID SHEED

This mold-breaking Washington memoir came from the woman who crafted some of President Ronald Reagan's most memorable speeches.

THERE MAY BE SOMETHING TO BE SAID FOR keeping your eye on the enemy when the alternative is looking at friends like the Reagans. Ms. Noonan's all too brief description of these is wonderful social comedy, a kind of Frank Capra version of *Alice in the White House* or of *The Mikado:* Maureen is the classic boss's daughter, or Katisha character: one can imagine Edward Arnold or Eugene Pallette puffing over at any moment to smooth her feathers and fire whoever is bothering her. Nancy would be the Red Queen, sailing ominously through the White House with her entourage, glaring briefly, murderously at Ms. Noonan's work clothes. The President himself has to be the White King, a kindly old fellow who keeps falling off his horse and has to be helped up again. A Reaganite might protest that they're not really like that and he might be right, because one senses that this could just be Massapequa acting up again, cocking a snook at the nonsense outside, and that if Ms. Noonan had found herself on a bus full of Reagans instead of peaceniks at an impressionable age, the Democrats never would have lost her.

And this is the great strength and pleasure of *What I Saw at the Revolution:* the glee it keeps giving one to find a recognizable human, a comrade, in truly preposterous circumstances, be they left or right. It wasn't just Ms. Noonan's clothes that Nancy was glaring at, but her very presence. You don't belong here. And Ms. Noonan, hailing from a real neighborhood and a real family, is struck by some lines of criticism she has heard from over the wall. If the young Reaganites are "so interested in the family how come none of them are married? How come none of them have kids? . . . You guys don't believe in God, you just believe in religion. I ponder this," she adds.

Ms. Noonan does her level best for Ronald Reagan in this book. After a meeting at which he has manifestly woolgathered, but not without point, she triumphantly reports that "he had opinions, he had something he wanted to do"—to which a voter can only respond weakly, "I should certainly hope so."

On dark days she would give up altogether. "I would think to myself . . . that the battle for the mind of Ronald Reagan was like the trench warfare of World War I: Never have so many fought so hard for such barren terrain." And it wasn't just his mind. "This White House is like a beautiful clock that makes all the right sounds, but when you open it up, there is nothing inside. . . . When I thought of him in those days, it was as a gigantic heroic balloon floating in the Macy's Thanksgiving Day parade."

Such was the indifference bordering on simplemindedness of the White House staff that they didn't even realize that it pays to be kind, or at least rudimentarily decent, to writers on their way out the door. Ms. Noonan is finally released without so much as a thank-you note or a photo-op with the Great Balloon—who, for his part, doesn't come down from the sky long enough to realize she's even missing.

And this is what is most astounding. Ms. Noonan had given him his very best words (written out as they are here they may sometimes seem as flat as unaccompanied song lyrics, but they sang pretty well at the time), and you would suppose that just this one thing he would keep his eye on and do something about. But no, it was all the same to him where the words came from—maybe the elves brought them. And indeed Ronald Reagan only noticed her absence when by some miracle her name got attached to George Bush's famous acceptance speech (in which she committed a minor fraud by disguising Mr. Bush's instinctive preference for weak phrases).

Suddenly she was a celebrity, somebody he could cope with, and he insisted on having this famous stranger write his final State of the Union message for him. Which is perhaps all you need to know about the role of the writer in Hollywood.

The best epigraph to the whole book appears, I believe, quite early on. Ms. Noonan is talking about a brutal round of layoffs at CBS, including some revered veterans, and the shudder it has sent through the ranks; ever since Ed Murrow had braved bombs to cover the London blitz, CBS News had considered itself something special; but suddenly, no more. CBS "spent loyalty as if it was going out of style," says Ms. Noonan, "which perhaps it is. Rather captured it. . . . 'Listen,' Dan said, 'this place has all the tradition of a discount shoe store.'"

That she sees, even now, no connection between this kind of scene and the Reagan White

Noonan in her Manhattan home, January 17, 1990.

House illustrates the infinite distance between a speechwriter's reality and a critic's. Subsisting on a diet of affirmations and debating points, a President's ghost would only complicate her life intolerably by doubting her own uplifting words for more than a minute, or looking on the downside of her lovely revolution. But what she can't criticize with her mind she more than makes up for with her eyes and ears, and there are some deadly word-pictures in here along with some highly admiring ones—perhaps in each case beyond the subjects' warrant. So long as Ms. Noonan is writing about it, the old shoe store fairly rocks with life, but one senses that she is investing the characters with her own vitality and making them a mite more interesting than they deserve.

At any rate, I am much more curious about what she does next than what they do next.

Sandra Cisneros, *Woman Hollering Creek*

BY BEBE MOORE CAMPBELL

Sometimes, the Book Review misses out on a stellar debut. "We are bound, being mortal, to overlook an unpopular idea, a new sound, a revolutionary rhythm, an original shape," an editor explained in 1956. "And so it goes— a hit and a miss and an occasional muff." The Book Review did not cover T. S. Eliot's *The Waste Land,* for example, or Sandra Cisneros's *The House on Mango Street,* now considered a classic of Chicana literature. This review of her second story collection brought her work to our pages several years later.

IN HER RADIANT FIRST COLLECTION OF STO-ries, *The House on Mango Street,* Sandra Cisneros propelled readers into the world of Esperanza Cordero, a wise little girl who yearns for a better life while growing up perilously fast in a poor Mexican-American neighborhood in Chicago. That book promised wonders to come from Ms. Cisneros. In her new collection, *Woman Hollering Creek,* she delivers.

These stories about women struggling to take control of their lives traverse geographical, historical and emotional borders and invite us into the souls of characters as unforgettable as a first kiss. These aren't European immigrants who can learn English, change their names and float casually in the mainstream. These are brown people with glossy black hair and dark eyes who know they look different, who know the score, and so they cling to their culture like the anchor it is. As Clemencia, the narrator of "Never Marry a Mexican," says, "But that's—how do you say it?— water under the damn? I can't ever get the sayings right even though I was born in this country."

Some of the vivid images in these stories are ironic and funny, as in "Mericans," when American tourists in Mexico are shocked to discover that the little Mexican children they have given gum to are, like themselves, American tourists. There is the humor of "The Marlboro Man," a conversation between two very hip young women who describe a mutual friend's affair with the Marlboro man of cigarette fame. Or at least that's who they think he is. In "Barbie-Q" we feel the tempered enthusiasm of two little girls who have learned early on how to make do and who sensibly buy coveted, albeit smoky, Barbie dolls at a fire sale.

There are darker broodings here. Ms. Cisneros thoroughly explores the rage Mexican-American women feel when their men choose white women over them, the accompanying feelings of rejection that such betrayal engenders. In "Pretty," when Lupe, a discarded lover, discovers that her former boyfriend's new woman is blonde, she rants, "Eddie, who taught me how to salsa, who lectured me night and day about human rights in Guatemala, El Salvador, Chile, Argentina, South Africa. . . . Eduardo. My Eddie. That Eddie. With a blonde. He didn't even have the decency to pick a woman of color."

Ms. Cisneros doesn't present too many nice guys here, and the perfidy of men is a motif in

Cisneros in front of her home in 1998. Her purple house caused a stir on the South Side of San Antonio, Texas, when the Historic Design and Review Commission ruled the paint historically incorrect. "What the house is saying," she told The Times, "is, 'I'm very Mexican, and I'm proud of it,' and that it's another way of being American."

several of the stories. But the author doesn't dabble in man-hating diatribes, nor does she waste words with explanations of machismo. Instead she uses the behavior of men as a catalyst that propels her women into a search deep within themselves for the love that men have failed to give them.

Such is the case in the title story of this collection. Juan takes Cleofilas, his new bride, from Mexico to *el otro lado*—the other side. As she accustoms herself to a drab blue-collar existence in a harsh border town, Cleofilas is fascinated by La Gritona, the creek behind her house. The rough translation is *Woman Hollering Creek,* and

Cleofilas wonders about the name. Is the woman yelling for joy or sadness?

Woman Hollering Creek is not without flaws, but even the stories that don't work satisfy because of the richness of the language. The author seduces with precise, spare prose and creates unforgettable characters we want to lift off the page and hang out with for a little while. In a land where our views of Hispanic people are often limited and distorted, Sandra Cisneros offers precious glimpses of the internal workings of their lives. She is an educator, unerring and relentless; she is not only a gifted writer but an absolutely essential one.

Jackie Collins,
Hollywood Kids

BY JOE QUEENAN

Jackie Collins and Joe Queenan:
a match made in literary heaven.

THERE IS A FLICKERING INSTANT IN THE
novel *Hollywood Kids* where Jackie Collins
threatens to introduce a principal character that
the average reader might find likable, and even
normal. The character is Michael Scorsinni, a
New York cop who has come to Los Angeles to
re-establish contact with his ex-wife and daughter.
Scorsinni arrives in a city that Ms. Collins has
populated with Zane Marion Ricca, a serial killer;
his former employer Mac Brooks, a movie director obsessed with oral sex; Jordanna Levitt, a slut
whom Zane is stalking; Jordan Levitt, Jordanna's
father, who drove his first wife and son to suicide;
Kim Levitt, now married to Jordan after a career
as a call girl; Brooks's wife, Sharleen, Jordan's
ex-lover, who is obsessed with oral sex, prefer-
ably in a moving vehicle; and Cheryl Landers,
Jordanna's best friend, who is pinch-hitting as a
brothel operator for a vacationing friend, and who
will soon get dressed up as a nurse and provide
Luca Carlotti, Brooks's mobster godfather and
Zane's uncle, with the best oral sex he has ever
experienced in his life. Thus, quite early in the
proceedings, Scorsinni emerges as the closest
thing to a moral anchor that the ordinary reader
can possibly cling to.

Alas, it soon develops that Scorsinni is a
recovering alcoholic who has been traumatized

Collins at a London hotel on September 4, 1990.

by the discovery that his soon-to-be-murdered ex
is a prostitute, by the revelation that his daughter is actually the child of his older brother, Sal,
and by the unfortunate experience of having had
richly gratifying oral sex in a Times Square hotel
with a mini-skirted woman who turned out to be
a man. Whatever empathy the reader might feel
for the furloughed policeman evaporates when he
beds down with a local harlot scant days after his
ex-wife's murder, begins a dalliance with a young
woman named Marjory Sanderson, who will, in
the fullness of time, slit her wrists after writing a
series of bogus death threats to herself, and then
himself falls off the wagon.

Readers impervious to nuance will be tempted
to dismiss *Hollywood Kids* as just another trashy
novel about a serial killer bent on murdering the
six young women who testified against him in

court after he strangled his co-star on the set of a movie being directed by a man who was forced to hire him by a godfather who likes hookers dressed as nurses.

But if we can look beyond Ms. Collins's glitzy, gory, grubby scaffolding, we can see that the real subject of *Hollywood Kids* is the death of the American family. The true object of Zane's bloodlust is not his six young victims, but his mother, who seduced him when he was a boy. Cheryl Landers, one of the Hollywood kids after whom the novel is named, becomes a hooker nurse only to get back at her father, who never loved her. Jordanna Levitt, another Hollywood youth, sleeps with an aging movie star to humiliate her father, who drove half his family to suicide before marrying a prostitute. Marjory Sanderson fakes death threats and tries to kill herself to avenge herself on her billionaire father, who cares only about his career. Mac Brooks despises his godfather, Luca, and despises him even more when he finds out that the mobster is his father, because this means that Zane is not just a disgruntled actor, former employee and rampaging psychopath, but a cousin. And Scorsinni, whose ex-wife is a dead hooker and whose daughter turns out to be his niece, is so shattered by fraternal duplicity in the boudoir that he falls in love with Kennedy Chase, a hack journalist whose husband was killed by terrorists in Northern Ireland. The center, it would appear, will not hold.

Hollywood Kids is not without its faults. Jackie Collins cannot actually write, and the only way the reader can tell any of the female characters apart is by keeping track of who has the nurse's outfit. Yet, in its own perverse way, *Hollywood Kids* is an admirable, ambitious dissection of the horrible times we live in. Ms. Collins's most ingenious conceit is the repetitive use of oral sex as a mirror held up to American society. How, one is left to wonder, did any of these youngsters even manage to get born, inhabiting as they do a world where their fathers seem interested only in non-procreative sexual liaisons?

This is what makes the scene where Jordanna congratulates her ex-hooker stepmother, Kim, on the birth of her child so unforgettable. In a universe as depraved as this one, the job of giving birth to the next generation of Hollywood glitterati must inevitably fall to a reformed hooker. That the child of the morally re-energized call girl will be raised by a man who drove his wife and son to suicide is a powerful symbol of the spiritual void that America is entering as it faces the 21st century. As Jordanna puts it when she drops by her father's house to make peace with him: "Whatever Jordan had done in the past, it was his life. . . . So Kim used to be a call girl. Big deal. At least she was making Jordan happy. Maybe that was all that counted."

Maybe that's all that ever really counts.

1995 ——————————————————

Amazon sells its first book, *Fluid Concepts and Creative Analogies: Computer Models of the Fundamental Mechanisms of Thought*.

1996 ——————————————————

Oprah Winfrey's book club debuts.

1996 ——————————————————→

George R. R. Martin publishes *A Game of Thrones*, the first volume in his Song of Ice and Fire series.

1971–1996

291

Anonymous, *Primary Colors*

BY MICHAEL LEWIS

When it was published, *Primary Colors*—a roman à clef about Bill and Hillary Clinton and the 1992 presidential race—caused a ruckus inside the Beltway. Who was Anonymous? A former Clinton aide or campaign staffer? Our reviewer, the author of *Liar's Poker,* speculated that it might be George Stephanopoulos. Six months after the novel came out, the *Newsweek* columnist Joe Klein fessed up: "I felt that there are times when I've had to lie to protect a source, and I put this in that category," he said at a press conference.

THIS BOOK WAS WRITTEN BY AN ARTFUL thief, someone who knew just how much he could steal and get away with it. Although it is advertised as a novel, it tells the story of the 1992 Democratic primaries pretty much exactly as they must have appeared through the eyes of George Stephanopoulos. Almost every character, incident and setting has been drawn directly from life, and the author does everything in his power to make sure that we do not miss the connections. Bill Clinton is recast as Governor (of a small Southern state) Jack Stanton, complete with bimbo eruptions, a draft problem and a strident

wife (here named Susan). The pious Governor of New York, Mario Cuomo, has become the pious Governor of New York, Orlando Ozio; Gennifer Flowers has become Cashmere McLeod (with tapes); Hope, Ark., has become Grace Junction (the state is unnamed). Even the journalists are impossible to miss: the oenophile R. W. Apple Jr. of The New York Times makes a cameo appearance as the oenophile A. P. Caulley of The New York Times. It is a strange reversal of the usual conventions of fiction. Only the identity of the author remains unknown to the reader.

The author, whoever he or she is, makes about as much effort to cover his tracks through literature as he does through life. He has lifted his emotional infrastructure—or at any rate the book's central relationships—from *All the King's Men*, Robert Penn Warren's fictionalized account of the rise of Huey Long. Again, he seems to want us to know that he has done it. The narrator Jack Burden has become the narrator Henry Burton. The central object of unfeeling politicosexual attention, Sadie, here has become Daisy, or Daise, as she is affectionately and anagrammatically known.

But the most startling piece of petty larceny is the book's central relationship: Henry and Stanton. (That is, Stephanopoulos and Clinton.) Henry watches his governor with the same blend of love, awe, resignation and revulsion as Jack Burden did The Boss. Even the cascading, demotic rhythms of his voice are modeled on Warren. Here, for instance, Henry (George) describes meeting Jack (Bill) for the first time: "We shook hands. My inability to recall that particular moment more precisely is disappointing: the handshake is the threshold act, the beginning of politics. I've seen him do it two million times now, but I couldn't tell you how he does it, the right-handed part of it—the strength, quality, duration of it, the rudiments of pressing the flesh. I can, however, tell you a whole lot about what he does with his other hand. He is a genius with it."

Of course, you cannot borrow wholesale from a novel of the early 1940s and remain credible in the mid-1990s. The author has had to make a number of minor alterations, some very clever, to tailor Robert Penn Warren's package to the Clinton campaign. As a scion of the Louisiana overclass, Jack Burden was unable to serve his rising populist governor without betraying class and family. You can't get away with that sort of aristocratic conceit any longer; the upper class has long abandoned its posture of moral superiority toward practical political climbers. The upper class now underwrites practical political climbers. The author solves this problem—and gives us a protagonist a bit more sympathetic than the average Yuppie in the bargain—by having Henry be the scion of black civil rights leaders. In working for Stanton, Henry is made to feel by nearly every black person he encounters that he is selling out both his class and his family.

The only trouble is that Henry seems occasionally to forget that he is black. Or rather he is black when it serves the author's purpose but not when it doesn't. He finds himself in bed with white women across the Deep South, for instance, without a passing mention of the color of his skin. And can anyone imagine Hillary Clinton reaching across and "tousling" the hair of an Afro-American? I can't. (Though I can easily imagine her reaching across and tousling the hair of George Stephanopoulos.) If nothing else, the author's tangle with fiction reinforces the impression that the more plausible and vivid passages, which seem to be pure invention, in fact

> "The most startling piece of petty larceny is the book's central relationship: Henry and Stanton. (That is, Stephanopoulos and Clinton.)"

come straight from inside the Clinton campaign. (For addicts of politics and conspiracy theorists, a brief list of new leads: Stanton/Clinton hides the fact that he has got a 17-year-old black girl pregnant; Susan/Hillary goes to bed with Henry/George in a moment of anger; Stanton/Clinton is acerbic about all his fellow politicians. Of Senator Bob Kerry he says, "He's a résumé in search of a reason.")

Primary Colors is an odd book. But maybe the oddest thing about it is how good it is. In spite of its sins it is far and away the best thing I have read about the 1992 campaign; it breaks all the rules and lives to tell about it. The author's portrait of Mr. Clinton is astonishingly powerful. I doubt that anyone who reads the book will ever again think of the President in quite the same way. I'm not quite sure why this should be, except there is a wonderful honesty about it, a refusal to give in to the conventional interpretation of people and events that cripples so much that is written about politics. There is a whole set of emotions lurking just below the surface in politics that for whatever reason almost never get described in print. Here, for instance, is how the author describes Susan Stanton, appearing in public to defend her husband's sexual transgressions: "Her strength in the face of this embarrassment was strange. She was drawing attention to her perfection, which only served to remind people of her husband's imperfection—it was, I realized, a vengeful act."

That strikes me as just about perfect, and there are dozens of passages that ring equally true.

The person who wrote this book has the not entirely respectable gift of the realist: he makes art out of what he has seen. So who did it? From what he steals and how he steals it the author offers you a literary equivalent of one of those computer-generated crime sketches. White, male, young, extremely observant, gifted with the language, a bit tortured and conflicted but not so much that he is unable to pursue his ambition. Above all, he was very close to the campaign (though it could be argued that anyone who watched C-Span was). Possibly a journalist, but if so one with unusual access to insiders. More likely an insider himself. If George Stephanopoulos was planning to write a novel to make sense of his experience, he's been beaten to the punch by some reporter or underling. Then again, maybe he wasn't. You never know.

Lincoln Center, 1985.

1996

2021

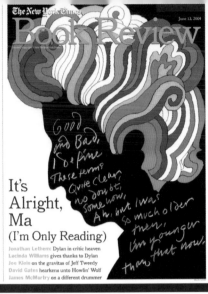

CHAPTER FIVE

The New York Times Book Review — June 13, 2004

It's Alright, Ma (I'm Only Reading)

Jonathan Lethem: Dylan in critic heaven
Lucinda Williams gives thanks to Dylan
Joe Klein on the gravitas of Jeff Tweedy
David Gates hearkens unto Howlin' Wolf
James McMurtry on a different drummer

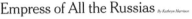

The New York Times Book Review — November 20, 2011

Empress of All the Russias *By Kathryn Harrison*

DAVID GREENBERG ON ANN BEATTIE PAGE 9 | REBECCA NEWBERGER GOLDSTEIN ON UMBERTO ECO PAGE 20

The New York Times Book Review — December 18, 2011 · CHILDREN'S BOOKS

Brainy Beauty
By John Adams

LUCInl SCHILLINGER ON P.D. JAMES PAGE 16 | BRAD LEITHAUSER ON STEPHEN SONDHEIM PAGE 17

The New York Times Book Review — April 8, 2012 · CHILDREN'S BOOKS

The Big Bang

FRANCINE PROSE ON NADINE GORDIMER PAGE 11 | JONATHAN LETHEM ON THOMAS BERGER PAGE 35

The New York Times Book Review

Eyes Wide Shut
By Michael Kinsley

The New York Times Book Review

Bride of Hades
By Stephen King

Book Review

O Captain!

By Jill Lepore

By Drew Gilpin Faust

The New York Times Book Review — February 8, 2015

Apocalypse Then

By Philip Caputo

The New York Times Book Review — January 25, 2015

Curses And Blessings

By Julian Lucas

For the publishing industry, this 25-year period was marked by head-spinning changes: the rise of Amazon, the decline (and, in some cases, the demise) of the big book chains, the consolidation of publishing companies, the proliferation of e-readers and tablets, the self-publishing boom. Publishers began to grapple with a lack of diversity, both in their workforces and in their book lists—and as they were doing that, in 2020, they had to figure out how to market books during a pandemic.

More than ever, books—and the Book Review— drove the culture and the national conversation.

During this time, The New York Times Book Review became the only freestanding weekly book review in the United States. Today it has a full team of editors who don't just cherry-pick likely books for coverage but survey the entire literary landscape, looking at every single galley that comes in. It isn't just about helping people find the next book they want to read (though that's certainly one of its primary goals). In a time of distraction, of online chatter and noise, people are seeking a deeper engagement, distraction from the distraction, context, the long view—and the Book Review is committed to providing exactly that.

Jhumpa Lahiri, *Interpreter of Maladies*

This luminous debut collection of short stories went on to receive the Pulitzer Prize in fiction.

A MARRIAGE IS EASY TO START. FATE, IN THE form of friends, relatives or lust, arranges a match. But after the wedding, how do you stay engaged? Books are easy to start, too, and they pose a similar challenge. No marriage is as arbitrary and accidental as one between a writer and a reader, set up by a brief infatuation in a bookstore or the enthusiasm of a third party. Perhaps because of this congruence, ill-advised marriages have been one of fiction's most fertile subjects, ever since Squire B. abducted Pamela.

Samuel Richardson's latest heir is Jhumpa Lahiri. Her debut collection of short stories, *Interpreter of Maladies*, features marriages that have been arranged, rushed into, betrayed, invaded and exhausted. Her subject is not love's failure, however, but the opportunity that an artful spouse (like an artful writer) can make of failure—the rebirth possible in a relationship when you discover how little of the other person you know. In Lahiri's sympathetic tales, the pang of disappointment turns into a sudden hunger to know more.

It is a hunger the reader will share, because Lahiri's characters are charmers. Only a heart of stone would not go out to Mrs. Sen, for example. The 30-year-old wife of a mathematics professor,

Mrs. Sen baby-sits and dices vegetables in gorgeous saris, the part in her hair properly powdered with vermilion. She is a fórmal, precise, modest woman, unsettled by only one thing: her unruly passion for fresh fish. Unfortunately, she does not know how to drive, and her husband is too busy to chauffeur her to market. "It is very frustrating," Mrs. Sen explains. Lahiri ingeniously finds a story about the ferocity of desire in what this indefatigable wife will do for the sake of halibut.

"Power," Emerson once wrote, "resides in the moment of transition from a past to a new state." Like Mrs. Sen, most of Lahiri's characters move between the Indian subcontinent and the United States. They date, vacation, emigrate and work across cultural and national borders. In the parallax of this double perspective, a shattered jack-o'-lantern may obscure a child's understanding of, say, Bangladesh's war for independence. Obscure, but not erase: Lahiri's stories are rendered more powerful by the sense of cultural transition and loss. "Everything is there," Mrs. Sen says of India, but her story begins with the fact that she herself no longer is. Lahiri's Indian-Americans struggle for dignity out of their element, like ornate shells left behind by the tide—still lacquered and colored with the wealth of the sea, incongruous on a beach of democratic sand where the only decorations are patterns of drift.

As is natural for a young writer, Lahiri spends some of her time exploring the terrain staked out by her literary precursors. Like Carver, she writes about a young couple who have fallen out of love and are playing a bittersweet game amid the detritus of their life together. Like Hemingway, she writes about a tour guide who has more heart than the bourgeois couple who hire him; he is seduced by the wife's glamour and then appalled by her cruelty. Like Isherwood, she writes about an earnest young man studying his landlady, whose calcified habits at first unnerve him and then draw out his tenderness. But none of her stories are apprentice work. Lahiri revises these scenarios with unexpected twists, and to each she brings her distinctive insight into the ways that human affections both sustain and defy the cultural forms that try to enclose them.

My favorite in the collection is "This Blessed House." The star of the story is Twinkle, a lackadaisical 27-year-old. An ambitious corporate vice president named Sanjeev has recently, rashly married her, because they both liked P. G. Wodehouse, they both disliked sitar music and Sanjeev was lonely. As her new husband soon learns, Twinkle cooks without recipes, leaves her undergarments on the floor when she gets into bed and feels no hurry to unpack the boxes in their new home. Her state of mind is "content yet curious," which drives the methodical Sanjeev nuts.

Serious trouble starts when Twinkle discovers a white porcelain Christ left behind by the previous tenants. Twinkle is charmed; Sanjeev, dismissive. The husband and wife are "good little Hindus," as Twinkle teasingly concedes, and Sanjeev hopes she will get rid of it. Sanjeev underestimates the tenacity of his wife's whim. He is also unaware that in the religious tchotchke department, their new home is a minefield. Twinkle's discoveries of St. Francis postcards and Noah's ark light-switch plates multiply into a treasure hunt. Fearing for the dignity of his home, Sanjeev finally threatens to dispose of a plaster Virgin Mary on their front lawn by force.

> "The reader finishes each story re-seduced, wishing he could spend a whole novel with its characters."

But ever since Pamela wound Squire B. around her little finger, force has been no match for sentiment, however defenseless sentiment may seem. During the showdown, Twinkle wears a bright blue facial mask while soaking in the bathtub. "I hate you," she tells her husband. Nonetheless, he insists on his threat, cruelly, until he notices that "some of the water dripping down her hard blue face was tears." Lahiri is not out to convert Hindus here, nor is she indulging in sarcasm at the expense of sincere belief. But not even religion is sacred to her writerly interest in the power of a childlike sympathy, going where it ought not go. Blue-faced Twinkle has become the Madonna statuette that she is so taken with. She has breathed her own life into the Christian icon's plaster, not deliberately and not ironically but humanely, and she demands that her husband respond to this achievement with mercy and respect.

Lahiri's achievement is something like Twinkle's. She breathes unpredictable life into the page, and the reader finishes each story re-seduced, wishing he could spend a whole novel with its characters. There is nothing accidental about her success; her plots are as elegantly constructed as a fine proof in mathematics. To use the word Sanjeev eventually applies to Twinkle, Lahiri is "wow." —*Caleb Crain*

A Real-Life Hogwarts

BY PICO IYER

The third book in J. K. Rowling's series, *Harry Potter and the Prisoner of Azkaban,* had just been published, and Pottermania was sweeping the globe when Iyer recounted the similarities between his British schooling experience and that of Harry Potter and his friends.

AS A BOY, I WENT FOR MANY YEARS TO THE Dragon School in Oxford. The rooms in which we lived were called "Leviathan" and "Pterodactyl" and "Ichthyosaurus"; the men who instructed us in dead languages were (through some arcane local custom) known always by their nicknames—"Guv" and "Plum" and "Inky." A few of the boys at the school, and they were nearly all boys, had come there from the Squirrel School, down the street; and once we'd mastered our secret runes, we would proceed, as Old Dragons, to another medieval castle, full of dungeons and towers, where boys in black robes, called "praepostors" (the word is the source of our own "preposterous"), would sweep into classrooms

at 11:40 each morning to summon malefactors to the headmaster's study.

I mention all this because, as Harry Potter's adventures conquer the nation, readers on this side of the Atlantic may not appreciate how much there is of realism, as well as magic, in the exotic tales of young sorcerers being trained at the Hogwarts School of Witchcraft and Wizardry. The classical boarding-school process favored by the English middle classes is esoteric—in fact, mad—to the point of resembling some Charms School for apprentice mages. The main languages we learned, from the ages of 7 to 14, were ones that had been out of use for 2,000 years or more, and Friday nights would find us bouncing up and down in our pajamas, reciting the principal parts of Greek irregular verbs. Every Sunday night, in our flowing black robes (we were known as "tugs"), we would gather in a classroom dating from 1441 to sing hymns in Latin, and whenever we passed a "beak"—i.e., a teacher—in the street, we were allowed to greet him only by raising one solemn finger silently into the air. What movies like *Heathers* (or novels like *The Virgin Suicides*) are to the American experience of growing up, the Harry Potter books, I suspect, are to the English.

The heart of magic realism is that if you describe the features of one culture to another, radically different, they will seem as strange and wonderful as fairy tale: the people of Aracataca, in Colombia, doubtless read much of García

1996	1998	1999
Jay McInerney finds David Foster Wallace's *Infinite Jest* to be "alternately tedious and effulgent."	José Saramago wins the Nobel Prize in Literature.	Stephen King, out for a walk near his home in Maine, is hit by a van and seriously injured.

Márquez as if it were the local newspaper; and my own mother treats the fantastications of Salman Rushdie's imagination as an unfailingly accurate account of day-to-day life in the Bombay of her youth. What J. K. Rowling has done, with considerable charm and inventive brio, is to take the traditional rituals of English public schools and show them in a light in which they seem as curious to outsiders as the rites of passage of tribal Africa. She makes it easy to overlook the fact that the most visible character going through Harry Potter's training even now is Harry Windsor.

For those who passed through these eccentric playgrounds, though, much in the Harry Potter universe can seem as familiar, and even as nostalgic, as passages in Cyril Connolly's *Enemies of Promise.* Here are all the rites I remember as vividly as lemon drops: the cryptic list of instructions that would appear through the mail, describing what we must—and mustn't—bring to school (the point of all the rules being not to make order so much as to enforce obedience); the trip to dusty old shops with creaky family names— New & Lingwood or Alden & Blackwell—where aged men would fit us out with the approved uniform and equipment, as they had done for our fathers and our fathers' fathers; the special school train that would be waiting in a London station to transport us to our cells.

It is precisely through the accumulation of such details that Rowling casts her spell, the names of her boys ringing out like hoofs on cobblestones—Crabbe and Goyle and Longbottom and Finch-Fletchley. (Many, in fact, are so nasty, brutish and short—Boot and Peeves and Weasley—that they sound like the product of Beowulf's liaison with Grendel's mother.) And even if Hogwarts didn't have a Latin motto on its crest involving dragons, even if it didn't have cruel little boys talking airily of the "wrong sort" and mocking anyone without the right family connections, I would be back in that realm of sick bays and tuck-shops where we mumbled the Lord's Prayer in Latin and thought it strange that some children didn't run a steeplechase through Agar's Plough.

Behind all this, of course, there is a somewhat sinister clannishness that makes all these private academies seem like secret societies—the English version of Skull and Bones—designed to train the elite in a system that other mortals cannot follow. When I was at school, it was always assumed that all the years of quasi-military training ("Hard work and pain are the best teachers if you ask me," the Hogwarts caretaker says) were meant to teach us how to rule the Empire and subdue the natives around the world. When we graduated, however, we found that the Empire was gone, and the only natives visible were ourselves.

One reason England has always been fertile ground for children's classics, I think, is precisely the fact that its training grounds are so ruled by dotty traditions and cobwebbed terms. Lewis Carroll and J. R. R. Tolkien looked around them, at Oxford's eccentric dons and the gargoyles above its chapels, and came up with the Mad Hatter and Bilbo Baggins; C. S. Lewis opened up a wardrobe near the Dragon School and discovered Narnia. What makes the Harry Potter books fly, so to speak, is not so much their otherworldliness as their fidelity to the way things really are (or were, at least, when quills and parchment were still more common than computers): wizards, Harry Potter's world suggests, are only regular Muggles who've been to the right school.

Zadie Smith: "I Wanted to Prove That I Was a Writer"

Shortly after her highly lauded debut, Smith played down its significance. "I have great ambitions of writing a very great book," she said. "I just don't think this is it."

ZADIE SMITH'S DEBUT NOVEL, *WHITE TEETH*, may have been sold for a considerable advance on the strength of 80 or so stunning pages. It may have inspired normally reserved British reviewers to fall all over themselves with enthusiasm. And it may have elicited a flattering telephone call (and a blurb, too) from none other than Salman Rushdie. But that doesn't mean Smith has to think it is any good.

"A lot of the book is an exercise in 'Look at me,'" she says with faint distaste, speaking of her work as if it were an embarrassing relic from her juvenile period, written decades ago (in fact, it was written three years ago, when she was 21). "I wanted to prove that I was a writer." And then, "It's like 100 other first novels I could pick up."

It's tempting to think that she's protesting too much. But over lunch at a Soho cafe that proves disappointing to the exacting Smith because of the way the place has abandoned its humble roots and tried to put on airs, she seems as hard on herself as she is on the state of current British fiction in general. That is, very hard indeed.

"So much of it is tedious and suburban," she says. "Of course, I absolutely include myself in that category."

Zadie Smith is spiky in manner, striking in appearance and very, very clever, though she gets strangely inarticulate when called upon to discuss *White Teeth*, a big, generous stew of a book that describes the lifelong friendship between Archie, a white, working-class Londoner, and Samad, a Muslim from Bangladesh, with issues of race, religion, generational conflict and genetically modified mice thrown spicily in to the pot.

"I'm so bad at this," she groans. "I'm reminded of Nabokov, who said: 'I think like a genius. I write like a man of letters. And I talk like a child.'"

But as lunch—soup and a salad, and cigarettes—wears on, she warms up and proves anything but childish. Brought up in Willesden Green, northwest London, to a young Jamaican mother and a far older English father, she was "a bit of a stoner" as a teenager, she says. When she announced at high school that she wanted to go on to Cambridge, the teacher literally threw a book at her in disbelief.

1999 ——————————————
The final *Peanuts* comic strip is published.

2000 ——————————————
A 1936 poll asked readers to predict which current writers would still be read in 2000. The winners? Sinclair Lewis, Willa Cather, Eugene O'Neill and Edna St. Vincent Millay.

2001 ——————————————→
The film version of *Bridget Jones's Diary* opens; Salman Rushdie, Julian Barnes and Jeffrey Archer have uncredited cameos.

Smith at Lincoln Center in 2016.

But go to Cambridge she did, and thrived on its competitive culture. After graduation, she applied for a number of jobs in journalism, didn't get even a single interview and found herself with a completed novel and a reputation for being the exciting new voice of youth and color in British fiction. Indeed, *White Teeth*—which is set in a neighborhood much like the one Smith grew up in—is as much a celebration of its mishmash of cultures and races as anything else.

"It is an area that works very well and in which people have been able to live their lives with the ideals that they have in their own community," she explains. "I wanted to show that you can live a life where Princess Diana isn't your role model, and the fact that David Beckham cut his hair doesn't matter at all," she adds, referring to a British soccer star.

The book, she says, presents "a utopian view" of race relations. "It's what it might be, and what it should be and maybe what it will be."

Smith's many fans will be happy to know that she is working on her second novel. It is about a man from a Jewish enclave in London who trades in autographs and whose adventures lead to an examination of the nature of fame and fortune, things the author has learned a great deal about in recent months, though they don't sit particularly well with her.

"It's the oddest thing in the world, having money," she says. "I don't really know what you're meant to do with it. In the end, you kind of shuffle off the planet. But now I've made enough and I don't need any more."

Nor does she need the goods that companies seem eager to provide her with, now that she is very successful and modestly famous (not to mention being young, black, tall and extremely stylish, in a white hat and fashionably cuffed jeans on this particular day). "People are always trying to give me stuff," she says. "I got an e-mail the other day. Someone wanted me to carry around a $450 handbag. Great: free stuff for rich people."

Smith says she is writing her new novel in a radically different style from that of *White Teeth*, and that it is going to be spare and sharp, rather than extended and gently satirical. "English writing tends to fall into two categories—the big, baggy, epic novel or the fairly controlled, tidy novel," she says. "For a long time I was a fan of the big, baggy novel, but there's definitely an advantage to having a little bit more control."

She returns to the subject of *White Teeth* and concedes that it was perhaps a good start, if nothing more. "I have great ambitions of writing a very great book," Smith says. "I just don't think this is it." *—Sarah Lyall*

2001 — Michael Chabon wins the Pulitzer Prize in fiction for *The Amazing Adventures of Kavalier & Clay*.

2002 — Upon learning that his novel *Life of Pi* had been awarded the Man Booker Prize, Yann Martel says, "It feels like winning the lottery."

2003 — Stephen Glass, fired from *The New Republic* for plagiarism, publishes a novel, *The Fabulist*, based on his own life. (In an author's note he says he regrets his "misconduct.")

Alice Sebold, *The Lovely Bones*

Sebold's fiction debut—which opens with the unforgettable lines "My name was Salmon, like the fish; first name, Susie. I was 14 when I was murdered on December 6, 1973."—blazed to the top of the best-seller lists in the summer of 2002. In a Times interview, Sebold wondered why it had struck such a chord: "It's the hardest question. I mean, I hear different things at readings. For me, I really do want to hear stories about what I think are the large issues, like love, hate, grief and loss."

IT TAKES A CERTAIN AUDACITY TO WRITE AN uplifting book about the abduction and murder of a young girl. But consider that the bones of *The Lovely Bones* belong not to the victim but to an abstract and quite positive idea—namely, that bones are the structure on which living things are built. Alice Sebold's accomplished first novel takes the metaphor of "bones," tainted by overuse, shakes off the thriller trappings and turns not only this but many other clichés upside down.

It also takes a certain daring to write a book narrated by someone who's dead. Not only dead but murdered, and not only murdered but murdered at the age of 14. Susie Salmon is in heaven. And, yes, she's looking down—but with a fishy eye.

All is not well in the world Susie has left behind. Her grief-stricken mother has an inappropriate fling and flees to California. Her distraught father attacks her best friend, Clarissa, in the cornfield where Susie was murdered, inexplicably mistaking Clarissa for Mr. Harvey, the creep who lives nearby.

Mr. Salmon suspects—and we know—that Mr. Harvey is the murderer. But the police fail to solve the crime and Mr. Harvey leaves town, turning up here and there over the years, observed by Susie but, alas, rarely by the authorities. I won't reveal whether he's caught, but setting the novel in the early 1970s does avoid the necessity of dealing with what one suspects would be a quick resolution in the age of DNA analysis.

Susie has a younger sister and a much younger brother, as well as a boyfriend, Ray Singh, with whom she is on the verge of a sweet first romance. She also has a strange friend named Ruth, who plays a greater role in Susie's life after it's over than during it. Susie will appear to each of them over the coming years. Her brother, Buckley, takes the sightings more or less in stride. "Do you see her?" he asks a playmate not long after the murder. "That's my sister. . . . She was gone for a while, but now she's back." But Ruth's sightings of Susie affect her increasingly deeply. As she grows up, acting as witness to crimes past becomes her obsession.

This is a high-wire act for a first novelist, and Alice Sebold maintains almost perfect balance. There are a couple of faltering moments: It seems implausible that Susie's grieving father would implicitly encourage his surviving daughter to nose around in the murderer's house looking for clues. And in a scene toward the conclusion of the book that strains credulity, Ruth does a kind of involuntary channeling that allows Susie one last moment with Ray. But Sebold catches herself in

1996–2021

307

Sebold on August 29, 2002.

"This is a high-wire act for a first novelist, and Alice Sebold maintains almost perfect balance."

the nick of time, and the book ends on the same appealingly plain-spoken note that it opens with: "I wish you all a long and happy life," Susie says.

Why did Mr. Harvey kill Susie Salmon? Sebold, perhaps wisely, stays away from this tricky territory, though his mother's early abandonment of him seems to be a contributing factor. Susie's chilling description of the crime opens the novel. In brief, dispassionate sentences she tells us how Mr. Harvey lured her into his secret cellar under the cornfield, how she fought back, how "hard-as-I-could was not hard enough." "I wept," she writes. "I began to leave my body; I began to inhabit the air and silence. I wept and struggled so I would not feel." It's a difficult first chapter, and a mesmerizing one.

Susie is our guide through the maze of grief and dysfunction that follows her brutal death. Her

dispassionate, observant young voice and poignant 14-year-old view of life don't change much. But she comes to understand things as she might have if she had grown up. Sebold's book is about the mind of a young girl, the reactions of a family to tragedy, the flaws that become enormous rifts under the pressures of grief. And it's about heaven.

This book happens to have been published at a moment when a real-life kidnapping of a 14-year-old girl, Elizabeth Smart, taken from her comfortable middle-class bed in the dead of night, haunts the news. The very idea of Sebold's subject matter might make a reader queasy. But there's nothing prurient or exploitative in *The Lovely Bones.* Susie's story, paradoxically, is one of hope, set against grim reality.

Sebold is also the author of a well-received memoir, *Lucky,* about the harrowing experience of being raped as a college freshman. In *The Lovely Bones,* as in that book, she deals with almost unthinkable subjects with humor and intelligence and a kind of mysterious grace. Like Anna Quindlen's *Black and Blue* and Russell Banks's *Sweet Hereafter, The Lovely Bones* takes the stuff of neighborhood tragedy—the unexplained disappearance of a child, the shattered family alone with its grief—and turns it into literature.

—*Katherine Bouton*

The "It Books" of Summers Past

DURING THE SUMMER OF 2002, NO matter where you went—the beach, the pool, the park—you saw the same book. Clad in a pale-blue jacket, its author's name a slash of blood-red ink, *The Lovely Bones* was in the very ether, what everyone was reading and everyone was talking about: the "it" book of summer.

What, exactly, is a summer "it" book? It's usually written by someone you've never heard of before. It appears out of nowhere, often having been published quietly the previous winter or spring, and has spent months gathering steam—hand-sold at bookstores, passed from one friend to another, recommended by librarians. Then one day, all of a sudden, it's the book you see wherever you look.

The thing about these books is, they often don't sound like something you'd want to read. A novel narrated by a murdered teenager? The history of a racehorse? But no matter the subject, "it" books distill something essential about the country at a particular moment. Some of them capture an economic or political mood; others piggyback on a cultural trend or ride the wave of a big news story. Most of all, though, they have to be compulsive page-turners, the kind of books that go down like an ice-cold milkshake on a hot day.

"It" books don't come around every summer, but when they do, they're impossible to forget. Here's a list of favorites from the last 50 years—pluck a tattered copy of any of these books off your shelf, and memories of the summer you read it will come roaring back.

LOVE STORY, BY ERICH SEGAL
1970

Segal ticked a lot of boxes with his tear-jerker—passion, sex, dying young, poor Radcliffe girl, rich Harvard boy. The country, battered by the events of the late 1960s, was still at war with Vietnam. Social tensions were running high, and the moment was ripe for a transporting romance. After Barbara Walters said on the *Today* show that she'd been up all night reading it and sobbing, sales took off.

THE NAME OF THE ROSE, BY UMBERTO ECO
1983

It was the year the *Challenger* flew its first space mission, the year cellphones first went on sale and arguably the year the internet began. So it's both completely surprising and not surprising at all that the summer of 1983's hot book was a cerebral murder mystery steeped in medieval history and set in a 14th-century Benedictine monastery.

PRESUMED INNOCENT,
BY SCOTT TUROW
1987

It was published at the end of 1986, but sales of this brainy legal thriller—about a Chicago prosecutor accused of murdering his lover—soared throughout the spring, and by the summer of 1987, the book seemed to dot every beach towel and peek out of every backpack.

THE JOY LUCK CLUB,
BY AMY TAN
1989

The novel people couldn't get enough of in 1989 was an emotional one, told around the mah-jongg table, about four Chinese immigrant women and their daughters, all born in America. It was published at a time when social turmoil was roiling China (the events of Tiananmen Square unfolded not long after it came out).

WAITING TO EXHALE,
BY TERRY MCMILLAN
1992

The blockbuster sales of this affectionate novel about the lives and loves of four friends in Phoenix were driven by African-American women, who had never found themselves portrayed in much commercial fiction before McMillan came along.

LIKE WATER FOR CHOCOLATE,
BY LAURA ESQUIVEL
1993

The English translation of this Mexican novel landed on best-seller lists just as the film version hit theaters; sales of movie tickets fueled book sales, and vice versa. Fans loved both versions of Esquivel's tender, all-consuming tale of forbidden love, in which a young woman wields fantastical powers through the food she cooks.

A man reads in Central Park
after work, on June 10, 1985.

Miguel de Cervantes, *Don Quixote*

BY CARLOS FUENTES

The Mexican novelist Carlos Fuentes celebrated Edith Grossman's new translation of the novel almost four centuries after it was written.

IN 2005, DON QUIXOTE WILL BE 400 YEARS OLD. Most epic heroes are young, from Achilles to El Cid. It was part of the genius of Cervantes to put an old man in the saddle and send him off to relive the heroic tales of the past. But Don Quixote is not alone in his mad quest for chivalry. He is accompanied by his opposite in figure, speech and temperament: the round, earthy, plainspoken Sancho Panza.

I stop right here, as the curtain goes up—or the pages open—to celebrate the great new translation of *Don Quixote* by Edith Grossman. Nothing harder for the *traduttore*, if he or she is not to be seen as the *traditore,* than to render a classic in contemporary idiom yet retain its sense of time and space. Up to now, my favorite *Quixote* translation has been that of Tobias Smollett, the 18th-century picaresque novelist, who rendered Cervantes in the style proper to Smollett and his own age. His *Quixote* reads much like *Humphry Clinker*, and this seems appropriate and, even, delightful. The family relationship is there.

Edith Grossman delivers her *Quixote* in plain but plentiful contemporary English. The quality of her translation is evident in the opening line:

"Somewhere in La Mancha, in a place whose name I do not care to remember, a gentleman lived not long ago, one of those who has a lance and ancient shield on a shelf and keeps a skinny nag and a greyhound for racing." This *Don Quixote* can be read with the same ease as the latest Philip Roth and with much greater facility than any Hawthorne. Yet there is not a single moment in which, in forthright English, we are not reading a 17th-century novel. This is truly masterly: The contemporaneous and the original co-exist. Not, mind you, the "old" and the "new." Grossman sees to it that these facile categories do not creep into her work. To make the classic contemporary: This is the achievement. And through it, Grossman can highlight Don Quixote's flight into heroic rhetoric with great comic effect.

If for many reasons *Don Quixote* is the first modern novel, it is pre-eminently because of the different languages spoken in it. Characters in classical literature all spoke the same language. Achilles understands Hector; Ulysses can even speak to Polyphemus. But Quixote and Sancho speak two different idioms. Why? Because the characters are engaged in what the Spanish critic Claudio Guillén calls "a dialogue of genres."

There has been some dispute about whether *Quixote* is indeed the first modern novel. Ian Watt gives primacy to the 18th-century English novel, which was responding to the rise of a middle-class, book-buying public. André Malraux thought of Madame de Lafayette's *Princesse de Clèves* as the first because it initiated inner exploration of character. But I believe that *Don Quixote* really inaugurates what we understand modern fiction to be—a reflection of our presence in the world as problematic beings in an unending history, whose continuity depends on subjecting

> "This *Don Quixote* can be read with the same ease as the latest Philip Roth and with much greater facility than any Hawthorne."

Illustration from the first English edition of *Don Quixote*, published in 1620.

reality to the imagination. Cervantes does it, as all writers do, in a precise time and space. This is Spain in the decadent reign of Philip III, a country that has conquered and plundered and built a New World in the Americas and returns, exhausted, to its native village in La Mancha with nothing but the memory of past deeds. It is also the Spain of the Counter-Reformation, where the Renaissance enlightenment brought to the court of Charles V by the Erasmist scholars had long been buried under the severe vigilance of the Inquisition and the edicts of the Council of Trent.

Don Quixote has so many levels of significance that I can set foot on only a couple of them. The first is the dialogue of genres. Cervantes inaugurates the modern novel through the impurity, the *mestizaje* of all known genres. Often criticized for ignoring the requirements of the well-made novel (recognizable characters, expert plotting, linear narrative), Cervantes audaciously brings into his book, first and foremost, the dialogue between the epic (Don Quixote) and the picaresque (Sancho Panza). But then he introduces the tale within the tale, the Moorish, the pastoral, the Byzantine modes and, of course, the love story. The modern novel is born as both an encounter of genres and a refusal of purity.

Out of this meeting, Cervantes proposes a new way of writing and reading whose starting point is uncertainty. In a world of dogmatic certitude, he introduces a universe where nothing is certain. The place is uncertain: "Somewhere in La Mancha . . . ." The authorship is uncertain. Who wrote *Don Quixote?* One Cervantes, "more versed in pain than in verse"? A gentleman called de Saavedra, mentioned in the novel with admiration for his love of freedom? (Cervantes's full name was Miguel de Cervantes Saavedra.) Is the author the Moorish scribe Cide Hamete Benengeli, who discovers, by chance, an anonymous manuscript? Or is it the despicable Avellaneda, who writes an unauthorized sequel to *Don Quixote* (in real life, and in the novel)? Or could it be, if we follow this rich, fantastical path opened by Cervantes, that the author of *Don Quixote* is really Jorge Luis Borges, who wrote a tale called "Pierre Menard, Author of the Quixote"?

If authorship is uncertain, so are names. *Don Quixote* is a veritable onomastic carnival.

Whoever enters Don Quixote's sphere changes names, furthering the uncertainty that brands this novel. The nameless horse becomes Rocinante; the magicians who haunt the Don are tongue-twisted beyond recognition by Sancho, whose wife can be Teresa, Juana or Mari Gutiérrez; Don Quixote's adversaries have to assume heroic names in order to be credible. And above all, Dulcinea, the knight's damsel, the epitome of gentility, is in all truth none other than the sweaty peasant girl Aldonza.

Don Quixote wants to live the books he has read, Michel Foucault pointedly observed. This leads the book to an extraordinary inaugural event and to a heartbreaking conclusion. The event is that Don Quixote, in pursuit of the malevolent plagiarist Avellaneda, rides into Barcelona and there visits . . . a printing shop. And what is being printed there? The book that we are reading. *Don Quixote de la Mancha.* They know all about us! exclaims Sancho, even the most private conversations. Cervantes and his ingenious squire have just inaugurated, de facto, the era of Gutenberg, the democratic society of readers and writers.

But then, the terrifyingly destructive, not evil but just plain and cruelly destructive, dukes invite the knight and his squire to their castle. And here the sadness of the book is brought to our hearts. For in the castle, Quixote's dreams are offered to him in reality. Where his wonderful imagination could turn an inn into a palace, here the palace is real. Where he could imagine scullery maids as highborn princesses, here the aristocratic women are real. Both real and cruel. Don Quixote is subjected to incessant mockery. Even Sancho, the levelheaded peasant, is lured into the political comedy of becoming governor of a nonexistent island.

The illusion comes crashing down. Books are no longer the grand, imaginative truth that moved Don Quixote through perils without end. So the windmills were not giants. So the armies were only flocks of sheep. So reality is shabby, gray, unarmed. . . . What can Don Quixote do but return home, get into bed, recover his reason and peacefully die? The "impossible dream" is over. No wonder that Dostoyevsky, in his diary, calls *Don Quixote* "the saddest book ever written." For it is, he adds, "the story of disillusionment."

That Edith Grossman has brought all these levels—and many more—to contemporary life is a major literary achievement. For to read *Don Quixote,* in an increasingly Manichaean world of simplistic Good versus Evil and inquisitorial dogmas, becomes one of the healthiest experiences a modern, democratic citizen can undertake.

2004 —————————————
Margaret Atwood, reviewing Orhan Pamuk's *Snow*, writes that it "is an engrossing feat of tale-spinning" and "essential reading for our times."

2004 —————————————
David Foster Wallace's review of *Borges: A Life*, by Edwin Williamson, which appears on the cover of the Book Review, is replete with his trademark footnotes.

2005 —————————————→
The writer JT Leroy is revealed as a literary hoax, the creation of a writer named Laura Albert.

Dale Peck,
Hatchet Jobs

BY JOHN LEONARD

In this review, headlined "Smash-Mouth Criticism," a former Book Review editor took on a controversial critic in a fittingly bold critique.

ALTHOUGH ROBERT SOUTHEY WAS THE POET laureate of England from 1813 until his death in 1843, and a Lake District buddy of Coleridge and Wordsworth, he is hardly read at all today. A wisecrack by Richard Porson may have done some serious damage. About Southey's epic poems, Porson said, "They will be read when Homer and Virgil are forgotten, but—not till then."

You will notice that I mosey. Some of us, when we are about to be unpleasant, are bothered by the feeling that it's almost as hard to write a bad book as a good one and lots easier to write a slash-and-burn review. So we walk around the block to suck up Randall Jarrell and perspective. Others, like Dale Peck, fall down out of the sky on the head of the pedestrian author like a piano or a safe. Peck is his own blunt instrument.

Which is why, in *Hatchet Jobs,* his Newgate Calendar of maledictions, he leans on words with primary colors, like terrible, bloated, boring and gratuitous; hate, resent, stale and slather; maudlin, dreck, drivel and insipid; muddled, pretentious, derivative and bathetic—not to mention scatologies that can't be reprinted here but

brought no blush to the bum of *The New Republic,* where most of Peck's fatwas first appeared and where most of American literature is generally considered a waste of the editors' warped space and deep time.

Peck is so hard on his elders that you suspect him of symbolic patricide, except that he is just as hard on his peers. Famously, of course, Rick Moody: "the worst writer of his generation." But Colson Whitehead gets it for his "stiff, schematic" first novel, *The Intuitionist,* and a second, *John Henry Days,* with "the doughy center of a half-baked cake." David Foster Wallace's *Infinite Jest* so much fails to amuse him that he wishes on Wallace an anal assault. Richard Powers, Dave Eggers and the Jonathans, Franzen and Lethem, are rudely dismissed for lack of "a true empathetic undercurrent" and what he elsewhere disdains as "pomo shenanigans." Nor is he impressed by the Dirty Realists (trailer homes), the Brat Packers (nightclubs) or the New Narrativists (sexual transgression).

This isn't criticism. It isn't even performance art. It's thuggee. However entertaining in small doses—we are none of us immune to malice, envy, schadenfreude, a prurient snuffle and a sucker punch—as a steady diet it's worse for readers, writers and reviewers than self-abuse; it causes the kind of tone-deaf, colorblind, nerve-damaged and gum-sore literary journalism that screams "Look at me!" The rain comes down—and the worms come out—and just what the culture doesn't need is one more hall monitor, bounty hunter or East German border guard.

It's the relish on this hotdog that turns the stomach. He promises never to do it again, but the very title *Hatchet Jobs* reeks of market niche, an underground service like fumigation or garbage

1996–2021

315

recycling. His alibi for being unfair is that he's a novelist, and they lie a lot. But his reputation would have long since earned him the right at his various pillboxes and lemonade stands to review any book he chose, out of hundreds of good ones needing discovery among tens of thousands cynically published, and yet he almost always seems to pick a punching bag, or draw his own bull's-eye on the passing chump. This is lazy, churlish and even demagogic.

I was going to suggest some hard-won guidelines for responsible reviewing. For instance: First, as in Hippocrates, do no harm. Second, never stoop to score a point or bite an ankle. Third, always understand that in this symbiosis, you are the parasite. Fourth, look with an open heart and mind at every different kind of book with every change of emotional weather because we are reading for our lives and that could be love gone out the window or a horseman on the roof. Fifth, use theory only as a periscope or a trampoline, never a panopticon, a crib sheet or a license to kill. Sixth, let a hundred Harolds Bloom. But instead I'll tell a story.

"It's the relish on this hot dog that turns the stomach."

Many years ago the editor of this publication asked me to review John Cheever's last, brief novel, *Oh What a Paradise It Seems*, after he had already been turned down by half a dozen critics who knew that Cheever was dying but thought his new book a weak one and didn't want to compromise their supreme importance with a random act of kindness. It never occurred to me that a thank-you note to a wonderful writer, a valediction as it were, would get me kicked out of any club I wanted to belong to, so I immediately said yes. At the time, besides that review, I wanted to write a message to those preening scribblers who thought they were too good for lesser Cheever. On a card, in small caps, I would have said what I say to Peck:

GET OVER YOURSELF.

2006 — Stieg Larsson's name appears in The Times for the first time when his novel *Men Who Hate Women* hits #1 in Norway. It will be published in the U.S. as *The Girl With the Dragon Tattoo* in 2008.

2006 — The Book Review podcast begins. Each episode starts "with a Letterman-esque tagline," such as, "A weekly conversation about books and ideas, and the ever-widening chasm that seems to separate the two."

2007 — Doris Lessing learns she has won the Nobel Prize in Literature from journalists outside her London flat. "Oh, Christ," she says.

Alison Bechdel, *Fun Home*

This droll and engaging graphic memoir—about Bechdel's childhood, coming out and relationship with her father—was later reimagined as a play and won the Tony Award for best musical in 2015.

IF THE THEORETICAL VALUE OF A PICTURE IS still holding steady at a thousand words, then Alison Bechdel's slim yet Proustian graphic memoir, *Fun Home,* must be the most ingeniously compact, hyper-verbose example of autobiography to have been produced. It is a pioneering work, pushing two genres (comics and memoir) in multiple new directions, with panels that combine the detail and technical proficiency of R. Crumb with a seriousness, emotional complexity and innovation completely its own. Then there are the actual words. Generally this is where graphic narratives stumble. Very few cartoonists can also write—or, if they can, they manage only to hit a few familiar notes. But *Fun Home* quietly succeeds in telling a story, not only through well-crafted images but through words that are equally revealing and well chosen.

A comic book for lovers of words! Bechdel's rich language and precise images combine to create a lush piece of work—a memoir where concision and detail are melded for maximum, obsessive density. She has obviously spent years getting this memoir right, and it shows. You can read *Fun Home* in a sitting, or get lost in the pictures within the pictures on its pages. The work is so absorbing you feel you are living in her world.

Bechdel is known to readers of the indie press as the author of a long-running comic strip called "Dykes to Watch Out For." She's a lesbian, and sexuality looms large in her memoir. Bechdel's father, Bruce, was gay (as she puts it: "a manic-depressive, closeted fag"), and *Fun Home* is at its heart a story about a daughter trying to understand her father through the common and unspoken bond of their homosexuality. The hopelessness of this desire is deepened by the fact that Bruce Bechdel was hit by a truck and killed shortly after his daughter wrote her parents a letter that announced, "I am a lesbian." As it happens, Bruce Bechdel was the town funeral director (hence the title, which comes from the family's name for the funeral home). His daughter believes his death was a suicide, brought on in part by her own confession. She draws herself beside his coffin, a thought bubble coming out of her head: "I'd kill myself too if I had to live here."

"Here" is the 800-person hamlet of Beech Creek, Pa., and, more specifically, the family home, a fetishistically restored Victorian mansion on Maple Avenue; the vessel into which her father poured his love and passion and repression, and the second ironic fun home of the title. The Bechdels lived in this museum in a state of profound isolation. "We ate together, but otherwise were absorbed in our separate pursuits." Alison's childhood was that of a small-town girl living in a big house where "astral lamps and girandoles and Hepplewhite suite chairs" were treated with more tenderness than she was. One of the few breaks from Beech Creek comes when the family takes a trip to New York City, with a babysitter (one of the boys her father also collected—and probably slept with) in tow. The post-Stonewall Greenwich Village is described, longingly, as a place where "a lingering vibration, a quantum particle of rebellion," hung in the air; it's a place, it is implied, where Bruce Bechdel could have had another life. But his daughter does not dwell on the possibility. Instead, with the humor that fills every sad moment in this story, she labels the smell on the corner of Christopher Street and Seventh Avenue South according to its constituent parts: "putrefaction" for a trash can; "diesel" for a bus; "menthol" for a cigarette; "pastry" for the exhaust from a chimney; "Brut" for a pedestrian; and "urine and electricity" for the subway entrance. New York City olfactory history in a single panel—and one that captures the effortless scope of "Fun Home." As a recent trip to this corner will attest, only the electricity remains.

My copy began with the following unmissable notation, titled "Alison Bechdel, on Creating *Fun Home*": "I've always been a careful archivist of my own life. . . . I've kept a journal since I was 10. I've been logging my income and expenses since I was 13. . . . All this detritus came in handy as I wrote *Fun Home*, as a corrective to the inevitable distortions of memory. I discovered that the actual documentary truth was almost always richer and more surprising than the way I had remembered a particular event. And it was certainly more interesting than any possible way I could have fictionalized it." This is one of the great truths of nonfiction writing, and I would amplify by pointing out that the emotion and depth of *Fun Home*, as with all honest memoirs, come entirely of watching Bechdel try to make sense of the confusing facts of her own life and history. If it were fiction (or fictionalized) it would be meaningless.

Depressingly, memoirists now seem compelled to pre-emptively defend the factuality of their works, under the assumption they will inevitably be questioned. Memory is no longer entirely credible in the genre of memory. In fact (and to ensure factuality), it seems possible that not only are the roles of memoirist and documentarian about to be combined, but the roles of reviewer and investigative journalist are as well.

With this in mind I took a trip to Beech Creek, Pa., shortly after completing *Fun Home*. Two hundred miles west of Manhattan on I-80, then south on Route 150, past the spot where Bruce Bechdel was killed (signs there now read "Special Enforcement Area," "Don't Tailgate" and "DUI: You Can't Afford It"). I pulled into a parking lot. Maps on Pages 30 and 146 showed me where I was. A memoir you can navigate by!

I took an odometer reading and compared it with Bechdel's assertion that "On a map of my hometown, a circle a mile and a half in diameter circumscribes: (A) Dad's grave, (B) the spot on Route 150 where he died, near an old farmhouse he was restoring, (C) the house where he and my mother raised our family, and (D) the farm where he was born." True. A conversation with a local established that Beech Creek is pronounced "Bitch Crick." I visited the cemetery. Bechdel's drawings of it are accurate right down to the almost unnoticeable radio tower on a mountain behind the graves.

Of course the true memoirist's mission, like the novelist's, is not so much establishing factuality as getting to the heart and truth of something—and there is no way to get there dishonestly. Having read *Fun Home* I believe that Bechdel's made the journey. But my certainty is blessedly un-fact-checkable.

Leaving town I drove up Maple Avenue, past the Bechdel residence. It is for sale: $279,900 and you can live in *Fun Home* full time. The real estate agent's exhortation on the front lawn: "Don't miss your chance to own a piece of history!"
—*Sean Wilsey*

Bechdel touring her childhood home in Beech Creek, Pennsylvania, while it was on the market in 2006.

"To Live a Proud and Decent Life"

Mary Karr, who rose to prominence with the memoir *The Liar's Club,* wrote to the Book Review in response to an essay on the form.

To the Editor:

I take issue with Benjamin Kunkel's rant against memoir ("Misery Loves a Memoir," July 16), specifically: "Where is the contemporary writer reporting honestly, ambitiously and without therapeutic cant or smug self-help recipes on his or her effort to live a proud and decent life? Contemporary memoirists have taught us mostly how to survive. They haven't begun to teach us how to live."

Who died and put Ben Kunkel in charge of what memoirists are supposed to do? I think few memoirists worth reading ever—St. Augustine included—set out to teach someone how to live. Kunkel mentions Thoreau with appropriate reverence, but Thoreau is most revered as a political philosopher—a fairly smug one at that—not as a riveting storyteller.

Would Kunkel ask for a memoir with no conflict? Instructional, morally righteous? He's describing a high-church service, a spoonful of cod-liver oil—not something you'd read for pleasure.

A more accurate critique of memoir would differentiate between the reductive, preachy, sound-bite memoirs that make good TV, and the literary memoirs that—like great novels—will endure in their complexities beyond our speck on the timeline. Plenty of those teach us how to live, and they do so through stories, grounded in conflict and evoking deep feeling. Nabokov's *Speak, Memory,* for one; Richard Wright's *Black Boy.* More recently, Tobias Wolff's *This Boy's Life,* Michael Herr's *Dispatches,* Michael Ondaatje's *Running in the Family,* Maxine Hong Kingston's *Woman Warrior* all instructed me, albeit subtly, as the great novels I've read have. Chekhov once said if a writer can describe a problem accurately, his work is done.

Underlying Kunkel's essay is a Calvinist distaste (it seems to me) for strong feeling unguided by moral principle, and a sense that these sad people with nasty lives should keep the mess to themselves. As for Kunkel's novel, which I read in one gulp and liked a boatload, did it teach anybody how to live? I sincerely hope not.

MARY KARR
Syracuse

Me, Myself and I

Karr's wasn't the only blockbuster memoir of the 1990s.

GIRL, INTERRUPTED,
BY SUSANNA KAYSEN
1993

Kaysen's memoir of mental illness and hospitalization, which was adapted into a film starring Winona Ryder and Angelina Jolie, has become a classic of the genre. Susan Cheever's review of the memoir pointed to a pressing double standard: "When women are angry at men, they call them heartless. When men are angry at women, they call them crazy. Sometimes it doesn't stop there."

PROZAC NATION,
BY ELIZABETH WURTZEL
1994

The Book Review's assessment of this story of depressive youth was less than flattering: "Instead of prescribing Prozac to depressive patients, doctors might now want to try something else first: Give them a copy of *Prozac Nation* and say, 'Read this; if you don't watch out, you could end up sounding like her.'"

ANGELA'S ASHES,
BY FRANK MCCOURT
1996

Denis Donoghue opened his review of this memoir of poverty and family strife with a bold (and familiar) claim: "All happy childhoods are the same; every unhappy childhood is unhappy in its own way."

BONE BLACK,
BY BELL HOOKS
1996

Thulani Davis, who reviewed this memoir, said that reading it "raised questions about the power of personal exploration to halt the tongue and impoverish an elegant vocabulary. I wondered if it was by design or by mishap that Ms. Hooks has created here a language devoid of the sensuality she so amply displays elsewhere."

THE DIVING BELL
AND THE BUTTERFLY,
BY JEAN-DOMINIQUE BAUBY
1997

This memoir about living in near complete paralysis "belongs to what might be called the literature of extreme circumstance, like the book of Job, moving and powerful in inverse proportion to the tone of brave understatement that Mr. Bauby manages to maintain throughout," wrote Thomas Mallon in his review.

André Aciman, *Call Me by Your Name*

Aciman's debut novel, which was later made into a highly praised film, received a rave.

THIS NOVEL IS HOT. A COMING-OF-AGE STORY, a coming-out story, a Proustian meditation on time and desire, a love letter, an invocation and something of an epitaph, *Call Me by Your Name* is also an open question. It is an exceptionally beautiful book that cannot quite bring itself to draw the inevitable conclusion about axis-shifting passion that men and women of the world might like to think they will always reach—that that obscure object of desire is, by definition, ungraspable, indeterminate and already lost at exactly the moment you rush so fervently to hold him or her. The heat is in the longing, the unavailability as we like to say, the gap, the illusion, etc. But what André Aciman considers, elegantly and with no small amount of unbridled skin-to-skin contact, is that maybe the heat of eros isn't only in the friction of memory and anticipation. Maybe it's also in the getting. In a first novel that abounds in moments of emotional and physical abandon, this may be the most wanton of his moves: his narrative, brazenly, refuses to stay closed. It is as much a story of paradise found as it is of paradise lost.

The literal story is a tale of adolescent sexual awakening, set in the very well-appointed home of an academic, on the Italian Riviera, in the mid-1980s. Elio, the precocious 17-year-old son of the esteemed and open-minded scholar and his wife, falls fast and hard for Oliver, a 24-year-old post-doc teaching at Columbia, who has come to the mansion for six weeks to revise his manuscript—on Heraclitus, since this is a novel about time and love—before publication.

The younger Elio has apparently been more or less heterosexual until Oliver arrives, but in fewer than 15 pages he's already in a state he calls the "swoon." He lies around on his bed in the long Mediterranean afternoons hoping Oliver will walk in, feeling "fire like fear, like panic, like one more minute of this and I'll die if he doesn't knock at my door, but I'd sooner he never knock than knock now. I had learned to leave my French windows ajar, and I'd lie on my bed wearing only my bathing suit, my entire body on fire. Fire like a pleading that says, Please, please, tell me I'm wrong, tell me I've imagined all this, because it can't possibly be true for you as well, and if it's true for you too, then you're the cruelest man alive."

But it is true for Oliver, and he does knock, and then things really heat up. What Elio and Oliver do to a peach might have made T. S. Eliot take a match to "The Love Song of J. Alfred Prufrock." Aciman, who has written so exquisitely about exile, loss and Proust in his book of essays, *False Papers,* and his memoir, *Out of Egypt,* is no less exquisite here in his evocation of Elio's adoration for the lost city of Oliver's body and the lost city of the love between the two men. He builds these lost cities with the extraordinary craftsmanship of obsession, carefully imagining every last element of Elio's affair with Oliver, depicting even the slightest touches and most mundane conversations with a nearly hyper-real attention to how, exactly, each one articulated a desire in Elio that

> "His narrative, brazenly, refuses to stay closed. It is as much a story of paradise found as it is of paradise lost."

Aciman on February 9, 2007.

felt "like coming home, like asking, Where have I been all my life?" Aciman never curbs or mocks Elio's unabashed adolescent romanticism, never wheels in repressive social forces to crush the lovers, never makes one the agent of the other's ruin. Even Elio's father is fairly "*que será, será*" about what he suspects has been going on (a lot) under his scholarly roof.

What unwinds the men from each other's embrace is none of these clichés; instead, Aciman, Proustian to the core, moves them apart, renders their beautiful city Atlantis, with the subtlest, most powerful universal agent: time. Nobody gets clocked with a tire iron. No one betrays the other. One becomes ordinary and marries; the other's romantic fate is vague but seems to be more patchy. They meet again, 15 years later, and they're not tragic; all they are is older.

In his essay "Pensione Eolo," Aciman writes, "Ultimately, the real site of nostalgia is not the place that was lost or the place that was never quite had in the first place; it is the text that must record that loss." In other words, Elio and

Oliver might give each other up, but the book that conjures them doesn't give up either one. In fact, it brings them back together, reunites them, for a glorious endless summer. In the book, the river can be revisited. The closing words echo the title: a phrase simultaneously of elegy and of invitation.
—*Stacey D'Erasmo*

Jazz Messenger

BY HARUKI MURAKAMI

The Japanese novelist
described how he learned
to write—through music.

I NEVER HAD ANY INTENTION OF BECOMING
a novelist—at least not until I turned 29. This is
absolutely true.

I read a lot from the time I was a little kid,
and I got so deeply into the worlds of the novels I
was reading that it would be a lie if I said I never
felt like writing anything. But I never believed I
had the talent to write fiction. In my teens I loved
writers like Dostoyevsky, Kafka and Balzac, but
I never imagined I could write anything that
would measure up to the works they left us. And
so, at an early age, I simply gave up any hope of
writing fiction. I would continue to read books as
a hobby, I decided, and look elsewhere for a way
to make a living.

The professional area I settled on was music.
I worked hard, saved my money, borrowed a
lot from friends and relatives, and shortly after
leaving the university I opened a little jazz club
in Tokyo. We served coffee in the daytime and
drinks at night. We also served a few simple
dishes. We had records playing constantly, and
young musicians performing live jazz on week-
ends. I kept this up for seven years. Why? For
one simple reason: It enabled me to listen to
jazz from morning to night.

I had my first encounter with jazz in

1964 when I was 15. Art Blakey and the Jazz
Messengers performed in Kobe in January that
year, and I got a ticket for a birthday present.
This was the first time I really listened to jazz,
and it bowled me over. I was thunderstruck. The
band was just great: Wayne Shorter on tenor
sax, Freddie Hubbard on trumpet, Curtis Fuller
on trombone and Art Blakey in the lead with his
solid, imaginative drumming. I think it was one
of the strongest units in jazz history. I had never
heard such amazing music, and I was hooked.

A year ago in Boston I had dinner with the
Panamanian jazz pianist Danilo Pérez, and when
I told him this story, he pulled out his cellphone
and asked me, "Would you like to talk to Wayne,
Haruki?" "Of course," I said, practically at a loss
for words. He called Wayne Shorter in Florida
and handed me the phone. Basically what I said
to him was that I had never heard such amazing
music before or since. Life is so strange, you
never know what's going to happen. Here I was,
42 years later, writing novels, living in Boston and
talking to Wayne Shorter on a cellphone. I never
could have imagined it.

When I turned 29, all of a sudden out of
nowhere I got this feeling that I wanted to write a
novel—that I could do it. I couldn't write anything
that measured up to Dostoyevsky or Balzac, of
course, but I told myself it didn't matter. I didn't
have to become a literary giant. Still, I had no
idea how to go about writing a novel or what to
write about. I had absolutely no experience, after
all, and no ready-made style at my disposal. I
didn't know anyone who could teach me how
to do it, or even friends I could talk with about
literature. My only thought at that point was
how wonderful it would be if I could write like
playing an instrument.

Murakami on October 5, 2018.

I had practiced the piano as a kid, and I could read enough music to pick out a simple melody, but I didn't have the kind of technique it takes to become a professional musician. Inside my head, though, I did often feel as though something like my own music was swirling around in a rich, strong surge. I wondered if it might be possible for me to transfer that music into writing. That was how my style got started.

Whether in music or in fiction, the most basic thing is rhythm. Your style needs to have good, natural, steady rhythm, or people won't keep reading your work. I learned the importance of rhythm from music—and mainly from jazz. Next comes melody—which, in literature, means the appropriate arrangement of the words to match the rhythm. If the way the words fit the rhythm is smooth and beautiful, you can't ask for anything more. Next is harmony—the internal mental sounds that support the words. Then comes the part I like best: free improvisation. Through some special channel, the story comes welling out freely from inside. All I have to do is get into the flow. Finally comes what may be the most important thing: that high you experience upon completing a work—upon ending your "performance" and feeling you have succeeded in reaching a place that is new and meaningful. And if all goes well, you get to share that sense of

> "Whether in music or in fiction, the most basic thing is rhythm."

elevation with your readers (your audience). That is a marvelous culmination that can be achieved in no other way.

Practically everything I know about writing, then, I learned from music. It may sound paradoxical to say so, but if I had not been so obsessed with music, I might not have become a novelist. Even now, almost 30 years later, I continue to learn a great deal about writing from good music. My style is as deeply influenced by Charlie Parker's repeated freewheeling riffs, say, as by F. Scott Fitzgerald's elegantly flowing prose. And I still take the quality of continual self-renewal in Miles Davis's music as a literary model. One of my all-time favorite jazz pianists is Thelonious Monk. Once, when someone asked him how he managed to get a certain special sound out of the piano, Monk pointed to the keyboard and said: "It can't be any new note. When you look at the keyboard, all the notes are there already. But if you mean a note enough, it will sound different. You got to pick the notes you really mean!"

I often recall these words when I am writing, and I think to myself, "It's true. There aren't any new words. Our job is to give new meanings and special overtones to absolutely ordinary words." I find the thought reassuring. It means that vast, unknown stretches still lie before us, fertile territories just waiting for us to cultivate them.

2008 —————
Asked about the death of his ideological foe William F. Buckley Jr., Gore Vidal replies, "I thought hell is bound to be a livelier place, as he joins forever those whom he served in life."

2008 —————
Suzanne Collins publishes *The Hunger Games*; John Green, reviewing it for The Times, calls it "brilliantly plotted and perfectly paced."

2009 —————→
Elizabeth Strout wins the Pulitzer Prize in fiction for *Olive Kitteridge*; Colum McCann nabs the National Book Award in fiction for *Let the Great World Spin*.

Junot Díaz, *The Brief Wondrous Life of Oscar Wao*

BY A. O. SCOTT

The Dominican-American author established his melodious style with this polyphonic novel about a young nerd from Jersey.

THE HERO OF JUNOT DÍAZ'S FIRST NOVEL IS an overweight Dominican-American man named Oscar, a "ghetto nerd" from Paterson, N.J., and a devotee of what he somewhat grandly calls "the more speculative genres." He means comic books, sword-and-sorcery novels, science fiction, role-playing games—the pop-literary storehouse of myths and fantasies that sexually frustrated, socially maladjusted guys like him are widely believed to inhabit.

In *The Brief Wondrous Life of Oscar Wao*, Díaz, the author of a book of sexy, diamond-sharp stories called *Drown*, shows impressive high-low dexterity, flashing his geek credentials, his street wisdom and his literary learning with equal panache. A short epigraph from the Fantastic Four is balanced by a longer one from Derek Walcott; allusions to *Dune*, *The Matrix* and (especially) *The Lord of the Rings* rub up against references to Melville and García Márquez. Oscar's nickname is a Spanglish pronunciation of Oscar Wilde, whom he is said to resemble when dressed up in his Doctor Who costume for Halloween.

"What more sci-fi than Santo Domingo? What more fantasy than the Antilles?" Oscar wonders. And the question of how to take account of his ancestral homeland—its folklore, its politics, the diaspora that brought so many of its inhabitants to North Jersey and Upper Manhattan—is one that explicitly preoccupies Oscar's creator. The way Díaz tells it, the Dominican Republic, which occupies the Spanish-speaking half of the island where Columbus made landfall, is the kind of small country that suffers from a surfeit of history. From the start, it has been a breeding ground for outsize destinies and monstrous passions.

Díaz's novel also has a wild, capacious spirit, making it feel much larger than it is. Within its relatively compact span, *The Brief Wondrous Life of Oscar Wao* contains an unruly multitude of styles and genres. The tale of Oscar's coming-of-age is in some ways the book's thinnest layer, a young-adult melodrama draped over a multigenerational immigrant family chronicle that dabbles in tropical magic realism, punk-rock feminism, hip-hop machismo, post-postmodern pyrotechnics and enough polymorphous multiculturalism to fill up an Introduction to Cultural Studies syllabus.

Holding all this together—just barely, but in the end effectively—is a voice that is profane, lyrical, learned and tireless, a riot of accents and idioms coexisting within a single personality. The voice belongs, for the most part, to Yunior, who only gradually slides from behind the curtain of apparently omniscient narration to reveal himself as a character. He's Oscar's sometime roommate at Rutgers, the would-be boyfriend of Oscar's sister, Lola, and in just about every imaginable way Oscar's opposite. While Oscar favors the stilted, thesaurus-fed diction of the fantasy-nerd autodidact ("I think she's orchida-ceous"), Yunior affects a bilingual b-boy flow, punctuated by bouts of didacticism. And while Oscar falls madly and chastely in love with a succession of not-quite-attainable women, Yunior is a chronic woman-izer. Though Yunior is, like Oscar, an aspiring writer, his preferred genres are more hard-boiled, "all robberies and drug deals and . . . BLAU! BLAU! BLAU!"

But *The Brief Wondrous Life* isn't Oscar's story alone. Indeed, he often seems like a bit of an exile in the book that bears his name. The recounting of his thwarted romances, his suicide attempt, his friendships and his literary projects is interrupted—and overshadowed—by episodes of family history that reverse the migratory path from the D.R. to the U.S.A. and concentrate on the women in Oscar's family. His sister, a punk rocker, runaway and track star, is in many ways a more vivid and magnetic character than her brother, as is their mother, Beli, whose remark-able biography forms the novel's true narrative backbone. In Baní, the provincial Dominican city where she was raised, Beli was a dark-skinned beauty, a scholarship girl at a fancy private school and eventually the lover of a notorious criminal. Her son's painful, familiar passage into adulthood is set against her own transformation, shown in reverse. When we first see her, she is an angry, borderline abusive immigrant matriarch, fighting with her daughter and furiously wearing herself out with work and worry. But later chapters show

"The island may be cursed and haunted, but it's also enchanted."

Beli as a rebellious daughter in her own right, struggling with La Inca, the poor yet respectable relative in whose home she was raised. Beli's parents—a doctor and a nurse, as La Inca never tires of reminding her—were members of the bour-geoisie who fell afoul of Rafael Trujillo, an impressively brutal dictator, even by mid-20th-century Latin American standards.

The island may be cursed and haunted, but it's also enchanted; even the bitterest memories seem softened by nostalgia. The evil spirits that are periodically invoked to explain Oscar's fami-ly's bad luck are also, for the novelist if not for his characters, lucky charms.

Without the horrors and superstitions of the old country, without the tropical sweetness that inflects Díaz's prose even at moments of great cruelty, Oscar Wao would be just another geek with an Akira poster on his dorm-room wall and a long string of desperate, unconsummated sexual obsessions. The incongruity between Oscar's circumstances and his background—a disjunc-tion Díaz solves violently and unconvincingly in the book's final section—is the real subject of *The Brief Wondrous Life of Oscar Wao*. This is, almost in spite of itself, a novel of assimilation, a fractured chronicle of the ambivalent, inexorable movement of the children of immigrants toward the American middle class, where the terrible, incredible stories of what parents and grand-parents endured in the old country have become a genre in their own right.

Jennifer Egan, *A Visit From the Goon Squad*

Egan won a Pulitzer Prize for this structurally inventive novel. Nominally about a record label executive and his kleptomaniac assistant, it features a sprawling cast of characters and hopscotches from New York to Naples to San Francisco. "Everything hangs together," our reviewer wrote, "connected by a tone of simmering regret arising from love's wreckage and time's relentless devouring."

IF YOU'RE LIKE ME, YOU TEND TO REGARD plot summaries as a necessary boredom at best. They're the flyover country between a reviewer's landing strips of judgment, revealing almost nothing about the way a book actually works, almost nothing about why it succeeds or fails. If plot were the crucial measure, there'd be no difference between a story about the fish that got away and *Moby-Dick*. Reading such summaries (or writing them) is usually as beguiling as listening to some addled fan of *Lost* explain what happened on that botched rune of a show.

At least this is how I felt until I read Jennifer Egan's remarkable new fiction, *A Visit From the Goon Squad*. Whether it is a novel or a collection of linked stories is a matter for the literary accountants to tote up in their ledgers of the inconsequential. What's actually kind of fun for once, however, is attempting to summarize the action of a narrative that feels as freely flung as a bag of trash down a country gully. That's because to do so captures Egan's essential challenge to herself: How wide a circumference can she achieve in *A Visit From the Goon Squad* while still maintaining any sort of coherence and momentum? How loosely can she braid the skein of connections and still have something that hangs together?

There is a madness to her method. She hands off the narrative from one protagonist to another in a wild relay race that will end with the same characters with which it begins while dispensing with them for years at a time. The book starts with Sasha, a kleptomaniac, who works for Bennie, a record executive, who is a protégé of Lou who seduced Jocelyn who was loved by Scotty who played guitar for the Flaming Dildos, a San Francisco punk band for which Bennie once played bass guitar (none too well), before marrying Stephanie who is charged with trying to resurrect the career of the bloated rock legend Bosco who grants the sole rights for covering his farewell "suicide tour" to Stephanie's brother, Jules Jones, a celebrity journalist who attempted to rape the starlet Kitty Jackson, who one day will be forced to take a job from Stephanie's publicity mentor, La Doll, who is trying to soften the image of a genocidal tyrant because her career collapsed in spectacular fashion around the same time that Sasha in the years before going to work for Bennie was perhaps working as a prostitute in Naples where she was discovered by her Uncle Ted who was on holiday from a bad marriage, and while not much more will be heard from him, Sasha will come to New York and attend N.Y.U. and work for Bennie before disappearing into the

Egan photographed at her home in New York on June 24, 2010.

desert to sculpture and raise a family with her college boyfriend, Drew, while Bennie, assisted by Alex, a former date of Sasha's from whom she lifted a wallet, soldiers on in New York, producing musicians (including the rediscovered guitarist Scotty) as the artistic world changes around him with the vertiginous speed of Moore's Law.

All of the above takes place in 13 chapters covering 40 years or so, ranging backward and forward across time, each composed from a different point of view, which means 13 different centers, 13 different peripheries. And yet everything hangs together, connected by a tone of simmering regret arising from love's wreckage and time's relentless devouring.

Is there anything Egan can't do in this mash-up of forms? Write successfully in the second person? Check. Parody celebrity journalism and David Foster Wallace at the same time? Check. Make a moving narrative out of a PowerPoint presentation? Check. Write about a cokehead music producer who demands oral sex from his teenage girlfriend during her friends' band's performance? Check. Narrate another chapter from the perspective of the above girlfriend's best friend, standing at the same performance on the other side of said producer? Check. Compose a futuristic vision of New York? Check.

For a book so relentlessly savvy about the digital age and its effect on how we experience

"A narrative that feels as freely flung as a bag of trash down a country gully."

time (speeded up, herky-jerky, instantaneous, but also full of unbearable gaps and pauses), *A Visit From the Goon Squad* is remarkably old-fashioned in its obsession with time's effects on characters, that preoccupation of those doorstop 19th-century novels. Hanging over Egan's book is a sense that human culture is changing at such warp speed that memory itself must adapt to keep pace.

The last chapter, which literalizes this sense perhaps a little too much, depicts a futuristic New York, in which babies signal their consumer choices with handsets and audiences are manipulated by selected enthusiasts known as "parrots." Here Egan attempts to bring a centrifugal narrative full circle, which, given the entropic exhilarations on display, isn't really in keeping with the story's nature. But this is perhaps the only shortcoming (and a small one at that) in a fiction that appropriately for its musical obsessions, is otherwise pitch perfect. —*Will Blythe*

2010
Mark Twain's autobiography is released 100 years after his death, just as he requested.

2010
Mario Vargas Llosa wins the Nobel "for his cartography of structures of power and his trenchant images of the individual's resistance, revolt, and defeat."

2011
Tina Fey publishes *Bossypants*, which rockets to the top of the best-seller list and inspires dozens of other comedians to try their hand at memoir-writing.

"This Story Is a Complete Invention"

To the Editor:

In her review of Nora Ephron's book *I Remember Nothing*, Alex Kuczynski refers to a chapter, called "The Legend," which relates a story about how Ephron's mother, Phoebe, once "put *The New Yorker*'s Lillian Ross in her place." The chapter describes a party at Ephron's parents' house in Los Angeles 60 years ago. According to Nora Ephron, I was brought to this party by the writer St. Clair McKelway and, after saying something that upset Phoebe Ephron, I was asked to leave. This story is a complete invention. I never went to a party at the Ephrons' house, and I never went anywhere with St. Clair McKelway.

LILLIAN ROSS
New York

Nora Ephron replies:

My book is about, among other things, the vagaries of memory. Lillian Ross's memory of this event is different from my mother's and mine.

Complaints From Other Writers

If Benjamin DeMott, your reviewer of my novel *Any Woman's Blues*, found "gorgeous, saving sass" in *Fear of Flying* 17 years ago, it is curious he did not say so when he reviewed the book for *The Atlantic* in December 1973, comparing it to a paperback called *John & Mimi: A Free Marriage*. How easy it is to beat an author over the head with her first novel, when she has the temerity to produce her sixth. It has taken Mr. DeMott 17 years to decide he liked *Fear of Flying*. Let's hope it doesn't take him that long to discover *Any Woman's Blues*.
ERICA JONG
NEW YORK, FEB. 25, 1990

Can't anybody ever review a certain kind of book for what it is and not for what it isn't? Judith Krantz is not Joan Didion or Doris Lessing or Penelope Mortimer or Alice Walker or Judith Rossner. What she is is an entertaining storyteller whose novels are well-constructed—very well-constructed—fantasies about people who are more beautiful, talented, sexy, rich, dramatic and occasionally depraved than the rest of us.

Couldn't a review just once acknowledge the excellence of a certain kind of book because you can't put it down—that you just read and read and read until your eyes drop out because it brings so much pleasure?
HELEN GURLEY BROWN
NEW YORK, JUNE 15, 1986

Oh dear. But since The Times *is* the paper of record, permit me the following sparse comments on Ruth Rendell's review of my novel *High Jinx*. If Mrs. Rendell has never seen a bosom alight with excitement, then she has not seen all the marvels of the world I celebrate in, and out of, *High Jinx*.
WILLIAM F. BUCKLEY JR.
NEW YORK, APRIL 27, 1986

Robert A. Caro,
The Passage of Power

BY BILL CLINTON

Caro, who has made the study of political power his life's work, began his massive, multivolume biography of the 36th president, Lyndon Johnson, in 1982—and three decades later, the 42nd president reviewed the fourth installment for us.

THE PASSAGE OF POWER, **THE FOURTH** installment of Robert Caro's brilliant series on Lyndon Johnson, spans roughly five years, beginning shortly before the 1960 presidential contest, including the Bay of Pigs, the Cuban missile crisis and other seminal events of the Kennedy years, and ending a few months after the awful afternoon in Dallas that elevated L.B.J. to the presidency.

Among the most interesting and important episodes Caro chronicles are those involving the new president's ability to maneuver bills out of legislative committees and onto the floor of the House and Senate for a vote. One of those bills would later become the 1964 Civil Rights Act.

You don't have to be a policy wonk to marvel at the political skill L.B.J. wielded to resuscitate a bill that seemed doomed to never get a vote on the floor of either chamber. Southern Democrats were masters at bottling up legislation they hated, particularly bills expanding civil rights for black Americans. Their skills at obstruction were so admired that the newly sworn-in Johnson was firmly counseled by an ally against using the political capital he'd inherited as a result of the assassination on such a hopeless cause.

According to Caro, Johnson responded, "Well, what the hell's the presidency for?"

This is the question every president must ask and answer. For Lyndon Johnson in the final weeks of 1963, the presidency was *for* two things: passing a civil rights bill with teeth, to replace the much weaker 1957 law he'd helped to pass as Senate majority leader, and launching the War on Poverty. That neither of these causes was in fact hopeless was clear possibly only to him, as few Americans in our history have matched Johnson's knowledge of how to move legislation, and legislators.

It's wonderful to watch Johnson's confidence catch fire and spread to the shellshocked survivors of the Kennedy administration as it dawned on them that the man who was once Master of the Senate would now be a chief executive with more ability to move legislation through the House and Senate than just about any other president in history. Johnson's fire spread outward until it touched the entire country during his first State of the Union address. The words were written by Kennedy's speechwriter Ted Sorensen, but their impact would be felt in the magic L.B.J. worked over the next seven weeks.

In sparkling detail, Caro shows the new president's genius for getting to people—friends, foes and everyone in between—and how he used it to achieve his goals. We've all seen the iconic photos of L.B.J. leaning into a conversation, poking his thick finger into a confidant's chest or wrapping his long arm around a shoulder. At 6 foot 4, he towered over most men, but even seated Johnson commanded from on high.

The other remarkable part of this volume covers the tribulation before the triumphs: the lost campaign and the interminable years as vice president, in which L.B.J.'s skills were stymied and his power was negligible. He had little to do, less to say, and no defense against the indignities the Kennedys' inner circle heaped on him. The Master of the Senate may have become its president, but in title only. He might have agreed with his fellow Texan John Nance Garner, F.D.R.'s vice president, who famously described the office as "not worth a bucket of warm spit."

Caro paints a vivid picture of L.B.J.'s misery. We can feel Johnson's ambition ebb, and believe with him that his political life was over, as he was shut out of meetings, unwelcome on Air Force One, mistrusted and despised by Robert Kennedy. While in Congress he may not have been universally admired among the Washington elite, and was even mocked by them as a bit of a rube. But he had certainly never been pitied. In the White House, he invented reasons to come to the outskirts of the Oval Office in the mornings, where he was rarely welcome, and made sure his presence was noted by Kennedy's staff. Even if they did not respect him, he wasn't going to let anyone forget him.

Then tragedy changed everything. Within hours of President Kennedy's assassination, Johnson was sworn in as president, without the pomp of an inauguration, but with all the powers of the office.

As Caro shows in this and his preceding volumes, power ultimately reveals character. For L.B.J., becoming president freed him to embrace parts of his past that, for political or other reasons, had remained under wraps. Suddenly there was no longer a reason to dissociate himself from the poverty and failure of his childhood.

For a few brief years, Lyndon Johnson, once a fairly conventional Southern Democrat, constrained by his constituents and his overriding hunger for power, rose above his political past and personal limitations, to embrace and promote his boyhood dreams of opportunity and equality for all Americans. After all the years of striving for power, once he had it, he said to the American people, "I'll let you in on a secret—I mean to use it." And use it he did to pass the Civil Rights Act, the Voting Rights Act, the open housing law, the antipoverty legislation, Medicare and Medicaid, Head Start and much more.

He knew what the presidency was for: to get to people—to members of Congress, often with tricks up his sleeve; to the American people, by wearing his heart on his sleeve.

Even when we parted company over the Vietnam War, I never hated L.B.J. the way many young people of my generation came to. I couldn't. What he did to advance civil rights and equal opportunity was too important. I remain grateful to him. L.B.J. got to me, and after all these years, he still does. With this fascinating and meticulous account of how and why he did it, Robert Caro has once again done America a great service.

Caro at his office in New York on January 9, 2018.

THEODORE ROOSEVELT ON *JUNGLE PEACE,* BY WILLIAM BEEBE
OCTOBER 13, 1918

"If I had space I would like to give an abstract of the whole book. As it is I merely advise all who love good books, very good books, at once to get this book of Mr. Beebe's."

"I cannot be suspected of seeking favors when I say that the little book is an important contribution to after-war history; that it is worth reading, and worth keeping in the library as the testimony of a soldier who could not harbor rancor against the children of a defeated foe, of a writer who was impelled to do his bit toward setting the world mind straight."

JOHN F. KENNEDY
ON *WHAT WE ARE FOR,*
BY ARTHUR LARSON
FEBRUARY 8, 1959

"Though the book's style is somewhat discursive and here and there perhaps a trifle condescending, Mr. Larson does succeed very well in portraying the dangers of analyzing American society in terms of class distinctions or rigid economic interests."

Celeste Ng, *Everything I Never Told You*

BY ALEXANDER CHEE

In her debut novel, Ng took familiar themes—families, secrets—and fashioned them into something fresh and unexpected.

CELESTE NG'S DEBUT NOVEL, *EVERYTHING I Never Told You*, is a literary thriller that begins with some stock elements: a missing girl, a lake, a local bad boy who was one of the last to see her and won't say what he knows. The year is 1977, the setting, a quiet all-American town in Ohio, where everyone knows one another and nothing like this has ever happened before.

This is familiar territory, but Ng returns to it to spin an unfamiliar tale, with a very different kind of girl from the ones we've been asked to follow before. If we know this story, we haven't seen it yet in American fiction, not until now.

The missing girl is Lydia Lee, apple of her father's eye, her mother's favorite daughter. A blue-eyed Amerasian Susan Dey, the most white-looking of her siblings in her mixed-race Chinese and white family, she is also so serious, so driven, so good and responsible, she seems the least likely to go missing.

The mystery for the reader is not whether Lydia is still alive, or where she's gone—we learn on the first page that Lydia is dead, her body found at the bottom of the lake. We watch instead as the police come to the Lees' home to ask the uncomfortable questions—Was she doing well at school? Who were her friends? Did she seem depressed? Did she ever talk about hurting herself?—and her parents, sister and brother all find themselves unable to answer honestly. The mystery is why they can't bring themselves to tell one another, or the police, what they believe is behind her disappearance.

The term literary thriller might make you scoff, but Ng has set two tasks in this novel's doubled heart—to be exciting, and to tell a story bigger than whatever is behind the crime. She does both by turning the nest of familial resentments into at least four smaller, prickly mysteries full of the secrets the family members won't share. Take the moment Marilyn, Lydia's mother, confidently goes to search the diaries she has given her daughter every year for over a decade:

"With one finger, she tugs out the last diary: 1977. It will tell her, she thinks. Everything Lydia no longer can. Who she had been seeing. Why she had lied to them. Why she went down to the lake.

"The key is missing, but Marilyn jams the tip of a ballpoint into the catch and forces the flimsy lock open. The first page she sees, April 10, is blank. She checks May 2, the night Lydia disappeared. Nothing. Nothing for May 1, or anything in April, or anything in March. Every page is blank. She takes down 1976. 1975. 1974. Page after page of visible, obstinate silence. She leafs backward all the way to the very first diary, 1966: not one word. All those years of her daughter's life, unmarked. Nothing to explain anything."

Ng at her kitchen table in Cambridge, Massachusetts on May 10, 2018.

What is Lydia keeping from herself? This is the true conundrum, and we catch a glimpse of it when her father, James, reads an article about his daughter's death: "As one of only two Orientals at Middlewood High—the other being her brother, Nathan—Lee stood out in the halls. However, few seemed to have known her well."

James finally starts to see his family as the town does: a living exhibit on the question of whether an Asian man and a white woman should marry, and the children he had hoped would be accepted as third-generation Americans seen instead as immigrants at birth, arriving from an America his neighbors can't yet imagine is possible.

Ng has structured *Everything I Never Told You* so we shift between the family's theories and Lydia's own story, and what led to her disappearance and death, moving toward the final, devastating conclusion. What emerges is a deep, heartfelt portrait of a family struggling with its place in history, and a young woman hoping to be the fulfillment of that struggle. This is, in the end, a novel about the burden of being the first of your kind—a burden you do not always survive.

Jacqueline Woodson, *Brown Girl Dreaming*

This memoir in verse captured Woodson's childhood in South Carolina and New York. She told The Times: "I grew up in a Southern family—there was a lot of talking. More than stories there was transparency: We talked about race, we talked about class, we talked about so much of what it meant to just be human in this world."

I WAS 14 YEARS OLD WHEN I FIRST READ NIKKI Giovanni's masterly collection of poetry, *Cotton Candy on a Rainy Day*. As with most everything I read between the ages of 12 and 16, there was so much I didn't understand. I was the first-generation daughter of people who came from a small country, a country so small that I had yet to meet someone from there who could not connect the dots to my family in five seconds flat. I didn't know a thing about Jim Crow, the American South, soul food or classic rhythm and blues. Yet like most kids who love to read, I understood the feeling behind the words, if not all of the meaning of the words. So when Giovanni wrote:

We are consumed by people who sing
the same old song stay:
as sweet as you are
in my corner
Or perhaps just a little bit longer
But whatever you do don't change baby baby
*   don't change*

I didn't really know what old song she was referring to, but the rhythm of her words drew me in. And because I was a teenage girl, I was fairly confident I knew exactly what Giovanni meant when she wrote:

If loneliness were a grape
the wine would be vintage
If it were a wood
the furniture would be mahogany
But since it is life it is
Cotton Candy
on a rainy day
The sweet soft essence
of possibility
Never quite maturing

I thought of Nikki Giovanni and the teenage girl I was, almost constantly, as I read Jacqueline Woodson's wonderful memoir in verse, *Brown Girl Dreaming*, because I suspect this book will be to a generation of girls what Giovanni's book was to mine: a history lesson, a mash note passed in

2012 Hilary Mantel becomes the first woman to win the Booker Prize twice, and the first person ever to win for two books in a series—*Wolf Hall* and *Bring Up the Bodies*.

2015 HarperCollins publishes Harper Lee's *Go Set a Watchman,* a sequel to (or perhaps an early version of) *To Kill a Mockingbird.*

2016 Bob Dylan is awarded the Nobel for "for having created new poetic expressions within the great American song tradition."

Woodson on July 8, 2015.

class, a book to read burrowed underneath the bed covers and a life raft during long car rides when you want to float far from wherever you are, and wherever you're going, toward the person you feel destined to be.

I will say first that the title seems to confine the book in too narrow a box. I wondered if the author and publishers, by calling the book *Brown Girl Dreaming*, were limiting its audience or, at the very least, the audience of girls who would pick it up right away. Why not call it *Home Girl Dreaming* or *Tall Girl Dreaming* or even just *Girl Dreaming*? I believe strongly in the words of that most expert of brown girl writers, Lorraine Hansberry, who said, "To create the universal,

you must pay very great attention to the specific." But I worry that such a specific title might lead a reader—especially a teenage reader—to miss what a big tent Woodson is pitching. Will girls who aren't brown know, without prompting, that they too are invited to this party?

> *We take our food out to her stoop just as the*
> *   grown-ups*
> *start dancing merengue, the women lifting their*
> *   long dresses*
> *to show off their fast-moving feet,*
> *the men clapping and yelling,*
> *Baila! Baila! until the living room floor*
> *   disappears.*

You can read *Brown Girl Dreaming* in one sitting, but it is as rich a spread as the potluck table at a family reunion. Sure, you can plow through the pages, grabbing everything you can in one go, like piling a plate high with fried chicken and ribs, potato salad and corn bread. And yes, it's entirely possible to hold that plate with one hand while balancing a bowl of gumbo and a cup of sweet tea with the other. But since the food isn't going anywhere, you'll make out just as well, maybe even a little better, if you pace yourself. If you know Woodson's work (which includes *Hush* and *This Is the Rope: A Story From the Great Migration*), read for her life story first:

> Good enough name for me, my father said
> the day I was born.
> Don't see why
> she can't have it, too.
> But the women said no.
> My mother first.
> Then each aunt, pulling my pink blanket back
> patting the crop of thick curls
> tugging at my new toes
> touching my cheeks.
> We won't have a girl named Jack,
>   my mother said.

For young readers in the process of discovering what Anna Julia Cooper so beautifully called "when and where I enter," there are poems galore. Poems about sibling rivalry, poems about parents who don't take no mess, poems about grown-ups who make a mess of things and, most poignantly, poems about the friends who help see you through. Such as this one, in "Maria."

> Late August now
> home from Greenville and ready
> for what the last of the summer brings me.

> All the dreams this city holds
> right outside—just step through the door
>   and walk
> two doors down to where
> my new best friend, Maria, lives. Every morning,
> I call up to her window, Come outside
> or she rings our bell, Come outside.
> Her hair is crazily curling down past her back,
> the Spanish she speaks like a song
> I am learning to sing.
> Mi amiga, Maria.
> Maria, my friend.

The short poems are a gift too and made me think of April when the Academy of American Poets leads a nationwide celebration called Poem in Your Pocket Day. I especially loved the series of numbered short poems, threaded throughout the book, called "How to Listen." This is No. 8:

> Do you remember . . . ?
> someone's always asking and
> someone else, always does.

In *Possession*, A. S. Byatt wrote about how we are transformed by the act of memorizing poetry "by heart . . . as though poems were stored in the bloodstream." Jacqueline Woodson's writing can seem so spare, so effortless, that it is easy to overlook the wonder and magic of her words. The triumph of *Brown Girl Dreaming* is not just in how well Woodson tells us the story of her life, but in how elegantly she writes words that make us want to hold those carefully crafted poems close, apply them to our lives, reach into the mirror she holds up and make the words and the worlds she explores our own.

This is a book full of poems that cry out to be learned by heart. These are poems that will, for years to come, be stored in our bloodstream.
—Veronica Chambers

Patter and Patois

BY WALTER MOSLEY

Mosley, best known for his crime fiction, offered this ode to Louisiana and its storytellers. "For me," he wrote, "there is little difference between the blazing sun, the nighttime jazz, the human flaws, the bound novels or the oral tales of this heroic land. It all comes together in my heart."

I AM WHAT YOU MIGHT CALL A GRANDCHILD of Louisiana. My father was born there as were many of his friends and relatives. Most of my neighbors in Los Angeles came from there too—black rural folk who had traveled west through southern Texas on their migration to escape the South's heavy hail of racial hatred. They came to California for the tattered shelter of mocking freedom that the Golden State had to offer people like them, poor people willing to work hard.

My father and his family brought the Deep South with them—barbecues and gumbos, dirty rice and soul food. They brought their strong accents and multiplicity of tongues, their histories from Africa, France, Native America mingled with generous drams of so-called white blood, European blood.

Louisiana flowed in that blood and across those tongues. Louisiana—a state made famous by Walt Whitman and Tennessee Williams, Ernest Gaines and Arna Bontemps, Kate Chopin and Anne Rice. These writers, from many eras, races and genres, took the voices of the people and distilled them into the passionate, almost desperate, stories that opened readers to a new kind of suffering and exultation.

I could talk about any or all of these writers with respect and admiration. But my relationship to the literature of Louisiana goes deeper, back to my childhood. Almost everyone in Watts came from Louisiana or Texas. They'd gather around kitchen tables, eating raw oysters swimming in Tabasco sauce, telling stories of the old days when death shadowed their every step.

There was the story of Alberta Jackson, bitten by a harbor rat and saved by a backwoods auntie who used the sliced-open body of a special toad to draw the toxins from the wound. There was my cousin Helen, who took my father's knife intending to kill the man he was getting ready to fight. She swung at the man but stabbed my father by mistake. Hearing the story again, 20 years later, my father laughed and laughed at the memory.

Another cousin, Willie, got a job as a porter on the Panama Limited that traveled between Chicago and New Orleans. When he got his first check, he proudly told his mother he was going to use it to buy a new pair of pants. "She socked me so hard," he told us one night, "that by the time I came to she had already cashed the check and spent it at the general store on Bywater Street."

They talked of sugar cane fields and light-skinned cousins who would stay once a year in fancy white hotels without getting caught. They told of lynchings—and retribution too. They talked about Africa, Italy, France and Germany, where their men had been shipped off to fight for freedom.

That war was won, but the conflicts at home, in Louisiana and Texas, continued to rage. Even up North, where black labor was vital, black skin

Mosley, circa August 2003.

was despised. My father told me that he returned home after the war to find that most of his neighbors had died, whereas most of the black men that shipped off to the largest conflagration in human history had survived. The tragedy of war played second fiddle to the experience of my people, most of whom were born near some bayou.

These people created an orally transmitted literary life out of a soil drenched by the blood of slaves and ex-slaves, Creoles, Cajuns and the French. Louisiana is my literary grandsire, the source of the content and dialect of my early stories. It is no surprise that, even though I was born in Los Angeles and then moved to New York, my first words in fiction were, "On hot sticky days in Southern Louisiana the fire ants swarmed"—or that the first character I created was Easy Rawlins.

Easy was born in early-20th-century New Iberia and knighted by the hard knocks of racism and poverty. His life maps the progress of a man struggling to maintain not only his personal dignity but also the nobility of his people, their inimitable tongues and stories, the fights and failures and victories that left their souls blasted and their bodies scarred.

Louisiana is my ancestor and the great mother, the Mississippi River, bore him slowly, out of sediment and over eons. For most of that time, the river has transported, fed and terrorized its residents. Hurricane Katrina was only the most recent catastrophe to challenge these people.

Recently I went down to New Orleans to accept an honorary Ph.D. from Tulane University. While hanging out around the Warehouse District I was reminded of how deeply my roots run among these people—the music in the accent and the mixtures of races, classes and cultures that appear to flow together as seamlessly as the currents of the Mississippi.

I met a man who told me how the hurricane had forced him to choose between his wife and his mother. He ended up staying in New Orleans during Katrina to protect his mother, who refused to evacuate, while his wife and young daughter made their way to safety. Everyone survived though the marriage faltered. But the man did not lament his loss. He said his teenage daughter comes down every summer to live with him, and she shares her dreams of a future in medicine or in the military. He explained to me how important it was for her to have a life and how brilliant she was, how talented.

Listening to him, and how the music of my family pulsed through his words, I remembered why I had loved the stories of my upbringing—those stories, no matter how brutal, were told by people who loved me, who wanted to share with me their experience. Like that man I met, my family made their way through the tragedies that gave form to the modern world so that I could tell their tales of heroism; tales that languished for centuries in shadows and darkness and enforced silence.

For me there is little difference between the blazing sun, the nighttime jazz, the human flaws, the bound novels or the oral tales of this heroic land. It all comes together in my heart. The black man whose mother survived and whose child now thrives expressed a loving pride, an endurance and bravery, that has been kept a secret from the rest of America, even from my own people, sometimes.

This is the literature of Louisiana. It has a beating heart and a spring in its step, eyes that watch the world and a real voice that reverberates in the word "home."

Lucia Berlin, *A Manual for Cleaning Women*

Berlin's rich, complicated life—she was, at various times, a socialite, a maid, an E.R. nurse—spills across the pages of these vibrant stories. As one of her sons later said, "Ma wrote true stories, not necessarily autobiographical, but close enough for horseshoes."

SOME SHORT STORY WRITERS—CHEKHOV, Alice Munro, William Trevor—sidle up and tap you gently on the shoulder: Come, they murmur, sit down, listen to what I have to say. Lucia Berlin spins you around, knocks you down and grinds your face into the dirt. You will listen to me if I have to force you, her stories growl. But why would you make me do that, darlin'?

Berlin's stories are the kind a woman in a Tom Waits song might tell a man she's just met during a long humid night spent drinking in a parking lot. They take place in the ragged borderlands on the outermost fringes of American life: West Texas ("the Holy Land," one character calls it), inner-city Albuquerque, the slums of Oakland— all dust and buses and late-night laundromats. Their characters are friendless children, pregnant teenagers, unmarried women past middle age in search of connection or just a bottle of vodka. More often than not, they are alcoholics. Many

of them might be the same person at different stages in her life.

The stories in *A Manual for Cleaning Women* are all linked, in that they're connected by the sensibility of the person who tells them, who has lived them. Nearly all the stories are told in the first person; when third-person protagonists surface, they tend to be a version of the first-person narrator. Characters fade in and out. Sometimes they share the author's name, or a variation of it; sometimes they have different names or go unnamed. What they all have in common is their rawness, as in knuckles rubbed raw, exposed. In one story, a man in a nursing home, a double amputee, screams constantly of the pain in his legs. The nurse tells him to hush—it's only phantom pain. "Is it real?" the narrator asks the nurse, who shrugs. "All pain is real."

All pain is real could be Berlin's mantra, the motto of this collection. It's no accident that one of her alter egos is named Dolores. The narrator is sometimes a cleaning woman (as in the title story) or an emergency-room nurse, two jobs that require constant contact with the messier aspects of being human: blood, vomit, colostomy bags, hemorrhoids. The agonizing moments relived here are often rooted in the physical. The time her grandfather, a dentist, took her into his office and told her to pull out all his teeth: "The sound was the sound of roots being ripped out, like trees being torn from winter ground." The trip across the Mexican border to an abortion clinic, where she couldn't go through with it but watched another girl hemorrhage on the hallway floor. Her arrest in middle age with her teenage boyfriend: After he is beaten by a policeman, she licks clean his eyes, fused shut with blood. "The best thing that could happen to you would be for you to be

Berlin in 1962.

"'All pain is real' could be Berlin's mantra."

uncomfortable once in a while," a teenage narrator, during a rare moment of privilege, is told by her teacher. In the context of this collection, it sounds like a bitter joke.

The emotions in *A Manual for Cleaning Women* are maximalist, but the language is sparse and unadorned. Sentences are fragmentary, sometimes just single words. They turn on the sudden flash of an image, not the elegance of the construction. The language is so precise that it paradoxically creates ambiguities. "The strange thing was that for a year or so we were always at Angel's at the same time. But not at the same times." "Everybody hated Grandpa but Mamie, and me, I guess." Sometimes the ugliness is tempered by a momentary lyricism, often in the form of an overheard sound. Before her grandfather makes her pull out his teeth, the girl in that story hears children next door playing jacks, the sound "magical . . . like brushes on a drum or like

rain, when a gust of wind shimmers it against the windowpane." In "Temps Perdu," with its incongruously romantic title, a young girl asks a boy her age what sex is like. "He held his hand up to mine so our fingers were all touching, had me run my thumb and forefinger over our touching ones. You can't tell which is which. Must be something like that he said."

These stories often feel more like stream-of-consciousness memories than like fiction. They are all beginnings and middles with no ends, which is to say that the end often comes the way it does in life, via a death or a departure rather than a well-turned phrase. In her foreword, Lydia Davis affirms that the stories conform in many of their details to the outlines of Berlin's life, which was "rich and full of incident," and describes her genre as similar to the French auto-fiction or "self-fiction": "the narration of one's own life, lifted almost unchanged from the reality, selected and judiciously, artfully told." One of Berlin's sons says something similar, but closer to the way she might have said it herself: "Ma wrote true stories, not necessarily autobiographical, but close enough for horseshoes." —*Ruth Franklin*

Colson Whitehead, *The Underground Railroad*

Whitehead won his first Pulitzer for this novel, a dazzling, dynamic, unflinching examination of slavery and its legacy.

COLSON WHITEHEAD'S NOVELS ARE REBEL-lious creatures: Each one of them goes to great lengths to break free of the last one, of its structure and language, of its areas of interest. At the same time, they all have one thing in common—the will to work within a recognizable tract of popular culture, taking advantage of conventions while subverting them for the novel's own purposes. *The Intuitionist,* with its dystopian concerns and futuristic mood, gave way to the folkloric past of *John Henry Days; Zone One,* Whitehead's contribution to the unquenchable American thirst for zombies, was his departure from *Sag Harbor,* with its coming-of-age feeling and concessions to nostalgia. His new novel, *The Underground Railroad,* is as different as can be from the zombie book. It touches on the historical novel and the slave story, but what it does with those genres is striking and imaginative. Like its predecessors, it is carefully built and stunningly daring; it is also, both in expected and unexpected ways, dense, substantial and important.

The central conceit of the novel is as simple as it is bold. The underground railroad is not, in Whitehead's novel, the secret network of passageways and safe houses used by runaway slaves to reach the free North from their slaveholding states. Or rather it is that, but it is something else, too: You open a trap door in the safe house or find the entrance to a hidden cave, and you reach an actual railroad, with actual locomotives and boxcars and conductors, sometimes complete with benches on the platform. "Two steel rails ran the visible length of the tunnel," Whitehead writes, "pinned into the dirt by wooden crossties. The steel ran south and north presumably, springing from some inconceivable source and shooting toward a miraculous terminus." The trains pass at unpredictable times and go to unpredictable places, but that is obviously good enough for those wanting to flee the misery and violence of slavery: its sheer inhumanity, a word that in Whitehead's unflinching explorations seems to fill up with new meanings.

Meet Cora, a young slave on a Georgia cotton plantation. Her mother ran away when Cora was a little girl, and that feeling of abandonment has haunted her ever since. When she is approached by another slave about the underground railroad, she hesitates; but then life, in the form of rape and humiliation, gives her the nudge she needs. (Whitehead does here as he will do several times in the book: He opens his eyes where the rest of us would rather look away. In this, *The Underground Railroad* is courageous but never gratuitous.) In order to ensure her escape, she kills a white man, and soon she is being pursued by a notorious slave catcher named Ridgeway, a man straight out of Cormac McCarthy, whose assistant wears a necklace made with human ears. What follows is Cora's uncertain itinerary through hell. The novel uses the architecture of

Whitehead at his home in Manhattan, July 28, 2016.

an episodic tale, each episode corresponding to a new stop in the journey—the two Carolinas, then Tennessee, then Indiana—each one introducing Cora to new incarnations of evil, or the evil brought out in everyone by the poisonous mechanics of slavery.

We begin to notice, as readers, slight departures from historical fact, places where *The Underground Railroad* becomes something much more interesting than a historical novel. It doesn't merely tell us about what happened; it also tells us what might have happened. Whitehead's imagination, unconstrained by stubborn facts, takes the novel to new places in the narrative of slavery, or rather to places where it actually has something new to say. If the role of the novel, as Milan Kundera argues in a beautiful essay, is to say what only the novel can say, *The Underground Railroad* achieves the task by small shifts in perspective: It moves a couple of feet to one side, and suddenly there are strange skyscrapers on the ground of the American South and a railroad running under it, and the novel is taking us somewhere we have never been before.

The Underground Railroad is also about the myriad ways in which black history has too often been stolen by white narrators. At a performance Cora sees from a distance, a slave is played by "a white man in burned cork, pink showing on his neck and wrists." Remembering the passages on slavery contained in the Bible, Cora blames the people who wrote them down: "People always got things wrong," she thinks, "on purpose as much as by accident." Whitehead's novel is constantly concerned with these matters of narrative authenticity and authority, and so too with the different versions of the past we carry with us. Throughout my reading, I was repeatedly reminded of a particular chapter from García Márquez's *One Hundred Years of Solitude,* to whose handling of time Whitehead seems to owe quite a bit. In that chapter, the infamous massacre of the banana plantation workers is denied by the official versions of history and soon forgotten. But one character knows what he saw—thousands of dead traveling toward the sea on a train—and goes around trying to find someone who will remember the story. He doesn't: People always get things wrong. In a sense, *The Underground Railroad* is Whitehead's own attempt at getting things right, not by telling us what we already know but by vindicating the powers of fiction to interpret the world. In its exploration of the foundational sins of America, it is a brave and necessary book.

—*Juan Gabriel Vásquez*

2017
A steamroller crushes a disk drive containing the unpublished works of Terry Pratchett, following instructions issued by the fantasy author before his death.

2017
Barack and Michelle Obama smash records with a joint $65 million book deal for their memoirs.

2017
The Chinese poet and Nobel laureate Liu Xiaobo, a prominent human rights activist, dies while serving an 11-year prison sentence for "subversion."

Tommy Orange, *There There*

BY COLM TOIBIN

In this vivid debut, a dozen Native Americans converge on an urban powwow in Oakland, Calif., where Orange grew up. "There's been a lot of reservation literature written," Orange told The Times. "I wanted to have my characters struggle in the way that I struggled, and the way that I see other Native people struggle, with identity and with authenticity."

IN GEORGE R. STEWART'S *NAMES ON THE Land: A Historical Account of Place-Naming in the United States,* there is a single mention of Oakland, Calif.: "Across the bay from San Francisco was a stretch of flat land scattered with magnificent California live oaks. In Mexican times it had been known as Encinal del Temescal, 'oak-grove of the sweat-house.' The Americans who planned a town there may not have known Spanish, but they could see the trees. In simple description they called it Oakland."

In Tommy Orange's *There There,* an ambitious meditation on identity and its broken alternatives, on myth filtered through the lens of time and poverty and urban life, on tradition all the more pressing because of its fragility, it is as if he seeks to reconfigure Oakland as a locus of desire and dreams, to remake the city in the likeness of his large and fascinating set of characters.

The title of his book comes from Gertrude Stein—who, one of the book's characters discovers, "found that she was talking about how the place where she'd grown up in Oakland had changed so much, that so much development had happened there, that the there of her childhood, the there there, was gone, there was no there there anymore."

Orange makes Oakland into a "there" that becomes all the more concretely, emphatically and fully so in a novel that deals, in tones that are sweeping and subtle, with what the notion of belonging means for Native Americans.

In an eloquent prologue, Orange writes of the relationship between Native Americans and the city: "Plenty of us came by choice, to start over, or to make money, or for a new experience. Some of us came to cities to escape the reservation. . . . The quiet of the reservation, the side-of-the-highway towns, rural communities, that kind of silence just makes the sound of your brain on fire that much more pronounced."

The idea of unsettlement and ambiguity, of being caught between two worlds, of living a life that is disfigured by loss and the memory of loss, but also by confusion, distraction and unease, impels some of the characters, and allows the sound of the brain on fire to become dense with dissonance. Orange's characters are, however, also nourished by the ordinary possibilities of the present, by common desires and feelings. This mixture gives their experience, when it is put under pressure, depth and a sort of richness.

Orange is fully alert to the possibilities that the pure lack of nostalgia, which he rigorously insists on, will offer his novel. He relishes the

Tommy Orange at
the Indian American
Institute of Art in
Santa Fe, New Mexico,
May 17, 2018.

paradoxes his characters inhabit and embody. "We are the memories we don't remember," he writes. "We know the sound of the freeway better than we do rivers."

Orange uses the word "Indianing" as though it were a choice, and something you have to be grown up to do, "like drinking or driving or smoking or voting." His character Orvil Red Feather discovers the word "pretendian" online, and later invokes the idea of "Indians dressed up as Indians."

Orvil looks in the bedroom mirror "with his regalia on all wrong. It isn't backward, and actually he didn't know what he did wrong, but it's off. He moves in front of the mirror and his feathers shake. He catches the hesitation, the worry in his eyes, there in the mirror." He knows that the woman who cares for him would disapprove if she saw him. He is deeply unsure of himself: "He's waiting for something true to appear before him—about him. It's important that he dress like an Indian, dance like an Indian, even if it is an act, even if he feels like a fraud the whole time, because the only way to be Indian in this world is to look and act like an Indian."

This idea of inauthenticity adds to the delicate drama of the book, makes Orvil's sense that he is "part of something" all the more poignant and credible, all the more dramatic and engaging.

No one in the novel is fully sure how to look or act, how to live or be. It is as though Orange has taken Orvil's broken, shadowy heritage and made it not only persistent and pressing, but also offers it as a way of enriching Orvil as a character, someone more fully present and "there" because

of the very battle going on in his being between absences and a shivering trace of something that comes sharply from the past.

Orvil, like most of the characters here, is what Orange calls in an interlude "a present-tense" person. And in this present tense, no one is pure. One of the characters ponders on the mixture of conquered and conquering in his own actual body: "You're from a people who took and took and took and took. And from a people taken. You were both and neither. When you took baths, you'd stare at your brown arms against your white legs in the water and wonder what they were doing together on the same body, in the same bathtub."

Within the cacophony of voices in this book and the chapters each told from the perspective of one of the characters, the structure is not only dictated by the sense of identity these characters share, but by the fact that many of them will meet at a great powwow to be held in Oakland. Thus they are all, as in Chaucer, pilgrims on their way to a shrine, or, as in Faulkner's *As I Lay Dying,* an extended family crossing the landscape.

The novel, then, is their picaresque journey, allowing for moments of pure soaring beauty to hit against the most mundane, for a sense of timelessness to be placed right beside a cleareyed version of the here and now, for a sense of vast dispossession to live beside day-to-day misery and poverty. Nothing in Orange's world is simple, least of all his characters and his sense of the relationship between history and the present. Instead, a great deal is subtle and uncertain in this original and complex novel.

2017 — Jesmyn Ward becomes the first woman to win two National Book Awards for fiction when *Sing, Unburied, Sing* nabs the prize.

2018 — The Nobel Prize in Literature is canceled after the Swedish Academy is engulfed in a sexual misconduct scandal.

2019 — In violation of their own rules, the judges of the Booker Prize give the award jointly to two novelists, Margaret Atwood and Bernardine Evaristo.

Books That Terrify

The Book Review asked authors to recommend the most frightening books they've ever read. Here's what they chose.

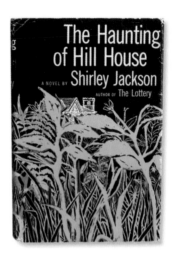

Carmen Maria Machado

The scariest book I've ever read is *The Haunting of Hill House* by Shirley Jackson. I read it one night next to my sleeping wife and found myself unable to move, unable to go to bed, unable to do anything except keep reading and praying the shadows around me didn't move.

Joe Hill

I never really recovered from *The Collector*, by John Fowles, a work of shattering brilliance and unbearable suspense—as well as the clear inspiration for *The Silence of the Lambs. The Collector* presents the reader with a pair of unforgettable adversaries, locked in a desperate yet restrained struggle: Frederick Clegg, the introverted kidnapper, and Miranda Grey, his prisoner. Writing before the F.B.I. created its criminal profiling unit—before the term "serial killer" had even been coined—Fowles was there, methodically exploring the reasoning of humanity's most terrifying predators.

Marlon James

I remember it—13 years old, in the suburban security of a life I took for granted. *Oliver Twist* snatched all of that away, when the boy was stripped of everything and left alone. I agonized over questions I never agonized over before. What if everyone died, leaving me alone? Adults were selfish and brutal, and in the case of Bill Sikes, evil incarnate. Sikes scared me right down to the bone and still haunts my dreams. I got goosebumps just typing this.

Neil Gaiman

The books that have profoundly scared me when I read them—made me want to sleep with the light on, made the neck hairs prickle and the goose bumps march, are few: Henry James's *The Turn of the Screw*, Peter Straub's *Ghost Story*, Stephen King's *It* and *Salem's Lot* and *The Shining* all scared me silly, and transformed the night into a most dangerous place. But Shirley Jackson's *The Haunting of Hill House* beats them all: a maleficent house, real human protagonists, everything half-seen or happening in the dark. It scared me as a teenager and it haunts me still, as does Eleanor, the girl who comes to stay.

Mariana Enriquez

Pet Sematary, by Stephen King. I got it as a gift when I was 11 or 12. I remember being so scared reading it that I threw the book away from me as if it were a poisonous insect. For the first time I felt a physical sensation with literature. It's so dark, so brutal. It's also very scary: the utter hopelessness, the way King just doesn't offer any relief.

Sarah Weinman

In the fall of 2001, I was working by myself on a weekend afternoon at a mystery bookstore in Greenwich Village. Traffic was slow and I had some downtime to read Sara Gran's *Come Closer,* which one of the bookstore's co-owners recommended highly. I generally shy away from horror—gore on film doesn't do it for me, and my imagination runs wild with the print versions— but once I began Gran's novel, about a young woman named Amanda who begins to behave in strange, inexplicable ways, I could not stop until I reached the very last line: "And that's all I've ever wanted, really: someone to love me, and never leave me alone." A common wish transformed into monstrous deed made me shiver in fear, a feeling that persisted until the end of my store shift, and in the years thereafter.

Tomi Adeyemi

The scariest book I've read in a long time is *A Reaper at the Gates,* by Sabaa Tahir. Though it has terrifying, fantastical monsters (picture the kind of face that would earn the name "Nightbringer"), the scariest part of this book for me comes in a hauntingly visceral portrayal of domestic abuse. Some scenes were so terrifying and hard to read I became physically nauseated!

Victor LaValle

The scariest book I've ever read is *The Autobiography of My Mother,* by Jamaica Kincaid. It's categorized as literary fiction, but it's a horror novel, too. It's narrated by a woman whose mother dies giving birth to her and death is the book's obsession. The book is bleak and venomous and yet it's written with such spare beauty. It's her masterpiece.

Tananarive Due

The scariest book I've ever read is Octavia E. Butler's near-futuristic *Parable of the Sower.* Much of Butler's work is frightening because it feels so plausible and true, even when she's writing about aliens or vampires. But this book's dystopia of walled-off communities, useless government, unchecked violence and corporate slavery feels like the waiting headlines of tomorrow—and too many of our headlines today. When I first began reading it, I could take glimpses of the teenager Lauren Olamina's world only a few pages at a time. But Butler forced me to grow stronger as I read. Despite the horror of its prescience, the stubborn optimism that burns at the core of *Parable of the Sower* helps me face our true-life horrors. As Butler wrote, "The only lasting truth is Change."

David Sedaris walking in Manhattan's Upper East Side,
June 9, 2020.

Brown in Atlanta, Georgia,
on July 30, 2020.

Jericho Brown, "Say Thank You Say I'm Sorry"

At a moment of profound national upheaval—shaped by the coronavirus pandemic and the death of George Floyd in Minneapolis—the Pulitzer Prize winner Jericho Brown wrote this poem for the Book Review.

I don't know whose side you're on,
But I am here for the people
Who work in grocery stores that glow in the
   morning
And close down for deep cleaning at night
Right up the street and in cities I mispronounce,
In towns too tiny for my big black
Car to quit, and in every wide corner
Of Kansas where going to school means
At least one field trip
To a slaughterhouse. I want so little: another
   leather bound
Book, a gimlet with a lavender gin, bread
So good when I taste it I can tell you
How it's made. I'd like us to rethink

What it is to be a nation. I'm in a mood
   about America
Today. I have PTSD
About the Lord. God save the people who work
In grocery stores. They know a bit of glamour
Is a lot of glamour. They know how much
It costs for the eldest of us to eat. Save
My loves and not my sentences. Before I see
   them,
I draw a mole near my left dimple,
Add flair to the smile they can't see
Behind my mask. I grin or lie or maybe
I wear the mouth of a beast. I eat wild animals
While some of us grow up knowing
What gnocchi is. The people who work at the
   grocery don't care.
They say, Thank you. They say, Sorry,
We don't sell motor oil anymore with a grief
   so thick
You could touch it. Go on. Touch it.
It is early. It is late. They have washed their
   hands.
They have washed their hands for you.
And they take the bus home.

2020
The poet Louise Glück wins the Nobel Prize in literature. Colson Whitehead wins his second Pulitzer Prize for fiction, for *The Nickel Boys*.

2020
Hachette cancels its planned publication of Woody Allen's memoir after a staff walkout. The book is later released by the independent publisher Skyhorse.

2020
Despite the coronavirus pandemic, the publishing industry thrives, with print sales growing by more than 7 percent over 2019.

1996–2021

The 10-Best Books Through Time

Each fall, the editors of The New York Times Book Review select the best fiction and nonfiction titles of the year. Our editors read, nominate, discuss and debate the merits of each year's books, working together to land upon our list. The practice of editors' sharing their picks of the year dates nearly back to the beginning of the Book Review in October 1896. But over the years, that list has taken many different names and forms. Now, we call this list the "Ten Best Books" and have done so since 2004.

2020

FICTION

A Children's Bible by Lydia Millet. *Deacon King Kong* by James McBride. *Hamnet* by Maggie O'Farrell. *Homeland Elegies* by Ayad Akhtar. *The Vanishing Half* by Brit Bennett.

NONFICTION

Hidden Valley Road by Robert Kolker. *A Promised Land* by Barack Obama. *Shakespeare in a Divided America* by James Shapiro. *Uncanny Valley* by Rachel Anna Wiener. *War* by Margaret MacMillan.

2019

FICTION

Disappearing Earth by Julia Phillips. *The Topeka School* by Ben Lerner. *Exhalation* by Ted Chiang. *Lost Children Archive* by Valeria Luiselli. *Night Boat to Tangier* by Kevin Barry.

NONFICTION

Say Nothing by Patrick Radden Keefe. *The Club* by Leo Damrosch. *The Yellow House* by Sarah M. Broom. *No Visible Bruises* by Rachel Louise Snyder. *Midnight in Chernobyl* by Adam Higginbotham.

2018

FICTION

Asymmetry by Lisa Halliday. *The Great Believers* by Rebecca Makkai. *The Perfect Nanny* by Leila Slimani; translated by Sam Taylor. *There There* by Tommy Orange. *Washington in Black* by Esi Edugyan.

NONFICTION

American Prison by Shane Bauer. *Educated* by Tara Westover. *Frederick Douglass* by David W. Blight. *How to Change Your Mind* by Michael Pollan. *Small Fry* by Lisa Brennan-Jobs.

2017

FICTION

Autumn by Ali Smith. *Exit West* by Mohsin Hamid. *Pachinko* by Min Jin Lee. *The Power* by Naomi Alderman. *Sing, Unburied, Sing* by Jesmyn Ward.

NONFICTION

The Evolution of Beauty by Richard O. Prum. *Grant* by Ron Chernow. *Locking Up Our Own* by James Forman Jr. *Prairie Fires* by Caroline Fraser. *Priestdaddy* by Patricia Lockwood.

2016

FICTION

The Association of Small Bombs by Karan Mahajan. *The North Water* by Ian McGuire. *The Underground Railroad* by Colson Whitehead. *The Vegetarian* by Han Kang; translated by Deborah Smith. *War and Turpentine* by Stefan Hertmans; translated by David McKay.

NONFICTION

At the Existentialist Café by Sarah Bakewell. *Dark Money* by Jane Mayer. *Evicted* by Matthew Desmond. *In the Darkroom* by Susan Faludi. *The Return* by Hisham Matar.

2015

FICTION

The Door by Magda Szabó; translated by Len Rix. *A Manual for Cleaning Women* by Lucia Berlin; edited by Stephen Emerson. *Outline* by Rachel Cusk. *The Sellout* by Paul Beatty. *The Story of the Lost Child* by Elena Ferrante; translated by Ann Goldstein.

NONFICTION

Between the World and Me by Ta-Nehisi Coates. *Empire of Cotton* by Sven Beckert. *H Is for Hawk* by Helen Macdonald. *The Invention of Nature* by Andrea Wulf. *One of Us* by Asne Seierstad; translated by Sarah Death.

2014

FICTION

All the Light We Cannot See by Anthony Doerr. *Dept. of Speculation* by Jenny Offill. *Euphoria* by Lily King. *Family Life* by Akhil Sharma. *Redeployment* by Phil Klay.

NONFICTION

Can't We Talk About Something More Pleasant? by Roz Chast. *On Immunity* by Eula Biss. *Penelope Fitzgerald* by Hermione Lee. *The Sixth Extinction* by Elizabeth Kolbert. *Thirteen Days in September* by Lawrence Wright.

2013

FICTION

Americanah by Chimamanda Ngozi Adichie. *The Flamethrowers* by Rachel Kushner. *The Goldfinch* by Donna Tartt. *Life After Life* by Kate Atkinson. *Tenth of December* by George Saunders.

NONFICTION

After the Music Stopped by Alan S. Blinder. *Days of Fire* by Peter Baker. *Five Days at Memorial* by Sheri Fink. *The Sleepwalkers* by Christopher Clark. *Wave* by Sonali Deraniyagala.

2012

FICTION

Bring Up the Bodies by Hilary Mantel. *Building Stories* by Chris Ware. *A Hologram for the King* by Dave Eggers. *NW* by Zadie Smith. *The Yellow Birds* by Kevin Powers.

NONFICTION

Behind the Beautiful Forevers by Katherine Boo. *Far from the Tree* by Andrew Solomon. *The Passage of Power* by Robert A. Caro. *The Patriarch* by David Nasaw. *Why Does the World Exist?* by Jim Holt.

2011

FICTION

The Art of Fielding by Chad Harbach. *11/22/63* by Stephen King. *Swamplandia!* by Karen Russell. *Ten Thousand Saints* by Eleanor Henderson. *The Tiger's Wife* by Téa Obreht.

NONFICTION

Arguably by Christopher Hitchens. *The Boy in the Moon* by Ian Brown. *Malcolm X* by Manning Marable. *Thinking, Fast and Slow* by Daniel Kahneman. *A World on Fire* by Amanda Foreman.

2010

FICTION

Freedom by Jonathan Franzen. *The New Yorker Stories* by Ann Beattie. *Room* by Emma Donoghue. *Selected Stories* by William Trevor. *A Visit from the Goon Squad* by Jennifer Egan.

Apollo's Angels by Jennifer Homans. *Cleopatra* by Stacy Schiff. *The Emperor of All Maladies* by Siddhartha Mukherjee. *Finishing the Hat* by Stephen Sondheim. *The Warmth of Other Suns* by Isabel Wilkerson.

2009

FICTION

Both Ways Is the Only Way I Want It by Maile Meloy. *Chronic City* by Jonathan Lethem. *A Gate at the Stairs* by Lorrie Moore. *Half Broke Horses* by Jeannette Walls. *A Short History of Women* by Kate Walbert.

NONFICTION

The Age of Wonder by Richard Holmes. *The Good Soldiers* by David Finkel. *Lit: A Memoir* by Mary Karr. *Lords of Finance* by Liaquat Ahamed. *Raymond Carver* by Carol Sklenicka.

2008

FICTION

Dangerous Laughter by Steven Millhauser. *A Mercy* by Toni Morrison. *Netherland* by Joseph O'neill. *2666* by Roberto Bolaño; translated by Natasha Wimmer. *Unaccustomed Earth* by Jhumpa Lahiri.

NONFICTION

The Dark Side by Jane Mayer. *The Forever War* by Dexter Filkins. *Nothing to Be Frightened Of* by Julian Barnes. *This Republic of Suffering* by Drew Gilpin Faust. *The World Is What It Is* by Patrick French.

2007

FICTION

Man Gone Down by Michael Thomas. *Out Stealing Horses* by Per Petterson; translated by Anne Born. *The Savage Detectives* by Roberto Bolaño; translated by Natasha Wimmer. *Then We Came to the End* by Joshua Ferris. *Tree of Smoke* by Denis Johnson.

NONFICTION

Imperial Life in the Emerald City by Rajiv Chandrasekaran. *Little Heathens* by Mildred Armstrong Kalish. *The Nine* by Jeffrey Toobin. *The Ordeal of Elizabeth Marsh* by Linda Colley. *The Rest Is Noise* by Alex Ross.

2006

FICTION

Absurdistan by Gary Shteyngart. *The Collected Stories of Amy Hempel* by Amy Hempel. *The Emperor's Children* by Claire Messud. *The Lay of the Land* by Richard Ford. *Special Topics in Calamity Physics* by Marisha Pessl.

NONFICTION

Falling Through the Earth by Danielle Trussoni. *The Looming Tower* by Lawrence Wright. *Mayflower* by Nathaniel Philbrick. *The Omnivore's Dilemma* by Michael Pollan. *The Places in Between* by Rory Stewart.

2005

FICTION

Kafka on the Shore by Haruki Murakami. *On Beauty* by Zadie Smith. *Prep* by Curtis Sittenfeld. *Saturday* by Ian McEwan. *Veronica* by Mary Gaitskill.

NONFICTION

The Assassins' Gate by George Packer. *De Kooning* by Mark Stevens and Annalyn Swan. *The Lost Painting* by Jonathan Harr. *Postwar* by Tony Judt. *The Year of Magical Thinking* by Joan Didion.

2004

FICTION

Gilead by Marilynne Robinson. *The Master* by Colm Toibin. *The Plot Against America* by Philip Roth. *Runaway* by Alice Munro. *Snow* by Orhan Pamuk. *War Trash* by Ha Jin.

NONFICTION

Alexander Hamilton by Ron Chernow. *Chronicles: Volume One* by Bob Dylan. *Washington's Crossing* by David Hackett Fischer. *Will in the World* by Stephen Greenblatt

Other Famous Reviewers and Essayists

Kingsley Amis reviewed *Honey for the Bears*, by Anthony Burgess

Martin Amis reviewed *The Andy Warhol Diaries*

Judd Apatow reviewed *Pops: Fatherhood in Pieces*, by Michael Chabon

Brooke Astor reviewed *Treasures of the New York Public Library*, by Marshall B. Davidson with Bernard McTigue

Saul Bellow reviewed *A Treasury of Great Russian Short Stories*, edited by Avrahm Yarmolinsky

Erma Bombeck reviewed *Free to Be . . . You and Me*, edited by Marlo Thomas

Ray Bradbury reviewed *The Home Planet*, edited by Kevin W. Kelley

Gwendolyn Brooks reviewed *The Life of Langston Hughes*

William F. Buckley Jr. reviewed *The Right People*, by Stephen Birmingham

James M. Cain reviewed *Our Man in Havana*, by Graham Greene

J. M. Coetzee reviewed *The Temple of My Familiar*, by Alice Walker

Misty Copeland reviewed *And Then We Danced: A Voyage Into the Groove*, by Henry Alford

Michael Crichton reviewed *How Doctors Think*, by Jerome Groopman

Simone de Beauvoir wrote an essay, **"An American Renaissance in France"**

Junot Díaz reviewed *Deacon King Kong*, by James McBride

E. L. Doctorow reviewed *The Unbearable Lightness of Being*, by Milan Kundera

Arthur Conan Doyle reviewed *Communications with the Next World*, edited by Estelle W. Stead

Lena Dunham reviewed *The Female Persuasion*, by Meg Wolitzer

Jennifer Egan reviewed *Eat, Pray, Love*, by Elizabeth Gilbert

Dave Eggers reviewed *All Aunt Hagar's Children*, by Edward P. Jones

E. M. Forster reviewed *The World Is a Bridge*, by Christine Weston

Mavis Gallant reviewed *From the Diary of a Snail*, by Günter Grass

John Galsworthy reviewed *Friday Night*, by Edward Garnett

Bill Gates reviewed *21 Lessons for the 21st Century*, by Yuval Noah Harari

Atul Gawande reviewed *A Fly for the Prosecution*, by M. Lee Goff

Roxane Gay reviewed *Dept. of Speculation*, by Jenny Offill

Nikki Giovanni reviewed *M.C. Higgins, the Great*, by Virginia Hamilton

Nadine Gordimer reviewed *The Flame Trees of Thika*, by Elspeth Huxley

Al Gore reviewed *The Sixth Extinction*, by Elizabeth Kolbert

John Green reviewed *The Hunger Games*, by Suzanne Collins

Jeremy O. Harris reviewed *Real Life*, by Brandon Taylor

Ethan Hawke reviewed *Self Portrait with Russian Piano*, by Wolf Wondratschek

Chris Hayes reviewed *The Impeachers*, by Brenda Wineapple

Seamus Heaney reviewed *The Poems: A New Edition*, by W. B. Yeats

Lillian Hellman reviewed *The Provincials*, by Eli Evans

Carl Hiaasen reviewed *Rush*, by Kim Wozencraft

Patricia Highsmith reviewed *First on the Rope*, by R. Frison-Roche

Christopher Hitchens reviewed *The Secret Man*, by Bob Woodward

John Irving reviewed *The Duke of Deception*, by Geoffrey Wolff

Shirley Jackson reviewed *Out of the Red*, by Red Smith

N. K. Jemisin reviewed *The Water Cure*, by Sophie Mackintosh

Tayari Jones reviewed *Men We Reaped*, by Jesmyn Ward

Michael Kinsley reviewed *Going Clear*, by Lawrence Wright

Henry Kissinger reviewed *George F. Kennan: An American Life*, by John Lewis Gaddis

Karl Ove Knausgaard reviewed *Submission*, by Michel Houellebecq

John le Carré reviewed *The Secret War*, by William Stevenson

Ursula Le Guin reviewed *War Fever*, by J. G. Ballard

Madeleine L'Engle reviewed *The Sunflower Forest*, by Torey Hayden

Elmore Leonard reviewed *Lines and Shadows*, by Joseph Wambaugh

Doris Lessing reviewed *The Inner World of Mental Illness*, edited by Bert Kaplan

Sinclair Lewis reviewed *The Narrow House*, by Evelyn Scott

Rob Lowe reviewed *Mad as Hell: The Making of 'Network' and the Fateful Vision of the Angriest Man in Movies*, by Dave Itzkoff

Rachel Maddow reviewed *Breach of Trust: How Americans Failed Their Soldiers and Their Country*, by Andrew J. Bacevich

Thomas Mann reviewed *Rehearsal for Destruction*, by Paul W. Massing

Hilary Mantel reviewed *Down by the River*, by Edna O'Brien

James McBride reviewed *The Cairo Affair*, by Olen Steinhauer

Colleen McCullough reviewed *The Sparrow*, by Mary Doria Russell

Jay McInerney reviewed *Infinite Jest*, by David Foster Wallace

Terry McMillan reviewed *Some Soul to Keep*, by J. California Cooper

Larry McMurtry reviewed *By Myself*, by Lauren Bacall

H. L. Mencken reviewed *The Financier*, by Theodore Dreiser

James Michener reviewed *Cosmos*, by Carl Sagan

Margaret Millar reviewed *Don't Look Now*, by Daphne du Maurier

Nancy Mitford reviewed *Bond Street Story*, by Norman Collins

Walter Mosley reviewed *Fugitive Nights*, by Joseph Wambaugh

Walter Dean Myers reviewed *Heart and Soul*, by Kadir Nelson

Vladimir Nabokov reviewed *Nausea*, by Jean-Paul Sartre

Gloria Naylor reviewed *Hidden Pictures*, by Meg Wolitzer

Leonard Nimoy reviewed *Whales*, by Jacques-Yves Cousteau and Yves Paccalet

Joyce Carol Oates reviewed *A Book of Common Prayer*, by Joan Didion

George Orwell reviewed Evelyn Waugh's *Scott-King's Modern Europe*

Cynthia Ozick reviewed *Carpenter's Gothic*, by William Gaddis

Orhan Pamuk reviewed *Updike*, by Adam Begley

Dorothy Parker reviewed S. J. Perelman's *The Road to Miltown*

S. J. Perelman reviewed *Benchley Beside Himself*

Ann Petry reviewed *I, Juan de Pareja*, by Elizabeth Borton de Treviño

Katherine Anne Porter reviewed *The House of Breath*, by William Goyen

Reynolds Price reviewed *Song of Solomon*, by Toni Morrison

Mario Puzo reviewed *Tell Me How Long the Train's Been Gone*, by James Baldwin

Ruth Rendell reviewed **High Jinx**, by William F. Buckley Jr.

Jason Reynolds reviewed **The Alex Crow**, by Andrew Smith

Anne Rice reviewed **Presumed Innocent**, by Scott Turow

Molly Ringwald reviewed **The Mothers**, by Jennifer Gilmore

Marilynne Robinson reviewed **Where I'm Calling From**, by Raymond Carver

Sally Rooney reviewed **Surprise Me**, by Sophie Kinsella

Arthur Schlesinger Jr. reviewed **"1984" Revisited; Totalitarianism in Our Century**, edited by Irving Howe

Maurice Sendak reviewed **Sid and Sol**, by Arthur Yorinks

Dr. Seuss reviewed **Homecoming**, by Jiro Osaragi

Paul Simon reviewed **Finishing the Hat**, by Stephen Sondheim

B. F. Skinner reviewed **The Proper Study of Mankind**, by Stuart Chase

Patti Smith reviewed **Colorless Tsukuru Tazaki and His Years of Pilgrimage**, by Haruki Murakami

Robert Stone reviewed **The Forever War**, by Dexter Filkins

Rex Stout reviewed **The Alice B. Toklas Cook Book**

Cheryl Strayed reviewed **Wave**, by Sonali Deraniyagala

William Styron reviewed **Fortunate Son**, by Lewis B. Puller Jr.

Ida M. Tarbell reviewed **The Hidden Lincoln**, edited by Emanuel Hertz

Touré reviewed **On Michael Jackson**, by Margo Jefferson

Diana Trilling reviewed **Marilyn**, by Gloria Steinem

Lionel Trilling reviewed **The George Eliot Letters**, edited by Gordon S. Haight

Scott Turow reviewed **Mr. Peanut**, by Adam Ross

John Updike reviewed **Franny and Zooey**, by J. D. Salinger

Gloria Vanderbilt reviewed **Harriet the Spy**, by Louise Fitzhugh

Gore Vidal reviewed **All's Fair: Love, War, and Running for President**, by Mary Matalin and James Carville

Derek Walcott reviewed **The Glorious Flight: Across the Channel with Louis Bleriot, July 25, 1909**

David Foster Wallace reviewed **Borges: A Life**, by Edwin Williamson

Jesmyn Ward reviewed **Gathering of Waters**, by Bernice L. McFadden

Robert Penn Warren reviewed **A Woman of Means**, by Peter Taylor

Wendy Wasserstein reviewed **Diary of a Mad Playwright**, by James Kirkwood

Jennifer Weiner reviewed **Know My Name**, by Chanel Miller

H. G. Wells reviewed **The Private Life of Henry Maitland**, by Morley Roberts

Cornel West reviewed **The Good Society**, by Robert N. Bellah, Richard Madsen, William M. Sullivan, Ann Swidler and Steven M. Tipton

Colson Whitehead reviewed **The Echo Maker**, by Richard Powers

Joy Williams reviewed **The Laughing Monsters**, by Denis Johnson

Garry Wills reviewed **All Too Human: A Political Education**, by George Stephanopoulos

Tom Wolfe reviewed **Cecil Beaton: A Biography**, by Hugo Vickers

Credits

FRONTMATTER

The New York Times (p.1); Carrie Boretz for The New York Times (p.4–5); The New York Times (p.10); The New York Times (p.13); Sam Falk/The New York Times (p.14); Fred R. Conrad/The New York Times (p.22–23)

CHAPTER 1 | 1896–1921

The New York Times (p.26); The New York Times (p.29); The New York Times (p.30); The New York Times (p.33); iStock.com/goir (p.33 background); New York Public Library (p.35); Corbis via Getty Images (p.36–37); The New York Times (p.40); The New York Times (p.41); Cleveland Public Library, Fine Arts & Special Collections Department (p.44–45); Rare Book and Special Collections Division, Library of Congress (p.46); The New York Times (p.48–49); Hulton Archive/Getty Images (p.51); The New York Times (p.53); Library of Congress (p.54); Library of Congress (p.58–59); Rare Book and Special Collections Division, Library of Congress (p.60); The New York Times (p.61); The New York Times (p.62); The New York Times (p.65); Type Punch Matrix (p.66); Moffett Studios (p.69); The New York Times (p.72); The New York Times (p.73); Fred R. Conrad/The New York Times (p.74–75)

CHAPTER 2 | 1921–1946

The New York Times (p.78); The New York Times (p.81); Everett Collection Historical/Alamy (p.82); The New York Times (p.83); Courtesy of the Getty's Open Content Program (p.84); The New York Times (p.85); The New York Times (p.87); Bettmann/Getty Images (p.88); Heritage Auctions (p.89); The New York Times (p.91); Courtesy Biblioctopus (p.92); The New York Times (p.93); Library of Congress (p.95); The New York Times (p.97); Carl Van Vechten/Van Vechten Trust, Courtesy Beinecke Rare Book and Manuscript Library, Yale University (p.98); Neal Boenzi/The New York Times (p.101); The New York Times (p.102); Rare Book and Special Collections Division, Library of Congress (p.106); Riverrun Books & Manuscripts (p.107); Triolet Rare Books (p.108); Hulton Archive/Getty Images (p.110); Bettmann/Getty Images (p.113); The New York Times (p.116); The New York Times (p.119); Raptis Rare Books (p.120); Jack Manning (p.125); Carl Van Vechten/Van Vechten Trust, Courtesy Beinecke Rare Book and Manuscript Library, Yale University (p.126); Jack Manning/The New York Times (p.129); The New York Times (p.132); The New York Times (p.135); Meyer Liebowitz/The New York Times (p.136–137)

POETS | P.130–131

Page 130, clockwise from top left: Chester Higgins Jr./The New York Times; Larry C. Morris/The New York Times; Corbis via Getty Images; Library of Congress; Paul Hosefros/The New York Times; Sam Falk/The New York Times; Carl T. Gossett Jr/The New York Times. Page 131, clockwise from top left: Library of Congress; Beinecke Rare Book and Manuscript Library, Yale University; Sam Falk/The New York Times; Meyer Liebowitz/The New York Times; Bettmann/Getty Images; DeGaston Studio/MPI/Getty Images

CHAPTER 3 | 1946–1971

The New York Times (p.140); Raptis Rare Books (p.142); Text: © 1949 The University of the South (p.144–145); Terence Spencer/The LIFE Picture Collection via Getty Images (p.145); The New York Times (p.149); Antony Di Gesu/San Diego Historical Society/Hulton Archive Collection/Getty Images (p.150); Everything But The House (p.151); Sam Falk/The New York Times (p.154–155); Rare Book and Special Collections Division, Library of Congress (p.156); Frederick Eberstadt (p.157); Jay B. Leviton–Atlanta (p.160); The New York Times (p.163); Raptis Rare Books (p.166); Meyer Liebowitz/The New York Times (p.167); D. Gorton/The New York Times (p.168); Interfoto/Alamy (p.169); Robert Doisneau/Gamma-Rapho/Getty Images (p.170); Courtesy L. W. Currey and John W. Knott (p.172); Raptis Rare Books (p.173); Jack Manning/The New York Times (p.177); Robert W. Kelley/The LIFE Picture Collection via Getty Images (p.178); Erich Hartmann/Magnum Photos (p.181); Raptis Rare Books (p.182); Neal Boenzi/The New York Times (p.184); Heritage Auctions (p.185); Rare Book and Special Collections Division, Library of Congress (p.186); The New York Times (p.187); Neal Boenzi/The New York Times (p.190); The New York Times (p.192–193); Text: Published by arrangement with The Estate of Dawn Powell (p.194); Sam Falk/The New York Times (p.196); Israel Shenker/The New York Times (p.199); Ernie Sisto/The New York Times (p.201); Everett Collection/Alamy (p.205); Courtesy Jill Quasha/Copyright the Estate of Marjorie Content (p.206); Sam Falk/The New York Times (p.209); The New York Times (p.211); Michael Evans/The New York Times (p.212); Marilyn K. Yee/The New York Times (p.213); Bob Peterson/The LIFE Images Collection via Getty Images (p.215); Barton Silverman/The New York Times (p.217); Jack Manning/The New York Times (p.219); Jack Robinson/Hulton Archive/Getty Images (p.220); Type Punch Matrix (p.224); Pach Brothers/Corbis via Getty Images (p.227); Louis Monier/Gamma-Rapho via Getty Images (p.229); The New York Times (p.230–231)

PLAYWRIGHTS | P.164–165

Page 164, clockwise from top left: David Attie/Getty Images; Marilyn K. Yee/The New York Times; Sam Falk/The New York Times; Arthur Brower/The New York Times; William E. Sauro/The New York Times. Page 165, clockwise from top left: Sam Falk/The New York Times; Sam Falk/The New York Times; Library of Congress; Sara Krulwich/The New York Times

CHAPTER 4 | 1971–1996

The New York Times (p.234); Text: "Bech Meets Me," copyright © 1971 by John Updike. First appeared in The New York Times; from PICKED-UP PIECES by John Updike. Used by permission of Alfred A. Knopf, an imprint of the Knopf Doubleday Publishing Group, a division of Penguin Random House LLC. All rights reserved. (p.236–237); Joyce Dopkeen/The New York Times (p.237); Text: © 1972, 2021 June M. Jordan Literary Estate Trust. Used by Permission

Saul Bellow on the New York subway, October 9, 1975.

Acknowledgments

It takes a village, right? So many people pitched in to help with this book, which would never have come together without their generosity and expertise.

At Clarkson Potter, our savvy, unflappable editor, Angelin Borsics, took our rough ideas and buffed them to a high shine, showing us what worked, what didn't, what needed to be added, what should be cut—and, while she was doing all this, repeatedly performed magic with the production schedule. Thanks to everyone else at Clarkson Potter for their full support, especially Ian Dingman, Jan Derevjanik, Stephanie Huntwork, Francis Lam, Mark McCauslin, Kim Tyner and Aaron Wehner.

At The Times, I'm especially grateful to Noor Qasim, who dedicated her year-long stint as an editing fellow at the paper to the Book Review's 125th anniversary. Her thoughtful, incisive editorial judgment helped me shape the book's content, and she took on a lot of detail work (like permissions!) that I did not have time for. Without her, this project simply would not have been possible.

Thanks, too, to John Cruickshank, who— calmly, and with great good humor—kept this book on track, even when schedules threatened to veer out of control (they never did, thanks to him!), and to Anika Burgess, photo editor extraordinaire, whose gift for excavating remarkable old photographs can be seen on almost every page. Anika's eye for the tiniest detail saved me again and again.

Many thanks to the head of the Books desk,

Pamela Paul—a passionate advocate for the project from the beginning—and David Kelly, our managing editor, for his encyclopedic knowledge of Book Review history. Other Books colleagues— John Williams, MJ Franklin, Emily Eakin, Gal Beckerman, Elisabeth Egan, Greg Cowles, Jude Biersdorfer, Alexandra Alter and Andrew LaVallee— gave me excellent advice and, when things got tough, unflagging support.

Also at The Times, thanks to Jeff Roth, who pulled dozens of old Book Review bound volumes from our photo morgue and delivered them to the photo lab, and to William O'Donnell and Sonny Figueroa, who painstakingly scanned countless back issues, negatives and prints, many of them old and fragile. Our thanks also go to our art production team, Steve Brown and David Braun, for so deftly handling such a massive amount of material.

Lee Riffaterre, Irina Starkova and Nick Jollymore provided invaluable advice on clearing textual permissions, a process spearheaded by the resourceful Nick Donofrio. Karen Sutorius, Aaron Tejada and Sarah Borell helped clear photo permissions.

A special thanks to Dara Hauser for feedback that helped make this book more accessible.

Finally, this book would never have come about without Binky Urban—who found the perfect home for it—or Jennifer Parrucci, M. Ryan Murphy and David Dunlap, who were all unstinting with their time when I first arrived at the Times and was teaching myself how to use the archives.

—TINA JORDAN